The Best American
Sports Writing
2020

The Best AMERICAN SPORTS WRITING™ 2020

Edited and with an Introduction
by Jackie MacMullan

Glenn Stout, *Series Editor*

MARINER BOOKS

HOUGHTON MIFFLIN HARCOURT

BOSTON · NEW YORK   2020

hmhbooks.com

ISSN 1056-8034 (print)   ISSN 2573-4822 (e-book)
ISBN 978-0-358-19699-0 (print)   ISBN 978-0-358-18183-5 (e-book)

Printed in the United States of America
DOC 10 9 8 7 6 5 4 3 2 1

Contents

Contents

Foreword

Don't expect a eulogy.

This is the thirtieth and last edition of *The Best American Sports Writing*, a series that began in 1991 and one that, accidently, commenced one year after the old *Best Sports Stories* series, which began in 1945, ceased publication. That makes this the seventy-fifth year an annual collection of sports writing has been published in the United States.

At such a time there is a great temptation, and maybe even an expectation, to provide some kind of grand summing up of the genre over the past three decades, charting the changes I have witnessed and noting the evolution that takes place in any field over time.

I might do that at some point, but it won't be here. Not that I don't have any thoughts about what has been taking place over the last three decades—*I do*—but right now this isn't about what I think, as I've never considered this book in any sense "mine." I've only thought of myself as the custodian of something that rightly belongs more to the readers of this book and, in particular, to the writers whose work has appeared in these pages. It is their effort and creativity that sustained this series and inspired a generation of writers and readers.

It has been an honor to serve as your caretaker. And I mean that. My role, from the start, has been to facilitate the process under standard Best American title guidelines and ensure that everyone—readers and writers—always felt welcome to submit material while surveying on my own as much other work as I could. In a business that is not always fair, I did my best to keep the process equitable and free of favoritism. After that, I tried to stay out of the way and allow the guest editors the latitude to make their own decisions according to their own standards and taste.

More than anything, I'm simply thankful to have been given both the opportunity and the responsibility. It's (mostly) been fun, or at least as much fun as living with a mountain of reading material chronically stacked in a corner or flooding My Pocket can be. And even on the occasions when the work has felt burdensome, there has always been the unexpected thrill of encountering a story that was an utter revelation. Apart from the entertainment this series provided over the years, I feel fortunate that it promoted some remarkable work from amazingly creative, resilient, and committed writers and reporters, and that it helped some of them get jobs, keep jobs, earn assignments, and, most important, share their writing with others. The ability of words to reach out is not finite and never ends.

When people learned that *The Best American Sports Writing* was coming to an end, it was gratifying to discover that this series has meant so much to so many. Knowing it mattered to you made it matter to me. Reader after reader and writer after writer sent me photos of their collection of the series. I appreciate that so many cared enough not only to buy the book year after year after year but to share it with others, save every volume, and return to read them again and again, just as I once did with the old *Best Sports Stories* series.

Before I thank all the writers who have shared these pages, there are a few others I must mention. Siobhan and Saorla have shared me with this book almost from the beginning. Every writer knows that a project extracts a cost from those who share your life; this isn't a nine-to-five job, and we are not always as present as we should be. I have no word for their love, patience, and understanding. Nor are there adequate words to express my gratitude to the many friends who shared beers and coffee and hours of conversation about writing, who gave counsel and criticism in equal measure. Some are writers and some are not, but at various times and in various ways you kept me moving forward on this project. Thanks in particular go to Howard Bryant, Richard Johnson, John Dorsey, Scott Bortzfield, Brin-Jonathan Butler, Kim Cross, Alex Belth, and everyone else who rewarded my faith in words.

I also thank the editors at Houghton Mifflin and Houghton Mif-

flin Harcourt I have worked with over the years: Steven Lewers—
who first took a chance on this wild-haired librarian and freelancer
—Alan Andres, Margie Patterson Cochran, Eamon Dolan, and Ol-
ivia Bartz. No one was more important to both *The Best American
Sports Writing* and my career than Susan Canavan, who supported
this series and placed her trust in me for most of the last two decades, not only for this book but for many others. My thanks go
out as well to the countless editorial assistants, copy editors, and
everyone else at HMH who have supported the series.

Beginning with the late David Halberstam, who, as the first
guest editor, set the standard, my thanks go out as well to all the
guest editors with whom I have worked, a list that includes some
of the most prominent names in writing and journalism: Thomas
McGuane, the late Frank Deford, Thomas Boswell, the late Dan
Jenkins, John Feinstein, the late George Plimpton, Bill Littlefield
(who supported this series for so many years on his National Public
Radio program *Only a Game*), Richard Ford, the late Dick Schaap,
the late Bud Collins, Rick Reilly, Buzz Bissinger, the late Richard
Ben Cramer, Mike Lupica, Michael Lewis, David Maraniss, the late
William Nack, Leigh Montville, Peter Gammons, Jane Leavy, Michael Wilbon, J. R. Moehringer, Christopher McDougall, Wright
Thompson (who, by a score of 13–12, was just edged out in total
appearances by the esteemed Gary Smith, but since Wright also
served as guest editor and wrote an introduction, I consider it a
tie), Rick Telander (unfailingly generous, Rick once, while visiting, came to see me play with an Irish band and drink Guinness),
Howard Bryant (whose frequent conversations and friendship are
invaluable), Jeff Pearlman, Charles P. Pierce, and Jackie MacMullan. This book could not have been what it has been without every
one of them. And to the thousands of writers acknowledged in the
"Notables" over the years, I wish there had been more room up
front.

I remember long ago, when I was young and dreamed of being
a writer, I'd see the stretch of *Best Sports Stories* lining the shelves of
my local library and feel overwhelmed. Now, in the old secretary
cabinet where I store my book titles, the span of *The Best American
Sports Writing*, including this edition, reaches a full three feet.

I initially intended to include a comprehensive index to the series in this edition, but space apparently precludes that. Instead,
since any impact this series has had belongs to the contributors,

after thirty years I'll end simply by acknowledging each of the more than 400 writers of the nearly 750 stories that have appeared here.

I hope I didn't miss anyone. It's quite a list and includes everyone from writers who have won Pulitzers and National Magazine Awards and National Book Awards and all sorts of other honors to inexperienced writers fresh out of the box who punched up.

Between the covers of this book you all belonged. It's been a pleasure to share the pages.

Alan Abel, J. A. Adande, Michael Agovino, Mitch Albom, David Aldridge, Marti Amis, Dave Anderson, Joel Anderson, Lars Anderson, Peter Andrews, Roger Angell, and Kevin Arnovitz.

Kent Babb, Katie Baker, Chris Ballard, Michael Bamberger, Bruce Barcott, Dan Barry, Dave Barry, Christopher Beam, Barry Bearak, Pam Belluck, Alex Belth, Ira Berkow, Jane Bernstein, Mike Bianchi, Burkhard Bilger, Jon Billman, Furman Bisher, Buzz Bissinger, Roy Blount Jr., Will Blythe, Jake Bogoch, Sam Borden, Ron Borges, Tom Boswell, Flinder Boyd, John Ed Bradley, Rick Bragg, John Branch, John Brant, Yoni Brenner, Jennifer Briggs, Chip Brown, James Brown, Larry Brown, Tim Brown, William Browning, Howard Bryant, Susy Buchanan, Bill Buford, Amby Burfoot, Timothy Burke, Bryan Burrough, Bruce Buschel, and Steery Butcher.

Matt Calkins, Tom Callahan, Gary Cartwright, Oscar Casares, Greg Child, Megan Chuchmach, Rene Chun, Tom Clynes, Richard Cohen, John Colapinto, Robert Cole, Steve Coll, Gene Collier, Bud Collins, Jeremy Collins, Pamela Colloff, Kevin Conley, Frank Conroy, Mark Coomes, Chloe Cooper-Jones, Jeff Coplon, Sara Corbett, Greg Couch, Lynne Cox, Daniel Coyle, Tommy Craggs, Virginia Otley Craighill, Richard Ben Cramer, Kim Cross, Paulo Cullum, Bryan Curtis, and Luke Cyphers.

Beth Davies-Stofka, David Davis, Frank Deford, Peter DeJonge, David DiBenedetto, Jack Dickey, Michael Dileo, Heather Dinich, Michael Disend, David Dobbs, Kathy Dobie, George Dohrmann, J. D. Dolan, Bill Donahue, Neil Donnelly, Larry Dorman, Geoffrey Douglas, Robert Draper, Evan Drellich, Todd Drew, Stephen J. Dubner, David James Duncan, Jeff Duncan, and Timothy Dwyer.

Mat Edelson, Scott Eden, Gretel Ehrlich, Tim Elfrink, and James Ellroy.

Jason Fagone, Steve Fainaru, Mark Fainaru-Wada, Michael Farber, Tom Farrey, Bruce Feldman, Nathan Fenno, Dave Ferrell, Bill Fields, Ron Fimrite, David Finkel, Michael Finkel, Robin Finn, William Finnegan, David Fleming, Sean Flynn, Bonnie D. Ford, Richard Ford, Pat Forde, Reid Forgrave, Roberto José Andrade Franco, Ian Frazier, Steve Friedman, Tad Friend, Tom Friend, and Ken Fuson.

Peter Gammons, Greg Garber, Emily Giambalvo, Elizabeth Gilbert, William Gildea, Bill Gifford, Malcolm Gladwell, John M. Glionna, Allison Glock, Michael Goodman, Adam Gopnik, Cynthia Gorney, Mark Gozonsky, Tim Graham, David Grann, Karl Taro Greenfeld, Vahe Gregorian, Alice Gregory, John Griswold, and Mike Guy.

David Halberstam, Michael Hall, Joshua Hammer, Travis Haney, Greg Hanlon, Jim Harrison, Nancy Hass, Nick Heil, Tony Hendra, Amanda Hess, Peter Hessler, John Hewitt, James Hibberd, John Hildebrand, Richard Hoffer, Bob Hohler, Skip Hollandsworth, Johnette Howard, Kerry Howley, Patrick Hruby, Robert Huber, Steve Hummer, and Dave Hyde.

Jeff Jackson, Dan Jenkins, Lee Jenkins, Sally Jenkins, Chantel Jennings, May Jeong, Cory Johnson, Bret Anthony Johnston, Bomani Jones, Chris Jones, Robert F. Jones, Ben Joravsky, Pat Jordan, Ron C. Judd, and Tom Junod.

Jennifer Kahn, Jay Caspian Kang, Karen Karbo, Donald Katz, Jesse Katz, Elizabeth Kaye, Andrew Keh, Garrison Keillor, Beth Kephart, Mike Kessler, Raffi Khatchadourian, James Kilgo, Dave Kindred, Melissa King, Stephen King, John Klima, Sam Knight, Dan Koeppel, Howard Kohn, Tony Kornheiser, Thomas Korosec, Pete Kotz, Jon Krakauer, Mark Kram, Mark Kram Jr., Aishwarya Kumar, and Mike Kupper.

Thomas Lake, Michael Lananna, Brook Larmer, Jeanne Marie Laskas, Guy Lawson, Tim Layden, Sydney Lea, Michael Leahy, Martha Weinman Lear, Dan Le Batard, Steven Leckart, Mark Levine, Ted Levin, Ariel Levy, Michael Lewis, Franz Lidz, Bill Littlefield, Mike Littwin, Jere Longman, Mark Lucius, and Mike Lupica.

Jeff MacGregor, Jackie MacMullan, Juliet Macur, Mike Magnuson, Jonathan Mahler, Erik Malinowski, Thomas Mallon, David Mamet, Steve Marantz, John Marchese, Jeremy Markovitch, Guy Martin, Jeff Maysh, Bruce McCall, Jack McCallum, Terrence McCoy, David McGlynn, Ben McGrath, Thomas McGuane, James McKean, Michael McKnight, Bucky McMahon, James McManus,

John McPhee, Rebecca Mead, Craig Medred, Andy Meisler, David Merrill, Elizabeth Merrill, Jonathan Miles, Kathryn Miles, Andrew Miller, Davis Miller, Sam Miller, J. R. Moehringer, Leigh Montville, Jon Mooallem, Michael J. Mooney, Kenny Moore, Eric Moskowitz, Doug Most, Lester Munson, and Jim Murray.

William Nack, Eric Neel, Dan Neil, Glenn Nelson, Tim Neville, John Paul Newport, Duane Noriyuki, Bob Norman, and Eric Nusbaum.

Henley O'Brien, Alexis Okeowo, Lisa Olson, Steve Oney, Susan Orlean, P. J. O'Rourke, Scott Ostler, Dan O'Sullivan, Jim Owczarski, and David Owen.

Ruth Padawar, Dave Parmenter, Nicole Pasulka, Avni Patel, Randall Patterson, Nick Paumgarten, Ben Paynter, Jeff Pearlman, Mark Pearson, Paul Pekin, Brian Phillips, Charles P. Pierce, Mary Pilon, Bill Plaschke, George Plimpton, Terry Pluto, Steve Politi, Neal Pollack, Brett Popplewell, Joe Posnanski, Shirley Povich, Padgett Powell, Robert Andrew Powell, John Powers, Joshua Harris Prager, Alan Prendergast, and S. L. Price.

Bridget Quinn.

Scott Raab, David Racine, Amy Ragsdale, Joel Reese, Elwood Reid, Jan Reid, Rick Reilly, David Remnick, Bill Reynolds, William C. Rhoden, Peter Richmond, Cinthia Ritchie, Amanda Ripley, Adam Rittenberg, David Roberts, Linda Robertson, Eugene Robinson, Stephen Rodrick, Ken Rodriguez, Michael Rosenberg, Ken Rosenthal, Tracy Ross, David Roth, Davy Rothbart, Karen Russell, Steve Rushin, Bob Ryan, and Joan Ryan.

Mike Sager, Robert Sanchez, Richard Sandomir, Eli Saslow, Grayson Schaeffer, Adam Schefter, Charlie Schroeder, John Schulian, Jason Schwartz, Tom Scocca, John Seabrook, Jay Searcy, Jonathan Segura, Josh Sens, Joe Sexton, Bill Shaikin, Sam Shaw, Dave Sheinin, Kevin Sherrington, Blackie Sherrod, David Shields, Florence Shinkle, Maggie Shipstead, Charles Siebert, Mike Sielski, T. J. Simers, David Simon, Mark Singer, Clay Skipper, Bryan Smith, Gary Smith, Jack Smith, Michael Sokolove, Christopher Solomon, Paul Solotaroff, John Spong, Charles Sprawson, Peter Stark, Alexandra Starr, Susan Sterling, Carlson Stowers, Donna St. George, Abe Streep, Kurt Streeter, Shelby Strother, Tim Struby, Mimi Swartz, and E. M. Swift.

Lisa Taddeo, Gay Talese, Jerry Tarde, Donna Tartt, Matt Teague, Rick Telander, Art Thiel, Louisa Thomas, Teri Thompson, Wright

Thompson, Ian Thomsen, Tommy Tomlinson, Pat Toomay, Touré, Wells Tower, and Tyler Tynes.

Karen Uhlenhuth.

Tom VanHaaren, Chris Van Leuven, Don Van Natta Jr., Kevin Van Valkenburg, George Vecsey, Bob Verdi, Tom Verducci, Craig Vetter, Katy Vine, and David Von Drehle.

Bruce Wallace, David Foster Wallace, Caity Weaver, Elizabeth Weil, Michael Weinreb, Patricia Wen, L. Jon Wertheim, Dan Wetzel, David Wharton, Ian Whitcomb, Peter O. Whitmer, Seth Wickersham, Chris Wiewiora, Michael Wilbon, Alec Wilkinson, Simon Winchester, Mike Wise, Gene Wojciechowski, Alexander Wolff, Woody Woodburn, and Brian Woolley.

Charles M. Young.

Mark Ziegler, Tim Zimmermann, Dave Zirin, and Derek Zumsteg.

After thirty years, I believe there is more TK, but for now, to each and every one of you, I say only this: Thanks for being a writer.

-30-

GLENN STOUT
Alburgh, Vermont

Introduction

WHEN I WAS nine years old, free to languish amid the lazy days of summer, I chose instead to meticulously lay out my clothes the night before I turned in, so I would be prepared. I lived on a quiet residential street shaped like a horseshoe, and it so happened that the straightaway section, the flattest part of the road, conveniently stretched along the front of my house. It was the ideal location for a makeshift street hockey game, an event that happened to be the center of my world in those days, but the rules were clear: first to the pavement were the first to play.

I wanted to be first. Not the first girl, because, as always, I would be the only one. It was paramount to me that while my sisters lingered at the breakfast table, cozy in their pajamas, I would be fully dressed, sneakers tied, peering out from behind the curtains of our dining room window, alertly awaiting my day's companions, who would soon be queueing up, sticks in hand, for an afternoon that promised to be splendid.

During adolescence, these were the moments when I felt most empowered, and most comfortable in my skin. Competition flooded me with confidence, and as long as I was running and jumping, or chasing, swatting, or shooting a ball, I was happy. In the sixties, my passion was occasionally met with curiosity, even skepticism. Is that girl out there again? Won't she get hurt? And yet, aside from my blond ponytail, I was indistinguishable from the rest of our group; T-shirts, shorts, knobby knees, and squeaky voices hollering "Caaaaarrrr!" whenever one of our family's station wagons lumbered down the hill.

Sports became my everything, allowing me to embrace an identity that seemed elusive in many of my alternate universes. It wasn't as nakedly simple as winning or losing, although when my team came up short, it was often me who quickly declared, "Let's go again!" even as the sun quit on us and our moms beckoned us to the dinner table. I knew I was different, but as long as I was immersed in sweat and the camaraderie of my male neighbors—my friends—I could navigate that.

It was only natural my love affair with competition would soon lead me to obsessively track the people who had parlayed their athletic talents into professional careers. There was a rule in our house regarding the newspaper: we were welcome to scour the sports pages and memorize the box scores, but only *after* we had dissected the news of the day. Once I waded through world affairs, politics, and daily crimes in the metro section, I was free to embrace the lyrical cadence of *Boston Globe* columnist Ray Fitzgerald, who so expertly enlisted humor and grace to spring my sports heroes to life.

In a major family breakthrough, my father purchased our first color television, enabling us to tune in to WSBK, the Boston station that broadcast the Bruins. (Yes, sporting events on television were free back then.) Like so many other New England kids my age, I worshiped at the altar of Orr. I carefully cut news clippings and photos from the *Boston Globe* and the *Boston Herald Traveler* and lovingly glued them into my Bruins scrapbook, smoothing each page, adding my own pointed comments (what would Ray Fitz write?), then tucking it under my bed. This was not a book for public consumption. It was my own deeply personal experiment.

When the Bruins won the Cup in 1969, the roars thundered up and down Stanford Drive, from the den of elderly Mrs. Corcoran, who always wore a dress, neatly pressed, with stockings, and charted how many goals Espo scored each night, to my pal Georgie Whalen two houses down, a ten-year old regular at our street hockey games who reminded us all of the value of a grinder like Wayne Cashman. We shared in our team's triumph as if we had suited up ourselves, as if we had anything to do with Orr taking flight in front of the net. Somehow, it felt as though we did, in part because of the way Fitzgerald and his cohorts drew us close, set the scene, and coaxed us into basking in the revelry.

In the decades that followed, I came to marvel at the power of sport, how it could draw together the most divergent of personalities—like an eighty-year-old widow and a preteen boy in love with the Bruins; two colleagues, a Muslim immigrant and his devoutly Catholic coworker, who discovered they both loved tennis and became partners on the court; the father and daughter who struggled to communicate, unless it was over football on Sunday; or a grandmother and grandson who found common ground by driving to the ballpark early to catch batting practice. The moment that remains forever etched in my soul is standing alongside two women, eyes shining, as they heaved a basketball toward a bent rim without a net on a dirt court in Rwanda. These women had been told their entire lives that exercise was just for men, only to discover, to their delight, that was a lie.

Rejoicing over common allegiances and heated (even hated) rivals is a bond that often transcends race, gender, religion, and economic status. As sports became increasingly politicized, we charted the awakening of our superstars, who decided Black lives did matter, kneeling was necessary, and skipping the White House ceremony could spawn meaningful dialogue. This led to debate, consternation, anger, and, once in a while, acceptance, but through it all the games continued, evolving along with society.

But then, last March, a most extraordinary event occurred: the entire athletic universe suddenly jammed on the brakes . . . and stopped. There we stayed, frozen in place, in uncharted territory for months, as a worldwide pandemic paralyzed our health care system, our economy, and life as we knew it.

The sports tipping point was when a seven-foot-tall basketball player from the north of France tested positive for the new coronavirus, COVID-19, a silent, deadly ailment that was seemingly impossible to corral. Days earlier, that same player, Utah Jazz center Rudy Gobert, had mocked the severity of COVID-19 by playfully touching the microphones and recorders of reporters. In an instant, he became the catalyst that brought all competitions across the world to a screeching halt. The psychological hand-wringing spread as swiftly as the disease itself. What will we do without sports?

The NBA shut down immediately, as did the NHL, on the precipice of the postseason. Baseball pushed back spring training, then opening day. Major golf and tennis tournaments were canceled or postponed—even the Masters, which for decades seemed impervious to outside forces, floating above it all in its own stratosphere. The Tokyo Olympics hit the pause button—for an entire year.

The annual NCAA spring basketball tournament was also a major casualty. The coronavirus served as the ultimate bracket buster, and for the first time ever during March Madness, *everyone* lost. There would be no fairy-tale ending for Sabrina Ionescu, the iconic Oregon superstar who returned for her senior season for one reason only: to win it all. There were no Cinderella highlights of the upstart Dayton Flyers, who were gunning for their first-ever men's championship; instead reruns from Villanova's 1987 upset over Georgetown and Christian Laettner's miracle shot from twenty-eight years ago attempted to plug the gaping hole.

We lamented for high school students from all over the country who were preparing for their state tournaments, until they were delivered the sobering news that no new champions would be crowned in 2020. For the spring warriors, track and field meets, lacrosse matches, and baseball and softball games were canceled before they were even scheduled. Pickup basketball was banned along with youth soccer, flag football, and impromptu games of street hockey on the flattest section of the neighborhood. Overnight, athletics went from a sanctuary to a hazard. It was unsafe to shake hands, exchange high-fives, or offer bear hugs at the buzzer. The danger was real—people died from the coronavirus by the tens of thousands—and the loss, even among those unaffected by the disease, was palpable.

As so often happens in a crisis, kindness and generosity emerged to help salve wounds. Franchises vowed to support workers who relied on the hourly wage from sporting events to pay their bills. Gobert donated $500,000 of his money to the cause; pledges followed from an array of familiar faces, among them Sixers big man Joel Embiid, Milwaukee Bucks star Giannis Antetokounmpo, Dallas Cowboys defensive end Demarcus Lawrence, Houston Texans captain J. J. Watt, and Florida Panthers goalie Sergei Bobrovsky.

The stories in this remarkable collection were written a year before COVID-19 rocked our world. They encompass a range of sports tapestries from some unlikely venues: a massage parlor in Jupiter, Florida, where the reputation of one of the most powerful men in the NFL was forever tarnished; a boulevard in southern Virginia in front of a Confederate statue that prompted tears of despair from author Kurt Streeter; a tiny apartment in Diest, Belgium, where a Paralympic athlete chose to end her life; and a courtroom in Somerset County, New Jersey, where a middle school baseball coach regained his.

None of these stories highlight exploits of stars from the major professional teams. Increasingly, elite athletes have opted to create their own "brand," churning out self-made glossy presentations shellacked with a veneer that lacks the authenticity of a story well told. Perhaps it's no coincidence that most of the subjects featured in this anthology are not household names who compete in mainstream sports for sizable cash prizes. As stars become less accessible and more protective of their "legacy," their stories also become less compelling.

Each of the gifted writers who grace these pages veered off the main path to craft rich storytelling that is gorgeous, pensive, and, in some cases, haunting. When I began the tortuous process of choosing which ones should be included, I promised myself to begin with a blank canvas of expectation—with no preconceived notions regarding writing style or subject matter. The plan was to open my mind—and, hopefully, yours—to a myriad of ways the written word can move us to tears, laughter, indignant rage, sorrow, regret.

Exceptional writing transports us on journeys we never imagined, immersing us so thoroughly that we can actually taste the dust from the desolate Angola Prison in John Griswold's "The Exiled and the Devil's Sideshow," his bleak account of the Louisiana State Penitentiary, where our country's last surviving prison rodeo is held. Angola's prisoners landed there for committing heinous crimes; for a few dollars, they provide fodder for a leering audience that seeks vengeance and violence in the form of twisted, gruesome entertainment. Griswold unveils this house of horrors that is equally abusive to the animals and the prisoners by introducing us to "convict poker," where four inmates sit at a table pretending to play cards as a snorting bull is released into the ring and does his mighty best to gore them all. Each rodeo "event" is crueler and more absurd than the next, leading Griswold to ponder, "Is this another joke, meant to parody what ignorance yields in the hardness of life? In any case, no one wins anything."

Elizabeth Merrill's thoughtful portrait of Shelly Pennefather, a former college basketball supernova from Villanova who gave up a lucrative overseas basketball career to become a cloistered nun, is less jolting, yet no less moving. Sister Rose Marie of the Queen of Angels, as Pennefather is now known, cannot email, call, or text her loved ones. Every twenty-five years she is allowed to enter a room and hug her family. Merrill's tender prose examines how her siblings and teammates grapple with this selfless decision, and how the enduring faith of Shelly's mother enables her to find peace with God, even as she embraces her daughter in quiet anguish, knowing it will likely be for the final time.

If you are surprised to discover accounts of a prison rodeo and a cloistered nun on these pages, then consider the Olympic hopeful who robbed twenty-six banks on his bicycle, and threw the stolen money in the nearest trash can during his maiden heist. Author Steven Leckart invites us on a rollicking ride with Tom Justice, whose self-destructive bent is at once perplexing and unfathomably sad.

In "Shooting a Tiger," Bryan Burrough transports us to a remote village in India, where the hunt for a female tiger who has mutilated thirteen villagers entangles doctors, environmentalists, hunters, bureaucrats, activists, lawmakers, veterinarians, and townspeople in a web of deceit and intrigue. It is a complicated quandary that weighs human life against the rights of an endangered animal who has been flushed from her habitat by the very humans who want her gone. Burrough's suspenseful storytelling, which masterfully unleashes tension throughout, left me vacillating back and forth between fervently believing the tiger should be shot, then reversing course and proclaiming the tiger should be spared.

While reviewing the entries for this anthology, there was one particular theme I hoped to discover, since it had thwarted me as a young writer struggling to find my voice. When I was a college student at the University of New Hampshire, I signed up for a magazine writing course and spent most of the semester desperately attempting to evade the red pen of professor Andy Merton, who was not for the faint of heart. With each submission, I remained tentative but hopeful that I had stumbled upon a winning formula, only to have my work returned with the telltale angry red slashes signifying my inability to accomplish Professor Merton's one simple objective: teach me something!

It became a mantra for me going forward, both as a writer and a reader. No wonder I was drawn to "The Grandmaster Diet," an intriguing story written by Aishwarya Kumar that details the grueling physical demands of becoming a world-class chess player. Did you know that the 1984 World Chess Championship was called off because the defending champion lost twenty-two pounds during the competition? I did not. How is this possible? Please read Aishwarya's story and discover why for yourself.

It is evident that these amazing pieces were carefully assembled through research, most of which was no doubt conducted face to face. Personal interaction is essential when it comes to capturing the mood of a subject, whether it's a slight hand gesture, a crinkle of the nose, or a vexed and furrowed brow. As any credible editor will inform you, there's no such thing as too many details, and when you think you've spoken to enough sources, it's time to reach out and tap into ten more. The most compelling stories are ones we can feel and touch and imagine, without much difficulty, that we are there.

This is precisely what Bill Plaschke accomplishes in his poignant column on patients with Alzheimer's disease, who gather at a Los Angeles office building to engage in what is called baseball reminiscence therapy. They swap stories about the game they love, slap a ball into their mitt, and hope to revive a snapshot of when the grass was freshly cut, the nights were warm and steamy, and their memories were intact. Plaschke unfurls a scene so vivid and visceral that I felt as though I had a seat in the therapy circle. Patients who sometimes go for weeks without engaging with anyone, who can't remember what they had for breakfast, draw strength from each other to unlock their minds and relive the simple pleasures of their past. As Plaschke notes, "Baseball has done it again. Baseball has wrapped its arms around unsettled souls and taken them out to the ballgame."

The hunt for such heartrending prose that so powerfully illustrates the impact of sport is a worthy one, even as our industry continues to shift dramatically. Access to the athletes of the major sports continues to shrink, and the challenge of connecting with them becomes more daunting each day. Practices used to be open to journalists, and players were free to converse before and after those workouts with the scribes who were regularly assigned to their team. If you wanted to foster a relationship, you arrived early and lingered late. Many teams still flew commercially, and the idle chatter and small talk at the gate or the coffee shop were building blocks for the writer to understand the athlete a little better—and vice versa. Those interactions were like tiny gold nuggets: priceless, and now, it seems, in high demand.

These days a private dialogue with an athlete feels like a major coup. Teams no longer rely on the airlines. Flying their own jets now, they can leave town immediately after their road game. Practices are scarce, and when they are scheduled, journalists are given no pre-workout accessibility. Often players are trotted out in group settings, or "scrums," as we like to call them. It is a disheartening way to do business, for both the athlete and the journalist, and it's nearly impossible to extract anything meaningful or unique from these sessions.

Yet even against that backdrop, superior reporting continues to emerge, as enterprising writers look elsewhere for meaningful content. The damning profile of Conrad Mainwaring, a former Olympic hurdler who became an Olympic training coach and was accused of molesting more than forty-one men over four decades, is shocking in its scope and the grim reality of its time line. Authors Mike Kessler and Mark Fainaru-Wada unsparingly peel back the layers of Mainwaring's alleged abuse with graphic and emotional testimonials from the many lives he ruined. It's a difficult story to digest and was even more challenging to report, requiring perseverance, courage, and persistence.

So, too, did Ken Rosenthal and Evan Drellich's groundbreaking reporting on the sign-stealing scandal that consumed the Houston Astros and ultimately cost both manager A. J. Hinch and general manager Jeff Luhnow their jobs. It was the most explosive story in baseball in 2018, and, one could argue, in 2019 as well. Its ramifications continue to shake the foundation of one of our country's oldest and most revered pastimes.

As I write this, the sports world is still "on hiatus," which, the dictionary tells us, is a pause or gap in a sequence, series, or process. It feels more seismic than that. It's impossible at this moment to quantify how the coronavirus has affected our culture, the quality of our lives, and our ability to do our jobs. For a brief time before the virus shut down sports completely, new safeguard regulations were put in place to protect the athletes, including closing the locker room to all reporters. It was a temporary measure, we were assured, but still, the alarm bells sounded. It was another obstacle to access, another hurdle in our quest to provide you, the readers, with the quality of work exemplified in *The Best American Sports Writing 2020* that rests in your hands. Sadly, this will be the final *BASW*, and my sincere hope is that we have selected stories that are memorable, and enduring.

As we navigate this haze of uncharted territory, there's one thing I'm certain of: exceptional reporters will continue to generate captivating stories, and superb writing will live on, from inside a convent, a village in India, or maybe even a massage parlor in a Florida strip mall.

JACKIE MACMULLAN

The Best American
Sports Writing
2020

BILL PLASCHKE

For People Suffering from Alzheimer's and Dementia, Baseball Brings Back Fun Memories

FROM THE LOS ANGELES TIMES

IT STARTS WITH a baseball.

Each person who attends the monthly BasebALZ program in a conference room at the offices of Alzheimer's Los Angeles is handed one, faded and scuffed.

For the next two hours, those suffering from Alzheimer's disease or other forms of dementia will hold that baseball.

Some will clutch it tightly as they listen to stories about former baseball greats. Others will roll it around in their palms as they watch presentations about baseball's historic moments. At some point, they will be asked to reach back into their own baseball history.

Through the magic of those 108 stitches, they will remember.

"My friends and I lived near each other, we'd play together," Al Hassan, eighty-two, says with a grin. "I wasn't very good, I played way out in the field. There was a little creek they put me near in case I had to jump in the water. It happened three or four times. I think they were agitating me!"

It's a bright Friday morning, and Hassan laughs, and across the table, Dolores Jones, eighty-nine, soon joins him.

"There was this St. Louis pitcher, I would stay up late to watch him on TV," she says with a grin. "He put his cap low; it was scary for hitters. They're looking for his eyes, they'd let a pitch go by."

Jon Leonoudakis, the meeting facilitator dressed in a gold vintage Pittsburgh Pirates jersey and cap, jumps in.

"Oh, you're talking about Bob Gibson," he says, pausing, then raising his voice in wonder. "And did you know he wore glasses?"

The room instantly buzzes with oohs and aahs and lights in eyes that have been growing dim. Baseball has done it again. Baseball has wrapped its arms around unsettled souls and taken them out to the ball game.

"Watching what happens here is like watching people come to life," says Anne Oh, manager of support groups and activity programs for ALZLA.

Even in a summer when the major leagues' best team plays at Dodger Stadium and its best player plays at Angel Stadium, nowhere is the power of baseball in Los Angeles better illustrated than on the fourth floor of this mid-Wilshire office building.

Led by members of the Los Angeles chapter of the Society for American Baseball Research, a group of as many seven dementia patients and their companion caregivers participates in what is known as baseball reminiscence therapy.

In sessions designed to elicit moments of clarity through a century-old connection with the national pastime, participants talk ball, sing ball, and even play a little ball. According to their caretakers, it is the first time some of them have engaged in weeks.

From talk of Little League to thoughts of autograph chases, delving deep into poignant childhood memories, there is something about the ancient sport that rustles the mind.

"Baseball is a game of storytelling; it's the heart and soul of the sport. Everyone has baseball stories, everyone has baseball memories," says Leonoudakis, sixty-one, a producer who brought the program here after hearing about its success in the Central/South Texas SABR chapter.

"These people grew up during the game's golden age, so it seems like such a natural fit."

Oh, whose office also hosts therapeutic programs involving art, music, gardening, and dance, says baseball touches a nerve.

"It brings them to the present," she says. "Individuals with dementia are often just home and not engaging in conversation, not being stimulated with activities. When they come here, it stirs up strong memories they have not thought about for a long time. It opens them up. It's real and important socialization."

It starts with a baseball, but officially begins with a song. On this Friday, after Leonoudakis passes out baseballs from a plastic grocery bag—they're remnants from his youth league coaching days —he pulls out a guitar and everyone stands up.

Because of the usual last-minute cancellations, and because the innovative program has been around only a year and still is gaining traction, there are only three participants today. But, along with their caregivers, they sing the national anthem like they are a group of 30,000.

"Play ball!" Leonoudakis finally shouts, marking the beginning of what is essentially an admission-free day at an imaginary ballpark.

There are concessions, with free pecan cookies, water, and coffee. There are bobblehead dolls, with Leonoudakis passing around tiny sculptures of the generation-spanning Clayton Kershaw, Randy Johnson, and Tom Seaver.

Then there are stories, plenty of stories, with this week's tales focused on legendary Negro Leagues pitcher Chet Brewer and that wonderful Pasadena historical institution known as the Baseball Reliquary.

But the best tales come from the participants themselves, spurred by a Leonoudakis question.

"When you hold that baseball in your hands, what does your heart and soul say?" he asks.

Hassan says, "Watch me, I throw pretty good."

Jones says, "I haven't been to a baseball game in a long time. I wanted to come here to see what it was like."

Then Richard Machinski, seventy-eight, speaks for the first time.

"It's what we did when I was eight years old," he says. "It keeps you alive."

Machinski is handed a photo by his wife Eva. It was from when he coached a youth league team in Bremerton, Washington, in the early '70s.

There are two girls on the boys' team, an odd sight for that era, and Machinski suddenly remembers why.

"I said, 'If they don't play, we don't play,'" he says.

As his health declined, Machinski has increasingly clung to his moments with this group. He constantly asks Eva about the date of the next session. One of his drawings from an art therapy session illustrated this longing.

Amid bright colors he wrote, "I draw pictures, I give them to my wife because I love her, it's now baseball time."

Machinski even recently brought in flour sacks that were used as baseball jerseys by his naval team.

"I played pitcher and catcher," he says, and when asked if it was fun, he exclaims, "100 percent!"

After the presentation and discussion ends, there is a seventh-inning stretch. Of course there is. Everyone stands and Leonouda-kis picks up the guitar and plays "Take Me Out to the Ball Game."

Afterward he shouts, with the excitement of a kid hollering at his neighborhood buddies, "Let's go play some ball!"

The group then moves to a patio where Leonoudakis pitches giant yellow and white Wiffle balls to participants, wielding a black Wiffle bat.

It is the first time some of them have swung a bat in more than fifty years. Some struggle with their coordination. They step into the box tentatively, and hold the bat carefully. But once they start, man, can they hit. Everybody makes contact, driving the ball off a brick wall, into a giant plant, rattling shots around the metal furniture and even off a patio umbrella.

The companions also take their hacks, and Eva Machinski swings out of her shoes. The program is designed not only to momentarily lift the cloud from those with Alzheimer's disease, but also offer a brief respite for those who care for them.

"That swing is for how hard it is to do this, to be a caretaker and companion, to live this every day. This gets the stress out," she says, clenching her teeth before regaining her smile. "We both need this."

The last participant to come to the imaginary plate is Jones. She doesn't want to do it, but her daughter Freda urges her, and so she steps up for her first at-bat in nearly a century.

And she crushes it. She lines a ball directly off Leonoudakis's leg as witnesses howl in delight, and for a moment, everyone is present, everything is clear, and Jones beams at this walk-off hit into a warm and familiar sunset.

"I felt like I was reaching for it, and I couldn't find it," she says of the pitch. "But I found it."

DAVY ROTHBART

The Believer

FROM THE CALIFORNIA SUNDAY MAGAZINE

IF YOU HAPPENED to tune in to the Winter Games last year during the women's halfpipe skiing competition, you might have caught one of the Olympics' most perplexing moments. Halfpipe, which was introduced to the games in 2014, features an adrenaline-soaked spectacle: skiers plummet down a steep track into a frozen ramp the shape of an empty motel swimming pool, before flying up the ramp's twenty-two-foot walls and launching high into the air for a series of bold tricks.

For years, the Olympics had been hemorrhaging viewers to the younger-skewing X Games. Adding halfpipe, among a slew of other freestyle skiing and snowboarding competitions, seemed like a clear bid to siphon back fans who craved big air. Last February, in the qualifying round in Pyeongchang, skier after skier hit the pipe ramp and soared into the sky, their bodies flipping and spinning. Then, Elizabeth Swaney—an Oakland native who'd been a last-minute add to the Hungarian team—started her run, and something really weird happened: she didn't do any tricks.

Instead, she rose neatly up and down the sides of the ramp in bizarrely underwhelming fashion, as the TV announcers, thoroughly confused, narrated the action: "Liz dropping in . . . just getting up to the top of the wall . . . Easing up to the top of the wall, showing the judges she can make it down this halfpipe clean." The overall effect was of a basketball player dribbling up and down the court while never shooting the ball, or a figure skater cruising in circles on the ice without a single jump.

When Swaney finished her run, she carved her way to a stop at the bottom of the course beside a throng of spectators in parkas, pumped her fist three times, and looked up at the scoreboard, waiting for the judges' tally, as though hoping she might have done well enough to advance to the medal round. After a minute, the numbers popped up: She'd totaled 31.4, one of the lowest scores ever recorded in the sport's Olympic history. She finished in last place.

A video of her performance quickly went viral and sparked polarized reactions. Many were furious, labeling her a fraud who had cheated her way into the games. "It's not some adult Disney World where you go to take selfies," someone posted on Swaney's Instagram account. "The Olympics are a showcase of the BEST athletes in the world and Swaney made a mockery of that. She made a mockery of people's life work." On Twitter, she was called the "worst Olympian ever," and a CBS Sports columnist said she'd accomplished "the real American dream: Scamming the system to achieve your life goals while doing the absolute bare minimum to get there." More than one commentator pointed out that by seizing her spot at the Olympics, she'd surely squeezed out people who were more deserving. Others had a more generous read, clumping her with past Olympians who lacked talent but had shown grit by competing in sports in which they were completely outmatched.

In an interview on the *Today* show, when the hosts pressed Swaney about the backlash, she danced around their questions, further mystifying audiences by acting as though there was nothing unusual about her runs. "I just fell in love with freestyle skiing and the opportunities for expression that it gives people," she told the hosts vaguely. Asked about those who would say she didn't belong in the Olympics, Swaney replied, "I thank them for their time . . . and I would just encourage positive vibes for everyone." Left with no satisfying answers, people continued to puzzle over who Elizabeth Swaney was and how this seemingly average athlete had managed to compete on the biggest stage in sports.

I found Swaney earlier this year at a gym in San Francisco called Flagship Athletic Performance, where she likes to train after work. (When she's not working out, she's a recruiter for the tech company Thumbtack.) The song "Happy," by Pharrell Williams, jangled from wall-mounted speakers, while a tattooed young woman led two dozen charges through a series of jumps, skips, and hops.

Between sets, people chattered about their work at Facebook and Apple.

In a quiet corner, Swaney, who is thirty-four, stretched, anonymous and unnoticed in her gray T-shirt, shiny silver leggings, and a pair of weightlifting Nikes that glowed hot pink. Nothing about her presence announced that she was an Olympic athlete; if you'd asked someone to guess who in the room had competed in the 2018 Winter Games, he might have pointed to ten other people first.

Done with her stretches, Swaney loaded weights on a barbell and began what struck me as a peculiar routine: For fifteen minutes, she lifted the barbell from her thighs up to her waist, then lowered it back to her thighs, a span of about three inches. Next, she held the barbell at her waist and spent ten minutes simply clenching her shoulders up toward her ears, again and again. Finally, she added more weight and all at once snatched a ninety-pound load from the ground and smoothly flipped it above her head. The bits she'd been practicing and perfecting, I realized, were micro-steps within a much larger (and more impressive) coordinated movement.

I asked her to explain her technique, since I knew nothing about weightlifting, and she broke things down for me in friendly, technical detail, invoking axioms of physics and the names of interwoven muscle groups.

"So it's all about gravity?" I asked, jokingly obtuse.

She flashed a smile, then zapped it. "I would say it's more about belief."

Swaney has a scientist's precise manner and a rock climber's focus. She's the type of person who listens to audiobooks at double speed (and is working her way up to 2.5 speed), attends Sundance screenings for documentaries like *Senna* and *Bhutto,* and thrusts her hand in the air to ask questions at post-show Q&As, and considers emailing the authors of a self-improvement book called *Designing Your Life* with suggestions on how they might improve their advice—the authors encourage people to focus on one thing; Swaney believes in attacking a variety of goals at once.

At nineteen, she mounted a campaign for governor of California in a race ultimately won by Arnold Schwarzenegger. In her effort to gather the signatures needed to get her name on the ballot, she stationed herself in front of a gym, sensing that people would be in a better mood—and more likely to engage—after a workout. Over the years, she's auditioned, unsuccessfully, to be a cheerleader for the Utah Jazz, Oakland Raiders, and L.A. Clippers, and trained in archery, gymnastics, piano, and flute. "If I'm going to do something," she told me, "I want to learn how to do it well. I might not become the best in the world at it, but I'll learn how the people who are the best in the world are doing it." Her diversified goals seem to function as some combo of self-challenge and intellectual curiosity.

During breaks from her workout, she slowly unspooled details of her unusual résumé. Swaney was born during the 1984 Olympics, she told me, and at age seven, after watching figure skater Kristi Yamaguchi—another Bay Area native—win the gold, she felt moved to pursue her own Olympic dream and began taking skating lessons. A few years later, Swaney's mom brought her to a luncheon hosted by Yamaguchi, and Swaney had a chance to meet her hero; she says Yamaguchi took the opportunity to hammer home the staggering hours of practice Swaney would need to devote to skating if she hoped to become an Olympian.

Swaney continued to train on the ice, but when her middle school teacher suggested that she try rowing, she fell in love with the sport and in college became the coxswain for the highly ranked University of California men's crew team. She had a talent for building friendships with her rowers and mined their personal stories for details she could use to help push them beyond their limits on race days. "She was the quiet assassin," Ivan Smiljanic, a team captain, told me. "Outside the boat, she wasn't loud. She wasn't rambunctious. But as soon as she stepped in the boat, she held the reins." After grad school at Harvard (she studied real estate), Swaney, like a space probe aimed toward faraway planets, relentlessly trained in various sports, including rowing, ice hockey, and skeleton (a luge variant where competitors hurtle headfirst at eighty miles per hour down an icy track). She was fixed on the idea of one day competing in the Olympics, in whatever capacity, making whatever sacrifices were necessary.

For many Olympic sports, the nation's elite athletes are nestled inside Team USA training programs, where the costs of their room, board, and coaching staff are largely covered. This allows them to devote themselves entirely to their craft. But a notch below these elite athletes subsists a layer of good but not great ones, who may not qualify for Team USA sponsorship but for whom the Olympics still feel tantalizingly within reach. Swaney was in this second tier. For these athletes, the challenge is multiplied—they need to prove themselves in their sport while finding a way to manage the entire financial burden of pressing toward their Olympic dream.

Swaney moved to Park City, Utah, a hub for Olympic hopefuls. To pay rent and cover the costs of coaches, gear, and lift passes, she worked a string of thankless jobs—collecting carts in the Whole Foods parking lot, selling cell phones for Sprint, and serving banquets at a five-star resort. "I greeted thousands of guests. 'Good morning, sir,' and 'Good afternoon, ma'am,'" she told me. "It was all in service of a larger goal." Her finances were stretched so thin that she sometimes got by on peanut butter and bananas.

Some athletes who can't make the cut for their home country's Olympic team are allowed to compete for other countries if they have legitimate ties elsewhere. In qualifying events for the skeleton —a sport in which Swaney believed she could land an Olympic spot—she represented Venezuela, where her mother grew up; it didn't hurt that fewer women competed, improving her odds. But after several years of intensive training and competition, she failed to make the 2014 Winter Games in Sochi, Russia. She shifted her focus to halfpipe, vying to become the first-ever freestyle skier in the Olympics to represent Hungary, the home of her grandparents. Halfpipe was known for its danger—four-time Winter X Games gold medalist Sarah Burke had died after a crash in Park City on the same course where Swaney began to train. Only the top twenty-four female halfpipers would be eligible for the 2018 Games in Pyeongchang. But with the dearth of halfpipe courses, and the relatively low supply of world-class competitors, the sport also presented Swaney with what could be her best chance to make the Olympics.

Here's the truth of it: Swaney hadn't trained relentlessly for years at a single sport in the way that her fellow Olympian hopefuls had. Although she could pull off impressive (if still lower-range) aerial stunts in practice on a water ramp, she couldn't complete the same tricks on the halfpipe, where a bad landing could lead to catastrophic injury. So she took another approach. The world rankings were based on points that skiers accumulated at a series of qualifying events in the years leading up to the Olympics in far-flung locales, ranging from California and Colorado to New

Zealand and China. If she attended every single qualifying event and skied a flawless, if simplistic, routine, she'd harvest a few points each time, outscoring those who tried for more-ambitious runs but couldn't land their stunts—a tortoise to their hare.

It was a clever, bluntly effective strategy, and by the time the 2018 Olympics drew near, she was on the cusp of qualification. When a few athletes pulled out due to injury just weeks before the games, Swaney got the call from the Hungarian Olympic Committee that she'd always dreamed of. She was in.

"She was just born that way."

This was Swaney's dad, Tom, who owns an insurance agency, talking to me over tea, as we sat with her mom, Ines, in Swaney's childhood bedroom. They lived in the same home in Oakland's Rockridge neighborhood where they'd raised Swaney and her brother. Swaney moved back in with them two years ago; she sleeps in the basement, workout clothes spread across the floor. Between her day job at Thumbtack, her multiple daily workouts, and traveling for competitions, they see her only fleetingly, although sometimes she rides the morning train into San Francisco with her dad.

In the year since Swaney competed in the Winter Games, Tom's colleagues had often asked him for parenting advice; they wanted to raise an Olympian as he had. But Tom told them he was surprised by his daughter's endless motor and that he had no advice to give. "She has an idea," he marveled, "and she just goes and does it. It's been that way since she was a kid. If only it was so easy for me and for everyone."

But the longer I talked to Tom and Ines, the more I had the sense that Swaney had absorbed some crucial, formative lessons from them. Ines is a Spanish interpreter who sometimes works for the courts. For decades, as a hobby of sorts, Ines and her friends have met monthly to enter a wide range of sweepstakes, which meant mailing in entry forms or postcards. And while she's never cashed in on a million-dollar payday, she's won countless smaller prizes—restaurant gift certificates; tickets to concerts, movies, and sporting events; and even two seats to the luncheon with Kristi Yamaguchi where she'd introduced her daughter to the Olympic star.

Tom was ritualistic in supporting whatever challenges Swaney dreamed up. Watching Yamaguchi at the Olympics ignited in

Swaney an interest in figure skating, so Tom arranged lessons. When she asked to play Little League baseball, he signed her up for a coed team, where she was often the only girl. Her teammates were reluctant to practice with her, but Tom took her to the backstop at a nearby grade school and taught her to throw, catch, and hit. In high school, when Swaney said she wanted to join a crew team called Oakland Strokes, Tom drove her to the estuary to train at 4:30 in the morning a few times a week.

When Swaney had qualified for the Olympics, her parents were thrilled that her persistence had paid off. They stayed up late, watching from their living room as their daughter appeared on their TV from Pyeongchang. "There she is!" Ines cried. But after Swaney performed the same kind of run that she'd been skiing at all of her qualifying events, and the video clip spread, they were heartbroken by the response. "It was shocking how unprofessional these news outlets could be," Tom told me. After an article in the Associated Press appeared, saying that his daughter "had no business competing in the Olympics," he felt that every other outlet had followed suit without digging deeper into her story. He mentioned English ski jumper Eddie the Eagle, the Jamaican bobsled team, and Tongan skier Pita Taufatofua, who had all become Olympic darlings as lovable underdogs and whose ineptness was at the core of their charm.

Ines and Tom's emotional reaction to the backlash was drastically different from Swaney's own response, which was, in essence, not to have a response at all. Whenever I asked her about the criticisms, she gave the same detached, deflective explanation she'd given countless times before: that she'd tried her best, that she had done some tricks, and that, ultimately, she doesn't listen to voices that aren't positive; there's no point.

The contrast reminded me of a story Ines had told me about a sweepstakes she'd won, which awarded her seats to a Golden State Warriors game and three chances to shoot a free throw during a time-out to win a $300 gift card. Before she took the shot, a courtside staffer told her, "Hey, if you make this, go absolutely nuts. Let the whole arena feel your excitement." Ines shot the free throw "granny-style," swished it, and jumped around in glee, like a World Cup player after a game-winning goal. Her reaction was partly genuine, but largely a put-on; she was merely doing as she'd been instructed. After all, it was just a free throw, and she'd only won a few hundred bucks. But the arena shook with applause, and over the course of the night, as she roamed the stands, Ines found herself trading high-fives with her newfound fans. It was a testament to the power of stagecraft: the facts of an event mattered less than their presentation.

But for Swaney, the very qualities that got her into the Olympics in the first place—the unadulterated belief that her hard work would somehow pay off, her refusal to succumb to, or even acknowledge, self-doubt—were the very things that prevented her from being an athlete the public could connect with. When the online trolling began, Swaney responded not as someone who understood what spectators needed—an acknowledgment of her underachievement—but as someone who felt pride in what she had managed to accomplish against long odds. "I just love challenges," she cheerfully told the hosts of the *Today* show, a couple of days after her last-place finish. "I'm always trying to do my best."

In Pyeongchang, Swaney's fellow Olympic halfpipers rose up to defend her; they'd witnessed firsthand her effort on the training slopes of Park City. "If you are going to put in the time and effort to be here, then you deserve to be here as much as I do," said Cassie Sharpe, who'd won the gold. Swaney told me that Maddie Bowman, a 2014 gold medalist, gave her a hug when they crossed paths right after the competition and told her, "We love you." And men's halfpiper David Wise, who'd struck gold in two consecutive Olympics, told a reporter he was "inspired by her."

After the run, she started reading through some of the hateful comments on YouTube and Instagram. Tom said he thought of his daughter as a fortress, eerily imperturbable. But one night when he asked if she'd read some new articles analyzing her story, she told him, "Dad, I don't think I can read any more of those," before disappearing into her room in the basement.

Within a few weeks, Swaney did what she always does—she focused on another goal: competing on the TV show *American Ninja Warrior*.

When she decided she wanted to train for *American Ninja Warrior*, energized by its range of physical challenges, Swaney sought out a man named Brian Kretsch, who operates a *Ninja Warrior* training gym called Apex, in Concord, California, a half-hour east of her parents' house.

On my last night in town, I drove with Swaney to Apex. We crossed over the Oakland Hills, winding past fast-food restaurants and chain stores into a misty industrial park, where Kretsch's gym was located inside a nondescript warehouse. *American Ninja Warrior,* the reality show where competitors try to complete an imaginative, death-defying obstacle course, spawned dozens of *ANW*-style gyms around the country, doubling as adult playgrounds and training centers for those who hope to become contestants on the show.

Kretsch, lean and tall, is one of the longtime stars of *ANW,* having appeared on all ten seasons. He stood with his arms crossed atop a high pedestal in the middle of the gym, beside a giant pit filled with foam fragments, calling out advice here and there to people fighting to get through the obstacle course and chastising a band of young teenagers for playing tag. "People see this on TV, and they think it's gonna be easy," he told me. "Then they come in here, and we never see them again. We call them 'one and dones.'"

Swaney was the opposite, Kretsch said. Supreme challenge was her prime motivation. "When something is hard, she shows up every day until she conquers it. She's a gym rat. And this sport is the ultimate test of patience and persistence." Swaney, he went on, was also highly coachable and extremely focused. "She wants to improve her technique because she understands that's where she'll make the biggest gains."

I watched Swaney try an obstacle called Rumbling Dice, four interconnected pull-up bars attached to a rolling cube. A few months before, she'd fractured her heel at Apex, and her strength had slipped a little. "See," Kretsch said, "most people try to muscle their way through that one. But it's all about technique." He said that Swaney had a stunning mind-body connection—she could receive advice and instantly translate it.

She moved to a "balance log" and crossed it a few times. She lost her footing once and crashed to the mat below. Instantly, she dusted herself off for another attempt, making it with ease. "Your turn," Swaney called to me. "Come try some of this stuff!"

She suggested I limber up with some pull-ups and lingered close by as I struggled to lift myself up to the bar. It was shameful to broadcast my weakness to a room full of athletes. "Okay," she offered generously, "if you can't do a pull-up, see how long you can hang there. That can awaken your muscles." I dangled there, arms burning, for as long as I could.

"Great!" Swaney said. She brought me to an area called the Floating Steps and demonstrated a path through the first few obstacles, hopping across the tops of four wooden posts of increasing height, before leaping to a thick rope, swinging to another platform, and crossing hand over hand along a steel horizontal ladder, until dropping to a stuntman's thickly cushioned mat below.

"I'm sorry," I said. "But there's no way I can do that." Then Swaney proceeded to show me the technique needed to conquer the first chunk, giving me tips on footwork and encouraging me not to allow my fear of failure and fear of looking foolish to mount. She patiently instructed me, looking for ways to make the impossible feel achievable, just as she'd done as a coxswain, just as she'd done her whole life for herself. Seeing her as this unflappable coach brought to mind something that a trainer, Zach Lemis at the Flagship gym, had told me about Swaney: he'd been in a weightlifting teacher-training course with her and was surprised to discover that she was learning to teach lifting while new to lifting herself. Swaney had also told me that when she'd learned to ski in Park City, within months she began training as a ski instructor. "Learning how to teach things," she told me, "helps me process how to do it myself."

Finally, after six failed attempts, I made it to the swinging rope and, adrenalized, managed to swing my way to the ladder, where I powered all the way across to the finish, letting out a cry of victory that echoed throughout the gym.

"Nice job!" Swaney cheered. All week, I'd never seen her smile so broadly. I lay on the mat, heaving for breath. Minutes earlier, the idea of completing even that minor section of the course had seemed ludicrous. But somehow, Swaney had chipped away at my skepticism. It's as if she knew something I was only beginning to understand: we're all amateurs at just about everything, and most of us will stay amateurs. But that only matters if you let it. Swaney extended a hand to pull me up. She wanted me to take a shot at the balance log next. Apex didn't close for another half-hour.

ROBERTO JOSÉ ANDRADE FRANCO

As the Border Bled, Juárez Watched the Game It Waited Nine Years For

FROM DEADSPIN

JUÁREZ, MEXICO — On a scorching hot Sunday afternoon, as you walk through the parking lot of Estadio Olimpico Benito Juárez, you can feel the excitement. Nine long years have passed since the last time Juárez had a team in Mexico's top soccer league. And now, Los Bravos of FC Juárez, are about to play their first home game.

People dance and smile, drink and eat. Kids and adults kick soccer balls between them. A *banda norteño* plays a cover of Fuerza Regida's "Sigo Chambeando"—a song in which the protagonist, after the tragic death of his daughter, begins moving drugs instead of working construction.

Walk among all of this, and it doesn't seem to matter that Los Bravos have yet to win a game. Or that in their last match, Santos Laguna outplayed them so thoroughly that the 3–0 score line didn't accurately capture the vast distance between the two teams. Coming into this first home game, Juárez had yet to score a goal, and sat dead last in Liga MX's standings.

As game time approaches, the thumping music moves inside the stadium, where the concrete seats are so hot their touch bursts the novelty balloons that were handed out to fans. Some of those fans come from El Paso. You can see a steady stream of Bravo jerseys walking to the stadium over one of the international bridges that connect Juárez to El Paso. And despite what's happened here over the past nine years, despite what happened here the day before, there's hope and excitement in the air.

Juárez hasn't felt this festive since February 2016, when Pope Francis visited a city rushing to transform itself. Workers scrambled to paint and clean the streets. The city government halted the sale of alcohol. Hardened prisoners rehearsed songs they'd sing for the Pope. In an open field next to the stadium, the Pope held mass. In front of hundreds of thousands, he called forced migration a "human tragedy."

Walk around Juárez and you can still see signs commemorating that day. They've been there for years; on *ruteras*—city buses—on cars as bumper stickers, or posters on a storefront. They're reminders of the day when people sang, prayed, cheered, and cried. A few carried crosses with the names of those lost to the violence.

"I think all people feel it is a blessing," one person said of the Pope's visit. "All of us think that the city is getting a new start because of his visit. Our family was affected by the violence. They killed four members of our family."

That open field where the Pope spoke and people carried signs is now a parking lot for the soccer stadium. It's the same place where, the night before Los Bravos' first home game, Juárenses gathered to hold a candlelight vigil and mourn the twenty-two people who had just been murdered in their sister city, El Paso, Texas.

Tension has always defined the United States–Mexico border. The most apt description of that tension comes from Chicana author, poet, and activist Gloria Anzaldúa. An *herida abierta,* she called it. An open wound where the two countries rub against each other. They irritate one another, and that grating brings blood. "And before a scab forms," Anzaldúa explains, "it hemorrhages again."

There's always something to make sure the grating never ceases: the proposal of a wall to further divide this place that shares a culture; a sudden shift in policy that demonizes a legal act and adds chaos to a place teetering on a delicate balance; a racist coming to power who legitimizes those with the same racist thoughts. Sometimes, and increasingly, those thoughts turn into violent acts.

El Paso is one of the safest large cities in the United States. Not coincidentally, you can see every branch of law enforcement here. There's an Army base, first established as a way of controlling the border, and now you can't drive out of the city without passing through a Border Patrol checkpoint. Across the border is Juárez, which is, as most know, one of the world's most dangerous cities. But not long ago, things felt different here.

At its most violent, Juárez averaged about eight murders per day. A few years after reaching that peak of bloodshed, though, it started to feel like things were changing. In 2015, city officials even started pitching Juárez as a tourist destination. "Juárez is Waiting for You," the slogan said.

"The purpose of this campaign is to vindicate the city's image abroad and demonstrate the levels of security and peace that we have reached," then-mayor Enrique Serrano said. At the core of this campaign was rebranding the city. Part of the plan was bringing tourists back.

During the darkest years of the violence Avenida Benito Juárez —or La Juárez as we call it—became a ghost town. That avenue is the artery connecting downtown Juárez to downtown El Paso; the two cities that were once one, and the place where I'm from.

On the south side of the divide, on La Juárez, bars, cabarets, casinos, and other types of tourist attractions once lined the street. In the 1930s, while the United States had a thirst for liquor, Juárez was the place to get a drink. The city became a Las Vegas deep in the Chihuahuan Desert, attracting the famous and infamous.

Jack Johnson fought here once as an old man. It was here that he took a punch to the gut and quit. Al Capone also came to Juárez once. He wore a silk, pinstriped suit and left a $50 tip back when cars cost $900. Frank Sinatra sang in one of the old downtown buildings. He divorced here too, as did Elizabeth Taylor and Marilyn Monroe. Conversely, John Coltrane came here to marry. Jim Morrison and John Wayne drank in Club Kentucky, a bar that's almost a century old. And Steve McQueen, dying of cancer, came here to find life. He died during a three-hour operation. Some say the once-strapping leading man had withered away to less than 100 pounds when his search for life ended.

At the height of the violence, La Juárez became a place you avoided once the sun set. A place where even during the day, you walked with your eyes straight ahead and stayed aware of everything around you. In that respect, it wasn't much different from the rest of Juárez. Once darkness came, in a city where well over a million people lived, the streets felt empty.

During the most violent of years, you'd hear rumors of El Chapo arriving at restaurants. His guards would take everyone's phones as he'd tell diners not to worry about their tabs. He'd tell them to eat and drink whatever they wanted. Relax, he'd suggest, because no one was leaving before him. These rumors persisted even when El Chapo awaited extradition to the United States while inside a Juárez prison.

But things got better. And as they did, so too did La Juárez. The city improved its infrastructure. It upgraded the streetlights, widened sidewalks and roads. It covered the outsides of once mismatched, multicolored buildings with a shared facade. Museums opened. Colorful murals brought a tinge of life to the drab desert landscape. Violence seemed to have passed.

One theory said the violence slowed because one cartel had established its hold on the city and with that came, if not peace, stability. A common joke said there was no one left to kill. By 2015, there were *only* 311 murders in the city. Several cities in the United States had more than that. Things felt different, like this wasn't the same place where 10,000 people had once been murdered over the course of four years. And those were just the confirmed dead. Many others disappeared. Gone, like so many things the desert swallows.

Saturday morning, there was a massacre in El Paso. A white nationalist terrorist entered a store and killed twenty-two people for no reason other than they existed. One woman, Jordan Anchondo, died protecting her child. Another woman, Elsa Mendoza Márquez, a teacher from Juárez, went into the store while her husband and son waited in the car. The victims were shopping. For back-to-school clothes and supplies, for milk, bread, eggs, and whatever other mundane necessities they needed. None of it mattered to their killer, who was threatened by their mere existence.

Four minutes before noon, a text warned of danger. "Active shooter in Cielo Vista area," it read. "All El Paso City/County residents are asked to shelter." Everyone from here knows that place. Most have shopped there. They've fought for parking during hot summer days when it feels like you won't make it across the asphalt lot without roasting alive.

Within a few hours, the highways were empty, as were restaurants and stores. Parking lots usually filled with life looked desolate. Like a ghost town. The absence of life made me dread the list of names that would eventually get released. I worried that I'd recognize at least one.

They say the killer drove upwards of ten hours to reach his victims, and I assume he took the same path I've taken many times —from Dallas to Fort Worth to Abilene to Odessa and then on to El Paso. From I-20 to I-10, from water, grass, and trees into the desert. I know this route because north Texas, where the killer came from, is my other home.

I've made that drive so many times I've lost count. I know where to stop for gas and which bathrooms are clean. As you drive into that open west Texas land, hours pass between glimpses of even moderate-sized cities. During that long, lonely drive it's impossible not to contemplate your own life, your beliefs, your future. Ten hours alone, and that still wasn't enough time for him to reconsider killing us.

The first time I took that drive back home, I returned a different person. After almost getting lost along the way, I figured out a few things with the help of some people. And every time I came home after that—taking that same drive—a little part of me had changed for the better. I eventually came back a father to a little girl who has my eyes.

On the day she was born, I began talking to her in Spanish. I told her things no one else knows. My deepest regrets. I told her I felt like a coward for saying these things to someone who can't understand. I told her I loved her and that I would always protect her. I said all of it in Spanish.

She's two years old now. She talks mostly in English, but I keep talking to her in Spanish. I sing to her in Spanish. I feel a sense of accomplishment when she sings to communicate with the side of the family that lives a long drive away from home. Recipes handed down, the stories that get told, the phrases with double meanings, the song lyrics so beautiful they make me glassy-eyed—she'll lose that.

Those are the things that make me who I am, a person from two

places, with two cultures living inside him. They are what make me
exactly like the people who were targeted in El Paso, those who
fled and fell to gunfire because of who they are.

In Juárez, professional fútbol in Mexico's highest league has only
survived for a few years at a time. In the late 1980s and into the
early '90s, there was Las Cobras. Towards the end, the team was so
awful Juárenses called them Las Sobras—The Leftovers.

More recently, Los Indios rose to Mexico's top division. They
reached the playoffs when violence was at its worst. The owner,
with some merit, said the team provided a social good. They were
a "civic vitamin, the one thing that works in Juárez," as Robert Andrew Powell wrote in his book about the city and team, *This Love
Is Not for Cowards.*

The team's improbable run breathed life into a city that was
dying, but the city's violence was eventually too much for Los Indios to overcome. Players refused to play here, and at one point
the team went twenty-nine games without a win. They became the
worst team to play in Mexico's top league. Eventually relegated,
they played in an empty stadium where only the most loyal fans
watched.

Among those who kept attending were members of the team's
barra—a word that doesn't have an English equivalent capturing
all that it means, but "fan group" comes the closest. Because of
Juárez's geographic isolation, that *barra* not only watched the team
play at home, but routinely traveled no less than ten hours to see
their Indios play away games. At these games, they carried signs.
Among them, a large one reading, "JUÁREZ NUNCA JUEGA SOLO."
Juárez never plays alone.

Noting their image among the rest of Mexico and the world,
they called themselves El Kartel. "It was kind of a reference to
crime and cartels, but with a "K"—something different," Angel
Juarez explains. "Making fun of the name itself . . . making fun of
the situation . . . we're not the bad guys. We're not those people
killing."

Angel was one of El Kartel's early members. He took those long
rides on rented buses that often sputtered early into a trip. He was
among a group of friends that grew up together. They turned the
various fan groups across Juárez and El Paso into something more.
Angel was there when they first took up a collection so the group

could buy their first bass drum to play at games. He remains one of three or four people who know the precise recipe for smoke bombs. The same recipe that, he thinks, a university professor gave them. Angel's always been there, and after traveling throughout the country with El Kartel, he can tell you how the rest of Mexico perceives Juárez.

"They only see when you get to a stadium," Angel says of the opposing fans. "But they don't see that you're a doctor. They don't see that you're a dentist. They don't see that this guy works in *el otro lado*." Here, *el otro lado* means El Paso, the other side of the border. Every day, people cross it to work or go to school.

"They see rapists," Angel continues. "They see drug dealers."

At some road games, the police stopped El Kartel's bus. They barred them from staying within city limits. They told them to stay out until it was time for the game. El Kartel was only there a few hours, but long enough to know they were unwelcome.

People see you differently when you're from Juárez. It wasn't always that way, but it is now. And if you're a member of El Kartel, you feel it as soon as you enter an opposing team's stadium. Police in riot gear escort them as they tell you to stand their colors, members of El Kartel stand out. Tens of thousands outnumber the few dozen that travel. And as police use their shields and nightsticks to push others out of the way, the hostility only increases. They feel nervous. Beer splashes on their heads and glass bottles break close to where they stand. Men and women of various ages, all members of El Kartel, begin talking. They sometimes yell because it's the only way others, standing a few feet away, can hear.

"*Ey wey, aqui ya valio verga*—we're fucked," Angel yells. "Whatever happens, it's all for one. *No mas a defenderse wey.*" Just defend yourself. Fighting has always been a part of this. And the illogical passions of sports only make things worse.

And because you are from Juárez, others will call you a rapist, a drug dealer, an addict, and a murderer. They will say you're an embarrassment to the rest of Mexico. They will yell that you should have stayed in Juárez, in your edge of the world.

The statistics say the murder rate increased, again, soon after Juárez began pitching itself to tourists. The same year they commissioned an artist to paint a mural on a nine-story building on La Juárez to help show how much everything had changed. The mural is of Juan Gabriel, the legendary singer and Juárez's favorite son. He began his career singing in *cantinas* along La Juárez. From an orphanage to feeling fame's bright lights, he traveled far but never forgot his home. "Congratulations to the people who are proud of being who they are," the mural reads, in Spanish.

2015 was also the year a new soccer team, FC Juárez, formed to replace the Indios, who folded and disappeared. To represent the spirit of the area, the team was named Los Bravos. Their crest includes a wild horse reminiscent of a statue that is one of the first things you see when you enter Juárez from one of the international bridges. It's of three galloping horses. Monumento a los Indomables—the Monument to the Indomitable—it's called.

Los Bravos were part of the city's rebirth. "Juárez is celebrating," former mayor Enrique Serrano said. "The passion for soccer returns and that revives Juárez."

But a year after that supposed revival, the murder rate swelled. First, it increased by a couple hundred in one year. The following year, a couple hundred more. Last year, Juárez had around 1,250 murders, enough to get called the twentieth most dangerous city in the world. And so, a few years after city officials proudly touted how much had changed, that Juárez no longer ranked among the world's most dangerous cities, they were right back on that dreaded list.

Unlike years past—back when there was an implication that, outside of deadly bad luck, those who died were part of the problem—this time felt different. The United States consulate in Juárez warned citizens against traveling downtown, the same place that used to symbolize just how much had changed. Murders were occurring there in broad daylight. The consulate also prohibited United States government employees from visiting downtown without permission. And if that permission came, travel had to include driving in armored vehicles.

Soon, news of murders again filled the front page of *El Diario de Juárez,* the local newspaper. The only reprieve came from soccer coverage. The day before Mexico defeated Germany in their first match of the 2018 World Cup, there were fourteen homicides. On the day after Mexico's historic victory, their win received more front-page attention than what the newspaper called "the most violent day of the year."

Experts say the increased violence in downtown Juárez comes

from former cartel allies turning against each other. They want to control the area leading into the United States, whose citizens have an insatiable appetite for Mexico's drugs. That area includes the bridge connecting Juárez to El Paso, and by extension, Mexico to the United States.

That's the bridge where, more than a century ago, authorities from the United States deloused Mexicans. They used Zyklon B. In 1938, a scientific journal in Germany praised the United States' method for dealing with their supposed infestation.

That's the bridge where, right before you cross north to the United States, you see a large black cross nailed to a pink board. "NI UNA MAS," a pink sign says in black letters. Not one more. It's a reference to the women who have disappeared in Juárez over the past years. A fair number of them worked in *maquilas*, those foreign-owned industrial plants that rely on cheap labor. The hope was that they'd not only help industrialize northern Mexico but also bring jobs. *Maquiladoras* were supposed to bring forth progress.

That's the bridge where, during the late summer of 2016, a hearse carried Juan Gabriel's lifeless body back home. He passed on the day he was to perform in El Paso. Tens of thousands gathered to cry, dance, and sing. His song "Amor Eterno"—eternal love—suddenly felt different. It punched you in the throat. People left flowers at Juan Gabriel's house. They contributed to a collection so mariachis could serenade Juárez's most beloved son. "Juan Gabriel promised that he was going to stay in Juárez," one man said. "And he did, although I never thought in this way."

That's the bridge where, a few months ago, Border Patrol held migrant families in what a local professor described as a "human dog pound."

It's one of the bridges fans cross to see Los Bravos play at home. It's the same bridge that, after the El Paso massacre, Juárenses going to the United States feared crossing.

You can't understand this place without understanding its past. This is where a man planned to assassinate both presidents of Mexico and the United States when the heads of state met in an attempt to settle a territorial dispute. This is the place that inspired Mariano Azuela to write one of the great novels of the Mexican Revolution, which ousted that same Mexican president, Porfirio Diaz, and became a seismic event in which both El Paso and Juárez played a pivotal role. *Los de Abajo,* or *The Underdogs,* tells the story of a revolution—once full of promise—that ultimately failed to resurrect Mexico.

You don't quite realize what this place is until you have distance between yourself and it. Once gone, you understand that living in the shadow of a border wall isn't normal. You also see how often this place is misunderstood by people who've hardly stepped foot here. Those who don't understand that "fútbol" and "soccer" can be used within the same conversation on either side of the border. Those who loudly worry over what that means. Those who live in fear of what is on the other side of the wall.

Humanity is the first thing that's lost. Read the statistics, headlines, and name—Juárez—and you have an immediate reaction. You may think there's nothing but despair here. And while there's certainly that, there's also life. People raise loving families that laugh and love. They cheer here. They have hope for this place that is home.

Juárez often gets used as a symbol, of what Mexico is and what the United States isn't. But if you're from here, Juárez is like a family member or friend, the one you love despite their problems. You love them because before those problems—some, but not all self-inflicted—you knew who they were.

Sometimes I feel guilty that I, by fluke occurrence, got out. I feel guilty that I left, and in doing so might have abandoned something existential about who I am. Something I can never recover.

Other times I worry that I'm just a tourist now. I go back to search for and find those with whom I lived. I worry because I've seen how it ends for most on that path. It's almost impossible to live here without an intimate understanding that not every story ends well. And yet, other times I talk to them and hear of their small but meaningful changes. They ask for pictures of my daughter. I watch them eat a full meal while they joke. They don't ask for money.

This is it, I think. Nothing ever comes easy in the desert. But, finally, this is them getting better.

Estadio Olimpico Benito Juárez—home of Los Bravos and Los Indios before them—is just off the banks of the concrete riverbed that is the Rio Grande. That river betrays the Mexican name, Rio Bravo, implying raging waters that fill the physical border. But with rising temperatures the melting snow from northern New Mexico and southern Colorado—a large part of the river's source—evaporates before it even gets here.

As Juárez plays Toluca in the third game of the season, members of El Kartel cheer and wave their flags like they did for Los Indios and before that, Las Cobras. Sitting in the southern part of the stadium behind the goal, they're together like they always have been, even when Juárez's past teams disappeared and left them to create their own events to attend.

The realistic expectations for this season are to maintain. "Next year," Angel says, "everything is going to start flowing how it's supposed to." It's that same hope that gives birth to talk of a new stadium. Something that will further attract tourism and transform this region.

Mexican culture has always been fatalistic. "*Cuando te toca, te toca,*" you often hear. And thus, at this moment and in this place, it's possible to forget there were twenty-two murders in Juárez the previous weekend. Or that a few days before that, in El Paso, a rumor on social media caught fire. It said a serial killer was to blame for the recent death and disappearances of several women on the north side of the border. The police department released a statement saying no such serial killer exists.

Here and now, you can forget, or ignore, that one publication now ranks Juárez, the perpetual underdog who fights mightily to live, as the world's fifth most dangerous city. But here and now I also realize some wounds are too fresh to even attempt to forget, let alone ignore. It's why today, on a hot Sunday afternoon, the food tastes a bit bland and the beer feels a few degrees warmer. It's why the sun feels that much hotter.

Death surrounds, again. But as always, the borderlands' duality means there's another side to that senseless death. It means there are long lines around buildings in El Paso, filled with people ready to give their blood. It means there are instances of people risking their lives to protect others. It means people in Juárez are fighting back tears, or letting them flow, alongside El Paso.

As the summer ends and the season remains young, families and friends laugh and dance together while in matching Bravos shirts and hats. On both sides of the border, fathers and mothers hold the hands of their small children. People laugh and smile, even if those expressions aren't as innocent for some as they once were. Strangers bond over their love for a team representing their city and home. They unite over what it means to be from here, a place where you can have two homes.

With Los Bravos' team flag resting at half-mast, there's a moment of silence before the game begins. "Talavera!" one fan screams at Toluca's goalkeeper, Alfredo Talavera, the second after that moment of silence ends. "Talavera! *Chingas a tu madre!*" That same fan who told the goalkeeper to go fuck his mother also held up a shirt that said, "PRAY FOR EL PASO."

On a day like this one, it's easy to imagine things that feel impossible. I imagine that Juárez and El Paso will be at peace soon. That Los Bravos will be champions of Liga MX. I imagine how this place would be different without the long history of racist violence brought on by those who aren't from here. From delousings to concentration camps, from Operation Wetback to Operation Fast and Furious. Without all of that, maybe I, and thousands upon thousands of others, wouldn't have left. Maybe the chain of trauma and hate that's looped its way across the border year after year, the same one that coiled itself around that store in El Paso on Saturday morning, wouldn't have become so hard to break.

For now, though, all there is to do is go on hoping. I'll hope for the day I can come back and not have to leave again, of the day when the border will bleed a little less than it always has. That's always been the way of this place.

Juárez won 2–0. Compared to last week, Los Bravos looked reborn.

KURT STREETER

Which Way, Richmond?
Which Way, America?

FROM THE NEW YORK TIMES

RICHMOND, VA — I wasn't ready.

As a reporter, I had seen death at the hands of street gangs, and life in the hands of a surgeon placing a new heart into the chest of a ten-month-old boy.

But nothing had ever made me feel like this.

My arms grew hot, prickly. My legs would not move. My stomach cramped. Was I going to throw up? I felt sweat on my forehead. Tears pooled in my eyes. They were tears of sadness, then despair, finally anger.

I had tried to prepare myself: "It's only going to be a statue."

But when I looked up and saw it, bronze and nearly three stories tall—Confederate general Stonewall Jackson sternly astride his horse in the middle of a Richmond intersection—I lost my moorings.

This is the Civil War capital of the Confederacy. I count slaves among my ancestors. This also is the birthplace and childhood home of my idol, Arthur Ashe, the first African American on the United States Davis Cup team and, so far, the only Black man to win the singles championship at Wimbledon, at the Australian Open, and at the United States Open.

My son, Ashe, eight, is named after him.

Early this year, amid opposition and racial tension, the Richmond City Council decided to rename Boulevard, one of its most historic thoroughfares, after Arthur Ashe. When new street signs were unveiled Saturday, it became Arthur Ashe Boulevard. It slices across Monument Avenue, known for its outsized statues of Confederate generals, at the very intersection where I was staring into the face of Stonewall Jackson.

Arthur Ashe Boulevard cuts through an avenue of ghosts, not all of them friendly. Richmond is checkered with bronze and stone tributes to the Lost Cause. At a time when this country is at a crossroads, this will become an intersection where the sordid, sinful, and divisive past meets an inclusive, hopeful vision for the future. Symbolically, it asks the question: Which way are we going?

Which way, Richmond? Which way, America?

Which way?

"Hello, Kurt," he said on the phone. "This is Arthur Ashe."

He was genial and calm. His voice was gravelly. It was 1983, and I was in high school. After watching Ashe win at Wimbledon eight years earlier, I had decided that I could dream his dream. I, too, could be a tennis champion.

By the time I was sixteen, I was pretty good—hardly a prodigy, but I was the top high school tennis player in Seattle; among the best in the Pacific Northwest, and one of the ranking Black players of my age in the country.

Ashe was reaching out. He was calling to say that he wanted to help me pay for a year at the Nick Bollettieri Tennis Academy in Florida. In a way, it was no surprise. He was always there for others.

After the academy, I won a tennis scholarship at UC Berkeley, became the first African American captain on its men's team, and helped lead the Golden Bears to an indoor national title. I played in the tennis minor leagues and was world-ranked in singles and doubles.

But I was no Arthur Ashe. I finally went into journalism, where I have tried to honor his legacy. His solicitude has prompted me to write often about the oppressed, the overlooked, and especially those who needed help.

There is another reason, though, that I came to Richmond.

I'm biracial. My late father was a tall, dark-skinned African American. Some of his ancestors were slaves in Virginia. My mother, eighty-seven, is a white woman whose forebears were English and Irish immigrants. Her paternal great-grandfather fought in a Union Army regiment that waged fierce battles near Richmond during the Civil War.

Growing up as I did, with a family like mine, tucked away in the far Northwest, the South was a boogeyman. My parents never traveled there. They feared they might be killed, especially in the 1950s, when they became one of the first biracial couples to marry in Oregon.

In 1964, three young civil rights workers, two white and one Black, were murdered near Philadelphia, Mississippi. Their bodies were buried in a dirt dam. A movie about the killings gave me nightmares for years. So did documentaries about the Ku Klux Klan. When I played tennis in the South, my family always warned: "Be careful. Mind yourself."

I needed to put away my fears. Perhaps because it was verboten, the South fascinated me. Over the years, I have traveled extensively through most of it, exploring its culture, its charms and nuances and stark divides. As an athlete, some of my best moments on the court happened there.

In the early 1990s, a Black, dreadlocked doubles partner and I marched to the finals of a professional tournament at an exclusive, all-white country club near Birmingham, Alabama, the kind of club that wouldn't have us as members.

We turned heads and raised eyebrows. It was the closest I ever came as a player to feeling some of the sting that Ashe had experienced growing up.

But despite my travels, I had never been to Richmond, where he is buried in a plot surrounded by a low iron fence on the outskirts of town.

Ashe died when he was forty-nine, of pneumonia related to AIDS, contracted from a blood transfusion during heart surgery. David Harris, a nephew, took me to his grave.

It was Harris who started a recent movement to honor his uncle with a newly named boulevard.

"It had been tugging at me for a long while," Harris said.

Last year, in the fallout of the deadly white supremacist rally in Charlottesville, Virginia, he came up with a plan.

Not long after the rally, white supremacists gathered at a four-story statue of Robert E. Lee on Monument Avenue. Harris wanted to counter their narrative. "I wanted to come up with a way to show there was another side to this place," he said. "A far different side. There's a lot of good happening here."

Richmond is enjoying a renaissance. At least 30,000 new

residents have arrived since 2000. Many are millennials from beyond the South, attracted by the midsize city's farm-to-table cuisine, craft breweries, art districts, inexpensive living, and downhome vibe.

Nonetheless, painful memories are stitched into the fabric of the city. Harris and I drove past shrines to generals who fought for slavery, as well as a former slave jail, slave burial grounds, and a market where thousands of African Americans were sold.

The city is trying to figure out what to do with its Confederate memorials, built around the turn of the twentieth century, in part to intimidate Black residents. Should the statues be destroyed? Put in a museum? Kept in place, but with added displays that provide context?

Indeed, in 1996, Richmond erected a statue of Arthur Ashe on Monument Avenue. But in size and prominence, it hardly matches the tributes to Confederates on the same street. Neo-Nazis showed up to protest its dedication.

Harris steered his truck to Byrd Park, a vast, tree-lined expanse including well-kept public tennis courts that figure prominently in Ashe's story. In the late 1960s, he played a Davis Cup match there. But in the Jim Crow days of his youth, he was barred.

Last year, Harris decided to renew old efforts to rename Boulevard.

Call it Arthur Ashe Boulevard.

Previous struggles to do so had been quashed during the 1990s and in 2003.

Harris approached Kimberly Gray, an African American councilwoman whose district straddles the street. "This change would seem like a slam dunk, right?" she said, when we met. "But this is Richmond."

Immediately, a group of white residents pushed back. They used old arguments: changing the name to Arthur Ashe Boulevard would be too inconvenient, cost too much—what about the price of new stationery? Some said City Hall was moving too fast; others complained change was occurring without enough citizen input.

Opponents of the name change said their protest had nothing to do with race. They seemed sincere. Also tone-deaf. This is the South, which is still suffering from racial wounds.

When I spoke with African Americans—and several white residents—they were skeptical of the opposition. Levar Stoney, Richmond's Black mayor, said it directly: "'No, no, no, go find another other space!' That is kind of Richmond's history. 'No, no, not here. Go somewhere else.' You can't continue to kick the can down the road if we are going to be an inclusive community."

For a while, Gray was not sure if she had enough votes.

Then came February, with scandals at the Virginia statehouse: a racist photo in the governor's college yearbook, the lieutenant governor accused of sexual assault, the attorney general's admittance that he appeared in blackface at a party in college.

The scandals, coming on the heels of the conflict in Charlottesville, "actually helped push this along," Gray told me. "It was like, 'In Richmond, what is the council going to do now?' The eyes of the world were upon us."

At a packed City Hall meeting, the proponents prevailed. Eight of the nine council members voted for the name change. One abstained.

"Relief," Harris recalled feeling. "It was like, 'Did that really just happen?' We went from being a close vote to nearly unanimous. Even some of our critics are on board now. We're showing what change can look like."

When the new Arthur Ashe Boulevard street signs were unveiled Saturday, thousands attended a celebration at the Virginia Museum of History and Culture. Representative John Lewis of Georgia, a civil rights icon, gave the keynote address.

On the last day of my visit, Harris drove me back to Byrd Park, where Ashe had been barred from playing tennis.

Older men, a group of women, and some children, a rainbow of races, were hitting tennis balls.

Harris and I joined them. When we finished, I walked slowly off the court. I looked beyond a small, grass-covered hill toward the boulevard that now bears Arthur Ashe's name. I felt tears again.

This time they were tears of happiness.

BRYAN BURROUGH

Shooting a Tiger

FROM VANITY FAIR

SHE WAS OUT there in the bushes, prowling in the darkness. He was sure of it. After all that had happened in those awful two years—the thirteen mutilated bodies, the riots, the court fights, the fruitless hunts—it had come down to this: a carload of five hunters and a man-eating tigress, alone on a lonely country road deep in central India.

The lead hunter, Asghar Ali Khan, had never killed such an animal. An open-faced thirty-nine-year-old, he was in charge this evening only because his father, the legendary hunter known to most in India by his colonial-era title, "the Nawab," had been called away on a business trip. Asghar did not have his father's aristocratic swagger, nor his years of experience tracking and killing rogue elephants, man-eating leopards, and wild boars. He did not even have a license to shoot the tigress. But after months of frayed nerves and missed opportunities, this was no time to hesitate.

Now, as the hunters sat in their open-air Suzuki Gypsy, a single mounted searchlight sweeping the night, Asghar saw a sudden movement in the brush. The man on the searchlight yelled that he thought he had seen the tigress cross the road—behind them.

Asghar turned and peered into the night. Nothing. Moments later, headlights swept across a rise in front of them, followed by the screech of brakes, and then screams.

Asghar barked at the driver, and the Gypsy surged forward. A carful of startled villagers were shouting and pointing to their left, into the shadowy trees by the roadside. They had seen the tiger just feet from their fender. As the spotlight again swept the night,

Asghar could see nothing. It had been market day in the nearby town of Ralegaon, and dozens of villagers, including people on motorcycles and small children, were streaming past them, heading home. Asghar knew he had to do something fast, or someone could be killed. The decisions he would make next would bring him headfirst into a confrontation unlike any in the subcontinent's long, fraught history with tigers.

For India, that night last November was the climax of a two-month-long national soap opera: a very public tiger hunt, roiled by bureaucratic infighting, courtroom drama, fatal accidents, and global protests. It devolved into a battle between old India and new: On one side were those who wished to save the tiger, led by a passionate young doctor and a dozen or so harried state veterinarians. On the other side were angry villagers and their unlikely champion, Nawab Shafath Ali Khan, India's last true "white hunter." The conservationists relied on Twitter and drones and tranquilizer darts. The Nawab, insisting that the tiger was simply too dangerous to be captured, trusted only in his gun.

"These activists and veterinarians, what they are doing was madness," he tells me two months after the hunt, as he shows me around his regal home in Hyderabad, India's fourth-largest city. "I knew I am the only person who can solve this problem. God has made me indispensable! There is no one in the country who is doing what I am doing. Out of 1.3 billion people, there is only me."

For centuries, Indian nabobs and the British elite hunted tigers for sport; an estimated 80,000 tigers were killed between 1875 and 1925 alone. By 1972, when Indira Gandhi outlawed hunting and began setting aside land for tiger sanctuaries, barely 1,800 animals remained in the wild. Since then, India has established fifty sanctuaries and waged a concerted battle against poachers, who supply tiger bones to the Chinese medicine trade. Today there are an estimated 2,200 tigers in India, and the number is on the rise.

More tigers, however, has meant more problems. Tigers, highly territorial animals, need a lot of acreage: an adult male may lay claim to more than thirty-five square miles, and will attack any rival that contests it. Tigers who lose this game of musical chairs in one of the state preserves are often forced to roam into the countryside, where they attack and eat cattle and, occasionally, humans. Since 2014, tigers have been blamed for 92 deaths—a rise from previous counts, but a fraction of the 1,052 people killed by elephants.

Without enough preserves to keep up with the rising population, tiger management has exposed a deep cultural rift between urban and rural India. Young urban activists want to save every tiger. Rural villagers—unable to work in their fields, and in fear for their lives—just want the tigers gone, dead or alive. Caught in the middle are the hard-pressed Indian bureaucrats tasked with protecting tigers and villagers alike; many have come to detest the "interference" of these new "armchair activists."

"These activists, it is a fashionable thing," spits A. K. Misra, the vinegary wildlife official who issued the kill order on the latest tigress. "Almost 100 percent of these people don't understand the issues. They just want to make a career out of this and generate donations for themselves."

Misra didn't name names, but there's little doubt about which wildlife activist in India is the most despised by villagers and hunters. In many ways, there would have been no controversy over the latest kill order had it not been for Jerryl Banait, an intense young doctor from the dusty city of Nagpur, at India's geographic center. A polite, poised twenty-five-year-old from a prominent Brahman family, Banait meets me at the Nagpur airport wearing French cuffs and patent-leather loafers. At my hotel, he unpacks several massive binders of his press clippings and explains that his parents, also doctors, were ardent conservationists. From the time he was young, they took him to camp in the countryside, where Banait saved monitor lizards and designed fiberglass water tanks for forest animals to drink from during droughts. But after a high school year in suburban Chicago, Banait had given up conservationism to focus on earning his medical degree.

Then, in June 2017, he read of a shoot-to-kill order issued against a tigress known as T-27, who had killed two men near the city of Bramhapuri. The hunting of "problem" tigers, Banait knew, is governed by strict regulations. For a kill order to be issued, the animal must first be declared a "man-eater." To do so, the government must form a committee to investigate and amass evidence, lots of it: swabs of the tiger's DNA in a human's wounds, human DNA in its scat, and a continuing pattern of attacks on humans. To his dismay, Banait realized that the government had done none of this.

"I was shocked and amazed," he recalls. "How can you label a tigress a man-eater when there are just two chance encounters with humans?" There and then, Banait decided, "I had to do something. I had to stop this. I had no idea how. So I called a lawyer and asked to discuss it."

With hunters already stalking the tigress, Banait was in a race against time. He and his lawyer decided to sue to stop the hunt. Neither had ever tried such a thing. As far as they knew, no one ever had. They drafted the papers in two days and filed them in Nagpur's high court. To generate media attention, Banait hatched the idea of naming the tiger. He dubbed her "Kismet." To his amazement, the judge quashed the kill order, ruling that the government had insufficient evidence to declare the tiger a man-eater.

Kismet was spared, but her odyssey was just beginning. A month later, after the Nawab subdued her with a tranquilizer dart to her neck, she was released into the Bor Wildlife Sanctuary. But, unable to establish her own territory there, she again roamed into the countryside. "She was looking for a new prey base," says Banait. "She traveled 550 kilometers in twenty-five days. She had two more chance encounters with humans. I say 'chance encounters' because she didn't eat their flesh."

Wait. "Chance encounters?" I ask. "You mean she killed more people?" In fact, the tiger had attacked three people, killing a farmer and an elderly woman who was relieving herself in a field. I ask Banait how he feels about that. Had he not saved the tiger, those people might still be alive.

He pushes his glasses up his nose. "I was heartbroken," he replies, his tone formal and a bit bloodless. "When there is a family member who, out of poverty and desperation, has to enter the forest to gather food, and gets unfortunately killed? As a doctor, I am more attached to human beings. But that doesn't mean you kill the tiger. There is a solution, which is not killing."

Another kill order was issued. Again Banait sued. But this time, with two more deaths, he lost. Gathering his papers, he booked a flight to Delhi to file an appeal at the Indian supreme court. At the airport, his phone rang. Kismet had been found dead, electrocuted on a farmer's fence. Banait was stricken. He decided to devote his life, or at least the next part of it, to saving tigers.

"I want to explain to people that we can save wildlife by involving ourselves," he says. "A common citizen can fight for the rights of the wild animal. I will be the voice of the voiceless. So I started delivering lectures, workshops. I gave a TED Talk. It was all very cool."

Even then, Banait had an eye on his next crusade, saving a five-year-old tigress that had killed nine villagers in a rugged area three hours south of Nagpur. The government called her T-1. Banait named her Avni. I'll call her the Tigress.

Lying just west of the modern interstate highway linking Nagpur to Hyderabad in the south, the area where the Tigress roamed encompasses some thirty square miles of rolling hills and patchy forest, home to roughly 10,000 people who live in two dozen villages connected by a web of paved roads. Cotton fields line the country lanes, but beyond them the terrain grows difficult: tall and impenetrable lantana bushes, crisscrossed by deep ravines.

At the epicenter lies Borati, a village of some 300 members of the Pardhi tribe. It's a study in contrasts. The people of Borati are poor, their shanties often lined with burlap bags. But the main paths, like those of many villages, are now made of concrete. Oxen stand roped to solar-powered streetlights. Even the poorest homes sport satellite dishes. "These people," my guide murmurs, "they *love* HBO."

The fear came to Borati in the spring of 2016, when a cow was found half-eaten. Tigers were unknown to the area, but from the claw marks on the carcass it was clear one had arrived. Then, one morning that June, an elderly woman named Sonabai Ghosale walked into the fields to collect the remains of her cotton crop.

"It was around seven," her daughter, Alka Pawar, tells me. "No one went with her. By noon we were a little concerned she had not returned. At that point her husband started asking around. No one had seen her. So I went to the field. I saw a pugmark"—the Hindi word for a large animal's footprint. "It was a tiger. I followed the pugmarks and I saw drops of blood. I followed the blood and I found the body. It was my mother. There were claw marks all over her back. And teeth marks on her neck. She had been killed, but not eaten."

State forestry officials, it turned out, had been tracking the Tigress since 2014. No one is sure where she came from, though most believe she wandered out of the Tipeshwar Wildlife Sanctuary, about forty-four miles south. At five years old, she was in her prime. Roughly 250 pounds, she measured eight feet long from her nose to the tip of her tail. Her colorings were striking: the fur on her face and forelegs a deep burnt orange, the rest of her a bright white and dusky brown with an overlay of vertical black stripes. She lived mostly on deer, boar, water buffalo, and the occasional monkey, and would return to feast on a large kill for as much as a week. Traveling with a male tiger dubbed T-2, she eventually gave birth to two cubs. And with more mouths to feed, she needed more food than ever.

Over the following year, seven more villagers in the area were found dead. After each kill, a wildlife warden would arrive to gather DNA evidence; angry villagers threw stones at him and set fire to his vehicle. Finally, one day in January 2018, an elderly couple, Ramaji and Kalabai Shendre, were working in their field outside the village of Loni. Kalabai was picking cotton when she heard a noise. She turned and, to her horror, saw a tiger emerge from the bushes and pounce on her husband. Ramaji was dead within seconds. Two days later, forestry officials issued orders to kill the Tigress.

Jerryl Banait and another activist, a Mumbai dentist named Sarita Subramaniam, persuaded a court to rescind the kill order, alleging that the conditions for declaring the Tigress a man-eater hadn't been met. But for the next six months, state veterinarians were unable to tranquilize her. "We saw her several times, but every time we failed," says Chetan Patond, a twenty-seven-year-old vet who was one of the Tigress's most determined pursuers. "I wanted to capture one of the cubs and get a radio collar on them. But what if the mother rejected them? They would die. It was decided we couldn't do that."

Last August, after six months without an attack, three more people were killed. In one village, locals went looking for a missing shepherd. "We started searching for my uncle," says Kapil, a thin young man with a rattail and an orange bindi between his eyes. "Someone found footprints. We followed them into the forest. That's when we saw the body." It was in pieces. Crouched atop the remains, snarling, was the Tigress. When the villagers shouted at her, she retreated, only to return moments later. "She came back, in front of 200 people," says Kapil, his eyes widening at the memory. "That shows how ferocious she was." Then once more she retreated, disappearing into the trees.

The villagers marched on the local forestry office, demanding something be done. Under intense public pressure, officials again issued a kill order on the Tigress. Banait filed to block it the next day. This time, though, there was enough DNA evidence to prove the Tigress was responsible. The court in Nagpur upheld the order, and on September 13 the supreme court refused to overturn it. "It was devastating," says Banait. "That's when I realized the only thing left was a lobbying effort."

That day, even as he began contacting conservation groups across India, Banait read the news he feared the most. The government had decided to call in the country's most revered and reviled hunter, a man notorious among activists as a kind of wildlife assassin. There was no one like him in India. They were bringing in the Nawab.

Nawab, which means viceroy, is a Hindustani title dating from the Middle Ages. The man himself, who turns out to be a trim, elegant sixty-one-year-old with a crushing handshake and no shortage of self-confidence, greets me at the gates of his home. He and his son, Asghar, wear gold-rimmed aviator glasses, pressed khakis, and camouflage shirts. They lead me into a grand salon dotted with worn divans, the walls lined with sepia-toned photos and framed articles documenting the Nawab's many kills.

"My grandfather built this home in 1933," the Nawab says with a sweep of his arm. "He was an adviser to Britain on animal issues, here and in Africa. When the British had problems, they called him. I grew up on my grandfather's tales. What I've done for years, yes, is controversial. But in England or the U.S., I would be known as a sportsman. What Ernest Hemingway did, or James Corbett, I do today in India."

For years the Nawab, who shot his first rifle at the age of six and was a national shooting champion at twelve, has worked with a number of Indian states, killing or tranquilizing their rogue elephants and man-eating tigers while training their foresters. "When hunting came to an end in the '70s, there was a vacuum of sportsmen who could read the forest," he says. "The nobility who enjoyed hunting hung up their weapons. A new generation of forestry officers didn't have that background. They were strangers to the forest. When man-animal conflict surfaced, they were at a loss. That's why we get called in."

Though he frequently works alongside the forestry officials charged with managing India's wildlife, the Nawab has little but contempt for them. He is often called in on massive, state-sanctioned culls of wild boars, which have overrun the country's farmland. "The government requests us to go and shoot two hundred animals here, or five hundred animals there, and we do it painlessly," he says with a smile. "We use the proper weapon and the proper bullet, which they don't know how to do. I have seen the police put forty bullets in a tiger, then throw down their guns and run. A lot of times the forestry officers sent with me, they have accidents in their pants. They don't know how to face an animal, or even shoot!"

The Nawab had actually scouted the T-1 search area in December 2017, when officials were considering the first kill order. At the time, the Tigress was traveling with her male consort. The Nawab and his son picked up their trail near Loni. "We went into a nullah," or dry creek bed, he recalls. "Suddenly, a tiger came charging out at us. He was ten meters from us. He stopped, and in a flash I knew it was not T-1. It was the male. He skidded to a halt. He stood there for three seconds. Those three seconds were like three days for us. And then it turned and left. Ninety percent of the time, the tiger withdraws without attacking, because it senses this is something entirely new."

The hunt's nerve center was a ramshackle base camp, typically spread across a roadside clearing, that moved every week or so as hunters tracked the Tigress. Yellow and green tarpaulins stretched between tree limbs were its only cover. Beneath them, state veterinarians and forestry guards hunched over laptops and maps that were spread across folding tables. Cars and jeeps lined the perimeter. Dozens of local men stood idly by, waiting to be sent into the field or on errands. Out in the countryside, the vets set up ninety camera "traps," which snap photos when a motion sensor is triggered.

The area's rocky hills, impassable lantana bushes, and fields of tall cotton, the Nawab informed the forestry ministry, made spotting a tiger difficult. Worse, it made the use of tranquilizer guns problematic. The guns, which are most effective in open fields, shoot low-velocity darts that are easily deflected by tree limbs and brush. In such terrain, the Nawab judged, the chances of tranquilizing the tiger were "very difficult." Privately, he advised that the animal would likely need to be killed. "If the government had listened to me then," he says, "four more innocent people would still be alive." The subsequent failure of state veterinarians to capture the Tigress, he adds, only made things worse. Their futility, in effect, trained the animal to avoid trackers, making it all the more dangerous.

The biggest challenge, in fact, turned out to be the rivalry between the Nawab and the veterinarians. From the start, everyone knew the two sides were in a race to find the animal first. "The hunters, they wanted to kill it," sighs Chetan Patond, the young vet. "We wanted to tranquilize. It was a battle."

The vets, however, faced severe limitations. They had few weapons and no professional trackers. Tigers are nocturnal, but the vets thought it too dangerous to venture out at night. They finished their work each day at six sharp, no matter the conditions. "The animal can see much better than we can," Patond tells me. "So it is not safe. We need to catch it in the open. She can be right there in that bush"—he points to one behind me—"and I couldn't shoot it. The dart will not go through a bush. Several times we knew she was in the lantana. She used to growl loudly, and we would back out of the area."

Under government orders, the Nawab's men cooperated with the vets during their daytime patrols. But the real work was done at night, when the Nawab himself, armed with rifles and searchlights, went out in his Suzuki Gypsy. "Moving the wheel of lethargy, getting the government to move, getting the job the way I wanted it was the most difficult thing," he says. "At base camp, they work nine to six. The tiger comes out at six! As their people are going home! This is madness!"

The problems began immediately. On September 13, two days after the supreme court ruled against Banait, the Nawab and a five-man team, having just arrived in the search area, responded to a report of a freshly killed cow near the village of Kishanpur. It had been dragged up a creek bed. Setting out on foot, the Nawab followed the drag marks for an hour or so until he found two sets of pugmarks, which he judged to have been made by the Tigress and one of her cubs. Another mile in, they found evidence that they were closing in. Water inside one set of pugmarks was still brown; the sediment had yet to settle. "We knew then she was just a few heartbeats ahead of us," the Nawab says. At twilight, pushing through deep brush, they came upon the half-eaten carcass of the cow.

They paused, listening. Asghar nudged his father, indicating he could hear a soft growling somewhere nearby. Then the Nawab heard it too. "I heard a *huff huff* sound, a cough-like growling," he says. "Then the pitch changed, louder and lower. In a few seconds we felt the ground shake before our feet as she broke into a charge. She came out of the lantana at an angle, then stopped and ran back into the jungle. We had no chance to shoot her. It was so surprising—it was one of the most terrifying charges in my forty years of hunting."

As darkness fell, they withdrew, reporting the incident to forestry officials. But when they returned the next morning, they were surprised to find a guard barring their way. The vets knew that the only hope they had of tranquilizing the Tigress was to keep the Nawab from getting a shot in first, so they had decided to block him from the search area.

The Nawab realized it was time to teach the bureaucrats a lesson. He called A. K. Misra, the ministry's wildlife chief, and explained what had happened. "I am leaving," he announced. "I don't want to be associated with this operation." Then he hung up. For the rest of the day, he ignored the calls lighting up his phone.

The hunt had already become a media circus; reporters hovered around base camp all day, and swarmed the Nawab's hotel in the highway town of Pandharkaoda at night. That evening, he was surprised to hear a soft knock on his door. It was the woman who oversaw the hunt, a wildlife staffer named K. M. Abharna. She apologized for the "miscommunication" and begged him to stay. Eager for scandal, the next day's papers expressed outrage that a married woman had been sent alone to the Nawab's room. "It's a very Indian thing," one journalist told me with a sigh. "It's something we don't do."

The Nawab agreed to stay on, but the infighting was just beginning. His main rival was a noted veterinarian named Akhilesh Mishra, a tall, animated man who had captured more than seventy tigers in the neighboring state of Madhya Pradesh. Mishra uses elephants to stalk tigers: they can tromp through bush humans can't, and a dart fired from atop an elephant faces fewer obstacles than one fired from low to the ground. Like many vets, Mishra views the Nawab as an egotistical relic of another time. "He doesn't know anything," Mishra scoffs, "yet he has created this aura. We always tried to ignore him."

It took only days for the tension between Mishra and the Nawab to boil over. On September 18, four cows were killed near Borati. Arriving at the area with his towering elephants, Mishra kept an eye on one of the kills until nightfall. Then he spotted one of the Tigress's cubs, presumably intending to feed. Some of the vets argued for capturing it, but Mishra waved them off. "No, let her go eat," he told them. "When she gets full, she will be easier to catch. And when you capture a cub, the mother is going nowhere."

Mishra suggested they get some sleep and return before dawn. He gave orders to forestry guards not to allow anyone into the area. With luck, they would spot and tranquilize the mother and her sated cubs in the morning.

But the Nawab cared nothing for Mishra's carefully laid plans. That night, he drove into the cordoned-off area. In a clump of woods, he managed to find the day's fourth kill. In the silence, he and his men followed their routine: they listened to the forest, straining to hear the animals known to emit warning cries when a tiger nears. Peacocks. Spotted deer. Monkeys. But this time, they heard something surprising: human voices.

It was two in the morning. Directing his driver to mount an adjacent hill, the Nawab was startled to discover a crowd of some forty villagers coming toward him. He knew what they intended to do—exactly what villagers had done to tigers for years: poison it. Tigers typically return several times over a period of days to feed on a kill. By sprinkling the kill with poison—usually pesticide—villagers give the tiger a long, painful death. It's the same method used by poachers of both tigers and African lions.

The Nawab called the police, and spent the rest of the night helping them clear the forest of people. He didn't especially care that he had spoiled Mishra's plan. "That night," he says, "those tigers would've been poisoned if not for me."

Returning to the cordoned area before dawn, Mishra was shocked to learn that the Nawab had spent all night inside. He grows animated just telling me about it. "He came back! He came back and drove all over! And scared her off! I couldn't believe it! He was there all night, driving around." Enraged, Mishra called wildlife officials and told them he was finished. "I quit," he said. "You can't control that idiot, so I'm going home."

The Nawab had succeeded at driving away his chief rival. But his victory sparked a backlash. The abrupt departure of Mishra and his elephants coincided with a surge in public interest in the hunt, triggered by a protest that Jerryl Banait led in Nagpur. Fifty activists, several with tiger stripes painted on their faces, marched on the forestry ministry and demanded the Nawab's removal, as did Maneka Gandhi, a government minister and the widow of Indira Gandhi's son. Stung by the unprecedented publicity, forestry officials convened an emergency meeting in Mumbai. The Nawab, they announced, was being sidelined to give the veterinarians a chance to tranquilize the Tigress. For the next two weeks, the vets would have the search area to themselves.

A new team of vets, along with five elephants, was dispatched to base camp. This time, they added a twenty-first-century touch, deploying a thermal drone to pinpoint the whereabouts of the Tigress. Unfortunately, the drone's sensors proved unable to penetrate the deep brush. The rocky terrain, meanwhile, retained the day's heat, preventing the drone's sensors from differentiating between a warm tiger and a warm boulder.

Then, on October 3, disaster struck. One of the elephants, apparently a female in heat, escaped its tether during the night and rumbled twelve miles to the village of Chahand, where it charged a thirty-year-old woman collecting cow dung beside her shanty. The elephant picked her up in its trunk and threw her into a cotton field, killing her instantly. That night, forestry officials decided to get rid of the elephants and bring back the Nawab.

And so, on October 7, the Nawab was given what he wanted: full control over the hunt. The veterinarians, who still believed they could save the Tigress from his guns, were allowed to stay. But even if they managed to spot her, they were ordered to do nothing until the Nawab appeared on the scene. "Five elephants, veterinarians from all over the country, drones—it had all achieved zero," he tells me. "Less than zero, actually, because their efforts had taught the Tigress new skills. Now, after all this, it was finally up to me alone."

In those first few days, the Nawab faced a more pressing problem than recalcitrant vets: the Tigress had vanished. For a solid week there was no sign of her or the cubs. Nothing on the camera traps, no scat, no kills, no pugmarks, nothing. The Nawab brought in a motorized hang glider and began flying sorties across the search area; a video of one of its crashes soon went viral. He tried a pair of Italian cane corso tracking dogs and hired a friend, a professional golfer, to lead them. Growing desperate, he had his men trap wild piglets, which he staked as bait. The Tigress ignored them.

Finally, on October 18, a shepherd outside the village of Sarati spotted the Tigress dragging a cow's carcass toward a tree line. As panic spread, the Nawab dispatched three veteran trackers. They had barely entered the woods when they spied the Tigress hunched over her kill. She charged. The three men sprinted for a tree and climbed it. As the Tigress paced below, they radioed for help. By the time Asghar and a team from base camp arrived, however, the Tigress had once again melted into the forest.

Back in Nagpur, a desperate Jerryl Banait knew the Nawab was closing in. The stress was getting to him. He had received death threats. Villagers had burned him in effigy. He was convinced he was being followed and his phones tapped. He was ready to try anything. He reopened his legal fight, asking the court to stop the hunt. This time, his attorneys packed the filing with every conceivable objection. The hang glider was illegal. The tracking dogs were dangerous. The use of piglets as bait was inhumane. But on October 22, Nagpur's high court refused to intervene. The hunt would continue.

Back at base camp, the veterinarians were starting to feel desperate. Most tigers are captured in a week or two; this hunt was entering its second month. "Our resources were exhausted, people were exhausted," recalls Chetan Patond. "This needed to be over."

Perhaps the strangest thing the vets tried involved luring the Tigress with samples of cologne: specifically, Calvin Klein's Obsession for Men. Obsession contains synthetic civetone, a compound derived from the scent glands of the civet, a tropical mammal resembling an otter. When it's sprayed in the wild, tigers have been seen taking deep whiffs and rolling around playfully. "I sprayed that perfume on a towel, twice, and tied it to posts near our cameras," sighs Patond. "Nothing happened."

On October 27, a new veterinarian, Sunil Bawaskar, appeared at base camp. A peppery forty-three-year-old who runs the zoo in Nagpur, Bawaskar had another idea for luring the Tigress: tiger urine. In the wild, tigers use urine to mark their territories. When sprayed from a container, Bawaskar believed, the urine—which smells like buttered popcorn—would arouse the curiosity of the Tigress and draw her in.

From the moment he arrived, Bawaskar, like the Nawab, made clear things would run his way. "I never listen to anybody," he tells me as we chat in his office, outside of which a tiger paces its enclosure. For years, he boasts, forestry officials have refused to invite him on hunts because he is "unmanageable." Now, at base camp, he found morale among the vets nearing a low point. "Everyone was telling me they could have gotten this tigress," he says. "But whenever they got signals and rushed to the spot, they were asked to step back and wait for the Nawab. But he sleeps all day and works at night. He took two hours to come when a spotting was made. So all attempts were failing."

To capture the Tigress, Bawaskar began spraying tiger urine on trees and bushes in remote areas, hoping to draw her away from places the Nawab could reach by car. Day after day, Bawaskar and his fellow vets waited in their blinds, known as machans, with tranquilizer guns readied. Then, on November 2—a day after the Nawab had left the search area on a business trip—the vets were having breakfast at base camp when they heard the news: a camera trap had snapped a photo of the Tigress near Borati. Racing to a spot not far from the village, they sprayed the bushes and trees with liberal amounts of urine. Then they took their tranquilizer guns and climbed into their machans. With the Nawab away, this was their chance.

The Nawab may have left the search area, but his son, Asghar, remained behind with a full team of guides and trackers. When I spoke with Asghar at the family home in Hyderabad, he seemed less the wild-eyed killer of some Indian press accounts and more an earnest, guileless young man who clearly worships his father.

As Asghar tells it, his team of six reached the area where the Tigress had been seen around 1:30 on the afternoon of November 2. Striking out on foot, his little column pushed through heavy brush for ninety minutes before finding a pugmark. "We knew where she was heading," Asghar recalls. "To the agricultural lands around Borati. Up there, there were people out in the fields, 360 degrees, people everywhere. It was a dangerous situation."

At one point, as they emerged from the brush into a tall cotton field, the tracker at the rear snapped his fingers. When Asghar looked back, the man pointed toward a bush-covered hillock on their left. With his eyes, he made clear: the Tigress was there.

Everyone froze. Minutes ticked by with no movement from the bushes. Finally, sensing that the tiger had left, they crept up the hillock. In the dirt they found the outline of where she had been lying. She appeared to be approaching the area where the veterinarians were waiting in their machans. "She is heading your way," Asghar radioed the vets. "Be ready."

As Asghar and his men returned to base camp, anticipation rose among the vets. But after an hour the sun began to set with no sign of the Tigress. It was, like the fifty before it, a wasted day. As the vets gathered at the roadside, preparing to leave, Chetan Patond wondered whether, with the Nawab away, it might be safe to spray urine along the blacktop. They suspected the tiger was prowling the roads at night, but they hadn't sprayed them, knowing the Nawab also used the roads.

"I was so frustrated, we were all exhausted, so we did it," Bawaskar recalls. "We said we can come back and tranquilize her in the morning. The Nawab is gone. It will be fine. We assumed the animal was safe that night. At least until the Nawab returned."

Later that evening, back at base camp, Asghar began getting frantic calls. As night fell, scores of villagers from Borati were returning from market day in the town of Ralegaon. Now, many on the road reported seeing a tiger in the brush. "We were not aware urine had been sprayed on that road," Asghar later tells me. "We had no clue. And villagers were driving right into it." The Nawab, as ever, was less diplomatic. "They were trying to draw a man-eater right beside a village!" he exclaims. "This is a great way to get these poor people killed."

Asghar says he was instructed to return to the village by A. K. Misra, the wildlife chief. "Misra urged us to get people off the roads and out of the fields and back into the houses," says Asghar. "No more human kills: that was the most important thing." (Misra denies having this conversation.) A little after six, with darkness falling, Asghar and his team piled into their Gypsy and drove to the first nullah on the road west of Borati. For two tense hours they slowly patrolled the road, their spotlight sweeping the gloom. Cars and motorcycles packed with laughing villagers—more than a few of them inebriated from market-day festivities—streamed past, heading home to Borati. Twice they heard screaming, and raced forward to find a carload of terrified villagers shouting and pointing into the darkness. But the hunters could find no sign of the Tigress. It was like chasing a ghost.

Around 8:30, as the traffic began thinning, Asghar and his men headed back to base camp for dinner. They had just begun eating when their cell phones suddenly lit up with calls, all from villagers on the road southwest of Borati. "There was call after call, SOS's, all sightings on the road," Asghar says. The veterinarians, who were midway through their own dinner, debated whether to return to the search area, but concluded they couldn't track the tiger in the darkness. "It would be suicide," Patond says.

Asghar and his team returned to the village, stopping to check the road along the way. At the first creek bed, the darkness was still. They swept the searchlight all around but saw nothing. Driving to the second nullah, they again swept the searchlight through the darkness. Nothing. They listened to the night. Silence.

It was 10:30. They cruised forward a few hundred yards, rounded a lazy curve, and coasted downhill to the low-water crossing spanning the third nullah, where they stopped, the Gypsy's engine running. White posts lined the aging road, its asphalt crumbling away to reveal cement beneath. Overhead stretched the limbs of an azan tree. Again, the searchlight cut through the inky night. To the left and right nothing moved among the worn stones of the nullah. Ahead, up a rise from the creek bed, dense brush lined the right side of the road.

Suddenly, one of the trackers motioned forward, toward the brush. "Something moved," he said.

The car began to ease forward, inching up the rise. They trained the searchlight on the right side of the road.

And then she was there, fifty feet in front of the Gypsy, stepping from an unseen trail in the bushes onto the road: the Tigress, T-1, Avni.

She began walking slowly across the pavement.

Two of the team's trackers had memorized the tiger's markings. "It's the man-eater!" one yelled.

"It's T-1!" shouted the other.

At that point, everything happened in a matter of seconds. "She was in the headlights," says Asghar, who sat on the left side of the front seat, cradling his rifle. "The forestry guard behind me, he instantly fired the tranquilizer gun. By this time she had crossed half the road. He hit her."

According to an official report, the Tigress was struck in the left thigh at a distance of forty-two feet. She snarled but continued crossing the road. Crucially, the Gypsy, now moving along the pavement's right shoulder, continued moving up the road, toward the Tigress. In seconds it drew even with the animal, which paused, just off the left shoulder, nineteen feet across the asphalt.

Asghar was nearest her. He could see her teeth. "In a second, she turned toward the vehicle," he says. "By the time we realized what was happening, there was almost no time to react. She was right beside my window. We had no protection. We were totally exposed. The important thing was the safety of my team. I was expecting she would leap into the vehicle in a fraction of a second. If I didn't shoot, we would've lost control of the situation. It would have gotten out of our hands. She was that close."

Between two and five seconds after the tranquilizer dart had been shot—and long before its chemical agents might have sedated the tiger—Asghar raised his rifle and fired a single bullet. It struck the Tigress behind the left shoulder, pierced her heart, and stopped beside her right shoulder. "The moment the bullet hit her, she went down," Asghar says. "She made no noise. She didn't even move her tail. She just went down."

The Gypsy kept moving as the tiger fell, coming to a stop a hundred yards up the road. The hunters trained the searchlight on the motionless animal for a long minute or two. When she didn't stir, they returned to find that she was dead.

The hunters radioed base camp with the news. In the time it took the vets and others to reach the site, Asghar stood staring at the lifeless body, so still and majestic. He insists he was saddened. "I didn't want to shoot her," he tells me. "I didn't. We tried to tranquilize her to the end. We were all disappointed. There was no way we could've saved her. There wasn't. One of us would've gotten killed."

When Sunil Bawaskar arrived, he took one look at the motionless corpse and walked away in disgust. Back in Nagpur, Jerryl Banait, having just returned from a meeting in Mumbai, took the call at his parents' home. "I was devastated," he says. "I was so close to her. I had named her. I was in tears. I didn't sleep that night. There was anger, frustration, sadness. And I felt like a failure. After everything we had done, I lost. Whatever I did, they had done whatever they wanted to do. I was furious."

The tiger's two cubs were eventually captured and taken to a sanctuary. But reaction to the killing, both in India and around the world, was visceral. Maneka Gandhi called it a "ghastly murder" and "patently illegal." PETA India called it a "wildlife crime." Protests, many of them initiated by Banait and his new allies in 168 conservation groups worldwide, broke out in thirty-three cities across eleven countries. Hundreds took to the streets in Mumbai and Delhi, and candlelight vigils were held in cities across India. The country had never seen anything like it in the long history of tigers and man on the subcontinent.

The public debate revolved around whether the killing of the Tigress was, in effect, murder or justifiable homicide. As critics have pointed out, there was no overwhelming need for Asghar to pull the trigger. Simply pressing the Gypsy's accelerator and moving the car ahead would have put the team safely out of the tiger's reach. A month after the killing, a report by the National Tiger Conservation Authority cast doubt on Asghar's version of events. It found numerous violations in the actions of his team, from using an expired tranquilizer dart to failing to bring along a wildlife biologist. An autopsy, meanwhile, found no evidence that the dart penetrated the tiger's muscle, suggesting, at least to activists, that it had been applied only after her death in an effort to cover up its circumstances. Whatever the case, Asghar, the report concluded, was unauthorized to kill the tiger—a finding disputed by A. K. Misra, the wildlife chief. "I authorized him," Misra tells me. "To criticize what Asghar did, it is hairsplitting."

In the end, however, such finger-pointing may miss a deeper and more complicated truth. Perhaps Asghar was neither a cold-blooded murderer nor justified in his actions. Unlike his famous father, he had never killed a tiger. The report, in fact, concluded that Asghar was a "totally inexperienced person." Perhaps, in that fatal moment, he did what most of us would do in the face of danger. Perhaps he simply panicked.

Sad as the Tigress's death may be, there is hope in India that some good may come from the publicity surrounding her plight. Some call it the country's "Cecil" moment, an allusion to the elderly lion in Zimbabwe that was killed by an American dentist with a bow and arrow in 2015. "The one thing both incidents did was to grab attention globally of people who may have otherwise never cared, resulting in public mourning and public shaming," says Sumanth Bindumadhav, the wildlife campaign manager of India's Humane Society. "One can only hope that the sacrifice these animals made will result in public-policy changes, as opposed to a onetime outrage."

But publicity alone, however well intended, won't save India's tigers. Only more land and more money can do that. The real threat to tigers isn't hunters like the Nawab, or even the poachers who profit from selling their body parts. The real threat is humanity itself. Every time a tiger is killed, it's a reminder that humans have overrun the creatures' habitat, leaving them without the space and prey they need to survive. Tigers attack people out of the desperation people have caused them.

Knowing this, wildlife officials in India have resigned themselves to the almost daily loss of the animals they are charged with protecting. The Tigress may be gone, but there are others still to save. "There are many tigers—this is just one," says Chetan Poland, the veterinarian. "In our park, poachers have killed four tigers in four days. This is a cycle, you know. Her death is sad. But at the end of the day, it's okay. She lived six years. She had a good life."

JOSHUA HAMMER

Chaos at the Top of the World

FROM GQ

IT WAS MORNING and bright, and Reinhard Grubhofer, depleted and dehydrated, hoisted his body over a crest and rose uneasily. There, from the summit of Mount Everest, he could see everything. How the earth curved gorgeously in all direction; how wisps of clouds sailed beneath his boots. The view—out beyond his worries—was beautiful. But closer at hand, he could see trouble taking shape.

He could feel it too, shuffling with a dozen other climbers onto a slim patch of ground roughly the size of two Ping-Pong tables. The space was crowded. Shakily, Grubhofer held up a small flag and posed for photos with his climbing partner, a fellow Austrian named Ernst Landgraf, who'd made the slog to the summit uneasily. It had been a brutal day. Their thirteen-man party had awoken at eleven the previous night and trudged through the darkness up the icy incline of Everest's north side. Along the way, the temperatures dipped to well below zero. At some point, the water bottle that Grubhofer packed had frozen into a solid brick. He was thirsty and exhausted. But he tried not to pay attention to any of that now. After weeks of waiting and years of planning, Grubhofer had made it. It was 9:30 a.m. on May 23, and a less experienced climber might have thought that the hard part was over. Grubhofer knew better.

As he jockeyed for a place to stand at the top of the world, his Sherpa's radio came alive. Kari Kobler, the founder of the Swiss mountaineering agency that had organized Grubhofer's expedition, was radioing urgently from base camp. Bad weather was moving in fast. They had to descend, quickly.

Grubhofer looked down toward Nepal and could see gray clouds sweeping across the southern face of the mountain. There was something else down there too: a line of a hundred or so climbers in brightly colored suits snaking up the side of the mountain. The crowd seemed incredible—like a bag of Skittles had been scattered down the slope. On the north side, Grubhofer knew, more climbers were tracing his trail up the mountain from Tibet too.

He hopped off the summit and crossed two windswept snow-fields, digging unsteadily into the crust with his crampons. Whenever Grubhofer encountered somebody ascending the mountain, etiquette forced him to unclip himself from the rope to step around the climber. Each time he did so, he was aware that a gust of wind or a misstep could send him hurtling to an uncertain fate.

Grubhofer had tossed his goggles after they'd frozen in the night and now was wearing Adidas sports sunglasses, which fogged over constantly, requiring him to remove his down mittens in the cold to clean the lenses—a tiny reminder of the multitude of dangerous unpleasantries and unforeseen challenges that crop up on Everest.

None of this was new to Grubhofer. A wiry forty-five-year-old with a thatch of reddish-blond hair, he'd taken up mountaineering fifteen years earlier at thirty. That's when Grubhofer, depressed following a divorce, vowed to restart his life. He set out for the Himalayas and scaled 21,250-foot Mera Peak in Nepal. "I was not fit enough, but it got me hooked in," he recalls. Over the following decade, Grubhofer ticked off three of the Seven Summits—the highest peaks on each of the seven continents.

Everest would be his fourth. He took his first shot in 2015, but the adventure was cut short. He was dug in with his team at 21,300 feet, at what's known as Advanced Base Camp, when an earthquake hit the region, setting off an avalanche that killed over a dozen people at the Nepalese base camp. Grubhofer's expedition was untouched, but no one from either the Tibetan or the Nepali side of Everest summited that season.

Returning to the mountain hadn't been cheap. Grubhofer, who works for a sightseeing company in Vienna, paid $65,000 for a package that included travel to and from Tibet, visas, guide and Sherpa fees, and the $11,000 permit issued by the Chinese government. Reaching the summit this time around represented a special kind of thrill, but he refused to celebrate until he was safely down the mountain. Late in the morning, as he made his way along the crowded trail, a fog rolled in, the wind whipped up, and snow began to fall.

Around noon Grubhofer arrived at the most dangerous obstacle on the northern side: step two, a roughly 100-foot drop, negotiated this time by three rickety ladders placed against the rock-and-ice facade. The first ladder was about 30 feet long. To reach it, a climber had to twist his body to face the mountain and extend his heavy, crampon-covered boot past an overhang, feeling blindly for the first rung. It was here that the half-dozen climbers ahead of him ground to a sudden halt.

Why the hell aren't we moving? Grubhofer wondered. *What's holding up the line?*

He swiftly identified the problem: a woman in a red climbing suit adorned with the emblems of a Chinese mountaineering group perched just before the drop-off, unwilling to go forward. The woman's two Sherpa guides were firmly encouraging her to descend the ladder, but she remained paralyzed in apparent fear. For those in the logjam behind her, there was no going around. Everybody was stuck, freezing in the storm. Nearly six miles high in the Himalayas, Grubhofer knew, conditions were unforgiving: standing still for long periods in the so-called death zone above 26,000 feet dramatically increased the risk of frostbite, heart attack, stroke, pulmonary or cerebral edema—and death. Grubhofer knew that Ernst Landgraf, the member of his climbing party whom he had seen on Everest's summit, had been exhausted at the top. He could just make out Landgraf—obscured by snowfall, clouds, fog, and people—a few climbers behind him, but Grubhofer didn't know how the sixty-four-year-old was holding up.

"Move it!" shouted a climber behind Grubhofer.

Oh, shit, Grubhofer thought, *this is getting serious.*

This Chinese woman, he was sure, had no business being on the mountain. *Why hadn't her guides screened her ahead of time?* Thirty minutes crawled by. Forty-five passed. Still she wouldn't go down the ladder.

"For God's sake," another climber exclaimed, raising his arms in disgust. "Why is she not moving?"

*

For much of the year, climbing Everest is an impossible idea. But each May the roaring jet stream that torments the mountain subsides just enough to allow alpinists a shot at reaching the top. Should the weather suddenly turn, the results are often deadly. Jon Krakauer's *Into Thin Air* made famous the May 1996 disaster during which eight climbers—caught in a blinding whiteout—perished from exposure or plunged to their death. The book was a tale of the vicissitudes of nature, the hubris of climbers, and the ineffable lure of the mountain, as well as a reminder that, though Everest had been summited by hundreds, it remains an incredible and dangerous challenge. It was also a scathing portrait of irresponsible guides catering to wealthy, out-of-their-depth dilettantes who were floundering around in what had become an increasingly commercialized enterprise. It was greeted as a wake-up call.

But two decades on, the Everest experience often seems to have devolved even further into a circus-like pageant of stunts and self-promotion. In April 2017, DJ Paul Oakenfold outraged mountaineering purists by hosting an EDM concert at the base camp in Nepal; this year three Indian climbers returned home to celebratory crowds after they supposedly summited on May 26, only to be accused of fraud after other mountaineers claimed that they never made it past 23,500 feet.

And then there are the growing crowds. For this year's climbing season, Nepal handed out 381 permits to scale Everest, the most ever. The Chinese government distributed more than 100 permits for the northern side. According to the Himalayan Database, the number of people summiting Everest has just about doubled in the past decade. And in that time the mountain has become accessible even to relative novices, thanks to a proliferation of cut-rate agencies that require little proof of technical skill, experience, or physical fitness. "Some of these companies don't ask any questions," says Rolfe Oostra, an Australian mountaineer and a founder of France-based 360 Expeditions, which sent four clients to the summit this year. "They are willing to take anybody on, and that compounds the problems for everyone."

On May 22—the day before Grubhofer reached the top—a long line near the summit had already begun to form. One of those pinned in the throng was a Nepali climber named Nirmal Purja. That morning, Purja snapped a photo of the chaos. The picture showed a near-unprecedented traffic jam on the popular southern side: a column of hundreds of climbers snaking along the knife-like summit ridge toward the Hillary Step, the last obstacle before the top, packed jacket-to-jacket as if they were queued up for a ski lift in Vail. The image rocketed around the world and, as the events on the mountain were still developing, raised an urgent question: what the hell is going on atop Mount Everest?

In the Himalayan Mountains, calamity frequently takes shape off in the distance. Events have a way of cascading. Everest was clogged with climbers in late May because of—among other things—a cyclone that had struck weeks earlier, several hundred miles away.

Earlier that month, Cyclone Fani made landfall in India as a massive Category 4 storm, blasting warm, wet air westward into the Himalayas. For weeks snow and wind buffeted Everest, and the climbers and crews who'd come to the mountain hoping for clear, calm skies dug in to wait.

At base camp, Kari Kobler, who was directing Grubhofer's expedition, was feverishly consulting the forecasts, hoping for a break. When the skies finally cleared, suddenly the race was on. "We were waiting for good weather at the base camp until May 19," says Dendi Sherpa, one of the lead Nepali guides in the Kobler group and one of seven Sherpas hired to help the team. It was apparent to him what was going to happen: "We have only a two-day window, and all the people are going to summit at the same time."

Grubhofer joined the caravan, and by midafternoon on Wednesday, May 22, he'd ascended to Camp 3, a bleak and windswept slope at 27,390 feet. At these heights, the low air pressure means that the vascular system is receiving far less oxygen than it would at sea level; most climbers rely on supplemental oxygen. After arriving at camp, Grubhofer hunkered down to sleep. At eleven o'clock that night, he pushed off toward the summit along with some eighty climbers from a dozen other groups—twice as many as usual, according to one veteran Everest climber.

Grubhofer's aim was to arrive at the summit shortly after dawn on Thursday morning, giving him plenty of time to make the descent before encountering the bad weather that typically sweeps in during the afternoon. He carried a bottle of oxygen that would last him between six to nine hours; his Sherpa guide carried two spares for Grubhofer as well as one tank for himself. But one hour above the camp, Grubhofer ran into trouble: the snow cover had melted, exposing treacherous patches of bare rock and gravel. "You are try-ing to dig in your crampons, but you are often sliding back, fight-ing to keep your balance, expending a lot of energy," Grubhofer says. "And I asked myself, for the first of a thousand times, 'Should I turn around?'"

After wasting precious time struggling up the rock slope, Grub-hofer reached the first of the three difficult steps just below the summit. At least ten other climbers lined up ahead of him, waiting to make the ascent. To do so, climbers had to squeeze sideways into a rock crevice and pull themselves up by a fixed rope. Grub-hofer watched several of them flounder and thought, *Oh, Jesus— what are they doing here?*

Two hours later, on the ridge above the second step, he came upon two frozen corpses lying beside the path. Judging from their torn and faded snowsuits and the patches of snow that covered them, Grubhofer could tell that they had been on the mountain for years; one was missing gloves, and the exposed hands had twisted into claws. "They seemed to be reaching toward me," he says. The bodies were among as many as 200 corpses abandoned on Ever-est, most left behind because of the high cost—up to $100,000 —and dangers of recovering them. They're grim reminders of the mountain's perils, and they're likely to become more noticeable: as climate change thaws the mountain, the melting snow and ice are exposing additional corpses each year. Grubhofer looked away. "You just move on," he says. "You refuse to let it affect you."

On the north side as well, Kuntal Joisher, an Indian alpinist famed for summiting Himalayan peaks while subsisting on an all-vegan diet, was trying hard to maintain a similar stoicism, despite what he was seeing. Joisher was attempting his fourth summit of Everest and had fallen in behind three Indian teenagers who seemed to have no idea how to negotiate the ascent of the second step. Fearful and slow, they took over half an hour to cross the step —usually a ten-minute climb for a strong alpinist. "I was thinking," Joisher recalls, "*Man, I'm freezing to death, and you guys are causing a traffic jam.*" There was nothing to do but wait his turn in the frigid wind. "You are standing at the ledge of a giant boulder, and it's just wide enough to hold your boots, with a sheer drop on one side," he says. "You are totally exposed."

Above step three, the scene got worse. Joisher encountered a Sherpa guide, sprawled in the snow, separated from his client, and utterly exhausted and delirious. His oxygen bottle was empty, and, says Joisher, "he had been there a while, and he had no idea what to do." Joisher's Sherpa searched the man's bag, found a full bottle, attached it to the man's regulator, and waited for the oxygen to flow. "After ten minutes he was able to form good sentences and was in good spirits, and he said, 'Okay, I'm ready to go up now.'" Joisher made the summit at 5:30 in the morning on May 23. "It was jam-packed at the top—it was crazy," he says.

He stayed only ten minutes in the cold and wind before heading back down—desperate to avoid the crush of eighty or ninety people whom he could see approaching from both sides.

Among those who'd also expected to be near the top by daybreak on Thursday morning was Chris Dare, a dentist with the Canadian Armed Forces. Like Grubhofer, he had started for the summit Wednesday night, falling in with a long line of headlamps snaking through the darkness.

One of those headlamps belonged to Dare's buddy Kevin Hynes, a gregarious fifty-six-year-old from Galway, Ireland. But Hynes made it only a hundred yards out of Camp 3 before he turned around. He wasn't feeling up to it and decided the prudent move was to head back. Dare pressed on, figuring he'd reach the top by six o'clock in the morning. But long, debilitating waits at each step delayed him until just before 9:30. Soon after his moment at the summit, of course, the weather Thursday afternoon began to turn ugly.

At around 10 a.m., Dare was heading back toward Camp 3 when he encountered a member of his team, Kam Kaur, a British yoga instructor, still inching toward the summit with her guide. Kaur was an experienced mountaineer, but, says Rolfe Oostra, the Australian guide leading the group, she wasn't in top physical condition—and it was dangerously late to be making the summit push. She was determined to go forward.

Covered with ice, short on oxygen, and physically spent, Dare made it back to Camp 3 at 7 p.m. and collapsed in his tent. He was barely conscious later, when a commotion erupted outside. The Sherpa whom Dare had seen earlier that day helping Kaur up the mountain had staggered into camp, incoherent and alone. They'd run into trouble, he said. According to Oostra, the Sherpa's oxygen ran out and he'd been forced to leave Kaur to seek

help. Oostra had been to the top once before but had abandoned
his summit push that morning at the second step, after a faulty
regulator valve had blocked his oxygen flow. "Where's Kam?" he
demanded when he saw the Sherpa.

"She's up there," the Sherpa gasped.

Oostra strapped on his crampons and grabbed an oxygen cylin-
der and a headlamp. As he prepared to climb, he spotted a light
high on the ridge and flashed his headlamp three times; three
flashes returned. Oostra locked onto the point in the darkness
where he'd seen the light and set out up the icy slope. When he
found Kaur, she was curled into the fetal position. Her oxygen had
run out, and she was drifting in and out of consciousness. It hadn't
been Kaur who'd signaled Oostra—her light was nearly dead—
but rather another man, a badly weakened Indian climber, who
flashed for help and then staggered away. (Kaur disputes Oostra's
timeline, though she told *GQ* that she's not yet ready to publicly
share her story.)

In Oostra's telling, Kaur was practically helpless when he found
her on the rock. "Can't move my hands, babe," she whispered.
"They're frozen." Oostra strapped her into a sling, clipped it to
his harness, and rappelled with her down the buttress. Then he
pushed and dragged her back to Camp 3, shouting above the wind
to keep her awake.

For the first-timers on the mountain—the multitude of climbers
who had never been to Everest—the crowds and the chaos might
have seemed normal. But the Sherpas knew better. Hundreds of
them were scattered on the high slopes that night, and many of
them understood that the mountain had never seen anything like
this.

Each year, in the months before the climbing season, mountaineering agencies identify the most agile and fearless men from
high-altitude Sherpa villages—and then hand them awesome responsibilities. Sherpas lay the fixed ropes that guide climbers to
the summit, lug the heavy oxygen bottles that keep their clients
alive, and closely monitor their clients' physical and mental states.
The work is risky—in April 2014, sixteen Sherpas died in an ice
avalanche on the Nepali side of Everest; two Sherpas would die
this spring in the Nepali Himalayas—yet the money, as much as

$10,000 per season, provides an escape from the poverty of rural Nepal.

The men often form an emotional bond with their clients, living beside them for weeks, sharing their victories and their setbacks. The finest walk a faint line between being helpful and being obedient—between bowing to their clients' wishes and saying no when those wishes seem dangerously misguided.

On Grubhofer's expedition, one of the lead Sherpas was Dendi Sherpa, a thirty-seven-year-old veteran who had worked for Kobler & Partner since 2008 and had summited Mount Everest six times. Having worked his way to a top guide spot on Kobler's team, Dendi had remained behind at Camp 3 on the day of the summit push.

Now Grubhofer—inching his way down, just past the second step—was headed in Dendi's direction when he heard agitated shouts and cries right behind him. His immediate thought was that his teammate, Ernst Landgraf, was in trouble. Landgraf was an experienced summiteer, but he was exhausted at the top. As he and Grubhofer sat on the summit that morning, congratulating each other, Grubhofer noticed that Landgraf seemed particularly spent.

A Sherpa on his team had the same impression when he confronted Landgraf the night before they set out for the top: "He was weak, but he said, 'This is my goal, I have to go to the summit.' And I thought, *Let him do it.* It's quite difficult to tell him, 'You cannot.'"

The Sherpa faced a dilemma confronted by many guides on Everest: how to respond to the determination of an apparently ailing or unfit climber. Only rarely, many experts say, will a Sherpa demonstrate the force of will to override a client's decision to summit; for new recruits trying to make a mark in a competitive business, getting a client to the top often becomes the priority.

Grubhofer listened again for the shrieks. *Please don't let it be Ernst,* he thought.

But it was. Later, Grubhofer learned that Landgraf had slipped while trying to plant his foot on a ladder. Grubhofer was told that because Landgraf had been clipped by his carabiner to the fixed line when he fell, he banged into the ladder and then dangled limply on the line. Guides quickly attempted to free him. The wind was blowing, the temperature was dropping, and the climbers behind Landgraf's suspended body were desperate to get off the mountain.

Later, Kuntal Joisher heard that the waiting climbers were getting agitated. "Cut him off the rope!" some yelled. "We're getting blocked—we'll die."

The rescuers struggled to get Landgraf off the line. After determining that he was dead, they pushed him aside and left his body hanging there. The exact cause of his death is unknown, but Kuntal Joisher says that at that altitude, with a weakened body under intense stress, the slightest stumble can be disastrous. "A small slip or fall can cause your heart rate to shoot up to such a level," he says, "that you will have a massive heart attack."

On the other side of the mountain, the Nepalese approach was turning into its own scene of confusion and death on Thursday. Gyanendra Shrestha, a Nepalese government liaison officer at the Everest Base Camp, had foreseen the trouble, watching days earlier as over 200 climbers milled around the tents waiting to set off for the top. One of them was an old friend of his, Kalpana Das, an Indian attorney who had summited Everest in 2008.

Das had been given a hero's send-off by thousands of admirers in her hometown before she set out for Everest in April as part of an all-women's team of climbers. But Shrestha, having observed her during acclimatizing runs up the mountain in mid-May, saw that she was off her game. "She was very slow, and she was a decade older this time—fifty-four," Shrestha says. "I told her at the base camp, 'Don't push yourself much. I have a sense you cannot do it this year.'"

Das struggled on the Khumbu Icefall, the first obstacle beyond the base camp. She eventually made it to the summit at around 1 p.m. on Thursday, but she collapsed on the way down. When Shrestha received a Mayday call from Das's Sherpa, Das was unconscious, barely breathing. The guide said that he was too exhausted to bring Das down alone. A four-man rescue team was dispatched, but by the time they reached her, hours later, Das had perished.

Shortly after dawn the previous morning, Donald Cash, a Utah software salesman who had quit his job in December to devote himself to high-altitude climbing, had also reached the top. The achievement marked the completion of Cash's Seven Summits project, and overjoyed, he performed a little victory jig at the summit. Then, without warning, he sank to his knees and toppled over. Cash's guide raced to his side and opened wide the valve on his oxygen.

The rush of air revived Cash, and the Sherpa helped him down to the Hillary Step, a 40-foot-high rock outcropping at 28,800 feet. A group of Sherpas had been dispatched to help bring Cash down, but when they arrived, it was too late. Cash had collapsed again and never got back up. Cash's body was left on the mountain, as his family wished.

Largely unaware of the tragedies unfolding around them, the other teams on the route raced higher up the mountain. Anjali Kulkarni, an experienced marathoner and high-altitude climber from Mumbai, and her husband, Sharad Kulkarni, summited on the same day as Cash, according to an account in the *Times of India*. After leaving the summit with her husband, Kulkarni fell ill. Above Camp 4, the paper said, she collapsed and died. A video shows a pair of rescuers, presumably Sherpas, attempting to move Kulkarni's limp body. She lies unresponsive, her right arm extended, hand still clutching the fixed rope.

The surviving members of Anjali Kulkarni's team staggered, mourning and half dead, into Camp 4. Nearby, another exhausted Indian climber from a different expedition, twenty-seven-year-old Nihal Bagwan, who according to the *Times of India* had abandoned a 2014 Everest climb 1,300 feet below the summit, would die of altitude sickness just before midnight on the twenty-third.

Bagwan had been climbing with a Nepalese agency called Peak Promotion, which had already lost three other climbers in the Himalayas the week before. (The manager of Peak Promotion told *GQ* that the deaths in 2019 represent the first time the agency lost clients in its twenty-seven-year history. She also said that Peak Promotion has guidelines in place to ensure that Sherpas have extensive mountaineering experience.) Another Nepalese agency, Seven Summit Treks, founded by four Sherpa brothers in 2010 and now one of the biggest mountaineering companies in Nepal, had an even worse record this year. On May 16, a client of theirs named Séamus Lawless, a thirty-nine-year-old computer-science professor at Trinity College in Dublin, unhooked himself from the safety rope to relieve himself near Camp 4, according to Seven Summits. A climbing companion speculates that a freak gust of wind blew him off the mountain, and he apparently fell hundreds of feet to his death. His body was never recovered. That same night, Ravi Thakur, a twenty-seven-year-old Seven Summits client from Haryana, India, died in his tent at the same camp. And in the days that followed, disaster struck three more times on expeditions led by Seven Summits on nearby Makalu, the world's fifth-highest mountain.

When I met with him this summer, Tashi Sherpa, one of the founders of Seven Summit Treks—and the youngest person ever to reach the top of Everest without using supplemental oxygen—defended the company's safety record. Seven Summits had sixty-four clients on Everest this year, led by one hundred Sherpas—and all but two had returned safely. He conceded that the climbing season had not been good, but he insisted that the company's practices are sound.

Last May's tragedies involved a wide range of outfitters from all over the world—including elite European agencies like Kobler's. It's not the case that companies from poorer countries are inherently more troubled or lax in their safety considerations. Still, Kuntal Joisher, the Indian climber, told me that the industry had become inundated with inexpensive agencies that cater to budget clients—Seven Summits' Everest trips generally cost $38,000, according to Tashi Sherpa. The cheaper companies often have less to pay for guides and are said to employ more inexperienced crews. (Seven Summits insists that it rigorously trains its Sherpas and pays them higher than the market rate.)

These agencies have found a steady clientele among Indian climbers, who typically have much less money to spend than Europeans and Americans and are dying on Everest at a greater rate than anyone else. Four out of the reported eleven who died on Everest this year were Indians; of the seventeen who died on Nepal's 8,000-meter peaks, eight were Indian. "Indians are showing up who have not even climbed a 6,000-meter mountain," Joisher says. "So many got frostbite, four died this year—clearly there is something wrong."

Grubhofer spent the last dreadful hours of May 23 in his own kind of agony. He'd staggered down the north side at a dreadful pace, exhausting his oxygen while waiting for others to move. Within sight of the cluster of domed tents of Camp 3, Grubhofer collapsed. He inched forward on his hands and knees in the gathering darkness, shredding his jacket on the rocks, begging for tea, water, and oxygen. "He was in terrible shape," recalls Dendi Sherpa, who revived him, replenished his oxygen, and placed him in his tent with another climber.

Too late to escape from the death zone, Grubhofer slept fitfully for hours, with his oxygen mask strapped over his mouth and nose, then sat up at around three o'clock in the morning, gasping for air. He felt terrible. With effort he removed his gloves, found his headlamp, scrounged around the mess of the tent for his oxygen bottle—and checked the meter. The tank was empty. It had been nearly full when he'd crawled into bed. He realized he must have accidentally opened the valve all the way.

"Fuck," he said. He tore off the mask of his regulator and retched.

"Dendi," he croaked as the wind howled outside. "My oxygen." Grubhofer again rasped out a plea for help.

Moments later, Dendi Sherpa began his standard check of his clients' oxygen supplies. Entering Grubhofer's tent, he saw Grubhofer motioning desperately for assistance. Dendi looked at the meter, saw the needle was on zero, and hurriedly attached a new bottle. Grubhofer drew deep breaths through his respirator and settled back in his sleeping bag. Without the new tank, says Dendi Sherpa, "Reinhard would have died."

A few dozen yards from Grubhofer, Chris Dare was thrashing about sleeplessly in his tent that night. All he could think about was getting below the death zone the next morning. He was ready to be done. He was eager to reunite with climbing buddy Kevin Hynes, who had turned around before the summit push. With Everest behind them, the two were looking forward to meeting up at the cabin Hayes had built in the Maine woods.

In the morning, as Dare and the group headed down the mountain, a Sherpa received a radio dispatch from Camp 1.

"Kevin's gone," he told Dare.

"What do you mean?" Dare asked, confused.

Hynes, Dare learned, had died in his tent at dawn. It might have been a coronary or a stroke or any one of the fatal afflictions that can overwhelm a climber's heart, brain, or lungs at Everest's merciless altitudes. Oostra says the coroner's report would attribute the death of the vigorous Irishman to "natural causes."

*

In Katmandu in August, long after the last mountaineers had returned home, I found the local climbing community consumed by a debate about what had gone wrong. At least four climbers died in the twenty-four hours that followed Grubhofer's moment at the top—casualties of interminable lines and tragic miscalculations, victims of one of the deadliest seasons the mountain has ever seen. In all, eleven would die on Everest in May. By the time I visited, the Nepalese government had proposed a new set of rules requiring, among other things, that prospective climbers provide proof of high-altitude experience. But skeptics doubted that the government would seriously enforce such reforms and risk reducing its millions of dollars in permit-generated revenues. "At the end of the day, the changes that Nepal talks about never happen," Rolfe Oostra tells me. "At the end of the day, money talks."

Reinhard Grubhofer shares the assessment that something has to change. When I meet him in Vienna, it has been three months since he scaled the mountain and he is still basking in the achievement. "I cannot go anywhere without being the one who has just done Everest," he says with a smile.

Sure, more people were climbing the mountain than ever before, but reaching the top of the world continues to offer unique bragging rights, he tells me. That will never go away, he thinks. "If I would meet you here and tell you I climbed, say, Annapurna, knowledgeable guys would say, 'Wow,' but 99.9 percent don't know what you're talking about," he says. "Mount Everest is such a fascinating mountain, this huge monster. It is still one of the biggest adventures on the planet. It is a prestigious place."

And yet the disasters that struck on the day he reached the summit cast a shadow. Nirmal Purja's infamous photo of the traffic jam on the summit ridge, he admits, has diminished the achievement in some people's eyes. "I was asked about the photo when I came back," he tells me. "People said, 'Oh, you've also been queuing up there,' like it was the supermarket." New rules have to be implemented, he says, to weed out the incompetent and the inexperienced, to reduce the crowds, to remove the Disneyland illusion and bring Everest back to something approximating its pristine state. Too many people, he says, have died needlessly because of sliding standards. "Let's not make it a tourist mountain," he says. "Let's not spoil it even more [and] reduce it to dead people and tourists."

Of course, Grubhofer also knows that the high stakes are part of the mountain's attraction. A note of humility creeps into his voice when he acknowledges how close he had come to asphyxiating in his tent—and how a single slip had been enough to end the life of his climbing partner, Ernst Landgraf.

Two days after Landgraf perished, Grubhofer tells me, a small team from Kobler & Partner returned to the site and gently removed the body, which was still hanging from the line. Grubhofer says they pushed and dragged it away from the trail and then found a niche in the rocks where they laid Landgraf's remains to rest—another haunting reminder of Everest's fatal allure.

NICK PAUMGARTEN

The Symptoms

FROM THE NEW YORKER

THE FIRST CONCUSSION in the year of concussions was delivered by the right fist of a man whose name I either don't know or can't remember. You could say it was a mild concussion, and I always will, but many experts say that there's no such thing. You have a concussion or you don't. You can't be mildly pregnant. But a brain injury is not a baby. We know what a baby is.

I didn't lose consciousness, or even my footing. When it was over, I skated away, with a ludicrous grin but without every item of my equipment or all of my wits. I had a sudden headache and a sense already of an alteration in the fabric of the world beyond the confines of my skull. Teammates leered at me. Aluminum rink light glinted off a thicket of surfaces: ice, plexiglass, helmets, sticks. The referee bent to report the infractions to the timekeeper, through a slot in the glass. In the penalty box, I fought the urge to lie down.

This was men's league—beer league. You play hockey, then you drink beer. Beer in the locker room, beer in the parking lot, beer at the bar. Specifically, this was Game One of the league final, best of three, early July 2016, after a sixteen-game season and a couple of playoff rounds. We all cared more than we should have. We ranged in age from just-out-of-college to my-kid's-applying-to-college, with varying degrees of organized-hockey experience. I was one of the oldest, and one of the least experienced—I'd quit in freshman year of high school—but I'd never stopped skating in pickup games. I'd been a beer leaguer for twenty-five years and could still contribute here and there, and even, with crafty editing, create a mind's-eye reel of my highlights to play as I drifted off to sleep.

Our team was called the Intangibles, for the sports cliché describing that unquantifiable quality of grit and attention to detail which valuable players, especially older ones, are often said to have, and which we reckoned was all we had left, amid a general decline in fitness and skill. On our jerseys, black, with a little orange and white, the word "INTANGIBLES" ran diagonally from top left to bottom right. On the back: numbers, but no names. Most of us wore matching socks, black with orange trim. The rest of the gear—helmets, gloves, pants—was ragtag. A motley militia, in the reeking regalia of past schools and teams. The games were at night, sometimes as late as midnight. We got a little nervous on game day. We perfected the timing of the nap and the meal. We stretched at home. We knew we were ridiculous, and made fun of ourselves constantly, but approached it all with enough sincerity to wring real gratification out of it. A good beer-league team consists of players who take it no more or less seriously than you do. Ours was a good team. Afterward, we could talk about a game for hours —about our own failings, in front of the others, and about the others' failings, behind their backs.

What led to the first concussion? I'd decided to repay an opponent who had, during a battle for a loose puck, shoved me into the boards headfirst. I'd been having neck issues, and this had made them instantly worse. Ours was a no-checking league, and yet we were allowed to play the body, as they say, and hostilities bubbled up from time to time. Now the game was basically over, and we were losing by several goals with a minute left. Fuck it. As the guy stole the puck from our captain and bore in uncontested on our goalie, I came off the bench on a line change (a player substitution, often midplay) and skated toward him as hard as I could. I came at him from his blind side, and arrived just as he slowed up a touch to execute a feint on our goaltender. My check blew him off his skates.

This was an uncool thing to do. Even in the pros, it would have been at least a charging penalty; in a middling no-hit beer league, it was beyond the pale. Also, the guy was much bigger, stronger, and younger than I was. He rose to his feet and rushed at me. I stood still, hands at my sides, in wonderment at the size of him, and at the purity of the grievance. I had an inkling that I deserved what was coming. His head was the size of a bucket. He shook his gloves off and quickly landed a series of right hooks before my teammates swarmed him, like rodeo clowns. The punches caught me behind the left ear, below the edge of my helmet. The thud was thicker than I'd expected. It felt as if my head had been slammed in a car door.

I had never punched, or been punched by, an adult before. The last time I'd used my fists was on my younger brother, during a tussle in our early teens; he retaliated by pelting me with a boom box. It got me in the mouth. I should have learned then: put up your dukes. The next morning, a dentist levered my teeth back into place with a tongue depressor and cemented them in line. I showed up for freshman year of high school with a mangled upper lip and a smile made of grout.

After the Game One punch-up, I sat out the rest of the series. I didn't feel right. We won without me. The rink manager handed the guys a yard-tall plastic trophy, which wound up on the bar of the tavern where we hung out after the games. I was a longtime fan of the Philadelphia Flyers, who in their heyday and my formative years were known as the Broad Street Bullies, for their use of physical intimidation as a tactic. So I allowed myself to believe, half seriously, that I'd contributed something. The boys encouraged me in this. I'd sacrificed my services, and my head, to change the complexion of the series. One intangible is knowing when to be a jackass.

I skate low, torso over toes, head turtled forward. It's not awful, but it's not ideal either. I catch a lot of stray elbows. It's hard to count the times, after those late-night games, that I've felt dazed the next day. Headaches, stiff neck, trouble finding words. But then there were always other variables: beer, dehydration, a severe shortage of sleep. Stay out or go home, six pints or two, I always needed four hours, from the time of the opening face-off, before I could fall asleep. Midnight games on Mondays left a mark.

After a day or two, the fog would lift. Nothing ever stuck, and so I decided that those passing head shots, the little dings, weren't anything at all. It seemed a small price to pay for the weekly company of the boys. There was the Brad, a master rigger of industrial cranes, whose gruff diatribes against bankers, bike lanes, hipsters, and "harelips" we surreptitiously recorded, for laughs. Pat (Patty) Patterson had grown up down the block from me; in the late seventies, our local street-hockey game had made the *Daily News*. We had a couple of smooth Minnesotans—Scoobs, a soulful bull of a kid who ran a charter school in Harlem, and Mahonze, our ringer from Duluth, lanky and shy. And some spicy Mainers too: Brawny, who was always grumbling about the libs; Bix, who smelled like a dead animal; and Junta, whom I met playing roller hockey in Tompkins Square Park, in the mid-nineties, and who had a thing about the size of his own wrench, which, admittedly, was prodigious. New recruits were always amazed to learn that Phish had named its first album for him. He came up with a lot of the nicknames, some of which only he used. Our goalie, whom we called Z, had eight children and lived in a shoe. Or so it was said.

Hockey nicknames are determined by an esoteric set of principles, the most basic one being that you add a long "e" to a name that does not have one, and drop it if it does. Clarke was Clarkie, Gretzky was Gretz. The Intangibles called me Dickie, for Dickie Dunn, the beat writer in the movie *Slap Shot*. For us, as for a generation of hockey players, *Slap Shot* was both a mirror and a prompt, in the way that *The Godfather* was for the Mob. There's a scene in a bar in which Dickie tells Reg Dunlop, the player-coach played by Paul Newman, "I tried to capture the spirit of the thing." We were all about the spirit of the thing. We took turns doing the postgame writeups: mock heroics, gong shows, choice chirps. Our team's captain, for a while, was a handyman for a bunch of wealthy tenants of Upper East Side town houses; reared in Detroit, he'd played college hockey at Liberty University, during a born-again-Christian phase, and then, as a pot-smoking apostate, had been Woody Allen's superintendent. He made paintings and signed them "Evryman." We called him Reg. One year, after we won a league championship, I emailed my brother a team photo. The trophy, the flushed faces, the thinning hair. My brother singled out a Philly kid we called Murph—for Audie Murphy, because his surname contained the letters "a-u-d" (and no long "e")—or Jesus, because he performed miracles. "That guy looks like a tough dick," my brother wrote. I shared this email with a few of my teammates. From then on, Reg implored us from the bench to play with an edge: "Tough dicks, boys. Tough dicks." Hockey, it needs to be said, brings out the dickishness in us all. It may even require it.

In New York City, in the 1970s, when I was a kid, recreational ice hockey was a curiosity, an obscure pastime of hard-nosed Long Islanders, Massholes, preppies, and Hell's Kitchen roughnecks. There was a men's league at the old Sky Rink, on the sixteenth floor of an office building near the West Side rail yards; one mis-remembers it now, with its steamed-up windows and its hothouse violence, as a kind of puckhead's Plato's Retreat. There were rug-ged barns at Coney Island, Long Beach, and the World's Fair site in Queens. During the winter months, I skated in Central Park and the Bronx, getting just a handful of weekend games in the suburbs each season. In summer, I went to hockey camps for a couple of weeks, in New England and Nassau County. But mostly I played roller hockey—pre-Rollerblades, on the old quads. The city had a lot more open asphalt than open ice. We used garbage cans for goals, a roll of electrical tape for a puck, and wooden sticks with the blades worn down by the pavement to the width of paint stirrers. The pace was slow, and nobody wore shin pads or helmets. Still, the games got chippy. My sharpest memory is of a full baseball swing I took to the back of a knee from the stick of a neighborhood bully known as Fat Allie.

Thirty years later, I was out mucking it up on the ice two or three nights a week—at Chelsea Piers, mainly, but also in Long Island City, Flushing, and Central Park, in leagues and in regular pickup games. It was my outlet, my social life, my private map of New York. One team blended into the next: Flin Flon, Team X, Red Army, Blind Justice, Lady Blue, Wheat Kings, Rink Rats, Polar Bears, Blackjacks, Hit Factory, Triple Canopy, LCHC (Lamb Chop Hockey Club), and THC, which, of course, stood for The Hockey Club.

Meanwhile, my sons got deep into organized travel hockey, the weekends a blur of games and practices. For a number of years, I helped out as a coach. To do so, I had to take a series of seminars and online modules, including a perennial refresher devoted to concussions, with strategies for getting children to provide an ac-curate accounting of their symptoms. But, when it came to self-diagnosis, those were superfluous.

I got the next concussion that fall, in a game in Central Park, at the outdoor rink where I'd learned to play, four decades earlier. This was a league for players older than forty. The team was called Tiger Williams, for a notorious goon. On a chilly night under the lights by the Harlem Meer, with friends on both teams, the mandate was to play it cool. Skating backward, defending, without much conviction, against an onrushing forward, I leaned to execute an over-fortyish poke check. The forward, maybe with too much conviction, cut hard and caught the side of my head with a shoulder. The contact helicoptered me into the air and then down to the ice. I stayed prone awhile, then made my way to the locker room, where I undressed and zombied my way home. Headache, vertigo, unrelenting fatigue: the symptoms reminded me of altitude sickness. I acclimated after a moment or two. I took six weeks off, and then resumed skating after Christmas.

The third concussion came months later, in another Intangibles game, the clock running out on a late-night midseason loss. A freak accident, a collision with a teammate: we hadn't seen each other. I got the worst of it. The light dimmed, the ringing kicked up, and the fog rolled in again.

In the following weeks, my skull felt as though someone had draped a towel over it and was pulling down on all four corners, or maybe cinching tight a bank robber's stocking. I had trouble concentrating. If I tried to exercise, the headache came galloping in. I couldn't handle crowds or concerts or the ordinary din of New York. The thought of playing hockey, the sight of men playing football on TV: it seemed as reasonable to stroll on foot across the New Jersey Turnpike. After an hour or two in front of a computer screen, a kind of dizzy fatigue washed over me. I began napping a couple of times a day. The Advil stopped working. My moods darkened. My work stalled.

At the urging of family and friends, I went to see a doctor, who said that the symptoms were consistent with post-concussion syndrome. Still, a diagnosis is an approximation. An MRI showed nothing, except some other things, which had nothing to do with concussions or my symptoms, and which I'd probably have preferred not to know about: *White matter intensity is generally preserved, however a solitary probable chronic lacunar infarction is present in the right caudate head, and trace probable microangiopathy is present in the parietal region on the left.* A neurologist told a friend, to whom I had sent the report, "He shouldn't freak out (too much)."

I was familiar with the murk of concussion science. Like anyone who follows sports, I'd been reading for years about professional athletes undone by head injuries, marooned in the dark,
mulling suicide. One knew about CTE, the disease of progressive
neurodegeneration, brought on by repeated blows to the head,
that seemed disproportionately to afflict boxers and football and
hockey players, such as the linebacker Junior Seau, who shot himself in the chest, at the age of forty-three, or Todd Ewen, the NHL
enforcer known as the Animal, who shot himself in the head, at
forty-nine. One of my son's coaches, a retired NHL player and a
gentle giant who participated in more than a hundred fights as
a pro, had several episodes a year of overpowering vertigo that
lasted for days. Of course, I hadn't done any of this. I hadn't even
played high school hockey. I was just a mildly rambunctious boy
on planet Earth: bicycle crashes, skiing accidents, pitiless shore
breaks, a drunken tussle or two. But it was widely accepted that the
damage accrues.

I bore witness as the kids opened their own accounts. In a
peewee practice, one of my sons collided with a teammate, and
the other boy had to quit hockey and miss months of school. I
attended a concussion-awareness fundraiser at his parents' apartment, featuring a former professional football player and the former pro wrestler Chris Nowinski, who suffered sixteen concussions
and now runs a research-and-advocacy group called the Concussion Legacy Foundation. This is an epidemic, they told us. There's
so much we don't know. When in doubt, keep them out. The
youth-hockey organization my sons played in adopted something
called the King-Devick test. At the beginning of the season, we
took the kids aside, one at a time, and had them perform cognitive
exercises while an adult timed them with a stopwatch. Patterns of
numbers on flip cards, read aloud, in sequence. This established
a baseline. The idea was that, if a player was suspected of having a
concussion, we'd administer the test on the bench and compare
it with the previous result, and thereby have some basis for a decision about his continued participation in the game.

One day, during a game on Long Island, a boy on our squirt
team (squirts are nine- and ten-year-olds) got clocked in front of
our bench. The referee saw it but gave no indication that he considered it a penalty. Home cooking? The visitors always think so.
Our player lay on the ice. From the stands, his father started shout-

ing at the referee, who skated over and told him to knock it off. The father yelled, "That's my son!" Then he let loose with some obscenities. The referee ordered him to leave the rink. The father went quietly, which was a relief, because he had a black belt in judo. Another father went with him, to make sure.

On the bench, I took the boy aside to administer the King-Devick test. He had put up a conspicuously slow time on his baseline. He was immensely talented but easily distracted: sometimes, when a coach explained a drill to him, his vacant expression brought to mind the badger sidekick in the movie *Fantastic Mr. Fox*—eyes just spirals. Now the boy sat on the bench, facing away from the ice, and read out the number patterns. He got through them much faster than he had for his baseline. This scenario hadn't come up in the pre-season tutorials. We sent him back on the ice, which was almost certainly the wrong thing to do. The game ended in a tie.

During a bantam game (bantams are thirteen and fourteen), at a rink on the top floor of a mall in West Nyack, one of our players got rifled into the boards. His head bounced off the plexiglass. He stayed down. The referees blew the play dead and stood nearby, dawdling like a pair of plainclothes detectives at a crime scene. The players retreated and took a knee. In street shoes, I made my way across the ice. This boy's father had played in the NHL and was in the Hall of Fame. Hundreds of goals, thousands of penalty minutes, dozens of fights. A legend. But he wasn't there that day. His son was lying face down, as though on a massage table. I asked the boy how he was doing.

"I'm done," he said.

"Do you know where we are?"

"Some shitty mall."

Lucid. Droll. Good to go? We held him out, without subjecting him to the numbers.

Years before, I'd been in the stands at Madison Square Garden when his father, playing for the Rangers, collided with an opponent head on head, neither seeing the other. Paramedics spent more than five minutes trying to revive him, as the arena went quiet. "Is he dead, Daddy?" my older son, then six, asked.

"I don't know," I said. I could hardly speak, being somehow on the verge of tears. After a while, the crowd started chanting the man's nickname. That's what brought him back to consciousness, he later said. He was wheeled off on a stretcher. He missed fifteen

games, then returned in time for the playoffs, and played for another two years. He stayed in the city and signed his son up for our
program. He helped coach. You could see the opposing coaches
and parents sneaking glances. On tournament trips, as kids raised
hell in the corridors of the hotel, the hockey dads and moms gathered around him at the bar and pumped him for insights and an-
ecdotes, a prince among the plebes. He liked to stay up late too.
An old habit, perhaps, from his playing days.

The symptoms lingered and mutated and became almost commonplace, and I began to contemplate retirement. That word, however
facetiously it was deployed—because to consider the beer leagues
a career, even in jest, was grandiose—had a finality that got mar-
bled up with whatever depression the concussions had brought
on. I missed skating, making plays, throwing my body around. I
missed the boys. I missed the postgame high, endorphins giving
way to beer and refrigerator raids.

   A few months after my third concussion, a teammate, Mango,
got one too. We had chemistry on the ice, and liked talking and
thinking about the game, on our way to and from the rink. We
were nerds for puck support and a methodical approach in the offensive zone. He was attacked in a melee at the final buzzer. Such
things were much rarer than I have made them out to be, but
here it was, violence that was not cartoonish. This time, there were
no rodeo clowns. Maybe the Intangibles had lost sight of the intangibles. A lot of guys had moved away or stopped showing up.
Injuries, work, babies, the burbs. Colorado, Chicago, Minneapolis.
Ribs, disks, ankles, brains. Jesus had a heart attack. Scoobs's house
burned down. The spirit of the thing: catch it if you can.

   Mango's symptoms lasted for more than a year. Before long,
he had to quit. So did Junta and Mahonze. The team disbanded.
Now we were the invisibles, a chunk of our city life eliminated by
blows to the head. My sticks stand blade down in a corner of the
apartment; now and then, I catch a whiff of the old hockey-glove
stink that still saturates the knob of cloth tape at the butt end of
each one. I feel well enough to entertain the idea that there's got
to be a game for me somewhere out there in the city, one peppy
enough to make it worthwhile yet so moderate as to be safe. Will
I never again collide with another human being? The thought is

hard to bear. When I can't sleep, I have a habit of imagining my-self, over and over, crossing the red line and, with a flick of the curved blade, flipping the puck high in the air, over the opposing defensemen and into the corner, but then, instead of chasing it, swerving toward the bench to get a line change.

AISHWARYA KUMAR

The Grandmaster Diet

FROM ESPN.COM

ONE WEEK IN early March, on a blustery, windswept day, Fabiano Caruana decides to get away. He drives three hours west from his St. Louis apartment over winding gravel roads to reach his destination, a 2,000-acre compound in rural Missouri owned by a wealthy friend.

At 7:30 the next morning, he pulls on gray Mizzou sweats and matching running shorts, rubs the sleep from his eyes, and heads out for his hourlong run with his training partner, Cristian Chirila. They jog up and down the hills around the farmland, whispering during water breaks about openings and effective chess permutations.

At five-foot-six, Caruana has a lean frame, his legs angular and toned. He also has a packed schedule for the day: a five-mile run, an hour of tennis, half an hour of basketball, and at least an hour of swimming.

As he's jogging, it's easy to mistake him for a soccer player. But he is not. This body he has put together is not an accident. Caruana is, in fact, an American grandmaster in chess, the No. 2 player in the world. His training partner, Chirila? A Romanian grandmaster. And they're doing it all to prepare for the physical demands of . . . chess? Yes, chess.

It seems absurd. How could two humans—seated for hours, exerting themselves in no greater manner than intermittently extending their arms a foot at a time—face physical demands?

Still, the evidence overwhelms.

The 1984 World Chess Championship was called off after five months and forty-eight games because defending champion Anatoly Karpov had lost twenty-two pounds. "He looked like death," grandmaster and commentator Maurice Ashley recalls.

In 2004, winner Rustam Kasimdzhanov walked away from the six-game world championship having lost seventeen pounds. In October 2018, Polar, a U.S.-based company that tracks heart rates, monitored chess players during a tournament and found that twenty-one-year-old Russian grandmaster Mikhail Antipov had burned 560 calories in two hours of sitting and playing chess—or roughly what Roger Federer would burn in an hour of singles tennis.

Robert Sapolsky, who studies stress in primates at Stanford University, says a chess player can burn up to 6,000 calories a day while playing in a tournament, three times what an average person consumes in a day. Based on breathing rates (which triple during competition), blood pressure (which elevates), and muscle contractions before, during, and after major tournaments, Sapolsky suggests that grandmasters' stress responses to chess are on par with what elite athletes experience.

"Grandmasters sustain elevated blood pressure for hours in the range found in competitive marathon runners," Sapolsky says.

It all combines to produce an average weight loss of two pounds a day, or about ten to twelve pounds over the course of a ten-day tournament in which each grandmaster might play five or six times. The effect can be off-putting to the players themselves, even if it's expected. Caruana, whose base weight is 135 pounds, drops to 120 to 125 pounds. "Sometimes I've weighed myself after tournaments and I've seen the scale drop below 120," he says, "and that's when I get mildly scared."

But there is literally nothing for Caruana to fear but fear itself. Stress and anxiety, in fact, are the greatest drivers of the phenomenon. Here's how it works:

Grandmasters in competition are subjected to a constant torrent of mental stress. That stress, in turn, causes their heart rates to increase, which, in turn, forces their bodies to produce more energy to, in turn, produce more oxygen. It is, according to Marcus Raichle, a neurologist at Washington University in St. Louis, and Philip Cryer, a metabolism expert at the school, a vicious, destructive cycle.

Meanwhile, players also eat less during tournaments, simply be-

cause they don't have the time or the appetite. "The simple explanation is when they're thinking about chess, they're not thinking
about food," says Ewan C. McNay, assistant professor of psychology in the behavioral neuroscience program at the University of
Albany.

Stress also leads to altered—and disturbed—sleep patterns,
which in turn cause more fatigue—and can lead to more weight
loss. A brain operating on less sleep, even by just one hour, Kasimdzhanov notes, requires more energy to stay awake during the
chess game. Some grandmasters report dreaming about chess,
agonizing over what they could have done differently for hours in
their sleep, and waking up exhausted.

To combat it all, today's players have begun to incorporate
strict food and fitness regimens to increase oxygen supply to the
brain during tournaments, prevent sugar-related crashes, and sustain their energy. In the 1980s and '90s, smoking, drinking, and
late-night parties were common on the chess circuit—that's right,
chess had a *Boogie Nights* phase—but that scene has all but disappeared.

"Physical fitness and brain performance are tied together, and
it shouldn't be a surprise that grandmasters are out there trying to
look like soccer players," Ashley says.

According to Ashley, India's first grandmaster, Viswanathan
Anand, does two hours of cardio each night to tire himself out so
he doesn't dream about chess; Kasimdzhanov drinks tea only during tournaments and plays tennis and basketball every day. Chirila
does at least an hour of cardio and an hour of weights to build
muscle mass before tournaments.

But not one of these grandmasters has perfected his fitness routine like the current world champion, Magnus Carlsen.

In 2017, Magnus Carlsen realized he had a problem. The reigning
world No. 1 for four years felt his grasp on the title loosening. He
was still winning most tournaments, but his matches were lasting
longer, the victories seemingly less assured. He was beginning to
wane in the last hour of games. He noticed younger players catching up to him.

So it was that Carlsen visited the Olympic training center in
Oslo, Norway, with his father, Henrik, seeking advice from performance specialists. Their suggestion was deceptively simple: "You

need to cut back on the orange juice you drink during tournaments."

Carlsen had relied on a mix of half orange juice, half water for an energy boost since he was a child. But now, in his late twenties, his body was no longer breaking down the sugar as quickly, leading to sugar crashes. The nutritionists suggested that he instead drink a mixture of chocolate milk and plain milk, which contained far lower levels of sugar but would also supplement his body with calcium, potassium, and protein.

"It kept his blood sugar at a reasonable level without too big a variation, and he felt less tired during key moments in tournaments that followed the change," Henrik said.

But that was merely the beginning of Carlsen's makeover: since then he has trained his body for chess, down to the very last detail. Before tournaments, he works out for hours—running on the treadmill, perfecting asanas on his yoga mat, playing soccer with his friends. Before the world championship last year, he went skiing every day and tweeted that it strengthened his legs and his willpower to get to the finish line. He hired a personal chef, Magnus Forssell, who travels with him to ensure he's eating the right combination of proteins, carbs, and calcium. (Says Forssell: "Before tournaments, you need a lot of energy, so I am trying to trick him to eat some pasta so he gets some reserve energy.")

These days, during tournaments, Carlsen focuses on relaxing and conserving energy instead of training. Caruana spends at least three hours before a match prepping his moves, but Carlsen does only fifteen to thirty minutes of prep. His reasoning: last-minute preparations are an unnecessary use of energy.

"When you allow your body to relax more during a tournament, it means that it will ask for more food, it means you can eat normally, you're not stressed, so your appetite is normal—that's what happens with Magnus," Carlsen's father says.

There's more: Carlsen chews gum during games to try to increase brain function without losing energy; he taps his legs rhythmically to keep his brain and body alert between moves.

He has even managed to optimize . . . sitting. That's right. Carlsen claims that many chess players crane their necks too far forward, which can lead to a 30 percent loss of lung capacity, according to studies in the *Journal of Physical Therapy Science*. And, according to Keith Overland, former president of the American

Chiropractic Association, leaning 30 degrees forward increases stress on the neck by nearly sixty pounds, which in turn requires the back and neck muscles to work harder, ultimately resulting in headaches, irregular breathing, and reduced oxygen to the brain.

"A chess player can develop chronic neck and upper back pain, as well as sore shoulders and backaches," says Overland, who has worked with the New York Mets and the U.S. Olympic Training Center. "This is particularly concerning considering how much energy they are exerting on playing a competitive game of chess at the highest level."

Not Carlsen. The Norwegian rests his lower back against the chair so it retains a natural curve, his knees slightly apart at the edge of the seat, feet firmly on the ground, and leans forward at about a 75-degree angle. In this position, which he arrived at through reading studies and trial and error, he's not too far forward to lose alertness and not too far back to use extra energy.

"A lot of times you see Magnus winning games in the fifth hour of play," says Ashley, who has commentated on most of Carlsen's games in the past decade. "He looks like he's just starting out while his opponents are burning out."

Since he became a world champion in 2013, Carlsen has even practiced a strategy familiar to fans of Kawhi Leonard or LeBron James: load management. Although the average elite player will play twelve to fourteen events a year to maintain his ranking and earn money, Carlsen has typically reduced his schedule to six to eight tournaments, taking months off to recuperate after each one.

"Even if he doesn't lose substantial weight like his peers, Magnus understood early on that his nervous system is stressed after every tournament and takes weeks at a time regaining that balance," Henrik says. "He understands his body well enough to know when he's achieved equilibrium before he goes out to play for another title."

Back in Missouri, Caruana and Chirila hole up in the dining room for six hours of chess, the room soundproofed for secrecy. Caruana is especially careful after screenshots of openings he'd planned to use against Carlsen leaked before last year's world championship. (It's only paranoia if they're *not* out to get you.)

Afterward, he looks exhausted, his glasses askew. Still, he grabs a handful of nuts and heads out for a final hour of tennis before dinner.

Kasimdzhanov and Chirila, after a dinner of salad, boiled shrimp, beef stew, and mashed potatoes, walk into the kitchen for a serving of chocolate pudding pie. Caruana does not join them. "No dessert for me today," he says.

Before big tournaments, Caruana usually goes into detox mode. Last year he gave up alcohol for three months before the world championship. This time, he has chosen sugar. It's a habit he picked up from Carlsen, who is showing signs, at long last, of possibly being mortal. After a run of eight consecutive tournament victories, the Norwegian dropped ten games at a competition in August and confessed to "constantly doubting" himself.

Carlsen's wobble on the eve of the Chess World Cup, however slight, is the opening Caruana has been waiting for. In his mind, Caruana knows what he has to do; like all grandmasters, he just needs his body to hold up.

"Sometimes you have to shock your body into listening to you," he says.

MARK GOZONSKY

Gritty All Day Long

FROM THE SUN

MOST OF THE other baseball players at the Pacific Coast League tryouts were half my age. Nobody said the league was for guys in their twenties, but that was the deal. Some goofuses showed up in shorts and tennis shoes. Not me, though. I own four different pairs of baseball pants. I didn't have on cleats, however. I was getting by with turf shoes, because I had not yet earned the exalted status bestowed by cleats. It really makes a difference to have your feet a quarter inch off the ground. Also, the clackety-clack of cleats on concrete is clear confirmation that you are a ballplayer, not a hapless schmo just going through the motions.

I thought it was a sure thing I would be drafted, probably drafted high. Everybody needed a fifty-seven-year-old catcher who hadn't played in twenty-five years—and who, on the late-August day of tryouts, was still seeing double from brain damage in April. Not severely double right in front of me. I'd been able to teach high school English up until the AP exam in mid-May and then take medical leave. But double, as in: isn't it weird how the walls are intersecting twenty feet down the hallway, and the students and the lockers and the floors are all looking more than a little bit swervy?

The trick, which I learned after going back to playing tennis in early August, was to keep the ball in front of you. If you let the ball get in on you, you (a) lose power and control and (b) have to pick which one of the two balls to hit.

My brain damage was not from a stroke, by the way. It was a "cavernous malformation" that leaked in my brain stem: a blob of blood-vessel cells that never quite form veins nor arteries nor capillaries; a vascular Creature from the Black Lagoon of your brain. You could have one and never know, like I did, until one day a little mutant blood vessel inside my brain stem suddenly oozed some goop. If the brain is like a computer, then this is like spilling coffee on your keyboard. I can't say what your keyboard feels, but I felt whacked by a two-by-four that didn't hurt but left me seeing some

> serious double
> and also
> a little
> wobbly, what
> with that
> numbness in
> my left

leg

from foot to calf. For a while there, the tingling went all the way up my thigh and into my balls, which was alarming, but, still, it could have been much, much worse.

I slept a lot. Deeeeeep sleeeeeeeep. My wife was *very upset* and demonstrated her love in both conventional and unconventional ways. For example, she went two-for-two in passing out during my initial medical exams—first in the emergency room and then again a few days later at the neurologist's office. If that's not love . . . well, it is.

She also did not yell at me one single bit when, fitted out with prism glasses, I backed my car out of the driveway and scraped her Volvo up nicely. Not a peep.

It is true that she was *very concerned* about how mean I was to her during this period. I wrote her two poems explaining that I wasn't being mean, but she wasn't buying it. For evidence of my mean-ness you will have to read her essay, if she ever writes one. What I felt was grateful and eager to recover so she would not feel mean-ness but rather l-o-v-e.

Over the course of my medical leave and summer vacation the tingling retreated back the way it came, down the quads and the calves and then around the ankle to one last holdout in my left foot, which still sometimes tingles to this day—my own personal memento mori, disconcerting but not enough to keep me side-lined. It's a reminder, if you will, to do it now, whatever *it* may be.

In my case *it* was playing baseball—actual hardball, not softball—with seventeen other guys and an ump and uniforms. The real thing.

I thought tryouts went great. I played catcher, just catcher. You may ask, How solid was my receiving with that lingering double vision? Well, I'm happy to report that squatting behind the plate was a miracle cure. I saw completely normal and snagged a whole lot of balls in the dirt. Each time I did, I was like: Looky here, pure gold. That whooshing hardball crashing into the grit, chaos about to explode, but no! My mitt swooped down and snagged it, and a satisfying *thunk* transmitted deep satisfaction direct from the web of the glove to the left prefrontal cortex.

Of course, plenty of balls also skipped right by me, but these were mainly wild pitches—i.e., the pitcher's fault, not mine. At least, according to me. I'm not really into whose fault it was. Let's just say a nontrivial number of pitches had destinies other than being caught. That feels like the truth. I also made no attempt whatsoever to field any pop-ups behind the plate. Too many balls lying around back there; you could break an ankle. In retrospect maybe I should have jumped up, turned around, and flung off my mask before I looked in dismay at the scattered balls and reluctantly abandoned what would have for sure been a dogged, ultimately triumphant pursuit.

To be honest, I cannot recollect ever in my entire life catching a foul pop fly as catcher, but I was in no mood to let such obvious limitations hold me back. There were about a hundred guys who needed to hit and just me and one other, obviously way-better-than-me guy taking turns behind the plate. This guy was Robo-Catcher, but perfectly friendly. He was like, Go ahead, and I was like, No, you go ahead. Me and Robo took turns. He was younger, of course, and I knew if it was just between him and me, he'd get picked first. But I could live with that. On my turn catching I was very encouraging to all the batters: "Whoa, dude, you nailed that one." One batter, built like a rustic cabin, swatted a ball that dented the outfield fence. *Kablam!* Another guy—jitteriest person I ever saw in my entire life, a downed power line in human form—batted lefty and made plenty of contact. This guy had eye-black all over his cheeks: an impressively deranged look.

In my own at-bats I got some hits, nothing Ruthian but nevertheless undisputed line drives to the outfield. I had no regrets. I did what I'd set out to do. Solid contact—that's my brand. When you need a line drive up the middle, call me.

After everyone had hit, it was time for the managers to pick, which was done playground style—brutal, merciless, fair: pick the best guys first, then the middle guys, and then we'll just have to see. Everybody needs a catcher who can hit, I thought. This is going to be redemptive. Watch me now.

And yet when the picking started, the coaches didn't pick me, and they didn't pick me, and they didn't pick me. Time slowed. My heartbeat amplified. All these other guys were getting picked, but not me. At first it was humbling, and then it was alarming. What if I didn't get picked at all? I had told all my students I was trying out. What would I say to them? It was too harrowing a thought to consider. The possibility of not getting picked blotted out everything except the green, green grass while I contemplated the question of whether to stand up straight, or lean against the fence, or gradually disappear.

I became full of mercy for the outcasts of the world. In the future I would treat them with compassion, show an interest, listen to their stories. In particular when kids failed in my classroom, I wouldn't secretly roll my eyes in exasperation: No! Never again. I couldn't go back and change the past, but from now on I could and would be kinder to the not-good-enough.

Then I got picked.

This tall, sad-eyed guy, who a couple of months later would hit two grand-slam home runs in the same game, approached me unnoticed (so preoccupied was I with how to stand) and said, with what in retrospect sounds like a note of apology for the long wait, "Hey, do you want to play with us?"

Whatever I actually said, what I felt was: *Whoop whoop!* I shed all trepidation like a snakeskin as I followed my new manager back to the chosen circle, leaving behind the remaining half dozen or so not-yet-and-maybe-never-picked players. One guy, as old as I am if not older, kept tossing the ball into his mitt: *thump, thump.*

I wonder even now what I would tell that guy, if I could tell him something encouraging but real. I keep thinking about that guy, who could so easily have been me; who, let's face it, *is* me in the alternative universe we all know is right there waiting for us whenever we don't catch a lucky break.

Among my instantly beloved teammates I recognized the cabin-sized guy who had hit the mightiest clout of tryouts, and the hyper guy with eye-black spread all over his cheeks. A guy with a long black beard told me there was a pitcher on our team who could throw ninety-plus miles per hour, and I should get ready for my hand to hurt.

This was the best news I'd ever heard, although it turned out not to be true. That guy maxed out in the high seventies. Also I was our team's fourth-string catcher, which is really not a thing unless you make it one, which you must do if you are to be true to your inner game. So I hung on to that role and played maybe twenty-something innings over a fourteen-game season. I could see where things were headed early on and floated a complaint about it to my wife, who said, "As long as they let you play sometimes and you have fun, it's okay," so I went with that. I did not see a ton of action, but I also did not see none, and furthermore I made a contribution. From the dugout with the other subs I did a lot of hooraying for our side and also talked some pretty vicious trash about the other team. Everyone plays a role.

We went undefeated and won the championship by a wide margin in a game in which I did not play at all. Yet there was one midseason game where none of the other three catchers could make it. So, yeah, I caught all nine innings, ending with us up 3–2. When you win 3–2, you know the catcher had to have been doing something right, and that was me, with a hand on the ground behind home plate so I wouldn't keel over but rather maintain a steady squat. *If this is where I go from a malformed blood vessel, then bury me right here.* That was my exact thought. It kept me going through innings seven, eight, and nine.

I am not going to tell you that I was a stellar catcher. Gritty, sure. Gritty all day long. But now I know: Those balls that get by you in practice? They also get by you in a game, and while a couple of passed balls here and there is okay, more than a couple is not. I got taken out of one game, mid-inning. With the bases loaded we got the runner out at third, and the throw home was there in my mitt, then gone. That was a real gut-clencher.

I told my students about it the next day. What's the point of failure if you don't make use of it? We share personal news at the start of each class, to get off on a human note before I tell them to put their headphones away. So I told them about being taken out in the middle of the inning, and nobody said anything. The room was still. The moment lingered.

This was the one game where my wife was watching. The games were way out in the wilds of the San Fernando Valley, but my wife came to this game on a sunny Sunday morning with sunglasses and dimples glinting, and you know what she said?

That I looked like a ballplayer.

I think that's what I would tell that unpicked guy thumping the ball into his mitt back at tryouts. I would tell him he's a ballplayer for sure.

ELIZABETH WEIL

Did Venus Williams
Ever Get Her Due?

FROM THE NEW YORK TIMES MAGAZINE

VENUS IS HITTING the ball, still, after all these years. Venus, the dutiful Williams daughter, who actually followed the seventy-eight-page playbook her father wrote even before she was born to make her a tennis champion. Venus, who in following that playbook delivered on the dreams of the old man now sitting courtside on a bench watching her practice in the syrup-thick West Palm Beach morning.

Serena is doing whatever it is that Serena does in addition to her training—attending the royal wedding or dancing in a Beyoncé video or organizing the Met ball. Venus's mother, Oracene, divorced Richard Williams in 2002. Richard's latest wife, Lakeisha, is gone as well. Richard, white-bearded and diminished by age, reportedly had a stroke, and in its wake he and Lakeisha have been dragging each other through a messy divorce. But Venus is here. Venus is loyal. Richard and Serena will tell you Venus is the most loyal person in the world. "There's your average loyalty," Serena told me. Then there's Venus loyalty, which "for lack of a better word is mind-boggling."

Earlier that September morning, before Venus's alarm rang, Richard called and woke her up. Richard likes to do this, and Venus lets him. She's secure and generous that way. Venus's schedule for a normal day is: "I get up, I go practice, I go to the gym. I go to the office normally. I visit my dad. I get home at eight or nine." If the sun is too hot, Venus avoids doing drills that spray balls all over the practice court. Richard likes to come and pick them up. Venus doesn't want him to scurry around and get heatstroke.

"There you go, V.," Richard said from the bench. "There you go. More wrist, less arm."

A few minutes later: "There you go, V. Whatever you're doing, just keep doing it."

That day, both Williamses were dressed in the same palette: Venus in black leggings, white top; Richard in fresh white sneakers, fresh white socks, black shorts, and black polo. After Richard paid Venus a third compliment, Venus turned to her father and said, "Thank you, Daddy."

Richard said, "You're welcome, baby."

The exchange was so tender, so easy and full of love, that if my daughter, when she is thirty-nine, speaks this way to me it will burst my heart.

Between drills, as Venus's young, male hitting partner jumped rope, Venus sat and wiped her brow on her pink-and-yellow Wimbledon towel. Venus's body, not in motion, looks strong but languid, weary even, the Statue of Liberty with her arm down to take a rest—right up until 0.1 seconds before she hits the ball, at which point she explodes. At six-foot-one, with limbs that span time zones, she has self-containment that's unexpected and beguiling, a stillness that seems to emerge not only from her muscles but also from a calm, unruffled space inside, a clarity about who she is. "I'm tall. I'm Black. Everything's different about me. Just face the facts," Venus said to reporters at age seventeen when, in 1997, preternaturally self-possessed, she would become the first unseeded women's player in the Open Era to reach the finals of the U.S. Open.

Three years later, in 2000, when Venus first won the U.S. Open, President Clinton called to congratulate her. "So what happened?" she asked the president, who had been at the stadium but left before her match started. "Where'd you go?" Venus went on to press Clinton as to why he, in his motorcade, was allowed to zip through the gridlock between Queens and Manhattan while she had to sit in traffic. That Clinton was widely considered the most powerful person in the world didn't matter. She did not believe the president was superior to her.

Every piece of Williams arcana has been studied, repeatedly, to decode how this happened: how these sisters from Compton,

California, became two of the greatest tennis players of all time and transformed not just the game but our understanding of what's possible for women in sports, maybe even what's possible period. It's easy to stand in the present and get distracted, even a little blinded, by the klieg light of Serena. She's flashy; she's extroverted. Her talent is so singular that it feels as if it dropped whole from the heavens, a dense, crystalline meteorite of athletic prowess and drive. Venus, a year older, seems more earthly and understated. If you're not deliberately looking through Serena's glare —if you don't hold up a prism and refract Serena's achievement into its constituent parts—you'll lose sight of what a star Venus is.

Venus is at peace with this. She has been ranked No. 1 in the world. She has won seven Grand Slam tournaments, including five Wimbledon championships. She projects Thich Nhat Hanh levels of equanimity. Venus is not aggrieved. When, on that humid day, I asked Richard, who is seventy-seven, what he saw when he looked at Venus, he said, "She's perfect."

As Richard knows well, and Venus too, the girls were always a two-stage rocket: Venus igniting first, blasting herself up through the worst of the gravity and the grittiest friction, then separating and falling away as Serena lit up and shot into orbit alone.

Venus is ranked fifty-second in the world. This year, so far, she has lost in the first round at the French Open, Wimbledon, the Rogers Cup, and San Jose; the third round at the Australian and Italian Opens and at Britain's Birmingham tournament; the fourth round at the Miami Open; and the quarterfinals at the Auckland Open, Indian Wells, and the Cincinnati Masters. Some days she brings her serving arm up and over her head like a black belt about to chop a plank of wood with her bare hand and hits an ace. Other times she seems to lean back and take a micronap before she completes her swing.

A totally reasonable question is: why does Venus keep competing? Not counting Serena, Venus is more than four years older than any other woman ranked in the Top 100. She last won a Grand Slam tournament eleven years ago. The oldest woman ever to win a Grand Slam tournament was Serena, in 2017, at age thirty-five. Venus also lives with Sjogren's syndrome, the energy-sapping autoimmune disorder that was diagnosed in 2011. The illness causes fatigue and joint pain and requires Venus to stick (mostly) to a raw, vegan diet.

Yet Venus was never just a player. Her job was never simply to swing a racket and win sets, though that was required. Her job was to change the game. "God blessed me with Oracene to be able to bring Venus down," Richard said in his mad-genius (but often prophetic) way in a segment on the *Oprah* show in 2002. "She came down and saved tennis!" Tennis, Richard felt, was "very boring," stuck in a staid, snobby, moribund past. "Tennis is so far back in the Dark Ages, it's disgraceful," he said. "It's the only sport that you can play" in which people say: " *'Shhhhh shhhhh be quiet, be quiet.'* Who wants to come to something you got to sit there like you're a baby and be quiet?" he said on the show. "Let's stomp some feet and get this tennis thing going to BOOMING! If not, Venus and Serena gonna be gone and your game gonna be dead."

Tennis had never seen such a tall woman with such an epic wingspan move with such speed and grace. Tennis had never seen a skinny limby Black girl who, by her own estimation, looked like "a baby giraffe," so proud of her own dark skin that she wore a backless dress. Tennis had never seen a female player from a neighborhood like Compton—"Let me tell you something: there was nothing remotely un-hood about it," is how Isha Price, the middle of Oracene's three daughters from her first marriage, once described the place—confident enough to stand up and say in public, I will be the greatest, and then back that bravado up on the court.

Venus brought to tennis her 129-mile-per-hour serve and a brick-wall volley game. But more important, as Courtney Nguyen, a senior writer for WTA Insider, the news department of the Women's Tennis Association, told me: "Venus brought, not trash talk, but the idea that if you don't believe in yourself, no one is going to believe in you. She brought not apologizing for being good, not apologizing for what you want. 'I'm here to win it. I'm not here to make friends.'" This is not to say Venus was impolite—she had to be polite. Every time she won, she waved to fans and twirled before leaving the court, among the sweetest, least threatening exits imaginable.

It seems inevitable now, but it was not. Venus, out front, alone, was followed by Serena, and behind her Sloane Stephens, Madison Keys, Taylor Townsend, Naomi Osaka, and Coco Gauff. Venus was the lead rider breaking the headwinds in the peloton, the rabbit pulling the runners behind her to world-record pace. Venus allowed young women, "African American women especially, to feel there's a pathway for them to the top of the tennis world," Pam Shriver, who won twenty-two Grand Slam doubles titles between 1981 and 1991, told me.

You could hear direct echoes of Venus in female athletes all year long. In Megan Rapinoe, the soccer star who was so sure that she was going to win the World Cup that she turned down an invitation to celebrate at the White House before the final game. In Naomi Osaka, who just before the start of the French Open said, "I always thought I would be No. 1 and win a Grand Slam when I was eighteen." In Coco Gauff, who at age fifteen refused to bow her head and tell reporters that she'd met her goal once she'd beaten her idol, Venus. Because, as a true Venus protégée, she had not. "I said this before: I want to be the greatest," Gauff told reporters after her victory in the first round at Wimbledon. "My dad told me that I could do this when I was eight."

This is the current story of women in sports. But Venus was first.

Last September Venus walked into a Mexican restaurant in West Palm Beach, Florida, set her little Havanese dog, Harry, in a bag at her feet, and told me a story. As is true for many pets, Harry is a surrogate and a way to discuss things—sometimes intentionally but often not—that Venus doesn't want to say, which for her is a lot. She has spent thirty years in the public eye trying to maintain her privacy, and at this point her courteous-but-nonresponsive Q. and A. jujitsu is top-notch. The International Tennis Federation expects each player to sit for a news conference after each Grand Slam match. These days, in response to a reporter's multipart question about, say, a younger woman she has just played and how that opponent makes Venus feel now that Venus must obviously be at the end of her career, Venus will typically utter something along the lines of "I've never thought about that," and then let the awkward silence hang in the air as the room sorts out who was just rude to whom. Still, as Venus told me in the Mexican restaurant (while avoiding the guacamole that fits her anti-inflammation diet but that, texture-wise, freaks her out), one day, eleven years ago, she saw a puppy with funny curly hair in the window of a pet store. She thought the dog was adorable, so she called Serena. Serena, not the equanimity expert in the family, said: "Get him! I love him already!"

"So if you're in a pet shop, do not call her," Venus said, her arms and legs ribboning out like plains-state freeways from her shorts and tank top. "You need adult supervision, and she's not an adult." Yet Harry, more than a decade later, has worked out great. "I think Harry mirrors me well," Venus said. "He's chill. Then he gets excited. He stands up for what he believes in." Less simpatico to Venus, however, is Harry's habit of walking into Serena's house and eating all of Serena's dog Chip's food, and then standing over the empty bowl waiting to fight Chip or Serena's other dog, Laura, if one of them comes near.

"Serena has grown to love it," Venus said, referring to Harry's bullying. "I don't know why she likes it!"

Even a casual reader of the Williams family oeuvre may know that Serena, as a preteen, happily took Venus's lunch money if she forgot her own and did not want to eat one of the free jelly sandwiches offered at school. "It's almost embarrassing when you're at that age," Serena told me. "Ugggghhh, you have to eat the sandwich in the bag." But Venus always had a far sturdier internal bulwark against the judgment of others. "She never really cared about people's opinions," Serena said. Serena also took Venus's first-place trophy if Serena came in second, saying she just preferred the color gold. She sneaked extra hotels onto her properties when playing Monopoly. If their three older half-sisters complained, Venus—reflexively, almost professionally, protective, like the Secret Service—told them Serena didn't understand the rules.

A more thorough student of Williamsiana may also remember the orange episode, which Serena describes in the first of her two memoirs, *On the Line* (2009). (Venus has published zero memoirs, only a business book in 2010, called *Come to Win: Business Leaders, Artists, Doctors, and Other Visionaries on How Sports Can Help You Top Your Profession*, which features others' voices far more than her own.) In the orange episode, Serena is eight or nine. One day a friend of Richard's brings a big bag of oranges to the practice court. He leaves them in the shopping cart Richard used to store tennis balls. At the end of practice, when the girls are supposed to be working on their serves, Serena opens the bag, hits a couple of oranges over the fence, and then smashes the fruit into a sticky, oozy, fleshy pulp. "I was like a wild child," Serena writes, with the help of her cowriter, Daniel Paisner. "I unleashed on these defenseless oranges. I didn't think about it. I just went a little crazy." Looking back on this scene, Serena sees an impetuous jerk, but she also sees greatness. "You need a wild streak if you hope to be a serious competitor. You need a kind of irrational killer instinct. You need to put it out there that you're reckless and unpredictable—not just so your opponents take note, but so that you notice too."

It was a transformative moment, "really the first glimpse I had of the passion I'd soon develop on the court," Serena writes. "The passion I'd need to develop if I meant to grow my game."

Venus, an introvert and internalizer, is a knight by nature, not a gladiator. She was never an impetuous jerk.

Besides the Williams family's own primary texts, an incredible amount has been written over the past twenty-five years about Venus and Serena, and in that deluge of prose it has been easy to lose sight of how radical Richard Williams's original vision was. There had been Black American tennis champions before, the first among them Althea Gibson, the daughter of sharecroppers who was denied entry into tennis clubs because of the color of her skin, even into a hotel hosting a luncheon in her own honor. She won both Wimbledon and U.S. Nationals in 1957 and 1958, but at that time she came to feel overwhelmed by the idea that, in addition to playing, she was supposed to address racism directly. "I tried to feel responsibilities to Negroes, but that was a burden on my shoulders," she said. "Now I'm playing tennis to please me, not them." The next two major Black American tennis champions, Arthur Ashe and Zina Garrison, likewise kept their focus primarily on the seventy-eight-foot-long court.

But for Richard Williams, tennis was always political, always a vehicle for change. The epigraph of his 2014 memoir, *Black and White: The Way I See It,* comes from the 1926 Langston Hughes poem "I, Too."

> *I am the darker brother.*
> *They send me to eat in the kitchen . . .*

Richard grew up poor in Louisiana in the 1940s, the oldest of five children. To help feed his family, he writes, "I used to go out in the woods and hunt bullfrogs to eat, and fish, and shoot rabbits, and steal chickens." He also writes that his best friend was lynched by the Ku Klux Klan. After high school, he bounced around between Chicago and Shreveport. Then he moved to California, where he hustled odd jobs and started a security firm, because, he writes, "it was a natural for someone who knew as much about stealing as I did." Then in 1978, he saw the Romanian tennis player Virginia Ruzici on TV receive $20,000 (Richard remembered this as $40,000) for winning the final of the French Open, and he decided not just to learn to play the game so that his daughters, who had not yet been born, could become rich but to learn to play the game so those daughters could expose the idea that if you think you're the best in the world but that world is built on privilege and exclusion, you are lying to yourself.

Richard watched tennis videos. He look lessons from a man nicknamed Old Whiskey. He moved his family from Long Beach, California, to Compton so that, in addition to mastering ground strokes, etc., the girls could hone their mental game; he wanted them to learn to handle the stress and adversity that came from practicing in gang territory because they'd have to deal with the even worse stress and adversity when playing in front of white people.

Venus, born on June 17, 1980, fifteen months before Serena, was taller, stronger, and more tactical, and was thrust into the public eye first. She was profiled in this newspaper at age ten. She quit the junior circuit at age twelve after winning all sixty-three of the sixty-three matches she played. She turned pro at age fourteen. Serena clung to the hem of Venus's tennis shorts in every conceivable way. "If she laughed, you laughed louder," Oprah Winfrey said to Serena with a hint of sternness when the sisters appeared on her show in 2002. "If she cried, you cried harder. If she ordered food, you would order the same thing."

Serena, twenty-one, nodded and admitted that "only maybe two years ago" she stopped being Venus.

Oprah said, "You woke up at, what, eighteen or nineteen and said—"

"I said: 'I'm not Venus. I'm Serena!'"

Isha Price told me it is "absolutely more clear in hindsight" what a huge burden it was for Venus to be the first body on the baseline for Richard's larger-than-tennis operation, the first Williams holding a racket on center court. But while it was happening, nobody in the family talked about the pressure. They were just living their lives. All parents circumscribe a world for their children. Richard and Oracene strictly defined theirs. "If they told us something, there was no other," Isha said. *"You don't really have any friends. Okay I believe that. The only people you have are your family. If people don't know you, they're not going to do anything to protect you, but you guys can protect each other.* We really kind of had to be ride or die for one another, because as far as we were concerned there was no one else."

Richard was there with Venus all the way. Yet in those first professional years, Venus was also alone. Isha remembers watching Venus's matches on TV in college, and she'd see, even in U.S. tournaments, everyone rooting for a player "from Europe somewhere," not for her sister. Venus also had to handle being treated as an interloper by the other players. "Only she knows what was going on in some of those early locker rooms, but it couldn't have been easy," Isha said. In 1997, in the U.S. Open semifinal, the Romanian Irina Spirlea shoulder-checked Venus during a changeover. "She thinks she's *the* [expletive] Venus Williams," Spirlea said, explaining her behavior in the aftermath, though not in the way she intended to.

Richard, when asked about the incident the next day on the phone by a reporter, called Spirlea "a big, tall, white turkey."

Richard pushed cultural buttons like a kid in an elevator. He was not afraid to say to Venus, in earshot of all, "Meet the white lady." Sitting down with a white *Sports Illustrated* reporter in 1994, he said: "Don't be intimidated. We won't hurt you." He claimed when his daughters reached the Wimbledon finals that he was going to invite the Crips to the All England Club to watch his girls' matches with the queen.

In 1999, in the quarterfinals of the Australian Open, a strand of beads fell out of Venus's hair as she served on what would be a break point in the second set against Lindsay Davenport (the sisters' most formidable opponent for many years). By that time Venus, at eighteen, was already a Top 10 player. She had gone 17-4 in Grand Slam tournament play in the previous year. She hadn't won a final. She did not yet quite have consistent control of her powers, but she was getting close. When those beads fell out, the chair umpire penalized Venus a point for distraction, giving Davenport a 3–0 lead. Venus looked up at him, furious, belittled, exhausted, her teenage voice cracking as she argued her case to the white-button-down-shirted referee who'd emerged to support the umpire's call.

"I am not causing a disturbance here!" Venus said, plaintive, keeping her anger in check. "No one is disturbed!" She was right: nobody was disturbed on that point. But tennis was disturbed. Venus, back on the court, summoned the strength to contain her fury. It took a toll; she lost the set, 0–6.

Serena was coming up by then. She won the 1999 U.S. Open. Among the cognoscenti it was already clear that Serena would become a better player than Venus, as Richard always promised she would. But Serena was entering a significantly different world from the one Venus entered, if for only one reason: she was entering a world with Venus already in it. Venus did almost all the talking in their joint interviews, introversion be damned. She was the one who had to explain that she and Serena didn't smile more because they didn't want to smile more. She was the one who had to explain that they stuck together because they didn't like to hang out with people they didn't trust. (Richard had a more aggressive response to this last question: "I hear a lot of people say that my girls weren't very social. Let me ask you: Do you see Bill Gates out there socializing with a ball?")

In 2000 Venus and Serena played each other in a Wimbledon semifinal. At that point they'd competed against each other in four major tournaments. Venus had won three matches, but Serena had won their most recent one. The night before, the sisters shared a bedroom as they had all their lives. The semifinal the next day was intense and strange, almost too intimate to watch, filled with power, grunts, operatic points, and dozens of unforced errors. Both Williamses, at times, seemed to avert their eyes. They knew each other's weaknesses as well as they knew their own. They wanted to exploit those vulnerabilities to win, but at the same time they did not want those vulnerabilities exposed for consumption and entertainment to the world.

The match ended with Serena double-faulting on match point. After Venus won 6–2, 7–6 (3), she walked off the court with Serena, who was on the verge of tears. "Let's get out of here," Venus said. At the news conference later, Venus was still focused on Serena's pain. "Serena is a real competitor, probably even more than what I am," Venus said. "So that really hurts deep."

Thus began Venus's prime. Two days after that Wimbledon

victory over Serena, Venus won her first Grand Slam championship, defeating Davenport. She won her second Grand Slam two
months later at the U.S. Open, again defeating Davenport. That
year Venus also won two Olympic gold medals—women's singles
and women's doubles (with Serena). She scored a $40 million en-
dorsement deal with Reebok, the largest a female athlete had ever
signed.

The following year, 2001, Venus again won Wimbledon, beat-
ing Justine Henin. She played Serena in the finals of the U.S.
Open. That match was another internecine war. It felt intrusive,
nearly transgressive, to watch. But who could look away? One of
Venus's serves blew the racket out of Serena's hand. Venus won,
6–2, 6–4. At the net, at the end, Venus said to Serena: "I love
you. I feel so bad. I feel like I haven't won." But Serena knew she
would not return her sister's fealty, and at the trophy ceremony,
before the cameras and the crowd, Serena put Venus and the
world on notice.

"She always goes extra, sometimes too much, worrying about
Serena," Serena said of her sister. "But she's got to realize: I didn't
win this time. Enjoy it, because it might be my time next time."

Four hours after she finished her muggy Florida practice, Venus
arrived at her office. (She'd driven home to take a shower and
fallen asleep.) Tennis was always a family obligation, deep at the
heart of the world laid out by Richard and Oracene. The world
also included Richard's driving the girls around in the maroon-
and-white family VW van, schooling them on the merits of buying
foreclosed houses and the necessity of becoming not just athletes
but entrepreneurs—all part of the plan to win not just on the
court but in all of American life. He had a deep, intuitive understanding of the American dream and an ability to see that dream
for what it was truly about: money, status, winning. Still, V Starr
Interiors, the interior-design company that Venus started in 2002,
and EleVen, the active-wear label that followed in 2007, were never
for Richard, or Serena, or anyone else. They were for Venus (one
of whose middle names is Starr) and Venus alone, and as such,
she loves them more than you might expect for a woman who has
been extraordinarily successful doing something else.

"They always stay babies, businesses," Venus told me. "Even
when they're big, they're still a baby and they need so much."

Venus has been known to take work calls at tournaments shortly before she plays. "If the need is there, I will do what it takes. You can't just leave your baby alone. I'm a good mama."

V Starr specializes in hotels, condo developments, and athletic clubs and serves primarily corporate clients (plus Serena). EleVen makes active wear—largely tennis clothes, though it has recently branched into streetwear. (Venus did not answer questions about the companies' finances.) The two small companies, with about twenty-five employees combined, share space in one of Florida's zillion mini-mall-like office parks. The setup inside is profoundly generic, just groups of tables pushed together with computers on them, which had the effect of making Venus, when she arrives, appear all the more resplendent in her black dress with metallic green cuffs, gold accent headband like a crown. All athletes are beautiful, but with Venus the beauty stems not only from the contours of her face and body but also from her carriage. She has a poise that, paired with her long neck, makes her seem regal, almost mythically so, like the bust of Queen Nefertiti. The effect is diminished only somewhat when she carries Harry around like an infant in the crook of her arm.

The businesses are very, definitely, vehemently not just a retirement plan as Venus is very, definitely, vehemently not talking about retirement. She still loves the game. Why should she quit? Billie Jean King, who played into her forties, told me she wished she'd played longer. "You should have a fulfilling career," King said. "You should go up the mountain and down the mountain all the way, just like you do in real life. You don't have to go out at No. 1 if you don't want to. I think that's a mistake." Venus's only concession to talking about her age is acknowledging that "maybe I just stretch more." So for now, in addition to training and playing in tournaments, her day-to-day includes being involved in most decisions at both V Starr and EleVen. The day I visited, she was approving a palette of materials for a midrange condo project. The sample tray included pink corduroy; brown leather; blue, tan, and teal velvet; white and black marble.

In a windowless conference room filled with EleVen samples, a safe distance from the office candy bowl (which Venus insists stays full, though her sweet tooth tortures her), Harry sat in a chair at the table as Sonya Haffey, vice president of V Starr, ran through the status of various clients.

"He's not responding to me," Haffey said, running down the list. "I was going to see if you could work your magic with him.

"He said he met you. You were in a Range Rover. He even said what you ate, which was very disturbing."

V Starr does not want to work with people primarily interested in Venus's celebrity, though it's just true that if Venus calls a client the firm is courting, the client is far more likely to call back. With EleVen, Venus's stardom is an explicit part of the brand. The company's identity is built around excellence—10 is a number, EleVen is a lifestyle, or so the tagline goes—with Venus herself representing that goal. She always wears EleVen apparel when she competes.

That afternoon Venus also took a call on speakerphone from a producer in New York to kick around yet another off-court opportunity: a reality-TV show. The producer offered a few concepts that interested Venus not at all. Venus then presented her own, tentatively titled "Designing Doubles." The idea was Venus and Serena would go around together, fixing up places like women's shelters and schools.

"I don't want to pigeonhole us," Venus explained. So instead of a show focused on sports, the Williams sisters would spend time in the community, working to make spaces better for those in need. They'd do the redecorating themselves, right down to sewing curtains. Oracene used to make the girls' tennis skirts. "She taught me how to sew," Venus said.

The producer on the line was enthusiastic. This put Venus at ease. "It's a concept I'm a lot more comfortable with in terms of personality and being myself," Venus said.

"I like it," the producer said. "We love it. We'd love to have your sister."

Venus told me another story: She and Serena were living in an 8,500-square-foot mansion they bought together in Palm Beach Gardens, Florida. Then one day Serena announced, "I found a place for us to live!"

Venus said, "Okay, great." She checked out the lot. She thought it was fine. "Serena liked it or loved it, I guess," Venus said. They put in a bid.

A few weeks later Serena called again and said, "Actually, I thought we'd get two lots, side by side." Then she announced she wanted to move to another development.

At the time Venus was traveling in Asia. But lots were going fast, and she bought one. "I was like, I guess I better close," she said. Venus hired an architect and got to what she called "75 percent construction documents." Then Oracene wanted to buy a new place, so Venus took her mother to look for properties in nearby Jupiter. There Venus had an epiphany. "I said: 'I always wanted to live here! This is where I planned on moving!'" Venus found a lot for herself in Jupiter. "Then Serena is like, I want to move there too! And then she was upset because she didn't find anything."

A few months later—you guessed it—Serena called: "I know this sounds nuts . . ."

Venus said, "Please leave me alone."

"I saw this lot." Serena said. "I think you should look at it."

"I was like: 'This is ridiculous. I will never do that,'" Venus said. "Next thing I know I went to look at the lot and I thought, 'This is an amazing idea.' I bought the lot. Then I got halfway along and I realized, Shoot, I really want to move to Jupiter. I sold that lot. It was just the craziest thing. By that time I was just so tired. Then Serena yelled at me."

Venus now has a house on Jupiter Island. Serena has a house in Palm Beach Gardens. Both sisters also have houses in New York and California, among other places, and once again, they own adjacent lots. V Starr is helping Serena design her new home. "Serena wants something supermodern this time," Venus said. Venus wants her own to be "relaxed, pretty, understated. Not, 'Oh, my God, this house is so big.'"

The sisters text constantly. For a while they had hitting partners who were brothers, and personal assistants who were brothers too. (Naomi Osaka has since hired Venus's hitting partner, Jermaine Jenkins, as her coach.) Venus said of Serena, "We have the most codependent relationship you've ever heard."

Venus has never, and probably will never, cop to feeling any pain caused by sibling rivalry. But after Serena blasted off, Venus seemed wobbly and lost for a while. Who could blame her? Venus had been ranked No. 1 in the world for eleven weeks during the spring and summer of 2002. Then, in June 2002, Venus lost the French Open final to Serena. This was the first Williams-Williams Grand Slam final that Serena won. Then in July, at Wimbledon, Venus lost in the finals to Serena again. Serena proceeded to complete her so-called

Serena Slam, by winning the U.S. and Australian Opens. Venus lost the No. 1 ranking. Serena held onto it for fifty-seven weeks straight. Venus has never been ranked first again.

In the years that followed, Venus suffered abdominal injuries. She suffered wrist injuries. Her form fell apart. She often stepped onto the baseline as taped up as a book with a broken spine.

Venus did regain her footing at Wimbledon starting in 2005, both on the court and off. At that point, the U.S. and Australian Opens offered equal prize money to men and women; Wimbledon and the French Open did not. Larry Scott, then chairman and chief executive of the Women's Tennis Association, wanted Venus, along with many of the other top women, to represent the female players in negotiations with Wimbledon leadership. Most athletes beg off chores involving tennis politics. "When a player starts to get involved," King told me, "it takes away from her true focus: winning." But Venus was never a regular player. She said yes. The day before she was scheduled to play in the 2005 Wimbledon final, she walked into the meeting at the All England Club and told the committee members to close their eyes—"no peeking!" she recalls saying. She asked the assembled to imagine being little girls who had worked all their lives to make it to a stage like Wimbledon. Then she asked them to imagine those little girls once they made it being told that Wimbledon valued boys more. How could a girl retain full belief in herself under those circumstances? Why cut girls down?

The next day Venus played Davenport in the Wimbledon final. Venus lost the first set, 4–6, but then in an epic match that lasted two hours, forty-five minutes, came back to win 7–6 (4), 9–7. She fell to her knees. The performance in the meeting did not take away. This—the combined effort, on and off the court—was always Venus's game. It took a couple of years, an op-ed by Venus in *The Times of London* ("How can it be that Wimbledon finds itself on the wrong side of history?"), and an endorsement in Parliament from Prime Minister Tony Blair. But in 2007, in a bit of cosmic justice, Venus won Wimbledon again and became the first female champion to receive a check for the exact same amount as Wimbledon's winning man.

Venus won Wimbledon for her fifth—and final—time in 2008. Three years later, in 2011, she found out she had Sjogren's syndrome. She brushed off my questions about how her autoimmune disorder is affecting her life these days. "I definitely do make sure I get my rest even though I'm on a busy schedule" was just about all she would say. But between 2011 and 2016, Venus made it to only one Grand Slam semifinal—Wimbledon, in 2016, which she lost to Angelique Kerber. Venus's ranking dropped from No. 5 at the end of 2010 to No. 103 a year later.

Serena, meanwhile, kept on winning, and winning, and winning. Twenty-three Grand Slam titles. Three hundred nineteen weeks ranked No. 1. Considered by some to be not only the greatest tennis player ever, male or female, but quite possibly the greatest athlete ever, full stop. Serena, who was newly pregnant, beat Venus in the finals of the Australian Open in late January 2017. That was the last tournament she played before she gave birth to her daughter, Alexis Olympia Ohanian Jr., on September 1, 2017.

With Serena sidelined on maternity leave for most of 2017, Venus had her best year of the past ten. In addition to the 2017 Australian Open final, she reached the finals at Wimbledon and the semifinals at the U.S. Open. Venus finished 2017 ranked fifth. She earned more prize money that year than any other woman on tour.

Serena returned in 2018. Venus finished that year ranked fortieth.

This past March Venus played at Indian Wells, just outside Palm Springs, California. The tournament was the site of one of the most excruciating episodes in Operation Williams. In 2001, Venus, age twenty, and Serena, age nineteen, were to play each other in the semifinals. They warmed each other up. They walked out onto the court. Then Venus withdrew from the match with tendinitis in her knee four minutes before the match was to start.

The crowd—heavily old, white, and rich—was upset, justifiably so. They'd paid for their seats, spent the afternoon getting to them, and now . . . no match. But the crowd's anger seemed to be born of more than disappointment. The crowd's anger seemed hot, personal, and consensus at the pavilion quickly landed on the idea that Richard had fixed the match. This was Serena's tournament, according to Richard, or so the thinking went. The best thing for his family was for Venus to scratch and give her sister a bye to the finals. Afterward, Richard told reporters that angry fans called him "nigger." One, Richard claimed, said he wished he could "skin you alive." Two days later, in the final, Serena faced Kim Clijsters. The crowd booed Serena, loudly. Still she won. At a tournament a few weeks later, the press continued asking Venus about the episode.

"Do you have any comment on what they claim, racism and all that junk?" one reporter asked.

Venus answered, "I don't think racism is junk at all."

Both sisters vowed never to play Indian Wells again. Neither did for fourteen years. Then in 2015, Serena decided to return. She'd been reading Nelson Mandela, she said. She wanted to practice forgiveness. She had become, by then, the almost mystically powerful woman only Venus and Richard could have imagined, the second stage of Richard's fantastic, world-changing, two-stage rocket. There was never any Serena without Venus. There was never any second stage without the first. Venus was the mightiest female player anyone had ever seen. Serena rode her power through the atmosphere. Then she exploded, becoming propulsively excellent, a woman who knew how to harness energies that, in less masterful hands, burn out of control. She was the girl who smashed the oranges, all grown up. The woman who loved her sister's dog Harry for eating her own dog's food.

The following year, 2016, Venus decided to play Indian Wells too. To explain why, she published an essay in *The Players Tribune* that is essentially an open letter about being Serena's sister.

> For me, being the big sister meant that, when I made my professional debut, I was the only player on tour who looked like me. I was the only player with my skin color, with my hair, with my background, with my style.
>
> Being the big sister meant that, when I became world No. 1 in 2002, I wasn't just world No. 1. I was also the first black American woman to reach No. 1 . . .
>
> Being the big sister meant that, when my little sister made her professional debut, I became a lot of new things to her—her colleague, her competitor, her business partner, her doubles partner. But I was still, first and foremost, the one thing I had always been: her family. I was her protector—her first line of defense against outside forces. And I cherished that.

Venus closed the letter by acknowledging it was now time for her to follow Serena, to Indian Wells and elsewhere. She ended by calling Serena "the greatest player in the world."

This year, at Indian Wells, Serena dropped out with a virus and Venus made it five rounds, to the quarterfinals. The stands were mostly filled, still, with old, rich white people. The theme on the evening of Venus's quarterfinal was Rat Pack night. Sinatra blared from the speakers.

But now the crowd in Palm Springs adored Venus. She walked out in her white EleVen dress and taped right knee, self-possessed and elegant as ever. She played Angelique Kerber, then ranked No. 8, a player who defeats her opponents by running down and returning every single ball. Playing a match against Kerber is like racing a clock for time.

Between points Kerber bounced up and down on her toes, checking to make sure the spring in her legs was still there. Venus didn't bounce. She put her hands on her hips. She retied her shoe. She knows her spring is gone.

Through the first set, Venus was down, then Venus was up. She managed to battle Kerber to six games all, but after she lost the tiebreaker, Venus knew she was done. At the end of the second set, fans stood in reverence and appreciation, for today, for all of it, for her service in changing their world.

Venus raised her arm, waved, and twirled. Then she walked off the court alone.

CHLOÉ COOPER JONES

Champion Moves

FROM RACQUET

I TAKE A PICTURE of Roger Federer. His trophy half-obscures his face. The tournament official in charge of the press conference is waving angrily at me, motioning for me to put my camera down, but the camera is in front of my face, blocking, and so I don't notice. I keep taking pictures until a journalist sitting nearby taps me on the shoulder and points. The official is stiff-jawed, glaring. A few more swivel in their seats, following the trajectory of his look to me. I lower my camera, my head. Pictures are forbidden, I learn later, too late. I'm sure I hear a disapproving hiss go around the room, but when I look up again, no one is staring at me, the room is hushed, everyone listens as Federer speaks for the final time of the fortnight; there's a rise in the room as everyone sits a bit straighter, forward in their seats, necks stretched, silent, eyes on him.

When I first arrive at the Indian Wells Masters tournament, I do little else but hide. I hide in the bathroom. I hide in the hallways that snake below the stands.

In the press office, rows of journalists write diligently at their desks. Silent TV screens glow above them, displaying the same match unfolding live on the other side of a wall of glass windows. Few turn their head to the window to watch, and yet they know the score and how precisely the players are succeeding or failing. They murmur across the desk dividers to each other. They speak in tongues. "Moonball," one says. A whisper, a groan, "Bleh, such big cuts." Later, "Jammed to the body." Another: "Out wide, cross-court; one, two: point, point, point, game."

I pass through the glass doors and hide in the far corner of the stadium's designated press section. I'm too short for most chairs and so my feet dangle freely, tugging my spine and hips out of alignment. I shovel in painkillers. After one match there is another and then another. I'm tired and aching.

I don't understand anyone or my surroundings, and because of this I am doubly isolated: first by being ignorant and second by needing to pretend I'm not.

My veil of belonging stays mostly intact if I avoid all conversations. I keep my sunglasses on in the press box, I sit in the very back row at the press conferences, I eat alone in the far corner of the food garden. I alternate between these spaces for thirteen hours or so, speaking to no one, then I drive the long drive, alone, along dark desert highways, to a hotel and sleep alone and return to do the same the next day.

I hadn't considered the possibility that a tennis tournament could be a lonely place, but the Indian Wells Tennis Garden is the loneliest place I can ever remember being. It's a strange and specific loneliness, one that arises from knowing I share the same focal point with everyone around me — the same match, the same results, the same player sitting at the dais at a press conference — but that I am unable to fluently communicate about what I see. All day and into the evening, I bump along my limits.

I'd come to the desert to be physically closer to Roger Federer. He'd been battling age and injury for a few years and had been forced to end his season early in 2016, signaling what many assumed was the inevitable downhill slide toward retirement. But then he'd arrived at the start of 2017 playing some of the best tennis of his career. Some spoke — seriously and not — about witnessing resurrection. It was the second coming of the true messiah of tennis, said John McEnroe, tongue perhaps in cheek. It was a new age.

I'd once read in *The New Yorker* that rooting for Federer was rooting for a Platonic ideal. "It is like rooting for the truth." He was, claimed yet another journalist, "a permanent miracle." He was, to many, a True Genius. Article headlines, book titles, documentaries described him this way; I heard it — *genius!* — on the lips of commentators, opponents, coaches, crowds. The word was an evaluation, a comparison, an explanation, an exclamation. It was whispered in disbelief.

I loved when the cameraman zeroed in on Federer fans during a match. The agony and awe on the faces was acute. I wanted to understand that feeling.

The *New York Times* reported that tickets to the 2017 Australian Open final between Federer and Nadal had sold for as high as $20,000. One smart Federer fan had purchased tickets to the final months in advance and then turned down the chance to sell them for $15,000. "But it's priceless to me," she said. "It's pathological," said another fan, explaining his need. A woman from Hawaii had planned only to stay for the earliest rounds of the tournament and then had extended her trip when Federer kept winning. After the fourth round, she took a ten-hour red-eye home, but in the taxi that took her away from the airport, she began looking for flights back to Melbourne. From the article: "Her husband sensed that she would rather be somewhere else."

What did anyone gain from proximity to genius as opposed to watching it from a screen? I wanted to know what his fans knew, feel what they felt. I wanted to know if these ecstatic visions were available to me. But I didn't have hundreds of dollars to spend on a ticket to watch him play. I was working as a freelance culture journalist and wondered if I could persuade a magazine to send me to cover a tennis tournament. One problem was that I'd never written about tennis and I didn't really know anything about tennis, at least nothing that could be of use to any readers anywhere. But I decided to see if I could just wish my desires into reality and so I sent an email to the sports editor of *Rolling Stone* asking to be sent to the California desert to cover the tournament at Indian Wells. I'd met this editor once years before and we had mutual friends and, anyway, he was too busy to look closely at what I was asking for, maybe, and so he'd said yes.

I was alone in bed in a hotel when his response came through. The shallowness of my knowledge hit me all at once. The room got blurry and I began to levitate. Not knowing what else to do, I googled "tennis" and started to read, but stopped because suddenly I was light-headed and couldn't see too well. I slid off the bed and onto the floor and stayed there, my face down, inhaling the chemical cleaner in the carpet.

*

Federer has a bye to the second round and won't play until the middle Sunday of the tournament. The desk next to mine in the pressroom is occupied by a handsome Australian journalist who eats only vegetables. All day he eats vegetables and types furiously, filing six or seven articles at a time, it seems. On the third day of the tournament I notice he's looked up from laptop screen to TV screen, actually observing a match. I get the courage to ask if he's hoping one player will win over the other and he says he doesn't care when a player he likes loses. I stare at him, hungry for conversation.

"I used to care," he continues. His eyes hold steady on the match, but he smiles a polite smile meant for me. He eats a red pepper sliced thin as a fingernail. He keeps his vegetables separated in their own plastic containers, which he keeps stacked neatly on his desk.

"It's a job, though," he says. "There will always be another tournament. They'll all play again."

"Do you care when Federer loses?"

"Nope," he says.

"Do you care when he plays?"

"Not really," he says.

I can talk to the Australian the longest without revealing that I don't belong here, but I have to be careful. A minute is okay, but if I push it further, he'll question me about a player I've never heard of and I'll have to fake a phone call and run away.

My only friend is Cindy. Cindy runs the main press information desk. It's her job to assign work spaces and lockers to the journalists. Cindy welcomes me every morning by saying my name. "Don't forget your coffee, Chloé," Cindy says, and I say back, "I never do, Cindy." She hands me a player interview request form and I nod my head like interviewing a player is something that, sure, I'll definitely do.

In the afternoon, she brings us the schedule for the next day's matches. When she stops at my desk, she says, "Almost time for the afternoon cup, Chloé?" and I'll say, "You know what, Cindy? I think it might be just that time."

There's a certain "Lady of Palm Springs" look, and Cindy's got it—dyed hair, diamond rings, perfect nails, perfect makeup. Cindy has fewer wrinkles than me although she's likely thirty years my senior. She tells me that she volunteers every year at the tournament just to keep herself from "rotting away in her condo, ha ha!"

Each morning, I greet Cindy, pour myself a cup of coffee, and walk past the rows of desks in the press office, straining to make eye contact with someone who might recognize me from the previous day. Every time I pass by the rows, I stare at the focused faces of the actual journalists. If they so much as lift their gaze for a moment, I'll be ready with my acknowledging nod. The TVs blaze unseen above their heads. Everyone is very busy. A sports newsroom is a place where if I said, *I'm having a heart attack, please help me,* the response might be, *Quiet, I'm on deadline.*

When I get to my desk, my TV screen is dark and I can't get it to turn on. This is a new problem. I run my hand along the screen's cold, smooth edges. There are no buttons. Cindy, on a surveillance stroll, passes my desk and sees me struggling. She pats my shoulder gently and says, "Watch this, Chloé," and then she touches the center of the screen itself. Instantly it comes to life, bathing Cindy's face in its electric glow. I thank her profusely and she says, "You're very welcome, Chloé," and then she says, "Have a great day, Chloé." I'm so nervous and so alone. I want to get down on my knees in praise of Cindy.

After the matches and press conferences have ended for the day, I hear the handsome Australian journalist talk to the cool French journalist who also sits in our row about having dinner. My stomach growls. To her he whispers, "I'm terrible, I snuck some bread for breakfast and bread for lunch." I tidy my desk as they tidy theirs. A debate about where to eat slows them down, so I pretend an important email has come in and type random sentences in an empty Word document until they start winding up their laptop cords and then I wind mine and then they put their MacBooks in their sleeves and I dump mine into my backpack and when they are ready to go, I'm ready too, but they walk out, forgetting to invite me to dinner.

I drive back to my hotel with the windows down and I breathe in the air, which is deeply perfumed, something I didn't expect in the desert. I was sure it would smell hot and dry, which is to say I thought it would not smell like anything, certainly not gardenias and marigolds, but that's only because I know nothing about the California desert and did no research before flying out from New York.

In my hotel room, I find that my television no longer works and neither does the internet. The night clerk shrugs when I tell him. "Sometimes works, sometimes don't," he says. It's my second and last human exchange of the day. His dog sleeps behind the lobby desk, but wakes to bark at me every night when I return. The dog's name is Terrance.

The next morning, I pass a very tall tennis player on his way to the practice courts. I recognize him, and when he sees me he stops as if he recognizes me too, although that's impossible. He's confused by something and stares at me, looking up and down the brief length of my body. I'm walking toward him and he starts to mimic my swayed walk. My uncommon gait is the result of my misaligned hips, my unbalanced spine, my missing sacrum bone, my disability, and it, along with my diminutive stature, marks me to some as strange. I walk slowly, looking off-balance, leaning side to side. The tennis player nudges the person next to him and says, too loudly, "What the fuck is that?" as he passes me.

I forget I'm not supposed to cheer in the press box, Lord, do I forget. The very serious, very busy journalists glare. I whistle and gasp. Some move to sit farther from me. I forget myself again and again. I am unworthy of their forgiveness. I hide in the bathroom, looking in the mirror, smoothing my hair.

I return to the press box, composing myself with care. A young man sits next to me. It's the *Times* reporter who'd written the article about the great lengths fans had gone to see Federer in Australia. I think of introducing myself; I try to do just that. I make a noise and the young reporter turns to face me. I look beyond his face and I see other faces looking at me. I see the crowd looking up at me, some with their necks craned, staring. Play on the court below has stopped and the players are looking at me. The chair umpire points to me. Illness waves through me. All are ready to jointly expel me.

The young reporter points to my hands. Somehow, in my

nervous fumbling, I'd turned on my cell phone's flashlight and it was facing out, the distracting beam reaching down onto the court. The young reporter takes my phone from me. The flashlight blinks off. He sets the phone back into my open hands and retreats. Play resumes.

At lunch I'm walking the grounds and I see a huge crowd gathered by a practice court. I find a seat in the stands and I see him. The moment hangs suspended as if it caught itself on a nail. He's right in front of me, the real human, Roger Federer, for the first time. He's hitting casual ground strokes with Lucas Pouille, a young Frenchman on the tour. The crowds around the practice court are thick with people and raised cell phones. I see a large red sign. It has a Swiss white cross on it and reads "SHHH!! GENIUS AT WORK."

I squeeze my way into the stands. Next to me, a true Lady of Palm Springs, drunk on Moët, shouts her love out to Federer. She's likely fifty or so, but has the body of a teen, which she shows off in a tiny black romper. Federer tosses a ball into the air and his body floats up to meet it. The ball then appears to have been convinced, rather than struck, by his racquet to graze the upper corner of the service box and bounce beyond Pouille's reach. An ace. The woman in the romper makes a gargling noise and extends out her arms and legs, spilling her champagne down her front. One of her wedge heels comes loose. A man behind her, presumably her husband, hands her his full, plastic Moët champagne goblet and she sips.

"I love you, Roger," she shouts. "I love you so goddamn much." She nudges another lady near her and that lady lets out a long "whoo" sound. "Come on!" they say to others around them, and soon a whole section of Palm Springs Ladies is swooning and cooing sweet things out to Roger. He and Pouille continue to play an easy practice set during which a ball is shanked off the end of Pouille's racquet and goes into the stands. A young girl passing by the court catches it and is uncertain whether she's allowed to keep it or must throw it back. "Keep it," yells the lady in the romper, above her in the stands. "Fucking keep it. Roger Federer touched that ball. That's Roger's ball. Keep it or give it here." The girl looks unsure. A coach on the court extends his hand out to the girl.

"Leave her alone," screams the lady in the romper. "Let her

keep it." Then to the girl she snarls. "Don't you dare throw that ball back." The girl runs off, the ball tight in her hands.

The lady in the romper stands, blocking her husband's view, and she starts to dance. She gestures wildly to all around her and soon the chorus of middle-aged women have all resumed their "I love you"s.

I feel immediately the awe of proximity—to Federer, yes, but more so to the crowd. Among them, I'm free; I'm no longer an impostor; I can simply be a fan, ecstatic. I am so close, just one row back from where he stands, and I'm free to gasp and marvel and nod and shout and bake in the desert sun alongside the bronzed Palm Springs beauties, all of whom understand me, none of whom shun and forsake me.

I think of snapping my own fingers at the husband of the lady in the romper, certain that if I did, he'd produce for me a plastic goblet full of champagne. Me and the Ladies, we are together in this. We will wait and watch, together, until Roger leaves the court. We will shout and coo and applaud. Gone are the aches from shivering hours on end in the overly air-conditioned press office. My muscles warm and relax, release, my eyesight sharpens, my pores open and sweat coats me, cleanses me from the inside out. I am woozy, euphoric. The women hoot and so do I. In between games, Federer changes his shirt, exposing his soft skin, and the Ladies erupt in high-pitched pleasure and I smile my best smile.

The concept of creative genius is a modern invention. In our earliest conceptions, genius was characterized as an attendant spirit that guided you toward both good and evil—genius was the angel and the devil on your shoulder. In the early 1700s, literary critics Joseph Addison and Edward Young were among the first to write about human geniuses. They saw human genius as an innate capacity, occurring naturally in those who possessed it.

"Among great geniuses those few draw the admiration of all the world upon them, and stand up as the prodigies of mankind, who by the mere strength of natural parts, and without any assistance of art or learning, have produced works that were the delight of their own times, and the wonder of posterity," wrote Addison. "There appears something nobly wild and extravagant in these great natural geniuses."

For Young, the genius was a magician capable of wielding an

otherworldly power, able to create outside of the physical laws the rest of us must abide by. We could become good through learning or practice, but genius was a divine gift. Young wrote, "Learning we thank, genius we revere; that gives us pleasure, this gives us rapture."

I decide to go to a bar. I leave my press credentials hanging around my neck, hoping someone will see and ask me something and I'll have a chance to talk about my day. I see people and they are all happily talking to other people. The bar is in a hotel, not my hotel, and I fear a concierge looking me up and down, knowing I don't belong here, and I fear walking in the bar and having the room swivel to me and look me up and down the way the tall tennis player did, and so I sit in my car for what feels like hours, but isn't really, and then I drive back to my hotel.

I'm grateful for the cool darkness of the desert at night. I turn down all the windows in my rental car and drive. I pass my hotel once, double back, and then pass it again, just so I can prolong the feeling of being hidden away in the dark car, in motion, moving forward not in failure.

I've brought with me a collection of travel essays by the writer Geoff Dyer, and each night in the hotel I read the essays and pretend I am him. Dyer's love of tennis lurks in the periphery of other subjects. His expertise in a subject is rarely if ever the point of his essays, which often end up as odes to strange accidents, mistakes, failures. I try on his curiosity, his bravery, his humor, and wear it like a protective cloak. The next morning, I walk the grounds of the Indian Wells Tennis Garden believing I am Geoff Dyer, a tall, white, nondisabled man with a sense of purpose. I greet people as I imagine he would greet them, I get my coffee the way he would, I sit at my desk and open my computer and begin to write like I have a reason to be where I am. I begin to write a draft of a story about the crowds surrounding Federer's practice. Then I start writing a draft of another story, and another. I begin to believe it is possible to climb out of defeat.

Out of the corner of my eye, I see a tall figure with white hair pass my desk and I imagine for a moment that it is Geoff Dyer strolling by, checking on me, appraising my progress. I begin an email to the editor at *Rolling Stone* pitching these possible pieces, hoping he'll like at least one idea. I attach a full draft of one of the articles, just to give him a sense of how I'm able to put a story together. I'm alive within a flurry of competence.

Later I climb to the top of the stadium and look back over its edge down to the pools of people outside, drifting around the grounds, and I think I see Dyer; his white hair bobs above the crowd for a moment before sinking back into the masses and disappearing from my sight.

I realize that I can extend the three-minute conversation window I have with the handsome Australian if I, too, eat vegetables.

"They're so crunchy," he says, smiling at me as I pass gravely by, my salad extended in front of me like a head on a platter. I say, "Yes, crunchy," and force a weary grin, and then I say, "Good lettuce." I shrug. He looks at me, at my pudgy, wobbling body, and says, "Don't worry, when no one is looking I go around the corner and stuff my face with doughnuts." And I say, "I bought the salad because of you and your little boxes of vegetables," and he says, "I'm a great influence," and he winks and now I have a friend and the next day when I return, I touch his shoulder and say, "Good morning," and he looks at me like he might know me from somewhere.

Finally, Sunday arrives and Roger Federer is set to play his first match against the unseeded Frenchman Stephane Robert. I'm spoiled by how close I'd been all week to Roger on the practice courts and now I do not want to spend the match all the way up in the press box, forced to fake disinterest. I go to Cindy's desk and stand before her with a strange feeling. I'm both weak and angry at the thought of him being withheld from me; I am a walking whine. I ask Cindy if there is any way to sit closer to the court for his match. I garble my words like a drowning woman. She looks at me. Her pity is thick. Then she comes around the desk and places a hand on my shoulder.

"Okay, Chloé," she says and hands over a slim slip, a paper ticket, a seat for me, seven rows from the court. I flatten the ticket between my palms to conceal it. I skip past the rows of journalists, my hands clasped shut over the ticket. I'm a child hoarding my treasure. I go to a concession stand with no vegetables for sale and buy gummy bears and soda and I take my place in the stadium and I settle deeply into my seat, into myself, and I watch him roll right over poor Stephane Robert.

I notice the handsome Australian is staring at me. I have head-phones on and so he waves his hand in front of my face to get my attention. Once I've removed them he says, "What are you doing?"

Lunchtime, I think to myself. It's lunchtime and he thinks I like vegetables. I am certain that he's about to ask me to get a salad with him or walk the grounds or tell me about his articles or his life outside of the press boxes, outside of tennis.

"Transcribing the last press conference," I say. I try not to look too busy.

"Give me your email," he says. I write it down for him and he looks back at his computer for a minute. "Check your email."

I do. There's an email from him with a link. I click on the link and find transcriptions of all the press conferences. Every single one. The Australian's mouth is hanging open a bit.

"Oh," I manage to say. "I didn't realize—"

"You've seen that woman who sits in the very front of all the press conferences, right? Curly hair?"

"Yes," I say.

"And you've seen her typing away on a, well, perhaps to you, a rather mysterious machine?"

"Yes."

"And what did you think she was doing? What did you *think* she was doing?"

I stand in a concession line for my dinner. A couple ahead of me are discussing how Nadal awaits Federer in a future round, a re-match of the Australian Open finals. They are nervous for Federer, certain he will lose to his rival, but, at the same time, remain in deferential awe of him. One says to the other, "His grace! His grace! Like one of those old-fashioned skiers, hands behind his back, just floating down the hill."

At the hotel, my key won't open my door. I go to the front desk and the night clerk says, "Sometimes turn the handle up and turn the key and sometimes push the handle down and turn the key." Terrance growls at me from below his owner's feet.

I can't sleep. I pace the floor of my hotel room, imagining my-self in conversation with Federer. I write and rewrite questions. I sing a little to myself. I fall asleep in my clothes, and when I wake up there's an email from my editor. He doesn't want any of my pitches and is unhappy that I've sent him a draft of an article.

My feeling of embarrassment is so large, so palpable, that it be-comes a second person in the room. I get in the car for no other reason than that I've done just that for the past eleven days. I start to drive and think to myself, *I could just keep driving. I could drive all the way back to New York.* I can't think of anything I want more than to put miles between myself and the Indian Wells Tennis Garden. I feel as if a rope is tied around my throat and the only way to release its grasp is to face east, to leave, to flee, to say "fuck it" to the desert, to tennis, to writing, to Roger Federer, to the Ladies of Palm Springs. I long to be alone on the road, driving away from failure and toward—if not success—just a different thing.

Maybe it seems absurd that I'm so upset and maybe it doesn't. The desert is a bad place to be alone; one's thoughts can spiral out too far into the vast, open landscape. Whatever shield I'd had to keep out my worst thoughts had chipped itself out of existence. I am in physical pain too, and this makes every feeling, stupid or not, loom too large, binding my sight.

I enter the press office and go to pour my coffee and Cindy ap-pears at my side. She doesn't greet me as she normally would, but instead is eyeing me suspiciously.

She says, "Chloé, can I ask you something?" My head pivots weakly. "Is it really *Rolling Stone?*"

"I'm not sure what you are asking me," I say.

"You write for *the* magazine? Or do you just have a blog with a similar name?"

"I don't have a blog," I say.

"Have you ever done anything like this before? Covered a big tournament?"

"No, Cindy, I haven't. Nothing even close."

"Okay, that explains a lot then," she says and pats me on the bare shoulder and her palm is rough as if covered in scales.

The next day, Federer is back on the practice courts and I watch. I notice two women are staring at me and gesturing.

"Let us offer you an exclusive interview," says one. They've seen my press pass.

Before I can agree or ask a question, the other hisses, "His game is so beautiful!" She leans in to share this news with only me. "So beautiful," and then says it again. She points out to him playing in front of us and searches for a further thought, her mouth open. She keeps pointing.

"He's the classic player," says the first woman, working to present herself to me as the more serious of the two. "He can pull out what he needs to do and just execute."

"He dances on the court!" says the friend. "He's a dancer. He glides. When he plays it's just beautiful so beautiful. To see his strokes up close like this. To see the smoothness of his strokes . . ." and her voice trails off as Federer's just hit an effortless crosscourt forehand and she disappears momentarily into her observation of him.

We watch him quietly until the serious one regains her composure and says to me in her serious voice, "A lot of people can play, but will miss when it matters. People collapse under pressure."

Again we fall silent. The ball comes toward Federer and, as he sees it, his body is suddenly in the air, turning effortlessly, his arms unfurling like two waves moving in opposite directions, and he hits his one-handed backhand. As he extends through the shot, his chest opens wide and his arms keep reaching, away, and the movement ripples down through his fingers, which are so relaxed that they look weightless, fluttering briefly in the breeze, and it is beautiful so beautiful.

I observe Federer in a trance; my mind lulls and unlooses itself in the heat of the midday sun. The intricacy of the human body comes into focus. So many minute movements have to perfectly align to hit a ball the way he is able to hit a ball. Philosophers had looked for evidence of God in beautiful things. Lord Shaftesbury had written that beauty was "never in the matter, but in the art and design; never in body itself, but in the form or forming power." My body was a creaky, unfastened machine; a form conjoined by pain. I was a collection of eroding joints, torn and tense muscles. This could be plainly seen in my movements. That tall tennis player had seen it and mimicked the way I walk. Perhaps he'd wanted to try on a faulty design.

But Federer was full of grace. His movements pure, efficient; his body, a collection of disparate parts working together with unified intention. When people looked at him they saw a capacity, and when they looked at me they saw a lack.

The moment shifts and I become irritable. How absurd it is that we are all gathered here to admire a man hitting a ball over a net. I feel foolish and angry. Why did he get to be the genius, exalted for something as meaningless as getting clean strings on a fast-moving ball? But he hits the ball again and that feeling dissolves.

For German philosopher Immanuel Kant, a genius was someone capable of showing the rest of us the upper limits of human ability. And here was Federer exploring them right in front of me —the limits of perceptual processing, of movement, of harmonious interplay of mind and body. And that was awe-inspiring. A genius, said Kant, could create something that displayed the furthest edge of our humanity and, by doing so, give us a sense of what might lie beyond. Genius was the liminal space where God came into contact with man.

If Federer's ability occupied one liminal space, my disability occupied an opposite space. He was effortless and I was the embodiment of effort. I was laborious, strange, disconcerting, out of place, suspicious. In the eyes of some people, he was superhuman; me, something lesser. *What is that?* the tall tennis player had said, seeing me walk toward him. What *is* that?

Federer's feet flutter, then plant. He hits his backhand. A winner right past Pouille. The serious woman opens her mouth to comment, but I don't want to hear from her anymore and so I look at her excitable friend and smile and I say, "That backhand, huh?"

And she says, to me, "Can you imagine doing anything, anything at all, as well?"

Federer overwhelms Nadal. He's summited another peak. He's aglow in press. He walks through the room as if he's never in his life feared the arriving moment. I catch, from the corner of my eye, a head of white hair, and when I look over, I see Geoff Dyer. He's sitting in the front row, watching Federer with a reverent attention I recognize as my own. I'd been visualizing Dyer as a coping mechanism for so many days, and so when I see him my first thought is to be thankful that my mind has manifested his image to help me through my lowest moment. But then I keep looking back at the man. He looks exactly like the actual human writer Geoff Dyer.

When the press conference is over, the man stands and I follow him. I follow him down the hallway, through a door, down a second corridor that leads us back outside. The hot desert air envelops me and I feel sleepy. There's a sudden thinness to reality. My mind tunnels within itself and I'm certain that I'm dreaming. I've fallen asleep while reading Geoff Dyer's travel essays and surely I'm in bed, back at the hotel, maybe just waking, my semiconscious mind imagining him walking just ahead of me. Or maybe I'm dreaming this whole tournament. Of course *Rolling Stone* has not just allowed me, a nobody, to be credentialed in their name. Suddenly this whole experience reveals itself as a mirage, full of figures conjured up by a deluded mind, fantasies dancing before me but remaining out of my reach. This white-haired man floats ahead, reenters the press office, moves through the glass doors, and takes a seat alone in the press box. He looks out at the empty court. I stand behind him and wait to wake up. If I tap his shoulder, it will be a foreign face, I'm sure, that turns to me. I walk away from the door, toward my desk, but then I return and stand behind the man again and finally I hear my small voice say, "Excuse me," and the man turns to face me and I am awake and it is Geoff Dyer.

The first thing I say is, "I can't believe you're here." He tilts his head to the side and smiles. He does not look past me or around me for an exit. I ask him what he's working on and who he's writing for and he laughs and holds up the press credential hanging around his neck. It reads "Geoff Dyer—*Palm Springs Life Magazine*." He shrugs.

"I'm here with my friend from this magazine. I wanted to watch some tennis," he says. "Also, I just like to be in proximity to Federer."

Dyer tells me he wished to have dinner with Federer and that he thought they'd be friends.

"I think we'd get on well," he says. "He clearly has a sense of humor. It's part of his genius."

"I think he'd get on well with me too," I say, and Dyer scoffs a bit, but not begrudgingly.

"Well, that's the thing about genius," he says. "It can make people believe that they might be special too."

"I saw you in his press conference," I say. "Will you ask him a question?"

"Oh, no," says Dyer, laughing, "I wouldn't dare."

I go into the next press conference and sit right in the front row so that I can look straight ahead and pretend no one is behind me in the room, that no one is near, that it is just me.

Federer enters and takes his place behind the microphone. I signal to the official that I have a question. The official indicates that I'll speak third. The first person opens their mouth to ask their question and I hear nothing but a rushing in my ears. My body produces a noise like static. I silently practice the wording of my question. I repeat in my mind the question over and over. Now the second question is being asked and suddenly my arms go tingly, I feel light-headed, my chest is tight. I think it is literally possible that I might faint or throw up. My hands shake. I try to calm myself, but have you ever really tried to calm yourself when your body doesn't want to be calmed? Have you felt your heart fight its way out of your chest and have you just said to yourself, *Stop? Just stop it.* And did that work?

I know I am making things worse than they are—I am often the thing in my way. Of course, he can remember his mechanics on the court, in front of thousands of screaming people, no matter the pressure. I cannot, but I can be here, trying. His answer to the second question ends and then the eyes of the official are on me and it's my turn and with the official's eyes, so follow Roger's eyes, and he's looking directly at me and only me, waiting for me to ask my question, and I realize that the question I've been practicing in my head over and over is gone, but more than that, my grasp of language altogether is gone, and I wonder if it's possible to just walk out of this room. I open my mouth and I speak.

When I return to my desk, the French and Australian journalists are sitting at theirs and they turn and acknowledge me with a nod. "Nice question," says the Australian. The French journalist agrees and I restrain from asking them for a group hug. I tell them that I'd been very nervous.

"Of course," says the Australian to my surprise. "It's nerve-racking to ask questions in front of everyone, but you'll get used to it. It will soon seem very normal to you."

"I've been nervous about everything for days. Nervous even to talk to you two."

"Us? Come on," says the Australian, rolling his eyes. "Were you nervous to talk to the janitors too? The food vendors? The lizards scurrying past?"

Later, right before the final match of the tournament, I see Geoff Dyer in the press box again. He greets me like an old friend. I tell him about the press conference.

"Were you nervous? I'd be nervous," he says.

"Yes," I nearly shout. "I was so nervous I lost my English."

"Oh?" he says. "What's your native language then?"

"English." And he laughs and I laugh.

I sit with the journalists in the press box and watch the final match, and when Roger Federer wins, the Australian says, "He made that look easy," and then he digs around his bag and pulls out a bright orange package, opens it, and hands me one of his two Reese's peanut butter cups.

Does it matter, I ask the Australian—whose name is Matt—that Federer makes his wins look effortless?

"It's impressive," he says. "It means something to some people that tennis could be mastered or solved. It's not that they think they'll be able to master it, but people like to see it look easy."

"Why?" I ask.

"Maybe because life is hard." We both look out at the crowd. The stage for the trophy ceremony is being set up. Matt takes a deep breath: "Isn't it lovely when things just work? All these difficult bits of life, just flowing, easy. Because it doesn't really, in real life, all work, for all of us. But it does for Roger sometimes, and there's a pleasure in being alive, able to sit out here in the sun and see something perfect. There is—" and then Matt points out to the crowd where the big red sign with the white Swiss cross is waving in the crowd "—some great pleasure in getting to see a genius at work."

He Told a Kid to Slide.
Then He Got Sued.

FROM NJ.COM

JOHN SUK SITS with shoulders slouched and his head down at the defendant's table in Courtroom 301, a stuffy wood-paneled space inside the Somerset County judicial complex. The thirty-one-year-old middle school teacher scribbles in a notebook as his reputation is shredded.

The plaintiff's attorneys in Civil Docket No. L-000629-15 have spent two full days portraying the co-defendant as an inattentive and unqualified lout. He is, they argue, a villain who destroyed the future of a teenager he was supposed to protect.

"He must be held accountable for what he did," one of the plaintiff's two attorneys tells jurors during opening arguments.

The attacks intensify when Suk takes the witness stand to defend himself on a split-second decision he made seven years earlier. He is accused of taking a reckless course of action that showed a callous disregard for another person's safety.

He sounds like an awful person. Then you remember what Suk did to end up here.

He instructed a player he was coaching during a junior varsity baseball game to slide.

Not into an active volcano.

Not into a shark tank.

Into third base.

As I watch this unfold from the nearly empty gallery, I first am overcome with the ridiculousness of the scene. I chuckle when the words "bang-bang play" become courthouse vernacular, grimace when the quality of an opposing JV team is attacked as "awful," and marvel at the surreal image of an attorney labeling a crude drawing of a baseball diamond as "Defense Exhibit 1."

I had come to Somerville ready to ridicule, but it doesn't take long for the gravity of the situation to hit me. If this jury of four men and four women decides Suk was reckless as a third-base coach for making this most routine decision, who else will end up in a courtroom like this someday?

What about the gymnastics coach who tells an athlete to tumble on a mat? Or the swimming coach who instructs a teenager to dive into a pool? Or the thousands upon thousands of parents who volunteer every weekend on soccer pitches and lacrosse fields and Little League diamonds?

If Suk is found liable for an injury that took place because of that slide—and if a seven-figure check is written because of his actions—what will happen to high school sports? Who will sign up for these coaching jobs knowing their reputation and livelihood might be in jeopardy? And how long before school districts drop sports entirely rather than pay skyrocketing insurance premiums?

So, yes, I have found the intersection of our overly litigious society and our out-of-control youth sports culture. As Suk sits there, scribbling away, I am consumed with a sickening thought: if this JV baseball coach is found liable for telling a player to slide, there's nothing to stop the dominoes from falling everywhere around us.

In short: We're all f—ed.

Excerpt #1 from March 9, 2016, deposition. John A. Suk is questioned by Rubin M. Sinins, attorney for the plaintiff:

Q. You did signal for him to slide to third base, correct?
A. Correct.
Q. Okay. What was the reason for that?
A. The proximity of the ball to the runner approaching third base.
Q. Okay. Based upon your telling us that there was a play at third base.
A. Correct.
Q. Okay. How close was he to third base when you signaled for him to slide?
A. Approximately six feet.
Q. He was running at full speed, correct?

A. *Correct.*

Q. *Giving no indication that he was going to slide, correct?*

A. *He was running full speed around the bases. He—his eyes were not affixed on the ball. He did not see the ball coming. I did. Therefore, he was running full speed, but upon my decision and telling him at a safe distance to slide, he was able to do so.*

Edward M. Coleman, gray-haired and bespectacled, settles into his seat behind the bench in Courtroom 301. He is a retired Superior Court justice who has been called back to ease the heavy caseload, a longtime criminal judge who once presided over one of the biggest cases the state has seen.

That was the manslaughter trial of NBA star Jayson Williams, a two-month legal odyssey that attracted nonstop coverage from Court TV.

This one is a bit different.

When the jurors are seated for the first time, on June 17, there is exactly one person in the gallery: me.

Coleman instructs the jury to keep an open mind during the proceedings, so I resolve to do so as well. That slide, of course, did not end well for the kid, and the story of what happens to him over the days, months, and years after he hit the infield clay is awful in every way.

Jake Mesar steps down from the witness stand and, at the instruction of his attorney, rolls up the right pants leg of his tan Dockers. The jurors position themselves for a better look at the two nasty scars on his ankle.

Seven years ago, Mesar was a fifteen-year-old freshman at Bound Brook High School and the best player on his junior varsity team. He already had made the varsity basketball team that winter, and given his talent and passion for sports, this seemed like the beginning of an athletic career that might go down in school history.

Then came April 4, 2012.

We will hear—in excruciating detail—what the plaintiffs believe Suk did and did not do on that day when Bound Brook played its first game of the season, at Gill St. Bernard's in Gladstone. Before traveling down that rabbit hole, let's review the facts not in dispute.

The visiting team was leading, 6–0, in the top of the second inning when Mesar, batting for the second time, laced a line drive over the left fielder's head.

Two runs scored. Mesar rounded second and headed for third. And next, a sickening sound echoed across the diamond as he hit the ground.

"POP!"

As Mesar wailed in agony, Suk (pronounced SOOK) rushed to his side. So did the player's father, Rob Mesar, who was keeping the scorebook in the dugout. An ambulance arrived. No one knew it then, but that promising freshman—two innings into his high school career—would never play another baseball game.

"I felt bad for my parents," Jake Mesar, now twenty-two and attending Rutgers, testifies on the second day of the trial. "They would never be able to see me play."

Baseball was the least of his worries. Even after three surgeries, the ankle was not improving—one doctor even presented amputation as a possible outcome. A specialist from the Hospital for Special Surgery in Manhattan, Robert Rozbruch, found post-traumatic arthritis and signs of necrosis—evidence the bone was dying.

Mesar needed two more surgeries, including one to inject stem cells into the ankle tissue, and he was fit with an external fixator, a stabilizing frame to keep the bones properly positioned. The injury improved, but Rozbruch told the once-active teenager to avoid high-impact activities. Even jogging.

When it comes time for Rozbruch to testify, he abandons the clinical language of his profession and makes it clear that Mesar's baseball dreams died on third base that day.

"He will never recover fully," the doctor says.

It is more than a physical injury. Mesar has endured frequent bouts of depression and a pair of panic attacks, including one that sent him from a family party on Christmas Eve to the emergency room. The injury is, as his lawyer tells the jury, "something he has to live with every minute, every hour, every day of his life."

All of this, to use a decidedly non-legal word, sucks. How can anyone sit here, listen to his story, and not have your heart break?

Still, injuries happen. That is at the cold reality of sports. Did the coach sitting with his head down at the defense table really ruin this kid's life?

I could be John Suk. You could be John Suk. It isn't hard to imagine switching places with this former high school catcher, sitting there in his black suit and wrinkled gray shirt. He takes notes to distract himself from the constant verbal assaults.

Early during voir dire, it becomes clear that picking a jury without including someone who has coached on some level is nearly impossible. Who, when you reach a certain age, hasn't told a kid to dive for a ball and not worried as he or she hit the ground with a thud?

For most of us with kids, it's a short chapter. No one else will do it. Or a friend coaxes us into "doing it for the kids." The commitment runs a season or two.

Not so for Suk. That game on April 4, 2012, was Suk's first time coaching on the high school level. He was twenty-three, still not a full year removed from FDU-Madison, coaching at Bound Brook for just a few weeks after his predecessor abruptly resigned.

He is thirty-one when he walks into Courtroom 301. Do the math: this incident has hovered over him in some form for nearly a quarter of his life, always there, always grinding along without resolution.

"Was it hard to sleep some nights? Yeah," Suk tells me. "It was hard knowing that I had to explain myself, over and over and over again. It took the fun out of the job because I kept on thinking, 'He could be the next kid who comes up with a lawsuit.' You know? The odds are slim but you don't want to go through something like this again."

He learns he was named in the lawsuit when a claims examiner from New Jersey Schools Insurance Group, the firm that insures Bound Brook and 375 other public schools, showed up at his new job at North Brunswick High. This was in the winter of 2015, nearly three years after the injury.

His initial shock is met with assurances from the insurance rep that this case probably would never see a courtroom. He gave a deposition in 2016 and, when a judge granted a summary judgment to the defense on February 17, 2017, he figured he had put the entire episode behind him.

He was on his way to a freshman baseball game on May 2, 2018, when a friend texted him.

"Why are you getting sued?" the message read. Not only had Mesar's attorneys won the appeal, but a news story about the case was getting national attention because of the eye-popping headline.

"Baseball player sues coach for telling him to slide."

His sister heard his name on Jersey 101.5. His parents started to worry about the stain on his reputation. Suk, never a fan of attention, now had the incident tacked onto his life in a very public way. He had to explain what happened, at parties or at games or in school, whenever someone he knew made the connection.

"I have to tell you, my son was crushed," says his mother, Franca. "He told me that he was done with coaching if he lost this case. This changed who he is a little bit."

He was never going to lose any money out of his own pocket. But when NJSIG, as the insurance company is called, decides to draw the line in the sand and fight the case to the end, he knew he was facing a day like this in a courtroom. Eventually.

But "never for even a minute did I think it would take seven years for this to finally get to a trial," Suk says.

He says he isn't worried as he walks into Courtroom 301. He knows for Mesar to win, his attorneys must prove Suk's actions met a standard of recklessness under New Jersey case law that is defined as "an extreme departure from ordinary care in which a high degree of danger is apparent."

Common sense, he keeps telling himself, will prevail.

Surely, the eight people in the jury box will see that this accident—as awful as it has been for the kid sitting a few feet away—isn't his fault.

Right?

But, midway through the two days of testimony, I'll be damned if the opposite thought isn't creeping into my head: he's actually going to lose this thing.

Excerpt #2 from March 9, 2016, deposition. John A. Suk is questioned by Rubin M. Sinins, attorney for the plaintiff:

Q. *You gave him a signal to slide when he was approximately six feet from the base, correct?*

A. *Correct.*

Q. *And by your past answer, I take it that it's your position that being six feet from a base with a runner running full speed, that it's a safe distance to begin a slide?*

A. *Yes.*

Q. *What distance is not a safe distance for a runner to begin a slide?*

A. *Any distance inside two feet.*

> Q. *There would be no reason for a third-base coach to signal a player to slide into third base if there was not a potential play at third base?*
> A. *Correct.*
> Q. *Because sliding is dangerous?*
> *Defense: Objection.*
> A. *Sliding is a potentially dangerous activity, yes, but with proper training and teaching and the plaintiff's player experience, he could safely do so in an attempt to avoid injury.*

Suk ambles to the witness stand, raises his right hand and swears to tell the whole truth and nothing but the truth. The jurors sit up.

This is the person they want to hear testify.

They had spent the morning listening to testimony from Mesar, his father, and the surgeon who saved his ankle. They started the afternoon hearing from one of the umpires, a moment that ended in disaster for the defense when part of his testimony was struck from the record because he didn't remember the play at third.

Now, defense attorney William Bloom takes Suk through the play that led to the injury—the long hit to left field, the two runners scoring, the third baseman straddling the bag and, finally, Mesar rounding second at full speed.

"I see Jake approaching third base and I also see the ball traveling in flight," Suk says. "I make the decision for him to slide, to avoid injury and to avoid contact (with the third baseman), so he could approach the bag safely . . ."

"It was going to be a bang-bang play."

Bloom needs only nine minutes, and as he walks back to his seat, it seems so silly and simple. And then comes the cross-examination, and right away, I begin to wonder if we're talking about the same play.

The plaintiff's attorneys are no rookies. Eric Kahn and Rubin Sinins were involved in another of this century's highest profile cases in New Jersey, representing one of the Rutgers students accused of spying on a fellow student Tyler Clementi days before his suicide.

Sinins attacks Suk's qualifications and points out he never took courses in baseball instruction—"in hitting, fielding, throwing, catching, or sliding." He grills the coach on where he was looking when Mesar was charging to the base, hammering home the point at the core of the plaintiff's case:

That Suk was focused on the runners going home.

That he never looked toward Mesar until he was dangerously close to third base.

That there was never going to be a play at third base—"bang-bang" or otherwise—which means a slide was completely unnecessary in a blowout.

That Suk pivoted and made the signal to slide at the last minute, too late for Mesar to adjust his body properly and causing the injury.

That he knew sliding was unsafe and still instructed the freshman under his watch to do it anyway.

That all this, when factored together, was reckless.

"We have established that the fence is 315 feet, and that this is a JV game at Gill St. Bernard's," Sinins says. "And you've heard testimony that the Gill St. Bernard's team stunk. Is that fair?"

"Sir, my opinion of their team has no bearing—" Suk answers.

"You're telling this jury that the JV left fielder for the Gill St. Bernard's team reached the ball at the fence and threw a strike to the third baseman?" Sinins asks. "That's what you're telling this jury?!"

Sinins punctuates the grilling with a moment that seems stolen from a bad episode of *Law & Order*. He reads Suk's deposition testimony from three years ago, when the coach said a slide was safe anywhere from outside of two feet. Then he approaches the witness stand and stands with his body pressed against it.

"I am now two feet from you," he says. "It was your belief that a runner running at full speed from this distance that you could safely instruct him to slide into third base.

"Is that your position?"

By the end, the whole thing feels like an Abbott & Costello routine—second base, left field, I don't know, third base!—and I start to wonder if the jurors can follow the details. It has become a classic he-said/she-said case—or he slid, she slid—with the word of a father and son against that of a coach.

Then again, if they're debating blurry facts from a long-ago game at all, Kahn and Sinins have managed to steer them away from the only thing that really matters.

That Suk—or any coach in any sport—cannot be "reckless" when instructing a player to do something as routine as sliding into a base during a baseball game.

Would that jury agree?

*

Lauren Palladino stands in front of her seat in the jury box and leads four men and three other women into the deliberation room. The court officer closes the door behind them.

It is 1:30 p.m. on Wednesday, and everyone left behind in the courtroom agrees: the longer they spend behind closed doors, the better for the plaintiff.

Mesar and his attorneys find seats just outside the courtroom.

Suk paces before sitting near the elevators down the hall.

They wait.

Palladino knows that money—a lot of money—is riding on their decision. Coleman had told them that, if they found Suk had acted recklessly, to take into account Mesar's life expectancy when considering damages for his pain and suffering.

That number was 59.6 years. Any verdict in his favor easily would exceed seven figures.

She had arrived at the Somerset County courthouse on Monday hoping to get picked for a case, even if it meant missing a few waitressing shifts at California Pizza Kitchen at the Bridgewater Commons Mall. This was her first time called for jury duty, and she was curious.

"I had no idea what to expect," she will tell me after the trial.

She is twenty-two and a rising senior at Rowan University. She found herself connecting with Mesar during the trial. She was his age, and like him, an athlete; she played softball in high school.

She is ready to side with him—until those final minutes before walking into deliberations. It wasn't anything from the lawyers or witness testimony that starts to sway her, but the words from Coleman as he read the legal definition of recklessness.

"I don't think the coach had any intention of hurting the kid when he told him to slide," Palladino says. "It just . . . happened."

In the deliberation room, she quickly learns five jurors agree with her and two do not. Seven of the eight must agree to reach a verdict.

Thirty minutes pass.

The doors to the courtroom suddenly open and everyone rushes to their seats, but there is no verdict. The jurors have sent a note to the judge, asking for copies of the depositions of Mesar, Suk, and the umpire—information which is off-limits because it was not introduced at the trial.

The doors close again. It feels like a good sign for the plaintiffs. An hour passes, then an hour and a half.

Inside that room, they go back over the play at third base, grappling with an inconsistent and incomplete set of facts. It is clear, through interviews with six of the jurors later, that the personal experiences of the jurors play a large role in how they see this case.

Juror No. 1 is a soccer fan who broke his nose playing the game. Juror No. 7 is a grandfather who still plays recreational softball and rattled off a list of injuries during voir dire. Palladino herself leans on her experiences.

"How was the coach reckless?" she tells the seven others. "That's how you play the game."

A seventh juror, a nursing student, changes her mind and sides with the six others.

Nearly two hours have passed.

The doors to the courtroom open again.

This time everyone gathers knowing this seven-year legal odyssey is about to end.

When the foreman reads the verdict—"seven no, one yes"—I wait for a show of emotion, tears from the former baseball player or a fist pump from the vindicated coach.

Nothing comes.

Mesar turns to face his father. Suk picks up his notebook. The lawyers shake hands and the room clears quickly.

Palladino is back at California Pizza Kitchen the next day. When a bartender tunes a flat screen television to a baseball game, she tells coworkers about the trial that caused her to miss work that week. Their reply should come as no surprise.

"Wait. Are you serious?"

From the moment Jake Mesar made that fateful slide into third base until Civil Docket No. L-000629-15 was resolved, exactly 2,625 days passed. Jill Deitch, chief legal officer for NJSIG, estimated the insurance company spent more than $75,000 in legal fees to fight the case, and that doesn't include the countless hours it consumed her staff.

That is the price of drawing a line in the sand. She already has used the case at a New Jersey State Interscholastic Athletic Association workshop called "Legal Liability and Athletics."

"Coaches and athletic directors have so much to deal with," Deitch says. "This kind of lawsuit second-guessing a coach's direction to slide should not be one of them."

Rob Mesar, meanwhile, is convinced his own clumsy testimony doomed his son's chances to win the case. But it is the play at third base itself that consumes him, night after night, and he figures it will for the rest of this life.

I ask him: Was all this fair? Suing a coach?

He says he is a business owner who would never file a frivolous lawsuit. He believes his son was wronged, that too many of the facts of what happened on that ballfield didn't come to light in the trial.

He doesn't lay all the blame at Suk's feet. He wants accountability from administrators who gave him the job without, he believes, enough preparation to keep his son safe. What about the next kid? Who will protect him?

"You have people just taking the extra $8,000 who don't know what the hell they're doing," Rob Mesar says. "Somebody's got to be responsible. Nobody is!"

Suk, meanwhile, couldn't wait to get back to his house and clear out the folders and envelopes full of documents he has accumulated. As he leaves the courtroom, his phone lights up with texts from curious friends.

Well? Any news?

He answers a few on the courthouse steps, then he sits with me across the street in an otherwise empty deli. He says he is surprised the jury took as long as it did to reach a verdict.

I ask him to consider the other scenario: What would have happened if he lost?

"It's the end of high school sports," he says. "The coaching profession would be under heavy scrutiny for everything that happens. Coaches are going to have to have insurance like doctors have for malpractice. School districts are not going to want to take the risk of having sports."

He takes a long pull from his bottle of water.

The clouds that had covered the sky for most of the day are clearing, giving hope that North Brunswick's summer team might not lose another day off the calendar to bad weather.

The case is closed. The weight is lifted. He checks his watch, shakes my hand, then heads off to find his car. He has to hurry.

He has a baseball game to coach.

KEN ROSENTHAL AND EVAN DRELLICH

The Astros Stole Signs Electronically in 2017 — Part of a Much Broader Issue for Major League Baseball

FROM THE ATHLETIC

THERE IS A broad story about this era of baseball that has yet to be told.

To this point, the public's understanding of sign-stealing mostly rests on anonymous secondhand conjecture and finger-pointing. But inside the game, there is a belief that is treated by players and staff as fact: that illegal sign-stealing, particularly through advanced technology, is everywhere.

"It's an issue that permeates through the whole league," one major league manager said. "The league has done a very poor job of policing or discouraging it."

Electronic sign-stealing is not a single-team issue. Major League Baseball rules prohibit clubs from using electronic equipment to steal catchers' signs and convey information. Still, the commissioner's office hears complaints about many different organizations—everything from mysterious people in white shirts sending signals from center field to elaborate systems involving television cameras and tablets. But MLB has not punished any club, at least publicly, for violating sign-stealing rules since 2017, when the Red Sox were disciplined.

There was more going on that year.

Four people who were with the Astros in 2017, including pitcher Mike Fiers, said that during that season, the Astros stole signs during home games in real time with the aid of a camera positioned in the outfield.

Now, an MLB investigation into the Astros' culture in the wake of the team's firing of assistant general manager Brandon Taubman could be expanded to determine who in the organization was aware of the sign-stealing practice—and whether it continued or evolved in subsequent seasons. *The Athletic*'s confirmation of rule-breaking by Houston is limited to 2017.

"Beginning in the 2017 season, numerous Clubs expressed general concerns that other Clubs were stealing their signs," MLB said in a statement. "As a result of those concerns, and after receiving extensive input from the General Managers, we issued a revised policy on sign-stealing prior to the 2019 season. We also put in place detailed protocols and procedures to provide comfort to Clubs that other Clubs were not using video during the game to decode and steal signs. After we review this new information we will determine any necessary next steps."

The Astros declined to comment at the time of publication, and issued the following statement Tuesday afternoon: "Regarding the story posted by *The Athletic* earlier today, the Houston Astros organization has begun an investigation in cooperation with Major League Baseball. It would not be appropriate to comment further on this matter at this time."

Early in the 2017 season, at least two uniformed Astros got together to start the process. One was a hitter who was struggling at the plate and had benefited from sign-stealing with a previous team, according to club sources; another was a coach who wanted to help. They were said to strongly believe that some opposing teams were already up to no good.

They wanted to devise their own system in Houston. And they did.

"That's not playing the game the right way," said Fiers, who was with the team from 2015 to 2017 and was non-tendered in the offseason after the Astros won the 2017 World Series. "They were advanced and willing to go above and beyond to win."

Three other sources who were inside the organization in 2017 and had direct knowledge of the scheme discussed its existence on the condition of anonymity.

The Astros' setup required technical video knowledge and required the direct aid of at least some on the baseball operations staff, team sources said.

In an expected interview with Taubman, whom the Astros fired on October 24, during the World Series, for inappropriate comments and conduct toward three female reporters, MLB likely will attempt to learn as much as it can about the Astros' operation. The league also is expected to interview current and former Astros players and employees, according to sources.

MLB has heard of this specific system before, but to this point, the league has not gathered sufficient evidence to prove the Astros committed wrongdoing, sources said.

One challenge MLB will face if it expands its investigation to include the Astros' alleged sign-stealing: determining what is perception and what is reality with the franchise, which is viewed with mistrust by many in the sport.

Paranoia within baseball, particularly regarding the Astros, runs deep. In 2019, even after a full season of new, more rigid rules baseball enacted to clamp down on sign-stealing, the Nationals during the World Series employed a sophisticated set of signs against the Astros that they did not use in previous rounds of the postseason. During the American League Championship Series, the Yankees believed the Astros were whistling from the dugout to communicate pitches. But the league found no wrongdoing, a source said, and other rumors attached to the Astros might not be grounded in reality.

The Astros of this decade, under owner Jim Crane and general manager Jeff Luhnow, are a polarizing operation. In part, that is due to their success. But it's also because of how the industry views their modus operandi. The result might be that industry people are simply more willing to discuss Houston than they would be other clubs.

"People respect what they've accomplished," one rival general manager said. "They don't respect the culture they've created or some of the methods they choose to utilize to become what they've become."

The Astros' setup in 2017 was not overly complicated. A feed from a camera in center field, fixed on the opposing catcher's signs, was hooked up to a television monitor that was placed on a wall steps from the team's home dugout at Minute Maid Park, in the tunnel that runs between the dugout and the clubhouse. Team employees and players would watch the screen during the game and try to decode signs—sitting opposite the screen on massage tables in a wide hallway.

When the onlookers believed they had decoded the signs, the expected pitch would be communicated via a loud noise—specifically, banging on a trash can, which sat in the tunnel. Normally, the bangs would mean a breaking ball or off-speed pitch was coming.

Fiers, who confirmed the setup, acknowledged he already has a strained relationship with the Astros because he relayed to his subsequent teams, the Tigers and A's, what the Astros were doing.

"I just want the game to be cleaned up a little bit because there are guys who are losing their jobs because they're going in there not knowing," Fiers said. "Young guys getting hit around in the first couple of innings starting a game, and then they get sent down. It's (B.S.) on that end. It's ruining jobs for younger guys. The guys who know are more prepared. But most people don't. That's why I told my team. We had a lot of young guys with Detroit (in 2018) trying to make a name and establish themselves. I wanted to help them out and say, 'Hey, this stuff really does go on. Just be prepared.'"

And be on guard.

"I told the teams I was on, I didn't know how far the rules went with MLB, but I knew they (the Astros) were up to date, if not beyond," said Fiers, who became a free agent on December 1, 2017. "I had to let my team know so that we were prepared when we went to go play them at Minute Maid."

Two sources said the Astros' use of the system extended into the 2017 playoffs. Another source adamantly denied that, saying the system ended before the postseason.

One Astros source said he had a vivid memory of hearing the garbage can sound right before an Astros home run during the postseason. Yet, he also believed that during the World Series, it was probably too loud inside the park for the Astros' system to be effective. There was, after all, a basic requirement for the system to function: the batter had to be able to hear it.

The Astros did not use the same system in away games, sources said. The Astros won the World Series over the Dodgers in seven games, and the finale was a road game.

If the system was halted prior to the postseason, it was not stopped long before it, based upon an incident recalled by both an opposing pitcher and an Astros source.

Pitching for the White Sox in 2017, Danny Farquhar made two mid-September appearances at Minute Maid Park, just before the playoffs. One Astros source recalled that Farquhar appeared to visibly notice what the Astros were up to.

Farquhar, the source remembered, pointed to his ear on the mound.

"There was a banging from the dugout, almost like a bat hitting the bat rack every time a changeup signal got put down," said Farquhar, who is now the pitching coach with the White Sox's High-A affiliate in Winston-Salem, North Carolina. "After the third one, I stepped off. I was throwing some really good changeups and they were getting fouled off. After the third bang, I stepped off."

Farquhar said he and his catcher changed the signs to the more complex kind used when a runner is on second base — a situation where base runners have long been able to legally relay signs, using their own eyes.

"The banging stopped," Farquhar said. "My assumption was they were picking it up from the video and relaying the signs to the dugout . . . That was my theory on the whole thing. It made me very upset. I was so angry, so mad, that the media didn't come to me after."

The impact of the Astros' sign-stealing is difficult to assess. Not every player used it in Houston.

"There were guys who didn't like it," Fiers said. "There are guys who don't like to know (what's coming) and guys who do."

Players who did use it would not necessarily use it all the time either.

Yet, the Astros would probably not have employed the system if at least some players didn't perceive it as an advantage — or at least a leveling of the playing field.

Sources recalled the system being discussed around the team. One day in the cafeteria, a player lamented the fact that the screen had not been set up on time. Another time, a player said they were looking forward to going back to Minute Maid Park and the benefit of the trash can.

At least once, some on the Astros were worried enough that they would be discovered that, in the middle of a game, someone in the dugout ordered the screen hauled out of the tunnel and hidden.

For a long time, high-ranking executives with other teams have voiced their concerns about the Astros, in particular, as well as other teams, both to Major League Baseball and to reporters.

Some with Houston believed the effort to steal signs was, essentially, an act of self-defense. One Astros person called the electronic sign-stealing behavior in the sport "pervasive," and was surprised that more information had not come out sooner. That person suggested any potential accusers might also have dirty hands of their own, making them less likely to talk. If MLB looks more thoroughly into the Astros' actions, their employees might be forced to decide whether to tell the league about what they believed other teams were doing.

"I don't know if we really had any hard proof, but I'm sure there was (some evidence of other teams' conduct)," Fiers said. "Going into the playoffs, we had veterans like Brian McCann—we went straight to multiple signs (with our pitchers). We weren't going to mess around. We were sure there were teams out there that were trying certain things to get an edge and win ball games. I wouldn't say there was hard evidence. But it's hard to catch teams at home. There are so many things you can use to win at home."

Taubman, meanwhile, has been connected to the topic before.

Before he was fired, Taubman confronted a Yankees employee at Yankee Stadium in May of 2018, believing the Yankees were flouting the rules. During the 2018 playoffs, the Indians and Red Sox separately discovered a person connected to the Astros named Kyle McLaughlin taking pictures near the dugout. (McLaughlin was also with Taubman at Yankee Stadium in May.)

MLB publicly accepted the Astros' position that McLaughlin was on a defensive mission that October, trying to guard against other teams' efforts. That month, Jeff Passan reported the first accounts of Astros players using a garbage can suspiciously.

The 2018 playoffs were the first postseason in which MLB had dedicated measures in place to prevent electronic sign-stealing. The league then distributed new rules to all teams in the spring of 2019, outlining them in a six-page document and accompanying FAQ.

Among those rules: No camera installed beyond the outfield

fence and between the foul poles may capture an image of the catcher's signs. Any camera in that area needs advance approval from the commissioner's office. The league has also set rules about the placement and use of monitors and TVs, mandating that virtually every screen be on an eight-second delay. In addition, MLB placed league employees at the park to attempt to monitor what teams are doing.

However, the Astros' actions in 2017 were a violation of the rules even as written then: "Major League Baseball Regulations . . . prohibit the use of electronic equipment during games and state that no such equipment 'may be used for the purpose of stealing signs or conveying information designed to give a Club an advantage,'" commissioner Rob Manfred said in a 2017 statement.

That season, when MLB investigated the Red Sox for their use of electronic equipment against the Yankees, part of what MLB said it sought to learn was the extent of the Boston front office's involvement, a sign of what might be to come now. It was the first point listed among the league's explanations for the punishment.

"First, the violation in question occurred without the knowledge of ownership or front office personnel," Manfred said at the time.

The sport's history is laced with sign-stealing and various forms of cheating. The sport's present too. What separates this era from the past is the use of electronics, the arms race.

One Astros source was adamant: the team should not become the poster child for sign-stealing. Not when so much is going on with other clubs that MLB has not stopped, the source said.

Are the Astros more often a topic because they are disliked by some people around the league, and indeed, by some who walked through their own doors and clubhouse? Or is it because they are, in fact, at the forefront of the problem?

At this point, the commissioner's office might need to sort it out. All of it.

TIM LAYDEN

Disqualified

FROM SPORTS ILLUSTRATED

LOUISVILLE — They stood ankle deep in mud on the most famous racetrack in the world and they stood in the infield grass and they stood next to the little piles of manure in the long tunnel that separates the saddling paddock from the bowl inside Churchill Downs, beneath its ancient twin spires. They were thoroughbred horse trainers, they were jockeys, they were owners. It was dusk on the first Saturday in May, and a veil of gray twilight hung over the track and over the moment. Misty droplets of rain fell intermittently. The Kentucky Derby had been run for the 145th time and it had finished, and yet the outcome remained undecided. Minutes ticked past: Five, ten, fifteen, twenty. Forever, and then longer. On the giant infield screens, a single word was illuminated just brighter than the rest, or so it seemed: UNOFFICIAL.

They would wait and then wait some more and when it was finished they would all stand at the intersection of history and shock. Some of them would be deprived of the most important victory in American racing and others would be awarded that same victory. It would be a moment unlike anything before it, in this place, in this race, a moment that will outlive all of them and all of us. For the first time in the nearly century-and-a-half life of the Kentucky Derby, a horse would cross the finish line first, a horse named Maximum Security, and be disqualified for committing a foul in the race. Country House would be declared the winner at the second-longest winning odds in Derby history.

This is what had happened. Nineteen three-year-old colts had run one and a quarter miles around a giant oval inside this cathedral of racing, as they have done in the spring of the year since ten years after the end of the Civil War. On this day they ran on a racing surface turned to pale brown slop by the rain that began only in the ninety minutes before post time. They ran strangely, at first quickly and then in a beehive bunch, bumping and grinding along. "Like a little kids' soccer game," said five-time Derby-winning trainer Bob Baffert, whose three horses would finish fourth, fifth and fourteenth. One of them led by a tiny margin, towing the others. It was a bay named Maximum Security. He was one of those horses that should not win the Kentucky Derby, but sometimes does and sometimes becomes the favorite, as Maximum Security did on Saturday, at 4–1 odds. Just because.

Leaving the quarter pole at the head of the stretch, as more than 150,000 spectators, soaked by the rain, the bourbon, and the beer, rose and roared in full throat, Maximum Security opened up his lead. Last December 20, Maximum Security had run in a $16,000 claiming race at Gulfstream Park in Florida, the first start of his life. He won that race by nine lengths and was not claimed (anyone at Gulfstream could have taken him for sixteen grand, no negotiation). "I said, 'phew,'" said trainer Jason Servis, recalling that day. Maximum Security went on to win three more races, including the Florida Derby, to qualify for the Kentucky Derby as a genuine contender. There is no map for the trip from claimer to roses.

Maximum Security pulled away, ever so slightly, tiring less than the others. There was a moment of chaos near the top of the stretch. At least one jockey rose in his irons, a sign that a collision has been averted. In the mud and slop and in real time, it was difficult to interpret. Horse races are always difficult to interpret—giant animals running fast with brave and gifted small humans astride them. Maximum Security held together and won the Derby by one and three-quarter lengths over fast-closing Country House and three-quarters of a length over Code of Honor. The earth shook just a little as it always does and more so when it is the favorite who has won. He rides with more money on his back than the rest.

Maximum Security's owners, Gary and Mary West, forty years in the game and winners of many big races but never the Derby, were hustled from their trackside box seats to the infield, where the victory celebration takes place. Servis followed and stopped on the racetrack, standing in the mud in his windbreaker for an interview.

Then came the announcement, a part of racing everywhere that horses run, but so rarely in the Kentucky Derby: the jockeys on two beaten horses had claimed foul against the winner. Those jockeys were Flavien Prat, the twenty-six-year-old Frenchman who rode apparent runner-up Country House; and Jon Court, an ancient fifty-eight years old, the rider on Long Range Toddy, who had been in contention at the top of the stretch but faded to seventeenth place. Near the finish line, first Court and then Prat, bent over and talked into a landline telephone to the three racing stewards who would determine the veracity of their claims. Both men said they had been impeded by Maximum Security at the quarter pole, as the field straightened for home.

"It got pretty gnarly out there," said Court after hanging up the phone.

"When I was coming around the turn, he [Maximum Security] pushed me sideways," said Prat. "He kind of bumped me."

The OBJECTION sign was engaged on the board. The crowd gasped. In 145 Derbys, the horse that finished first had never been disqualified. A buzz fell across Churchill.

At the mouth of the tunnel, Country House's trainer, Bill Mott, stood at attention. A bespectacled, sixty-five-year-old man with a thinning shock of gray hair, Mott is among the most respected trainers in the game. He is a member of the Racing Hall of Fame and the winner of ten Breeders Cup races. But he had never won the Derby. After the midweek scratch of pre-race favorite Omaha Beach with a throat problem, and the departure of his much-liked trainer, Richard Mandella, Mott took the title of best trainer to have never won a major, as it were. But if he were to win the Derby, it was expected to be with Wood Memorial prep winner Tacitus, who went off at 6–1. Country House was 65–1. Mott had said three days before the Derby, "Tacitus is my best chance to win. Country House needs some things to happen."

Some things indeed happened.

Time passed. The stewards debated in their perch above the high-rollers' enclave called The Mansion, more than six stories above the track.

Mott was surrounded by media. "There was definitely a foul in the race," said Mott. "My horses didn't get bothered terribly, but there were a couple jocks that almost went down. There are 100,000 people [*sic*] here. The stewards don't want to make that call [to disqualify Maximum Security]. But I will say this: if this was a maiden claimer on a weekday, that horse [Maximum Security] would come down. It's the Kentucky Derby, but it's not supposed to matter."

Across the racetrack from Mott, near the inside rail, Servis waited for the decision. A slender man with short, wispy, blond hair, Servis is the older brother of John Servis, who fifteen years ago trained Smarty Jones to an immensely popular Derby victory and nearly to the Triple Crown. Servis has long played the racing game at the grittier levels, transforming claimers into winners and trying to make winners into stakes winners. The last two years have been the best of his life. As the minutes crawled past, he shook his head and grinned painfully. He knows the racetrack. He knows the stewards.

"This is a long one," he said of the delay. "I don't think that's a good sign." Behind him the race replayed from multiple angles. "I haven't seen a good angle," he said. "But I don't think my horse did anything to affect the outcome of the race."

Nearby, Maximum Security's jockey, twenty-seven-year-old Panamanian Luis Saez, was also surrounded, whispering short responses to incessant questions. He looked like a man in pain, holding roses (not literally) in his hands, sensing that they would soon be taken away.

At 7:16 p.m., three seconds shy of twenty-two minutes after the finish of the race, the UNOFFICIAL sign blinked to OFFICIAL and Country House's No. 20 was elevated to No. 1, winner of the Kentucky Derby. The crowd booed forcefully, perhaps at the perceived injustice, but more likely at tickets left uncashed. More than two hours after the finish of the race, the three stewards appeared at a press conference. Barbara Borden, the Kentucky Horse Commission's chief steward, nervously read a 107-word explanation of the disqualification of Maximum Security and did not take any questions.

Borden first confirmed what had been seen: "The riders of the 18 (Long Range Toddy) and 20 (Country House) horses in the Kentucky Derby lodged objections against the 7 (Maximum Security), the winner, due to interference turning for home, leaving the quarter pole."

Pause: Here is what the head-on replay (not the so-called "pan" shot that is commonly shown on television) seemed to show: That as the field began to straighten, Maximum Security darted to his right at least three "paths" (a path being a running lane). As he made this move, he passed directly in front of War of Will, who had been gathering for a potential move toward the front. This move caused War of Will's jockey, Tyler Gaffalione, to check his mount to keep both rider and horse from falling, which, given their place in the field, would have been disastrous. Maximum Security's move in front of War of Will forced War of Will in front of Long Range Toddy, a 55–1 shot who Court was forced to steady in similar fashion to Gaffalione. "I got knocked sideways," said Court, "and then I got knocked sideways again."

Finally, both War of Will and Long Range Toddy continued to slide sideways, nudging Country House at least one path wide, but less dangerously than the other two. All of this transpired in just more than a second. But it was a moment fraught with danger in a year when horse racing suffered mightily from too much death (the twenty-three horses who died at Santa Anita between December 24 and March 31).

Chief steward Borden said, "We had a lengthy review of the race." Indeed. More Borden: "We determined that the 7 horse (Maximum Security) drifted out and impacted the progress of the number 1, in turn, interfering with the 18 and 21 (Bodexpress, the longest shot in the field at 71–1). These horses were all affected, we thought, by the interference. Therefore we unanimously determined to disqualify number 7 (Maximum Security) and place him behind the 18, the 18 being the lowest-placed horse that he bothered, which is our typical procedure."

The result of the disqualification and replacing left Country House in first, Code of Honor in second, and Tacitus in third, giving Mott the first- and third-place finishers.

The decision is likely to be debated further, probably endlessly. What's unknown is unknown forever, but it seems unlikely that Country House would have caught Maximum Security no matter how far they ran. War of Will is another matter. But it's difficult to imagine the carnage that would have ensued if Gaffalione had not kept War of Will upright. However: it is baffling that the stewards watched that rodeo and did not instantly initiate a stewards' inquiry into the finish, which is standard practice when there might have been fouls. Also: for the stewards to refuse questions after changing the order of finish in the Kentucky Derby for the first time in history is a terrible look that will not age well.

Nearly an hour after the race, Gary West met with Servis. Both men claimed to have not seen a satisfactory replay of the race, which is surprising considering the number of times it was replayed on the giant infield screen. West is known throughout racing as a class act who has given more to the game than it has given him. His Derby pain goes back sixteen years to when contender Buddha was scratched in race week. But he was not immediately accepting of this outcome. "I've seen $5,000 claimers have much worse problems than this horse and not get qualified," West said. "I think it was a very bad decision. I might change my mind."

His mindset remained fluid. Minutes later, after Servis talked with the stewards, West and Servis both said they would consider any appeal of the disqualification. It is unclear what avenues would be available, but as night fell on Louisville, it remained possible that the Derby would be contested beyond the First Saturday in May.

In the aftermath of the decision, Mott moved slowly across the racetrack, in possession of the Derby, a race that he had listened to as a boy in South Dakota. He never envisioned it happening like this, and nor did the rest of us. "I really didn't want to win this way," he said. "I wish he had pulled away nice and clean and won by five." Mott shrugged. "This is what happened."

The mud pulled his feet deeper into the track and brown water pooled at his ankles. Fans shuffled toward distant parking lots and long rides home. A light wind whispered across the earth and the skies grew ever darker, a curtain falling noiselessly on a theater of the surreal.

KEVIN ARNOVITZ

How NBA Executive Jeff David Stole $13 Million from the Sacramento Kings

FROM ESPN.COM

THE MOVING VAN from Sacramento chokes its way through Miami's thick August air. It contains the objects of Jeff David's life, all destined for the Davids' new house in the affluent Pinecrest neighborhood. It is July 2018, and much of David's family is on hand to help with the move. Jeff's mother-in-law and her partner had arrived the previous night to help wrangle the kids while Jeff and his wife, Kate, led their family from their rental home in Coconut Grove.

Jeff, the former chief revenue officer of the Sacramento Kings, has taken the day off to move after landing a new role as CRO of the Miami Heat. His life is seemingly picture-perfect. He has an adoring wife of almost ten years, three healthy children. And after two stints with the Kings spanning more than a decade—while helping secure hundreds of millions of dollars in arena sponsorships for the team—he has joined one of the NBA's most respected organizations in an appealing, sun-drenched market.

On this Monday, walking through the Davids' new front door is a dizzying procession of cable guys, utility workers, and movers. Amid all of this, Jeff receives a phone call from a former coworker with the Kings. Her name is Stacy Wegzyn, and she works in HR. Jeff last remembers sitting in her office in Sacramento just months earlier, being told that the Kings were going to eliminate his position. After a few pleasantries, she gets down to business. She tells

Jeff she's been going through his old files, and in doing so she found one labeled "TurboTax" that references an entity called Sacramento Sports Partners.

"I was just curious what that is and if those are documents that should go to somebody else," Wegzyn says.

It's a seemingly innocuous inquiry from an HR lifer. But it's one that will dictate the rest of Jeff David's life. If he knows that—or senses it—he doesn't let on.

"No, no, no," Jeff responds. "That was a . . . man, this is taking me back. Maybe 2015?"

Wegzyn presses on. She asks Jeff whether the documents contain anything that anyone with the Kings needs to see. Jeff assures her they can trash them because the entity isn't around anymore. A few minutes after he hangs up, his mother-in-law, Nancy, is standing at the front door when an FBI investigator appears, asking to speak to Jeff.

This agent, John Sommercamp, finds Kate and Jeff in the kitchen, where he tells them they might be the victims of fraud. He says he's investigating a real estate title company. Jeff retreats to a back bedroom with Sommercamp, who wants Jeff relaxed and comfortable, a willing conversationalist. He does not believe Jeff is a victim. He strongly suspects he's the perpetrator of a felony. The longer Jeff believes the inquiry is about the title company, the more likely it is that Sommercamp can extract the details he wants.

Sommercamp has questions. A year earlier, Jeff had purchased an $8 million home in Hermosa Beach, twenty miles southwest of Los Angeles. Sommercamp asks Jeff how he found the money to buy it. Jeff explains that he's part of an investor group. Sommercamp wants to know who these investors are. Jeff volunteers that Golden 1 and Kaiser Permanente, two major sponsors with the Kings, are partners. The agent gets more specific, probing the mechanics of Sacramento Sports Partners' formation.

But it's when Sommercamp asks about how he obtained signatures from his partners in Sacramento that Jeff knows it's time to suspend his cheery front.

Jeff David knows he's cornered.

Back at the rental house in Coconut Grove hours later, Kate logs on to her personal banking app to discover a balance of $0.00. No alert, no explanation. Just zeros.

Kate dials Bank of America, whose reps bounce her around the after-hours customer service labyrinth. She finally learns that there's a freeze on the family account. Kate toggles over to the family's secondary account at Wells Fargo. It, too, is frozen.

"Why is all of our money gone?!" she screams at Jeff, who seems oddly sanguine for a man who suddenly doesn't have the liquidity to order takeout. "Does this have anything to do with those FBI agents today?"

Kate grasps for any theory, speculating that the agents might have been con artists posing as Feds to fleece the family. Jeff tells her that's unlikely. He pulls out the business card Sommercamp handed him when Jeff walked the agent out the door—after telling Sommercamp that he'd be more comfortable continuing the conversation once he consulted an attorney.

Jeff calls Sommercamp and puts him on speakerphone.

"Our money is frozen," Jeff says as Kate listens.

"You're probably not going to get that money back," Sommercamp says. "You know what you did."

When Jeff hangs up, Kate is apoplectic.

"What's he talking about?! What did you do?! *What's going on?!*"

Jeff sits on the bed next to his wife and places his hand on her knee.

"I'm going to tell you, but I need you to hear me out," he says. "I need you to listen to me."

The story Jeff David was about to tell his wife—of a years-long fraud, of millions of dollars stolen—was almost too absurd to believe.

In 2009, with the NBA in the headwinds of the global recession and rumors of a Kings relocation swirling, David was a man with growing concerns. Then Sacramento's vice president of corporate partnerships, David feared he'd have to make ends meet as a private sports marketing consultant. Motivated by such prospects, he'd set up a private entity—Sacramento Sports Partners. In its nine years of existence, SSP never undertook any consultancy work. But it did ultimately prove useful.

David left for a brief stint with the NBA league office before returning to Sacramento in 2011 as CRO. He was bright and self-motivated, with a keen understanding of the industry—not a man in need of micromanaging.

His style wasn't for everyone. One Kings coworker considered him the sort of oleaginous salesman who'd go into business with anyone. Another said David had a casual relationship with the truth, the type of person who claimed, semi-seriously, to be the inventor of phrases like "Cali Love."

"Jeff is white-collar meets surfer dude, the consummate bro," says a former Kings coworker on the business operations side. "He'd open meetings with 'It's Money Monday!' Then drop a silly rap lyric about an account."

Still, in a Kings organization often beset by palace intrigue, many colleagues found Jeff to be a reassuring voice who preached the virtues of "not sweating the small stuff." He was gregarious, fond of "hugging it out," able to laugh at himself when less extroverted spirits made light of that exuberance. "Let's close some phone numbers" in David-speak meant he wanted the Kings' sales team to craft some seven-digit sponsorship agreements.

In 2012, approaching his forties, David was earning a low- to mid-six-figure salary. But he had a desire for more.

His first opportunity came that year when Van Wagner, a New York–based sports marketing firm, placed a routine call to David. It was looking to broker courtside signage for Peak Sport, a sportswear company. When it came time to bill the buyer, David used the Kings' standard invoice template but had Van Wagner make three payments, totaling about $30,000, to SSP.

David had answered the unsolicited call from Van Wagner, so no one else with the Kings would have had knowledge of the discussion. The amount represented a relatively small sum for a franchise that would generate some $13 million in sponsorship revenue that season.

Because the advertising had been purchased by Van Wagner on behalf of Peak Sports, there was no suspicion that a check from Peak hadn't turned up in the accounting department. An inquisitive bean counter with the Kings could assume that any new signage in the arena must be part of a larger advertising buy.

The Kings had given David an autonomy he could exploit. He had launched the first in a series of grifts that would grow from thousands to millions of dollars. It was audacious and, in David's mind, airtight.

And in more than two dozen interviews, colleagues, friends, neighbors, family, law enforcement, and Sacramento businesspeople could offer no explanation as to why he did it. When asked for the motivation behind the theft, David, years later, gives no unified theory.

"Curiosity? Stupidity?"

The Kings entered 2015 celebrating their unlikely survival.

Led by David, they had begun discussions with several corporations for the naming rights for their new arena and training facility, which were under construction. Given the team's near-departure from Sacramento numerous times over the previous few years—including the stay of execution that had wrested the team back from Seattle in 2013—the Kings saw large-scale sponsorship deals as more than just an opportunity to cash some checks. They wanted to go local.

"The team almost left the city, and it was the people and companies of Sacramento that kept it there," David says. "It tells a better story."

It also gave David an opening. He spent the 2015–16 NBA season stealing more money than most Kings players earned on the court.

In June 2015, the Kings and California credit union Golden 1 agreed to a twenty-year, $110 million naming rights deal for the team's new arena. David and Golden 1 had a deal structure that included twenty annual payments averaging $5.5 million. During negotiations, Golden 1 CEO Donna Bland suggested that if the Kings needed more cash up front, Golden 1 could be in a position to accommodate. David filed this information away.

That August, the Kings also agreed to a ten-year, $28 million sponsorship deal for their new training facility with Oakland-based nonprofit health care provider Kaiser Permanente. Deals like this often have "escalators," an excess amount paid each year to account for inflation or increased operating costs—akin to a cost-of-living adjustment. David told his bosses that the Kaiser deal wouldn't include one, a condition they could live with given their satisfaction with the $28 million haul and the lengthy negotiation, according to David. But unbeknownst to the higher-ups, he kept negotiating.

Claiming that expenses were piling up as the Kings tried to complete construction of the new arena, David asked Kaiser if it would add a $4.4 million upfront payment in lieu of an escalator. Kaiser

agreed, and on August 19, 2015, David invoiced the company on
Sacramento Kings letterhead, payable not to the Kings but to his
SSP account.

He got to work revising the original paperwork, forging team
president Chris Granger's signature, and sending a digital file
back to Kaiser. The Kings, in possession of the original contract,
never saw the altered version.

In September, $4.4 million landed in the account of SSP.

A year later, David reached back out to Bland to inquire
whether her offer for an upfront payment still stood. On July 5,
2016, Golden 1 wired $9 million to SSP.

To offset the $9 million, David altered the payment schedule of
the initial agreement, again forging Granger's signature. Starting
in 2026, the annual installments due on July 1 of each year were
reduced by either $500,000 or $1 million for the duration of the
deal. To make up the shortfall, David says he planned to wire the
missing amount to the Kings.

How David Changed the Golden 1 Deal

Original		Amendment
$0	**Initial payment**	$9.0 million
$6.0 million	Years 1–3*	$6.0 million
$5.5 million	Years 4–8*	$5.5 million
$5.5 million	Years 9–13*	$5.0 million
$5.5 million	Years 14–17*	$4.5 million
$5.0 million	Year 18*	$4.5 million
$5.0 million	Years 19–20*	$4.0 million
$110 million	**Total**	**$110 million**

*Annual payments

The mutual trust between David and the sponsors was unassail-
able—enough to even navigate a snafu that could have derailed
his entire scheme. When Golden 1 remitted its first scheduled
annual payment, it did so to SSP—not the Kings. Like a bank
thief tossing away a dye pack, David reached out to Golden 1 and
explained that SSP was the account reserved for finalizing con-

struction of the arena. He promptly returned the $6 million and instructed Golden 1 to wire the funds to the Kings' primary account.

"I knew how the Kings operated," David says. "I knew how these other companies operated. We had an arrangement and we agreed upon it, then everyone moved on."

Less than four years after siphoning off $30,000 in courtside signage, David had now stolen $13.4 million from the Kings and their top corporate partners.

And nobody suspected a thing.

For Jeff David, the summer of 2017 was one of those times when the reality of a man's life surpasses even his dreams. The previous June, he had purchased a $3.8 million home just blocks from the Pacific Ocean in Manhattan Beach.

Now he had flown his wife and young family on a private charter to Southern California to spend July Fourth at the new four-bedroom house, which was half a mile from an even grander property in Hermosa Beach that Jeff had also purchased. He planned to rent these investment properties, but in the meantime, his young family could bask in the warm glow of one of L.A.'s most appealing coastal towns.

When Jeff had moved $250,000 of the family's savings into Sacramento Sports Partners, he told Kate the money was for a real estate fund with other investors. But the people she heard Jeff speaking with about floorings and fixtures weren't their co-investors—they were brokers and designers consulting with Jeff about how to improve the homes for maximum return.

The cash used in the purchases was almost entirely the millions sent to Jeff by Golden 1 and Kaiser Permanente.

As rewarding as sales work can be on behalf of a pro basketball team, it hadn't satisfied Jeff's thirst for more. Flipping these valuable properties—funded by his pilfering—gave him that chance. Now he was a part of the action with his most wealthy counterparts, demonstrating to himself that he could succeed at the art of investment. Kate, a chronic worrier about the Davids' growing family, could rest easier knowing he'd secured their future.

The next summer, David left the Kings for the Heat. But on his way out, he had left behind a digital trail.

*

It was only one document—one ordinary little document—that Stacy Wegzyn had needed from Jeff David.

In August 2018, the Kings' senior vice president of human resources had been looking for a copy of a commission structure to build out the corporate sales team. David had neglected to leave the digital document when he'd departed for Miami a few weeks earlier. Wegzyn figured a quick tour of his file directory would produce something, so on Tuesday, six days before the FBI sting in Miami, she'd had the Kings' IT department download an archive from their shared cloud system.

As Wegzyn navigated a morass of files in David's old directory, she hadn't been able to discern an organized system, so she'd had to open things one by one. Eventually, she'd stumbled onto a folder titled "TurboTax," whose first item was a depreciation schedule for a home. As someone who owned rental properties, the table of depreciating items looked familiar in its contents—furniture, a golf cart—but the name of the entity in question was odd: Sacramento Sports Partners LLC.

Wegzyn was aware of other entities associated with the Kings' basketball and real estate assets, but this one didn't sound familiar. Also, she wondered, why would a business whose name suggests it's an arm of the Kings write off a golf cart at a beach house near Los Angeles?

Before leaving the office that day, Wegzyn had asked John Rinehart, the team's president of business operations, and Gerri Guzman, the team's director of finance, whether they were aware of SSP. Neither was. Wegzyn had also found a couple of K-1 tax forms listing Golden 1 and Kaiser Permanente as partners in SSP, which seemed peculiar given that credit unions and health care consortiums don't make a habit of investing in beach houses with basketball executives.

She'd told the Kings' IT department that she needed access to David's email. She was leaving town in less than forty-eight hours to drop her daughter off at college in the Pacific Northwest, and she desperately wanted some clarity.

Now, in the wee hours of Wednesday morning, Wegzyn's husband, Mark, found her sitting at her kitchen table, hunched over her laptop.

"What's going on?" Mark asked.

"I've got something really crazy going on at work," she said. "I can't talk about it, but I'm obsessed. I have to stay with this. I'll be up soon."

She searched David's emails for any connection to the address in Manhattan Beach or Sacramento Sports Partners. She discovered that David had applied for mortgages and included a bank statement to a lender that showed a $4.4 million deposit from Kaiser Permanente. Later on, she found a $9 million deposit from Golden 1.

A surge of adrenaline jolted through Wegzyn's body. With each passing hour, she became increasingly convinced that she was headed down a path that would upend David's life forever. She was consumed by the chase but also suffering from periodic pangs of doubt. *What if I'm wrong? What if this is all legit?* Reading David's email felt invasive, even if Kings employees, like those at most companies, sign away their privacy to people like her.

Later that Wednesday, Wegzyn reached out to Golden 1 and Kaiser Permanente to learn more. She wanted to move quickly. In scouring David's correspondences, it appeared as if he'd been working to sell one of the properties.

"This is Stacy with the Kings," she told the rep in accounts payable at each organization. "We're partners. We're going through an audit, and I'd like to see if you can send me a list of all payments made to my organization over the last five years."

She was careful not to reveal her intention, not wanting to alarm either entity. When she found a receptive party at Golden 1, she emailed him the list of legitimate Kings entities, burying SSP in the middle.

One day later, as the family Ford Expedition charted its course northward, Wegzyn stayed in touch with Rinehart, trying to break through their partners' bureaucracy. Stacy and Mark bid schmaltzy parental farewells to their daughter, whom they settled at school, then reversed course back to Sacramento.

Just as Wegzyn returned to the office on Tuesday, confirmation arrived from Golden 1: it had sent a $9 million payment to SSP. Wegzyn and the Kings brass realized it was time to escalate this homegrown investigation. The team's new vice president of security operations, Dave Thomas, spent nearly thirty years in law enforcement with the FBI and Secret Service. Wegzyn asked Thomas to set up a meeting.

When the FBI arrived Wednesday afternoon, the Kings were

armed with troves of documents unearthed and organized by Wegzyn—a binder with all the correspondence, the tax documents, the bank statements, anything she could get her hands on. What Wegzyn didn't yet have were whatever contracts David had drawn up to lure Golden 1 and Kaiser Permanente into his scheme.

On Thursday, when the Kings were mining their network for additional evidence, a folder named "660" was uncovered—660 J Street was a temporary home of the team's business operations during construction of the new arena. Inside the folder were the contents of David's old laptop, which included a PDF with the signatures of Granger, Bland, and Rinehart, along with copies of the amendment for the Golden 1 deal and the revised contract with Kaiser Permanente.

One week after her first foray into David's underworld, Wegzyn had struck the mother lode.

"You could come work for us," Sommercamp told Wegzyn.

Back in Coconut Grove, in the living room of the house that Jeff and Kate had been renting, Kate lies shivering in a ball on the couch. Hours earlier, the FBI had stormed her house. Her bank accounts had been frozen. And now, after her husband has confessed to a monstrous fraud, her mother sits beside her and extends an arm, but she is virtually unresponsive.

"I'm in really big trouble," Jeff says to Kate's mother, Nancy, and her partner, Rich.

Kate is inconsolable.

Jeff explains—the visit from the FBI earlier in the day, the full breadth of the scam. Still, to Nancy and Rich, he seems oblivious to the depth of his crime.

"I'll just give the money back," Jeff says. "I can liquidate the properties. All the money's there. I'll give it back, and when I do, it'll be okay."

Rich shifts into fix-it mode, calling attorneys he knows back at home in Ohio, leaving messages because it's after midnight on a Tuesday morning. Rich tells Jeff it's imperative that he get legal protection.

"I think you're making too much of this," Jeff says. "I'll go to the FBI. I'll call them tomorrow. I'll tell them the whole story and show them where the money is. Everyone will get their money back, and it'll be okay. It's not going to be a big deal."

Rich and Nancy become incredulous. Does Jeff truly believe that the only item on his to-do list is restitution? As Rich pleads with Jeff, Kate rouses from her trance, shock replaced by resignation.

"You're going to go to prison," Kate says. "We're going to lose everything."

For several more hours, Rich tries to pierce Jeff's logic, while Nancy reassures the family that Jeff is redeemable.

"We went back to bed at four in the morning, and I said, 'I don't think he really gets it,'" Rich says nearly a year later.

After a short night's sleep, the family returns to the house in Pinecrest the next morning to rebox their belongings.

Says Nancy: "It was awful."

Two days later, David sits in Sacramento at a conference table between his two defense attorneys and across from a team from the U.S. attorney's office that specializes in white-collar crime.

Here, they begin with a directive to David:

"Anytime you want to confer with your lawyers privately, we're happy to step out of the room," says Assistant U.S. Attorney Michael D. Anderson. "But any half-truth will be considered a lie. Leaving out pertinent facts will be considered a lie. We expect you to tell us everything you know, and if you plan to do anything apart from that, let's go our separate ways, because lying is worse than telling us nothing at all."

David is operating under the hope that by cooperating, he can work out a favorable deal. He tries to establish a personal rapport with the government's lawyers, but few professions are more impervious to a salesman's charm than that of government lawyer.

David offers a broad outline of the Golden 1 and Kaiser Permanente schemes. When asked to recall the last time he spoke with someone from the Kings, though, he neglects to mention the call with Wegzyn on Monday. It occurs to the U.S. attorneys that David might not realize it's that conversation that implicated him. David also doesn't disclose information about the 2012 instance of fraud until Assistant U.S. Attorney Matt Yelovich brings it up.

David contends that from the moment he diverted funds from Golden 1 and Kaiser Permanente, he intended to repay the money. He says he had the mechanics worked out: On July 1, 2026, the Kings would be expecting $5.5 million (per the original payment schedule). And when Golden 1 would wire $5 million, David says he planned to open up a DBA ("doing business as") account called GoldenOne from which he'd wire the $500,000 shortfall. He says he believes that the Kings' finance department wouldn't have a concern that the $5.5 million had arrived in two payments as long as the full amount was present.

When asked whether David's scenario sounds plausible, business operations executives from six NBA teams say they find it farfetched. One executive in the finance department of an NBA team says, "We invoice everything—even signed contracts. So Golden 1 would be getting an invoice for $5.5 million weeks before the payment." Several of the executives note that it's not unusual for teams and sponsors to explore renegotiating their active agreements, which would require executives on both sides to review the paperwork. With David no longer present to service the Golden 1 account or run interference, the fraud would be nearly impossible to manage.

How Jeff David's scheme unraveled.

- **2009:** David sets up SSP
- **2011:** Named Kings CRO
- **2012:** Van Wagner fraud
- **2015–16:** Golden 1, Kaiser frauds
- **2016:** Purchases beach homes
- **Summer 2018:** Wegzyn finds the trail
- **December 2018:** David pleads guilty
- **2019:** Begins seven-year sentence

In the matter of Kaiser Permanente's $4.4 million, these executives are even more dubious of David's blueprint to make the Kings whole.

Unlike Golden 1's advance of $9 million, which produced annual shortfalls later in the deal, Kaiser Permanente's $4.4 upfront payment created no missing money. The cash went straight to David without the Kings knowing it existed. If he had truly wanted to return $4.4 million to the franchise, he would have needed to get creative.

How do you repay money to a team that doesn't know anything has been stolen? It's not uncommon in the NBA for one franchise to buy assets from another—suites, signage, logo rights—to construct a multimarket agreement for a corporate sponsor. David says that in his capacity as a top executive with another team, he could have called his counterpart in Sacramento several times over a ten-year period and brokered such deals.

One longtime team president finds David's plan unconvincing, noting that while franchises aggregate their market power, they're far more likely to swap data of pricing and then share the contact information for the sponsor. The notion that David could orchestrate, say, nine deals valued at an average of $500,000 is, the executive says, fantastical: "It doesn't work like that."

Furthermore, the U.S. attorney's office believes the debate over whether David could feasibly repay the funds is irrelevant because he had no intention to do so.

"If he really wanted to pay back the victims, he would've paid his earlier victims once he had a lot of money," Anderson says.

On September 7, 2018, the Heat dismiss David. In the following weeks, attempting to make restitution to the parties he victimized, he boldly pitches the prosecutors on the idea that he could help sell the properties based on his expertise and knowledge of the market.

But the forfeiture team has arranged to sell far more complex assets than beach homes. Given the circumstances, they're worried David might try to arrange a questionable below-market deal with a side payment to himself or a friend. The forfeiture team instead works with a real estate team in Los Angeles. The house in Hermosa Beach that David purchased in July 2016 for $8 million sells for $10.6 million; the Manhattan Beach house he bought for $3.8 million sells for $4.3 million. After restitution is paid to the Kings and other wronged parties, the remaining money goes to an asset forfeiture fund that compensates crime victims.

In December, David pleads guilty to wire fraud and aggravated identity theft charges. He returns to Columbus, where he, Kate, and their three children have relocated to a roomy cluster home not far from where Kate grew up and where most of her family resides.

He has six months before returning to Sacramento for sentencing.

In January 2019, top business-operations executives from the NBA and its thirty franchises congregate in Miami for the league's annual sales and marketing meetings. It's a schmoozy industry conclave where David had once thrived, and this year he is at the center of attention in absentia. Though his crime didn't make him a household name, David has become a cautionary tale among NBA front offices afraid they could fall victim to such a scam.

At group dinners and in casual conversations, execs who worked with David try to recall instances that might have marked him as a crook. CFOs swap accounts of stress-testing their team's internal checks and balances to protect against potential fraud. One team president says the franchise initiated a full audit of its operations days after the story became public.

Questions raged about how a credit union tasked with protecting the savings of teachers and a health care nonprofit could be snookered out of millions by a single individual. Golden 1 and Kaiser Permanente wired millions to an entity they hadn't vetted without asking David to loop in his legal and finance counterparts. Multiple sources in Sacramento portray Golden 1 as an institution eager to make a splash in the market it has championed passionately. In doing so, the credit union left itself exposed to a mistake a more sophisticated entity might have avoided thorough due diligence.

"What happened with Golden 1 and Kaiser probably doesn't happen with American Airlines or Bank of America," says a top NBA team executive.

Officials from Golden 1, Kaiser Permanente, and Van Wagner declined to comment.

The most persistent item for debate has been the extent to which this fraud could've happened to any team. The U.S. attorney's office and others in law enforcement praise the Kings for swiftly responding to what Wegzyn uncovered. But multiple sources who have come through the Kings organization over the past decade say the organization had systemic flaws that left it susceptible during much of David's tenure. Among the weak links, they say, was the Kings' finance department.

One NBA team controller says it's common practice at any well-run finance department, be it team or sponsor, to call when invoiced to pay an entity for the first time. Whether it's a $20,000 signage buy with Van Wagner, a shipment of basketballs, or a $110 million sponsorship deal, most NBA organizations have a rigorous system that tracks every purchase and sale.

The Kings take issue with this characterization.

"Any organization can suffer betrayal by a trusted employee," says Bill Portanova, a former assistant U.S. attorney who was retained by the Kings as an independent investigator. "Jeff David was a lone operator."

Jeff, Kate, and their families arrive at the U.S. Courthouse in Sacramento early on June 24, 2019. Jeff wears a double-vented navy suit, whiskey-colored shoes, and thick-framed glasses; Kate is in a black dress. Across the courtroom, the U.S. attorney's team readies itself to argue that Jeff David should serve nine years in federal prison.

David's lawyers counter that their client has cooperated fully and presents little risk of recidivism. They state that a lengthy sentence would be an act of vengeance with no practical purpose.

Nancy speaks with a measured empathy about a man whose adult life she admires. "It was particularly difficult for us because we had previously been witnesses to many occasions on which his strong moral compass was in clear view in far less profound situations," she says. This is the first moment when Kate, remarkably stoic throughout the ninety-minute sentencing, visibly cries.

David breaks down during the testimonial from his mother-in-law, removing his glasses and burying his head in his hands. And he becomes emotional when he speaks on his own behalf, pausing to collect himself as he conveys remorse to the court.

"I lost the respect I had," David tells Judge William B. Shubb. "I lost a job and a career I loved and excelled in. But I care less what has happened to me and I care more about making sure I've done the right thing for the people I've offended and I've hurt."

Anderson, the government's lead attorney at sentencing, lends no credence to David's unrelenting claim that he intended to compensate the Kings, and takes issue with the premise that David committed one or two indiscreet actions.

"This was a long, sophisticated course of conduct that required registering LLCs with the state, opening commercial mailboxes in the LLC's name, using the identities and the good names of prominent regional businesspeople, signing their names on LLC documents unbeknownst to them, and using their identities to perpetuate fraud," he says. "This happened over many, many years."

Shubb, an eighty-one-year-old who has presided on the bench in the Eastern District of California since 1990, expresses deep skepticism over whether David's contention that he planned to pay back the money is plausible.

"It's a fantasy," he says.

David and his legal team had hoped for a sentence not much longer than two years, but Shubb hands down a term of seven. When the session breaks, David's family and friends commiserate with him, but Kate doesn't move. From the front row of the gallery, she stares into the distance.

Fifteen days before David begins serving his sentence, a pressing matter lands on his docket. The family had spent the weekend at the Ohio State Fair, where two of his three kids won goldfish. This meant that one of his three kids was deprived of the innocent pleasure of toting home and choosing a name for this shiny, breathing doubloon swimming around in a plastic bag.

The pet stores are closed on Sunday evening, so soon after David mixes three glasses of chocolate milk and prepares breakfast, he corrals the kids into the SUV for a trip to equalize the great goldfish disparity of 2019.

"You have to put on real clothes, dude," he tells his five-year-old son, who finds the proposition that he can't wear pajamas to a suburban shopping mall entirely unconvincing.

David now lives at the Federal Correctional Institution in Morgantown, West Virginia, where pleasures are smaller and infrequent. Where, according to an article in *Fortune*, the prison currency comes in the form of tins of cooked mackerel.

Though his wife and in-laws still believe he's a good man, David won't enjoy their devotion in close proximity, except as official visitation rules permit. He won't see the children at all for the next several years. The family feels that seeing their father in a state of incarceration would be too traumatic for his kids.

Atherton, California, is the cradle of Silicon Valley, the second-richest ZIP code in the U.S. and the site of Kings managing partner Vivek Ranadive's 2016 Christmas party. Grapevines and Teslas lined the driveway of Ranadive's three-acre chateau; his glass-bottom pool was covered with flooring beneath an expansive tent. Tech titans helped themselves to sushi, while guests roamed downstairs on Ranadive's sunken basketball half court. Nearby, a shrine commemorated Ranadive's meetings with global celebrities. The party, say sources with knowledge of the event, cost between $150,000 and $200,000.

Jeff arrived at the soiree with Kate, who found the whole affair conspicuous, a bit ridiculous, a different kind of life. But this was the nerve center of Jeff's world. As the Kings' CRO, he had been the architect of multimillion-dollar sponsorship deals that were funneled to an ownership group whose managing partner was worth several hundred million dollars. The team's star, DeMarcus Cousins, earned $17 million. Even the head coach pulled in almost $4 million per season.

No milieu displayed this NBA abundance more than the Lexus Lounge at the Golden 1 Center half an hour before tipoff. There was nothing aesthetically unique about the Lexus Lounge. The masculine minimalism looked familiar to anyone who has walked into a boutique hotel in the past decade. But in Sacramento, where those with money are more likely to hide their affluence than flaunt it, this was the single most prominent accumulation of wealth the city saw.

Partners in the Kings' ownership group arrived to games via private jet from one of their multiple homes, while others showed up in limousines or $100,000 sports cars. Four blocks down L Street was the capital of the world's fifth-largest economy, and the lobbyists who grease the wheels of that engine were there at one of forty-one exclusive parties per season. On occasion, Ranadive walked into the building alongside celebrities such as Drake and Jamie Foxx.

From the exposed wall of the lounge, guests watched Kings players dash to and from the locker room and court for warm-ups. As the person principally responsible for selling associations to these famous athletes, David was a fixture on the event level too. And even though he was earning $360,000 per year plus bonuses, just about everyone in here made more than he did.

Jeff David's NBA was awash in wealth, yet in this rarefied air, he was the pauper.

STEVEN LECKART

The Bicycle Thief

FROM CHICAGO MAGAZINE IN PARTNERSHIP WITH
EPIC MAGAZINE

THE MAN IN the baseball cap and sunglasses waited for the teller to notice him. The morning of May 26, 2000, was quiet inside the LaSalle Bank in suburban Highland Park. Standing patiently by the velvet ropes, the man looked at his wristwatch. The second hand ticked slowly.

"May I help you?" said the young woman behind the counter, smiling. The man reached to the back of his khakis, as if to fish out a wallet. Instead, he presented her with a three-by-five-inch index card. The teller's smile wilted. She stared at the words handwritten in black marker: "THIS IS A ROBBERY, PUT ALL OF YOUR MONEY IN THE BAG." The man, who would later be described to the police as a slender, clean-shaven white man in his twenties wearing a light blue oxford shirt, returned the note card to his pocket. "Nice and easy," he said coolly, handing over a white plastic shopping bag from Sports Authority. While the teller anxiously transferred bundles of cash, the man held his hands at his heart, gently pressing his palms together as if he were about to whisper, *Namaste.*

"Thank you," he said before walking out the front door.

The street was empty: no cars, no pedestrians. Suddenly the man spotted a police officer riding a four-wheel ATV. Squeezing the shopping bag, he settled into a relaxed gait. As the ATV approached, the robber smiled and waved hello, as would anyone who had not just knocked over a bank. Returning a stiff nod, the officer kept rolling. And so did the man, descending into a parking garage.

Not sixty seconds later, he emerged, carrying an aluminum bicycle on one shoulder and a messenger bag over the other and wearing a red, white, and blue spandex bodysuit, a silver helmet, sunglasses with yellow lenses, and a pair of cycling shoes. He climbed onto the bike, clicked into the pedals, and began to ride leisurely. It had been less than three minutes since he exited the bank.

There were no sirens or alarms—only the sound of the 11:26 a.m. Metra rumbling into the station three blocks away. By the time the train was gone, so was the thief.

Fifteen minutes later, he was coasting south along Sheridan Road. He pedaled into Gillson Park in Wilmette and cruised up to a trash can. After fishing out two crisp $20 bills and shoving them into the pocket of his bodysuit, he removed the Sports Authority bag and held it upside down over the trash can. Several bundles of cash—what authorities would later reveal to be $4,009—tumbled into the garbage with a syncopated thud.

The man returned the empty sack to his messenger bag and pedaled away.

"Anyone interested in racing, bring your bike, and try your luck," a voice announced over the tinny loudspeaker at the Ed Rudolph Velodrome in Northbrook. Seated in the bleachers, thirteen-year-old Tom Justice was in awe of the cyclists careening around the outdoor track. Every time the pack whirled by, it cut the air, unleashing a concentrated whoosh.

Before that summer of 1983, Tom had never seen a bicycle race, let alone a velodrome. When his friend Kristin invited him to go, the skinny teen with straight black hair said yes only because he had a crush on her. But the moment they entered the stadium, he was transfixed.

The oval track measured 382 meters, with two long straightaways connected by curves banked at 18 degrees, allowing riders to maintain high speeds. While road races like the Tour de France play out over days on courses that meander for miles, track racing happens in a matter of minutes in tight confines. Cyclists aggressively jockey for position, bumping and elbowing as they fly around corners at fifty miles per hour. It's like NASCAR, except with no brakes. Crashes and multi-rider spills are common.

A week later, Tom returned to the velodrome with his maroon Schwinn. As the stadium lights buzzed, a dozen suburban kids gathered on the track. Everyone was wearing T-shirts and gym shorts except for Tom, who stood out in the professional-grade helmet, jersey, padded cycling shorts, and fingerless gloves his father had just bought him.

Tom won the twelve- to fourteen-year-old heat handily. Straddling his bike, his chest still heaving, he felt a surge of adrenaline. After trying basketball, baseball, and soccer and accepting he was unremarkable at any sport involving a ball, Tom had finally found something he excelled at. His father, Jay, a short, barrel-chested Navy veteran with an abundance of athleticism, was thrilled. "Get out in front," Jay began telling his son before races, "and don't let anyone get around you."

By Tom's junior year at Libertyville High School, his identity hinged on cycling. He was regularly shaving his muscular legs to try to make himself more aerodynamic. He was training at the velodrome on Mondays and Wednesdays, racing every Thursday, and pedaling for hours around Libertyville's winding back roads.

Nobody in town was surprised when Tom was selected to attend the Olympic training camp in Colorado Springs in 1987. It was a heady time to be an elite cyclist in America. After decades of embarrassing losses and zero appearances on the podium, the U.S. Olympic cycling team had capitalized on the Soviet Union's boycott of the 1984 Games, winning a record-breaking nine medals. In a tactical effort to prep for the Russians in 1988 and beyond, the U.S. coaches began grooming forty American hopefuls early. Tom received massages, soaked in hot tubs, had his bike fine-tuned by mechanics, and was subjected to a battery of testing to measure everything from body fat to oxygen efficiency.

A gifted sprinter, Tom had a knack for finding and accelerating through tight spaces to break away from the pack. His build was perfect for track cycling—he was tall, with thick, powerful legs, like a speed skater. And in the 1,000-meter match sprint, his favorite, he showed an instinct for overtaking the leader during the final forty-five seconds—the make-or-break moment.

That fall, Tom returned to Libertyville High, where he was elected senior class president. Girls pined after the guy with the shock of black hair flopping in his eyes. One of Tom's classmates even gave him a diary of her lovesick musings about him. "Tom was an attractive guy, but that wasn't what drew people to him necessarily," recalls Erika Zavaleta, who raced with Tom at the Olympic training camp and later made the 1989 U.S. national team. Tom wasn't a stereotypical macho jock. He was warm-hearted, silly, charming, and comfortable in his skin. "He came off as self-assured and really unthreatening at the same time," says Erika.

As Tom's senior year came to a close, his road map was clear: train at Southern Illinois University, where he had been accepted; stay focused; and be patient. Top track cyclists usually don't qualify for the Olympics until they are in their late twenties.

In the 1988 Libertyville High School yearbook, one page was dedicated to answering the question "What will your friends be doing in ten years?" The caption beside Tom Justice's name read: "On the cover of a Wheaties box, with his bike."

"*Je suis Américain?*" The drill sergeant was apoplectic. The Dutchman had been yelling ever since Tom arrived at the French Foreign Legion's candidate selection center in the South of France. It was the fall of 1997. Dropping to the pavement, Tom pumped out push-ups. Suddenly the sergeant's heavy boot walloped him in the stomach. The recruits around him laughed.

One of the few military outfits that accept noncitizens, the Foreign Legion tends to attract a menagerie of misfits. Men who can't even speak French arrive willing to endure hot-tempered drill instructors and five years of service in exchange for a French passport. At twenty-seven, Tom was on the older side for the legion, but he was still fit. He could bang out chin-ups, no problem. But he couldn't stand his superiors. One time, the stocky Dutchman forced Tom to spend three hours on his hands and knees, in shorts, picking up cigarette butts as the jagged asphalt burrowed into his kneecaps.

The legion tries to break recruits. The recruits, in turn, try to break each other. Tom was a frequent target of a wiry nineteen-year-old Moroccan. "Hey, big shot! Why don't you become American Navy SEAL?" the guy shouted one time. "Maybe you cannot make it?" Tom retaliated by grabbing the Moroccan's throat until they were separated. Both men were dismissed from the legion.

Tom's commanding officer encouraged him to enlist again in a year. But Tom would never return to France. Since high school, his commitment to cycling—and everything else—had lapsed. During the six years he attended Southern Illinois, Tom embraced the slackerdom that came to define Generation X. He switched majors, ping-ponging between philosophy and sociology and theater. He rushed a fraternity but never joined. When the film *Reality Bites* was released, Tom went to see it six times. Like Ethan Hawke's chain-smoking nihilist, Tom believed it was cool not to care.

He still talked about the Olympics, but he coasted on his innate talent. At college, he founded a cycling club, where he was surrounded with amateurs he could always best. Instead of training hard, Tom broke into empty tract houses to smoke cigarettes and chug beers with his buddies.

But deep inside, Tom still harbored wildly grandiose expectations. In college, he thought maybe he could become an artist. He dabbled in piano and sculpture, but nothing ever clicked for him the way cycling had. So after finally graduating in 1994, Tom moved to Los Angeles to train alongside the U.S. Olympic team. Racing around the famed 5,000-seat velodrome at California State University, Dominguez Hills, he did little to distinguish himself.

"Where's his head?" cyclist Bill Clay said to Tom's girlfriend, Laura, as they watched Tom loop around the track one day. A young sprinter who would compete in the 1996 Olympics, Bill could tell Tom lacked discipline. "Tom's fast, but he doesn't train right," he observed. "He needs to apply himself."

Tom soon washed out and returned to Chicago, where he and Laura shared an apartment in Ravenswood. He found a job as a social worker overseeing homeless schizophrenics. Helping people was a welcome distraction from his own issues. But after a while, it felt like a pointless slog—one with no finish line and no congratulations. As Tom's Olympic dream slipped away, he started fantasizing about identities he could substitute for the thrilling instant gratification of cycling. He made a list, hidden by his bed:

> helicopter pilot
> lock picker
> priest
> EMT

He started with the third, applying to a Catholic seminary. Tom wasn't even religious, but this seemed like a fresh start. He could be handed a rigid set of guidelines for a new life. Sitting down with an admissions officer at the University of St. Mary of the Lake in Mundelein, Tom admitted he couldn't remember the last time he'd been to confession. The man leveled with him: "Son, you really need to do some soul-searching."

Next Tom talked his way into an informational interview at the Drug Enforcement Administration's office in the Loop. He explained how he'd never worked in law enforcement but had plenty of experience frisking teenagers from a previous job at a high school for truants. "Can I be honest with you?" interrupted an agent. "You don't seem like the type of guy that's going to kick down doors fighting the war on drugs."

After watching *Repo Man,* Tom cold-called auto recovery companies for career advice. He toyed with becoming an underwater welder. He struck out with the French Foreign Legion. He wandered from interview to interview, growing increasingly unhappy with a life that to him seemed mundane. His relationship with Laura became strained. Whenever she mentioned marriage or kids, he grew uneasy. He couldn't see himself settling down—not yet and maybe never.

Late one night in 1998, Tom revisited his handwritten list. Over the years, he kept adding ideas and potential identities to it. Under "helicopter pilot" and "lock picker," he'd scrawled two letters: "B.R."

Bank robber.

The heist was timed around Halloween 1998. For a disguise, Tom went to Elim Wig & Beauty Supply in Uptown. In the 1930s, John Dillinger hid out in that neighborhood. Rumor has it he altered his appearance with help from a plastic surgeon who had an office above the Green Mill Cocktail Lounge. On the short list of notorious American bank robbers, several had spent time in Chicago. That rich history added to the allure for Tom.

At the wig shop, Tom considered his options: a hot pink Ziggy Stardust number, white-blond pigtails, or Afros in various shades of the rainbow. Ultimately, he settled on black braids with short bangs for $50. Only after he'd left did he realize it made him look like Rick James.

Three days later, on October 23, Tom entered his parents' garage and flicked on the light, which glimmered across his dad's white Porsche 928. The other parking spaces were empty. Tom's parents wouldn't be back for hours. His younger sister, Jennifer, was off at college. He grabbed his messenger bag and Fuji AX-500 and pedaled toward downtown Libertyville.

Tom coasted up to a tree-lined fence between two houses. Over his cycling spandex, he slid on a pair of khakis, a blue oxford button-down, a striped tie, and a navy blazer with a jack-o'-lantern decal pinned to it. He slipped on his wig, then a snug black baseball cap. For a finishing touch, he added dark, oversize sunglasses reminiscent of Jackie O.

As he walked to the American National Bank branch, teenage girls in a passing car catcalled. Tom pointed back like the Fonz retorting *Aaay!* He stopped at a pay phone and placed an anonymous call to the Libertyville Police Department headquarters, a mere two blocks from his target.

"Yeah, hi, I'm at Adler Park. There's a man with a rifle walking around the woods."

"Thank you, sir, we'll check it out," said the voice on the other end. One less patrol car near the bank.

A silver-haired sixty-something held the door when Tom arrived. As Tom approached a teller, she perked up immediately. Halloween had apparently come early this year. Then the love child of Rick James and Jackie O handed her an index card but wouldn't let go. Tom had no intention of leaving behind evidence. As an awkward tug of war ensued, the teller leaned in and read the message. Tense, she stared into Tom's dark sunglasses. He slid his white plastic bag across the counter, and she loaded it up with cash.

Tom strode outside, bag in hand. His heartbeat surged. His legs tingled. He looked at his wristwatch. The whole exchange had lasted forty-five seconds. Two minutes later, Tom was beside his bike, feverishly stripping down. He placed his disguise and the plastic bag onto a square piece of black satin and tied the corners to create a little bundle, which he shoved into his messenger bag.

After bunny-hopping gracefully into the street, Tom casually cycled back to his parents' circular driveway. Next door lived Pat and Denise Carey, who had moved in the previous spring. The forty-seven-year-old Pat was a meticulous mower, changing directions each week for a more uniform cut. He was also Libertyville's chief of police.

Tom parked his bike in the garage, kicked off his shoes, and tiptoed into the basement. He knew he'd never be able to tell anyone about this. Still, he wasn't remorseful. Banks are insured, and he didn't care about the money anyway. He'd choreographed, costumed, and delivered a flawless performance. His getaway vehicle was poetic. A sense of euphoria overwhelmed him. Years later, he'd compare the rush of robbing banks to the sensation of drinking four cups of coffee and taking an intensely hot shower while holding back the urge to pee. It had been a long time since Tom felt this alive—or this important.

Kneeling on the shag carpet, Tom removed the black satin bundle from his messenger bag. He looked at the money and began to weep.

When FBI agents arrive at a crime scene, they start with the details: how a suspect dressed and acted, what was said, how a note was written, whether a weapon was brandished. All these pieces fit together to create what former special agent William Rehder calls a "signature."

A suspect wearing one glove was dubbed the Michael Jackson Bandit. The Attila the Bun Bandit kept her hair in a topknot. The Clearasil Bandit's cheeks were dotted with acne. The Benihana Bandit gesticulated with a butcher knife. The Chevy Chase Bandit was—naturally—absurdly clumsy.

It would be many months before Tom Justice would even be considered for a nickname by the FBI. Armed robbers and violent offenders are the agency's top priority. And Tom had perpetrated just one nonviolent "note job" for a haul of $5,580. He wasn't going to draw heat, especially when the FBI was handling a record 171 bank robberies in the Chicago area in 1998. For now, Tom would stay under the radar. And he took precautions to keep it that way.

A few days after his robbery in Libertyville, Tom tossed his wig into the dumpster behind the Ravenswood apartment he now only sometimes shared with Laura. Ever since the Foreign Legion, Tom had established a noncommittal pattern of coming and going: one night, he'd crash with Laura; the next, his folks. For months, the $5,580 sat in a gym bag inside the closet of his old room at his parents' house. Tom assumed the bills were traceable, so he kept only two $20s as souvenirs. He separated the remaining cash into brown lunch sacks. Late one night, he tossed them into the dumpsters behind a few fast-food restaurants.

On October 27, 1999, nearly one year to the day after his first robbery, Tom hit the Lake Forest branch of Northern Trust. He wore a similar disguise and used his bike to escape with $3,247. This time he put the $20 and $100 bills into paper bags and discarded them in alleys where he knew homeless people would find them. He took all the $2 bills and hid them in the bushes outside his apartment. The Eastern European superintendent had two kids who used to play in the courtyard. Tom watched from his second-floor living room window as they discovered the money and screamed and giggled. Robbing banks and giving away the money was intoxicating. Tom saw himself as both mischievous and righteous.

But as time passed, that feeling faded. Tom's real life seemed mediocre and unfulfilling. He wrestled with depression. And so he returned to the one thing that would instantly lift his spirits.

On January 14, 2000, Tom pulled his third robbery: the LaSalle Bank in Evanston. The teller, a tall fifty-year-old woman, was neither frightened nor cooperative. "Are you serious?" she said, cocking her head. She glared at Tom as he slid the bag across the counter. Reluctantly, she filled it with all the cash in her drawer: $2,599. "Thank you, thank you so much," Tom said politely. She shook her head disapprovingly.

As the harsh winter winds blew off Lake Michigan, the streets became icy and impossible to navigate by bike. Cooped up that January, Tom brooded miserably, unable to shake the realization that at twenty-nine, his window of opportunity to become a world-class cyclist had nearly passed. If he wanted to pursue his Olympic dream, he had to do it now.

By the time he told Laura he was moving to Southern California to train for the Olympic trials, his plans were already in motion. He'd arranged to move into a house with an old college cycling buddy who lived near the San Diego Velodrome. Tom had won enough races to retain his classification as a Category 1 cyclist —the highest of five groupings—and so he would automatically qualify for the trials. All he'd have to do is show up and race.

Laura was skeptical about Tom's sudden urge to dive back into racing. But maybe if he made this one last push for the Olympics, he could then get on with his life. So she loaned him her mom's blue Honda Accord to drive to California. When Tom arrived, he looked into the mirror and told himself, "I'm not going to rob any more banks."

The stylist spun the chair around. Tom's black hair was bleached platinum blond, spiked, with the sides shaved. He was ready for his new life in a shared house in Encinitas, one of a constellation of beach towns near San Diego.

Since college, Tom's cycling buddy had become a Navy jet pilot. Now he lived in a two-story house with a bunch of military guys and a three-legged greyhound named Foxtrot. Tom slept on the top floor in a tiny twenty-square-foot space his housemates called the Turret. He hung his track bike—a red, white, and blue GT —on the wall above his mattress. The Turret was cramped, but its windows looked out over the Pacific. At night, Tom fell asleep listening to the waves.

"How's it going?" asked Laura, calling from Chicago.

"Well!" replied Tom. His skin was tan from his time on the outdoor velodrome. He'd bought his GT from Bill Clay, who'd given him a copy of the training manual used by the 1996 U.S. Olympic cycling team. Every morning at the YMCA, Tom worked through the Olympic strength-training regimen to build muscle mass. Within a month, he was squatting 500 pounds. At the velodrome, his already explosive dead start was getting deadlier. As the weeks passed in early 2000, Tom rounded into the best shape of his life.

But the monotony of training was setting in, and Tom's promise to himself was soon forgotten. His secret identity—and the instant rush that only a robbery could provide—called to him.

The day after Valentine's Day, Tom hit a bank in Encinitas. On February 29, one in Solana Beach. The next day, another in Encinitas. Two weeks after that, one in San Diego. On March 24, Tom robbed two banks: the Southwest Community Bank in Encinitas and the U.S. Bank in Carlsbad. "D-d-do you want the s-s-second drawer too?" the twenty-year-old blond U.S. Bank teller had nervously stuttered. She stuffed the bag with so much cash that it spilled out over the top. As Tom exited, a trail of bills flittered to the ground. It was his biggest score yet: $10,274.

He pocketed all the $5s and $1s and left the $20s inside public restrooms and porta-potties at beaches. He didn't need the money.

Then one morning, Tom awoke in the Turret and found he couldn't move. An intense pain surged through his lower back. He'd thrown it out overtraining. It would take hours before he could even get to his feet—and weeks before he could pedal without waking up in agony the day after. Muscle spasms kept causing his body to contort. His right shoulder was two inches higher than his left. His plan to race in the Olympic trials was over.

Soon after he returned to Chicago, Laura dumped Tom for good. He had changed. He wasn't merely devastated about missing the trials; he was colder, more distant, and secretive. "I don't know what's going on with you," she said. "But I know it's not right."

Tom moved into a two-bedroom apartment in Ukrainian Village with George, a 230-pound Greek hulk who blocked most of the doorway when Tom turned up, answering his Craigslist ad for a roommate.

"We won't see each other much," George explained. "I work nights."

"What are you—an exotic dancer?" Tom chuckled.

"No," replied George, "I'm a cop."

Tom couldn't resist. Sharing an apartment with a beat cop while committing federal felonies was an insane proposition. But with no girlfriend, no job, and no Olympics, all he had left was his unrelenting desire to feel exceptional, to prove to himself that he was too clever to get caught.

Once his lower back recovered, Tom robbed the LaSalle Bank in Highland Park—the heist in which he dumped his $4,009 haul in a park trash can. The next week, he hit three banks in three days, and it didn't always go smoothly. Outside a Bank One in Evanston, a dye pack exploded in his bag, ruining all the cash. Later that day, he hit an Edens Bank in Wilmette, where a heavyset fifty-something teller took one look at Tom's note and harshly scolded him in a Slavic language. She pointed sternly at Tom, who quickly fled without any money. The third robbery, at a Harris Bank in Wilmette, was a success, but when Tom rode up to his apartment, he saw two cop cars parked on the front lawn. His heart sunk—until he realized it was just his roommate, George. Tom went upstairs to his room, where he hid the $4,244 he'd stolen. George had no clue his roommate had just knocked over his thirteenth bank.

Two months later, Tom robbed the Bank of Northern Illinois in Libertyville. Chief Carey, who'd spent that winter helping blow snow from his neighbor Jay Justice's driveway, didn't have any leads—and neither did the FBI. The most interesting aspect of the robber's MO—his getaway vehicle—was still unknown.

No one suspected Tom, and so he grew cocky. Once, at a night-club, he met a twenty-something brunette in a midnight-blue cock-tail dress. Tom couldn't believe it when he learned she was a U.S. marshal. On the dance floor, as loud club music pulsed, she smiled playfully.

"So what do you do?" she yelled.

"I rob banks." He grinned and continued dancing.

She nodded and kept dancing too.

A custom bicycle frame is a wondrous blend of form and function. A precise network of triangles, diamonds, and curves, the frame must reconcile and, in turn, harmonize with a rider's body. To boost a cyclist's comfort and efficiency, a bike builder will spend hours measuring a client's body before carefully mapping out the geometry.

Once a blueprint is finalized, the builder embarks on a long, laborious process that begins with a pile of steel. After cutting spe-cific tubes into meticulously measured lengths, the builder con-joins two sections using a TIG welder, which uses a high-frequency electrical current to generate 11,000 degrees Fahrenheit. That in-tense heat creates a bond that cannot be broken. Only a skilled craftsman can fashion a weld that looks seamless and tidy.

The welds on Steelman bicycles were known to be exceptional. And Brent Steelman, the solitary builder at his company in Red-wood City, California, was known to be exceptionally selective. He preferred steel manufactured by Dedacciai, an Italian company re-vered by Tour de France riders. The stiffness of that steel imbues a properly built bike with a rigid yet responsive feel akin to a finely tuned Ferrari.

Working out of a cluttered garage in a suburban industrial park, Steelman built only fifty bicycles per year. He charged $2,500 just for the frame. Given the demand, he maintained a growing wait-list. If potential customers didn't strike his fancy, Steelman would decline them. This, of course, increased the cachet of owning a Steelman. As nearby Silicon Valley inflated with disposable in-come, Steelman bikes reached cult status.

In the summer of 2001, Tom joined a club cycling team run by

Higher Gear, a bike shop in Wilmette, not far from the LaSalle Bank in Highland Park, one of the nine suburban Chicago banks he had robbed at this point. Higher Gear's club riders all wore matching red, white, and blue spandex. One day, the bike shop's manager mentioned to Tom that a local rider was selling a used Steelman, a twelve-speed road bike built in 1996. Since Tom's bike had been stolen, he was looking for a replacement. The Steelman would be a welcome upgrade.

As soon as Tom saw the bike, he was torn. The Steelman was painted Day-Glo orange. But the construction was gorgeous. The bike was a tad larger than Tom normally rode. But he knew that a used Steelman didn't just magically appear every day. He bought it for $1,200.

Tom augmented the Steelman to cater to his own geometry. He swapped the seat post, situated the seat forward, and switched from 165 millimeter to 167.5 millimeter cranks. Despite the adjustments, the bike still seemed a touch big.

On group rides with the Higher Gear team, Tom was easy to spot atop his bright orange bicycle. Other riders consistently complimented the Steelman. It was, without question, the nicest bicycle Tom had ever owned. And not once did he ever ponder which was more amusing—a bike builder named Steelman or a bank robber named Justice.

"Dude, this is a bad idea," said Spider-Man. It was Halloween 2001 and Tom was walking with his friend Chris in Humboldt Park. Everyone on the street noticed the odd couple: Chris was wearing a homemade Spider-Man costume with bright red tights and a mask; Tom was a tuxedoed groom riding piggyback on a fake bride. As he walked, the dummy groom legs bounced cartoonishly from his waist.

"Man, what the fuck?" shouted a stocky thirty-year-old with a pick in his hair as Chris and Tom approached a street corner that had six people hanging around. "What are you supposed to be?"

"Uh, I'm Spider-Man, man," Chris replied, sheepishly pulling off his mask.

Guffaws rang out as a stout man wearing a Chicago Bulls hat and gold chain stepped forward. Shaking his head incredulously, he grinned.

Tom pulled out three $20 bills. By this point, he had stopped giving away the cash from his robberies. Tom exchanged the three crumpled bills for three small white rocks, each the size of half a sugar cube.

He and Chris walked away, heading into a dark alleyway, where they took swigs of whiskey. Tom pulled out a four-inch brass tube he'd purchased at Home Depot, stuffed one of the white rocks into it, lit the end, and took a deep drag from the makeshift pipe. The smell was wretched. Tom exhaled. For half a minute, he couldn't speak. His mind went blank. When he regained faint awareness, he smoked more crack.

Tom's descent into drug use had been steep. The previous Halloween, he'd tried cocaine for the first time. Then at a nightclub a few months later, he took some ecstasy. As he danced to thumping electronica, he felt a fantastic warmth surge over his body, like a down comforter that had been pulled from the dryer.

Tom began taking ecstasy every weekend. During the week, he was pursuing a master's in education at DePaul University. When Tom shared his grad school plans with his parents, they were optimistic. But they had no idea he was becoming dependent on drugs. On the weekends, Tom would swallow four pills of ecstasy, drink Red Bull and vodka for a few hours, then take another four pills. The sensation was magnificent. But as he increased dosages, Tom's post-high depression deepened. The only way he could shake the painful awareness that he was disappointing everyone who loved him was with more drugs.

"You look terrible," his mom would say at Sunday dinner. "You need to get some sleep."

Tom had no job, but he had pockets full of cash and cocaine. His friends assumed he was dealing. His sister certainly suspected as much. One afternoon, while Tom and Jennifer were at their parents' house, he asked her to go upstairs with him. There, in her childhood bedroom, Jennifer sat down on the bed and watched Tom shut the door behind him. Slowly he approached, holding his messenger bag. He turned it upside down, and three bundles of cash tumbled onto the floral bedspread.

"What's this?" Jennifer asked.

"I've been robbing banks," Tom replied.

Jennifer stared at the money.

"You want in?" Tom asked.

"Hell no!" she snapped.

"Well, I'm about to do another one tomorrow," he explained. "You could really help me."

"I can't," she said flatly. "And it's really shitty you asked me."

The next day, Tom pedaled away from the Northview Bank & Trust in Mundelein with $12,115, bringing his total at this point to $93,903 from twenty banks. Years later, he would admit to feeling ashamed about trying to recruit his sister. But at the time, Tom's addiction was fueling an increasingly destructive cycle of selfishness, entitlement, and loneliness.

To convince himself that he didn't have a *real* drug problem, Tom started attending Narcotics Anonymous meetings, joining a circle of admitted addicts sipping stale coffee on folding chairs in the basement of a hospital. When it was Tom's turn to share, he talked about merely experimenting with drugs. He was in denial.

"This is gonna be my last meeting," Tom announced to the group after just six weeks. He said he was moving back to California. He was planning to apply to grad school there. He wanted to become a teacher. Everybody in the room wished him luck—except one thirty-something with a weatherworn face. "Hey, man, just remember," the guy sighed, "wherever you go, there you are."

"Two-eleven in progress." The voice crackled through the radio in Officer Greg Thompson's squad car. Someone had just robbed the Union Bank near Main Street in Walnut Creek, California. It was March 7, 2002, and thick gray clouds were dropping intermittent rain on the quiet suburb east of Berkeley. The dispatcher described the suspect: a twenty-something white male—presumed armed—who was last seen fleeing on foot.

Thompson and his fellow officers were racing to set up a perimeter. The tactic rarely worked. Two intersecting freeways—Interstate 680 and Route 24—cross roughly a mile from downtown Walnut Creek, providing a quick getaway to thieves. Nevertheless, the forty-two-year-old Thompson wasn't one to break protocol.

Turning down an alley, he was passing a parking garage when a bicyclist shot out of the driveway. One second sooner, and the orange bike would've T-boned Thompson. Instead, the cyclist flew behind the cruiser. Thompson tapped his brakes and squinted into his side mirror. Dressed in red, white, and blue spandex, the cyclist looked like every other weekend warrior in Walnut Creek, except for one detail: the messenger bag draped over his shoulder.

Thompson sat for a moment. An eighteen-year police veteran, he didn't believe in mental telepathy. But as a field training officer, he taught new recruits to thrive on instinct. This was one of those moments. "If I don't stop that guy," he told himself, "I'm gonna wonder for the rest of my life."

But before he could flash his lights, the cyclist pulled over and hopped off his bike. When Thompson pulled up, the guy was fidgeting with his back wheel. It started to drizzle again.

"Can I talk to you for a second?" Thompson asked through the open window of his patrol car.

"Hey, yeah, sorry, it's gonna take me a second," Tom said, continuing to tinker.

Thompson parked a few feet ahead, turned on his flashing red and blue lights, and walked back to the cyclist.

"I live in San Ramon. I'm riding home," said Tom, pretending to adjust his brakes before climbing onto the bike and clicking his left foot into the pedal.

"Do you mind if I take a look in your bag?" Thompson asked the cyclist.

"Yeah, no problem. I just have to unclip," replied Tom. "These pedals are actually counterbalanced, so I need to click into both in order to get out at the same time."

There's no such thing as counterbalanced pedals. But Thompson didn't know that. He watched as the cyclist lifted his right foot, clicked down into the pedal, and—*whoosh!*—bolted into the street in a dead start as hellacious as any Tom had ever mustered on a velodrome.

"I knew it!" cried Thompson. He desperately grabbed his radio, but another officer was talking on the channel. The cyclist shot down Main Street and out of sight.

A few blocks away, Officer Sean Dexter was sitting in a squad car when he spotted a cyclist on an orange bike charging through traffic towards a red light. Dexter pulled into the intersection, but the cyclist didn't stop.

Tom swerved around the police car, crossed two lanes, and hopped the curb. Darting through a parking lot, he headed toward a tall fence bordering a dense thicket of fifteen-foot bamboo.

Dexter reached for his radio, but before he could even open his mouth, another cop hopped on the channel. "A guy on a bicycle just ran from me!" Thompson blurted.

Holy shit, Dexter thought, "I've got him right here!" he shouted into the radio.

Zigging through traffic, Dexter screeched into the parking lot. There was no sign of the cyclist.

Dexter got out of his car and paced toward the fence, drawing his Glock. He slowly cracked the gate and peered into the jumbled mess of vegetation. A creek flowed thirty feet below, amid fallen tree branches, dry brush, and piles of wet leaves. Following procedure, Dexter closed the gate and waited for backup.

Sirens blared as officers secured the perimeter. While Dexter and Thompson walked the upper banks, police dogs combed the creek. After about fifteen minutes, a detective spotted something in the leaves: an orange bicycle. Then a German shepherd from the K-9 unit led them to a pair of cycling shoes hidden under a concrete retaining wall beneath a bridge.

"He got out right here and went that way," the dog handler explained.

Dexter snorted in disbelief. If the suspect had crawled out of the creek, the police cordon would almost certainly have caught him. But as the sky grew bleaker and the air chillier, the search was called off. They had one good clue, though: the orange bicycle, which the police could tell wasn't some average Schwinn.

"This bike is special to somebody," Dexter said. "We gotta find out who."

The darkness was disconcerting. Tom was lying face-down in a cold, damp dirt tunnel. It was around 5 p.m. — six hours since he'd fled from the cops. With the sound of trickling water in the distance, Tom inched backward until his feet emerged just above the creek bed. He stood up, waist-deep in the frigid water, then looked and listened.

Nothing but the gentle noise of the creek.

Hours earlier, as the orange Steelman tumbled through the brush, Tom had slid down the embankment, crashing violently through the leaves. While Officer Dexter was awaiting backup, Tom trudged fifty feet upstream and took cover underneath a bridge, where he discovered a two-foot-wide hole at the water's edge. It looked as though a beaver had burrowed deep into the creek bank. Tom crawled in headfirst, thorny plants scratching his face and arms, and squirmed eleven feet to the narrow tunnel's end. Panting in the dark, he heard sirens, then faint voices and the jingling of a dog's tags. Tom assumed that was the end. But soon he accepted what seemed a miracle: the cops had given up the search.

It was dark outside when Tom emerged. He made his way to a high school parking lot and hid behind a dumpster there to change into the disguise he'd used during the robbery. With his messenger bag over his shoulder and his wallet to his ear, he walked down Main Street talking animatedly, pretending to be on the phone. Two miles away, Tom found his yellow 1983 Mercedes-Benz and drove to his apartment in Oakland.

"Is everything okay?" asked Tom's roommate, Marty.

"Yeah, just a rough couple of days," Tom replied, shutting his bedroom door.

Two months earlier, Tom had moved into Marty's two-bedroom apartment. Of all the respondents to Marty's Craigslist ad, Tom was easily the most appealing. He'd shown up to their first meeting wearing a blazer and collared shirt. Charmingly upbeat, Tom said he was a cyclist who'd once trained for the Olympics. He didn't have a job, but he offered to pay the first three months' rent up front, in cash.

Marty, a six-foot-five opera singer from Brooklyn, wasn't looking for a new friend, but he found one in Tom. During the week, Marty would cook dinner on his George Foreman grill and they'd watch movies on his sectional couch. On the weekends, they'd party at clubs. Marty knew Tom was snorting cocaine recreationally, but he was unaware of his other vices.

At night, Tom would drive his Mercedes near Oakland's empty shipyards. It was easy to find dealers. Tom would hand over $300 for twelve crack rocks. On the highway, he'd light his pipe and turn up the volume on melancholic electronica like Massive Attack's "Teardrop." He'd smoke crack for hours.

The drugs dulled his senses for days. He knew getting sloppy would get him caught. In early 2002, a pattern emerged: smoke crack, stay sober for one week, rob a bank, celebrate with more crack. After the botched robbery in Walnut Creek, Tom brooded in silence. He was anxious about the cops but also deeply disappointed in himself. A bank robber who gives away the money can

claim a certain nobility. Dillinger was branded a folk hero for re-
belling against the system. But Tom had devolved into a petty thief
stealing quick cash to cop drugs.

Days after his close call, he told his roommate he was leaving
Oakland forever.

"Tell me what's going on," said Marty.

"I really can't," Tom said.

"Tom, you can tell me *anything*."

"It's for your own good."

Soon after, Tom and all his earthly possessions were hurtling
east across Interstate 80. The landscape was a blur of snowcapped
peaks punctuated by occasional gas stations. Looking out across
the empty highway, Tom considered his future.

He wouldn't discover the extent of the forces conspiring against
him in Walnut Creek until many years later. But he knew one
thing: those cops were going to find the Steelman, which meant
that sooner or later, they'd trace it back to him. It was only a matter of time.

Officer Dexter was chasing leads. Normally in a bank case, it's the
police detectives, not uniformed officers, who help the FBI gather
evidence and interview witnesses. But in this case, after the suspect
had gotten away from him, Dexter made it his mission to follow up
on the best clue: the orange bicycle.

Contra Costa County, an 800-square-mile region that includes
Walnut Creek, had fifty to sixty bank robberies every year. Most
were perpetrated by small-timers with typical MOs. None had developed anywhere as ingenious a plan as the bicycle bandit. Which,
of course, made trying to ID him all the more alluring. "I'm gonna
find this dude," Dexter told Officer Thompson over coffee.

Although he didn't know anything about road or track bikes,
Dexter had a hunch that the orange twelve-speed was special.
The crime lab examined it for fingerprints but didn't identify any
matches. Dexter walked it from the station to a nearby bike shop.
A guy behind the counter said the frame was custom-made by a
man named Steelman in Redwood City, an hour's drive south.
Dexter called the company and spoke to Brent Steelman's wife,
who handled the bookkeeping. After digging through her records,
she told Dexter that the serial number he had might be for one of

two bikes: a blue one sold in California or possibly a 1996 orange one sold at a shop called Higher Gear in Chicago.

Dexter called Higher Gear, but the guy who answered said they didn't keep records that far back. There was no telling how many times that orange bike had changed hands. Dexter sent Steelman's wife a photo of the bike, along with a security camera shot of the suspect. She agreed to post a notice on the Steelman website and include the Walnut Creek Police Department's phone number.

A few days later, Dexter heard that a coach at the high school by the creek had seen something odd the night of the robbery. At 5:10 p.m., the coach was sitting in her car in the school parking lot talking on her cell phone when she saw a man rustling through the bushes by the bridge. He appeared to be wearing a wet suit. As he walked across the dimly lit parking lot, she noticed water squishing out of his sneakers. It was peculiar, but not peculiar enough to report—until she heard the news a day after the robbery.

Meanwhile, the FBI was doing its own investigating. Bob Schenke was one of two agents in the bureau's tiny satellite branch covering Contra Costa County. A matter-of-fact forty-something with a trim mustache and thinning hair, Schenke had been with the FBI since 1976. "Bank robbers are the stupidest people on the face of the earth," he liked to say. Once, Schenke busted a suspect who'd written his demand note on the back of his own deposit slip. Sooner or later, even the more sophisticated criminals trip up.

Before the Union Bank theft in Walnut Creek, Schenke had already tied a string of unsolved bank robberies to one suspect—what the FBI calls a "repeater." The crimes were committed in suburbs across Schenke's jurisdiction, including Lafayette and Concord. Schenke had gathered security cam images from each and noticed that the suspect had a habit of standing before the tellers with his hands pressed together. Soon after, the FBI nicknamed the unarmed suspect the Choirboy. Schenke noticed another pattern: each of the banks was near a train station. He had a theory that the unidentified man was using public transit to escape. He was just waiting for a new lead to break the case.

The orange Steelman was too good to be true. It had to be the Choirboy.

One month after the robbery, the manager of a bicycle shop in

Chicago called the Walnut Creek police. He'd seen the notice on Steelman's website. In 1996, he'd assembled the orange bike. He knew the original owner. He also knew the guy who'd bought the bike secondhand. It was a cyclist named Tom Justice.

The midmorning air in Tijuana was dry and dusty. It was April 2002, a month after the Walnut Creek robbery, and Tom was hoofing it along Constitución Avenue, a busy downtown street. The night before, he'd flown from Chicago to San Diego and strolled through the turnstiles into Mexico amid a throng of American spring breakers. Toting a backpack, Tom passed shops selling sombreros, ponchos, and decorative bottles of tequila. Drunk tourists posed for photos with donkeys painted like zebras. Tom kept sheepishly approaching bartenders with the same request: "*Necessito un passport illegal.*"

After his frenzied drive from California to Chicago, he'd decided to at least try covering his tracks. He phoned the original owner of the Steelman. "Uh, yeah, so your bike was stolen from me," Tom said cryptically. "Thought you should know." Then he called Higher Gear with the same story. His alibi was flimsy, and Tom knew it.

"*Necessito un passport illegal,*" Tom pleaded to a young man shining shoes on Constitución Avenue.

He nodded, and Tom followed him away from the tourist traps. When they finally arrived at a grimy motel, Tom was shown into a run-down room with a rickety bed and a TV. The shoe shiner requested $100. Tom handed him the cash, along with a picture he'd taken of himself in a photo booth in Chicago.

After the shoe shiner departed, Tom collapsed on the bed, anxiously chain-smoking cigarettes and flipping channels. Three hours later, the shoe shiner returned to say Tom's passport would be ready soon. Three more hours passed. The shoe shiner came back with a warm plate of carne asada but no passport. As Tom ate, the shoe shiner asked if he was interested in earning $500. The arrangement was simple: drive a car across the border with a little marijuana concealed in the gas tank.

Years later, Tom would learn this was likely a setup: as soon as he got in the vehicle, the cartel would've called the cops on him, and in exchange for having been provided someone to arrest, the cops would ignore the next several cartel trucks crossing the border.

In the moment, Tom declined the offer because he didn't need $500, let alone more trouble. What he needed was a fake ID. But the shoe shiner said it would be $100 more for the passport. As incensed as Tom was, he didn't see another option. He coughed up the cash, then lay back down on the bed. Strange noises were emanating from the bathroom window. It was a spooky cacophony of catcalls and whistles. Cartel lookouts were signaling that the streets were clear of cops and witnesses.

Turning over in bed the next morning, Tom accepted that he'd been conned. He was putting on his backpack when the shoe shiner returned—without a passport. "I'm outta here," Tom barked. The shoe shiner caught up to Tom in front of the motel and whistled loudly. A catcall echoed from a rooftop above.

"You don't know what you're doing," insisted the shoe shiner, pulling a knife. The five-inch blade wasn't far from Tom's stomach.

Panicked, Tom glanced down the street. A green taxi was bounding toward them. Tom flailed his hands wildly. Brakes screeched, and Tom bolted. "The border, *por favor!*" Tom said, leaping into the cab.

Tom crossed back into the U.S. in a pack of overweight retirees. Exhaling deeply, he knew he couldn't be alone, not now. He needed to be somewhere safe with someone he could trust. One person came to mind: Marty.

A few hours later, Tom flew from San Diego to Oakland. At an airport pay phone, he called his old roommate. Marty was at a cocktail party in San Francisco and invited Tom to join him. When Tom walked in, the guests gawked. Tom's collared shirt, blazer, and slacks were filthy. He looked like he hadn't slept in days.

Marty gave Tom a bear hug and suggested they leave. In the car, Tom reluctantly told him everything. Marty didn't believe him. It seemed more likely that his preppy friend was delusional. Maybe Tom had never trained for the Olympics. Maybe he'd embellished his racing. But as Marty listened, it all came together: The quixotic desire to feel extraordinary. The secret life. The drug addiction. "What are you gonna do?" Marty asked.

Tom said he wanted to see his parents before the cops found him. Marty wondered how Tom could be so sure he would be arrested. At his apartment, Marty opened his laptop and scrolled through an online forum for cyclists. Tom looked over his shoulder. There it was: a picture of the orange Steelman along with a security cam image of a guy in a baseball cap standing at a bank teller's window pressing his palms together.

"I need to buy a ticket home," Tom said.

Pat Carey was leaving work at 5 p.m. when the phone rang. It was a special agent with the FBI's field office in Chicago. There was a warrant out for a man whose parents lived in Libertyville—right next door to Carey.

"The Justices?" asked the police chief, stunned.

The agent explained that the FBI had been searching for Thomas L. Justice in and around Chicago for two weeks. His last known address in Illinois was the Ravenswood apartment he'd shared with his girlfriend two years earlier. The police had also tried staking out his old apartment in Berkeley, but he was long gone. The agent wondered whether Carey had seen Tom lately —and also, did he happen to know what type of car he drove?

Carey hadn't seen him in at least six months, but he seemed to remember Jay Justice's son drove an old Mercedes-Benz.

"That's the car we're looking for," the agent said. Then, before hanging up, he gave the police chief a heads-up: FBI agents would be traveling to Libertyville the next day to question Mr. Justice.

Carey headed to his car. His drive home took less than ten minutes. When he rolled up, he was astounded. There, parked in the Justices' driveway, was the yellow Mercedes.

As Carey scrambled for his phone, Tom and Jay sat in their kitchen finishing up dinner. The television was on, tuned to CNN. Tom's mom had cooked beef and green peppers. Now she was puttering around, packing up the leftovers for Tom.

"So how's that job of yours?" Jay asked his son.

It'd been a week since Tom's trip to Tijuana—not that his parents were aware he'd left town. As far as they knew, he was working as a bike messenger. It didn't sound like much of a career path.

"What's your plan for the future?" asked Jay, still watching TV.

"I'm gonna apply to some new grad school programs," Tom replied.

Jay nodded. *Sounds familiar.*

Tom grabbed his food and headed out the door. "See you guys later," he called, and climbed into his car.

When the first police car appeared behind him on Butterfield Road, Tom didn't think much of it. Then there were three more. After leading the procession for a mile, Tom glanced in his rear-view mirror again. Red lights were now flashing. He pulled over and reached for his wallet. As he leaned toward the glove box to grab his registration, a voice boomed through a bullhorn: "*Freeze! Let me see your fucking hands!*" Slowly, Tom glanced back. Five cops were aiming their guns at him.

"What is this about, Officers?" Tom asked, getting down on the ground. As the handcuffs tightened around his wrists, he felt a rush of emotion. He wanted to cry—not out of despair or fear but out of a much heavier sense of something he wasn't expecting: relief. After four years, his self-destructive cross-country loop was finally coming to an end. Ever since he'd traveled to Colorado for the Olympic training camp, Tom kept thinking that his life should be momentous enough to carry him far away from Libertyville. In between his escapades to France and Mexico, he'd robbed twenty-six banks in sixteen cities across three U.S. states. Now he was ly-ing face-down on the pavement back home, his hands bound be-hind him.

In the interrogation room, an FBI agent placed a photograph on the table. It was the security cam shot of the Choirboy. The or-ange Steelman had led them right to Tom. Had he been riding an average bicycle, Tom might never have been caught.

The agent encouraged Tom to cooperate. Tom gave a full con-fession.

Soon he was fingerprinted, photographed, strip-searched, handed an orange jumpsuit, and booked at the Loop's Metropoli-tan Correctional Center, where his parents came to see him before his hearing. In a cramped visiting room that smelled like sweat and microwave popcorn, Jay Justice asked his son the one question everyone is still asking seventeen years later: "Why?"

"I don't know," Tom replied. "It's just something I did."

Tom's parents hired him a lawyer, who rolled his eyes when Tom said he'd already confessed. He was facing a sentence of up to 120 years. But, as his lawyer pointed out to the prosecutor, Tom never carried a weapon, and he cooperated upon his arrest. Tom's confession helped the FBI sew together all twenty-six heists, including several that weren't even in the Choirboy file.

In the end, Tom pleaded guilty and was sentenced to eleven years.

In federal prison, he would spend hours walking the yard in circles, thinking back on his life, trying to make sense of everything. His four-year spree hadn't netted extraordinary money— $129,338. But Tom's MO was so unusual that, years later, even Officer Dexter back in Walnut Creek still felt an affinity for the bicycle bandit. "I have a certain respect for a smart crook," he says. "The whole changing clothes thing—his MO was *so* good."

After being released in 2011, Tom returned to cycling at the velodrome in Northbrook, where he still loves careening around the corners. He considered applying to grad school but eventually found a job at a doughnut shop. Little do the cops know that the forty-eight-year-old handing them their chocolate glazed is one of the most prodigious bank robbers in American history.

The notion that he wasn't some run-of-the-mill thief offers Tom a certain measure of satisfaction. His former roommate Marty interprets Tom's full confession not as an acquiescence to justice but as a statement of purpose: "'I'm not just a bank robber—I'm a *great* bank robber.' Even in that, he couldn't be ordinary."

The day of his arrest, Tom sat handcuffed in the back seat of the FBI car en route from Libertyville to Chicago.

"Man, what'd you do with all the money?" wondered one of the agents.

Staring out the window, Tom thought for a moment before replying.

"Nothing."

CHRIS BALLARD

Fumbled Recovery

FROM SPORTS ILLUSTRATED

I. The VP

ON THE MORNING of July 2, Eric Spofford awoke early, pulled on the gray suit he had bought the day before, and left for work by six. He wanted to be on site when the Secret Service arrived.

At thirty-four, with a buzz cut and thick, tattooed arms, Spofford is sometimes mistaken for a client of Granite Recovery Centers, the addiction treatment facilities he runs throughout New Hampshire. Growing up blue-collar in Salem, a town of nearly 30,000 just over the border from Massachusetts, Spofford started using Oxy at fourteen. By sixteen he was dealing heroin. By eighteen he'd have been dead if not for Narcan, the overdose-reversal drug. After getting clean in 2006, he started a sober living house, and in the decade that followed, as fentanyl poured onto the streets of New Hampshire, claiming close to 500 Granite Staters' lives annually, Spofford became an authority on the opioid crisis. He once testified before a U.S. Senate committee.

Even so, he was initially confused when a woman called in June, saying she was from the Vice President's office. "Vice president of what?" Spofford asked. She explained that it was *that* Vice President, and Mr. Pence wanted to highlight the opioid issue and was interested in doing that at one of Granite's facilities.

Now, ten days later, it was the morning of Pence's visit. Air Force Two was scheduled to land around noon, carrying the Vice President and the Surgeon General. Pence would meet at the facility with former patients, deliver remarks on opioids, and then head

back to the plane. An advance team had spent the better part of
a week securing the facility. A perimeter of dump trucks encircled
the empty parking lot as a barricade. An enormous white tent sat
atop Granite's rear loading dock, providing cover for Pence's fleet.
Employees working the event had submitted their dates of birth,
addresses, social security numbers, and driver's license numbers
for background checks.

Spofford had worked sixteen-hour days to prepare. Now, he had
his best people on site, including his mentor, Piers Kaniuka, and
his good friend and Granite's chief business development officer,
Jeff Hatch, who sat out front in slacks and a 3XL polo shirt, checking in visitors. At six-foot-six and 300 pounds, Hatch stood out in
any crowd. The thirty-nine-year-old, who was a third-round pick of
the Giants' in 2002, had his own comeback story: a first-team Division I-AA All-American Ivy League offensive tackle and a four-year
NFL vet, he got hooked on painkillers, got clean in treatment, and
joined the staff of a recovery center in Louisiana. Brawny and char-
ismatic, he appeared in documentaries—even acted in Hollywood
for a few years—then became an advocate, writing articles, speaking to students, and appearing with U.S. Senator Jeanne Shaheen
(D-NH) to promote a bill to fund awareness of opioids' danger to
athletes. If you were looking to put someone in front of cameras,
Hatch was a natural choice.

By eleven, the conference room had filled with 250 business
figures, media members, past clients, and politicians. Spofford
waited, anxious and excited. Then, a little before noon, a White
House staffer motioned him to the back. "There's been a situation," the man said. Pence's plane never took off. It wasn't going
to. "We're going to walk out on stage," Spofford recalls the man
telling him, "you're going to thank everybody for coming, introduce me, and I'm going to shut this thing down." And so he did.

Guests and staff speculated. A security threat? Russia? North Korea? A day later, the mystery deepened. "There was a very interesting problem that they had in New Hampshire," President Trump
told reporters. "I won't go into what the problem was, but you'll
see in about a week or two."

Spofford alternated between concern—*was it something they'd
done?*—and disappointment. Eventually, though, he moved on.
Until, that is, three weeks later, when, on the morning of July 22, a
distraught Hatch motioned him into his office.

At this point the two men had known each other for a decade. They had vacationed together, celebrated each other's sobriety at AA meetings, and spent long nights playing Ping-Pong and drinking Diet Coke. Spofford felt that he knew Hatch, or at least as well as anyone did.

"We have to talk some real s—," Hatch said. And then he began telling a crazy story—about drugs and cops and federal agents and a secret he'd kept for two years. When Hatch finished, Spofford hugged him and told him to go home. A couple of hours later, Spofford called his friend and fired him.

II. The Lineman

Hope Hatch's son stood out from the start. Jeff came into the world big in 1979, at eight pounds, six ounces, and twenty-four inches. By kindergarten he towered over his classmates, and a youth basketball coach was recruiting him.

The height came from Hope. She was six feet; she had played center for a small women's college. Jeff's brawn came from his dad Paul, a onetime linebacker at Rensselaer Polytechnic Institute. High school sweethearts in North Scituate, Rhode Island, each had served during Vietnam—Paul in the Army, Hope as a nurse at Walter Reed. They settled in the upper-middle-class suburbs north of Annapolis, Maryland, where Paul got a good job in computer science.

As the Hatches tell it, theirs was a 1980s idyll of American life: Saturday-night pizza parties, church and Redskins games on Sundays. Jen, their elder child, rode horses. Jeff was a Boy Scout, artist, and athlete, though not in that order. His friends included Mark Teixeira, the future Yankees first baseman, and Gavin Floyd, who would pitch for the White Sox. Every sport Jeff tried came easy. Tall, springy, and long-limbed, he excelled at tennis and swimming. Basketball was his first love, though. By his sophomore year, he was six-four and dunking.

That summer he transferred to Severn, a nearby private school with a strong sports program. The football coach, John Beckman, soon sought him out. Jeff said he'd consider playing, but only if his mom signed off.

Hope had a no-football policy. She knew the dangers of the game all too well. Paul had hurt his back at RPI, ending his playing days. The injury lingered and, by his late thirties he suffered numbness in his feet, requiring spinal-fusion surgery. He never fully recovered. (By forty-two he could no longer work. A lifetime of disability, prescription painkillers, and bouts of depression followed, but Paul remained active in family life. “He will always be my hero,” Jeff would later say.)

Beckman proved persistent, though, and Hope relented. Jeff took to the game immediately. Few defensive linemen are big, strong, and fast, but Hatch was all three, and he played with fire and joy. He was a sharp student too, with A’s and B’s, and a spot on the debate team. Colleges called. Good ones: Army, Navy, Brown. He chose Penn.

Doors opened, and not just in football. Jeff had started drinking as a high school freshman, invited to varsity parties. The alcohol filled a hole inside him, he’d later say in speeches. He’d been sensitive and awkward at times as a boy, despite his gregarious nature, and downing beers cured his feeling of not belonging. Now, away from home at Penn, he let loose: booze, weed, blackouts, moments of violence. Soon enough, he was selling a one-pound brick of weed out of his refrigerator.

Not that it affected his play. After switching to offensive tackle before his junior year, Hatch became a starter and an immediate force. In 2001, his senior year, Penn made the Top 25 and Hatch received an invite to the Blue-Gray Game, a predraft showcase, where he caught the eye of scouts. The *Baltimore Sun* described him as “a fist-pumping, headline-craving, limelight-loving offensive tackle from the usually staid Ivy League.” Hatch signed with an agent, Alan Herman.

Life spread out before him. He was a soon-to-be Penn grad with a degree in political science, philosophy, and economics. He was, he later told audiences, dating a former Miss Maryland. If his back ached at times, he assumed that was just par for the course. Besides, the media loved him. On draft night in 2002, an ESPN camera crew descended on the Hatch home, filming him for a special called *Hey Rookie, Welcome to the NFL.* With the seventy-eighth pick, two rounds after taking tight end Jeremy Shockey, New York selected Hatch. He joined a team of big personalities: Shockey, Michael Strahan, David Diehl, Tiki Barber. “The one thing I like about him is he’s mean,” Marv Sunderland, the Giants’ director of player personnel, told the *New York Post.*

On Herman's advice, Hatch refused to sign an injury waiver and sat out the first day of rookie minicamp. Only after general manager Ernie Accorsi guaranteed Hatch financial protection in the event of injury did he return, eventually signing a three-year, $1.4 million deal that included a $500,000 signing bonus.

Two weeks later, on the second day of training camp, Hatch left the field with what the team called back spasms. Two weeks later, the Giants announced he had a herniated disc and needed surgery. He would miss the entire season.

And that, he'd later say, is when the addiction began, at least in earnest. During recovery, his doctors gave him Percocet, or maybe Vicodin; Hatch couldn't later recall which. The pills took away the pain, quieted both his body and his mind. Soon enough, Hatch found a guy in a strip mall in New Jersey who could get him more. Other times, he doctor-shopped, trading Giants tickets for pills.

Returning in 2003, Hatch struggled to regain his form. The athleticism that had always defined him—"the big guy who moved like a small guy," as New York offensive line coach Jim McNally recalls—no longer existed. He spent much of the season inactive or on the bench. Finally, with the team ravaged by injuries, he started the final four games at right tackle.

They would be the only games of his NFL career. In March 2004, the Giants released him, "admitting to an embarrassing mistake," as the *Post* put it, calling him "the player yelled at more often than any other" by former coach Jim Fassel. Hatch latched on briefly with the Rams, then the Buccaneers.

Meanwhile, his back worsened. An NFL-affiliated doctor told him he needed spinal fusion, the same surgery that had debilitated his father. So in November 2005, Hatch underwent the procedure. That led to more pills. Alone, he lived in a rented apartment in Tampa, surviving on a cocktail of Soma, Xanax, and Oxy. In time his body rebelled. He suffered grand mal seizures from the benzodiazepenes.

Finally, after a call from Jeff, Paul and Hope flew down for a visit, and found their son in bad shape, having taken too many pills. They drove him to the ER and then flew with him to Louisiana, where, on February 6, 2006, at the urging of Martha Brown, another NFL-appointed doctor, Hatch entered Palmetto Addiction Recovery Center, in rural Rayville, where Brett Favre had previously sought treatment for his painkiller addiction. (Legend

has it that Favre rebuilt the gym while there.) In Hatch's case, he
agreed to detox for 14 days. Instead, he stayed for 104.

During that time Jeff made an impression, as he often did, for
he had a rare ability to empathize with strangers. Within nine
months of sobering up, he took a job at Palmetto as a marketing
rep, an uncommonly quick transition, shaking hands at conferences and meeting with therapists. It was then, at a 2010 industry
event, that he first met Spofford. The two hit it off and kept in
touch, but it would be years before they'd team up.

First, Hatch pursued an acting career. He moved to Venice,
California, and took classes in the Meisner technique at the Play-
house West. He appeared in commercials, on a show called *I'm
in the Band,* and as a stuntman in the comedy flop *R.I.P.D.* He
also costarred in *Brutal,* a low-budget MMA movie. More nuanced
roles, though, eluded him. He fell back on the stunt work, but old
injuries flared, in particular the meniscus he had torn in his right
knee years earlier. He became disillusioned, flaky. "It was obvious
he had some personal problems to deal with," recalls his movie
agent, Shawn Brogan, who says she generally liked Hatch. "We
can't represent talent that doesn't show up for auditions."

Out of money and in pain, he drove his Chrysler back home to
Maryland in 2013 to get knee-replacement surgery. When Spofford heard his friend's intention, he worried. Recovering addicts
fear surgery; one hit of an opioid in the hospital can lead to a
backslide. But Hatch assured Spofford he had a plan. He'd keep
the drugs in a safe at his parents' house, then flush them once he
no longer needed them.

As far as Spofford knew, that was what Hatch did. In the months
that followed, the two stayed in touch while Hatch recovered at his
parents' house for six months. Finally, Spofford called with an offer.
"Enough chasing this acting s—, man. We're getting old. Come work
with me." So Hatch moved to a crappy apartment in New Hampshire and, by 2015, took a job in marketing at Granite for $35,000.

At the time, the country was waking up to the severity of the
opioid crisis. The aggressive marketing and rampant overprescrip-
tion of drugs like Purdue Pharma's OxyContin had created addicts
from all walks of life: middle-class kids, moms, athletes like Jeff
Hatch. A 2018 study indicated that 26.2 percent of retired NFL
players who had used prescription opioids while playing were still
using them and that nearly half of that group was using the pills

without a prescription or not as prescribed. And in New Hampshire, where the death toll skyrocketed, it seemed as if everyone knew someone touched by the epidemic.

As Granite grew, expanding from its original facility, so did Hatch's profile. He spoke at health-care facilities, to students and athletes, and he wrote an essay for Yahoo Sports, questioning the NFL's approach to painkillers. In May 2017, he appeared with Shaheen at Portsmouth High School. "I remember getting that bottle of pills, and on that bottle it said you take one to two every four to six hours as needed for pain," he said. "And I . . . realized [if] that amount would cure my physical pain, a few more would kill the emotional pain."

Meanwhile, he and Spofford grew closer, cohosting a podcast and traveling together with their girlfriends. If Spofford noticed warning signs—like how he never met anyone else in Hatch's orbit or that Jeff seemed to disappear on nights and weekends—he'd laugh it off and joke that Jeff had a secret life. At work, the two proved complementary: Spofford was a grinder, while Hatch fed off human interaction. In 2018, Spofford elevated Hatch to chief business development officer.

And now, in July of 2019, here was Hatch, telling Spofford he had pleaded guilty to a drug crime. That he'd relapsed. Not a week or a month before but five years earlier. And that, as a result, he was in a lot of trouble. Trouble that was about to become public.

Politico had it first.

Vice President Mike Pence was one short plane ride away from shaking hands with an alleged interstate drug dealer, the story began . . . *If Pence stepped off the vice presidential aircraft, one of the people he would have seen on the ground was under investigation by the Drug Enforcement Administration for moving more than $100,000 of fentanyl from Massachusetts to New Hampshire.*

Court documents, which, along with the events they described, had been secret because Hatch was a cooperating witness, detailed the alleged chronology: How, on July 25, 2017, local, state, and federal agencies investigating a fentanyl supplier in Manchester, New Hampshire, had learned that Hatch had made a call to arrange a drug pickup in Lawrence, Massachusetts, and Hatch, by driving the drugs the twenty-plus miles back to his house, had crossed state lines and committed a federal crime, and how, after two years of silence, Hatch had then pleaded guilty the previous Friday in federal court to one count of using a communication device to facilitate the distribution of a controlled substance (fentanyl) and now faced up to four years in federal prison and a $250,000 fine.

Within hours, politicians rushed to condemn Hatch's duplicity. "Morally abhorrent," said New Hampshire Governor Chris Sununu. "If these reports are true, his cooperation in this investigation better have been sufficient enough to justify such a lenient plea agreement." Shaheen urged the court to "throw the book" at Hatch: "Granite Staters seeking recovery from substance-use disorders put their trust in Mr. Hatch, and it's incredibly disappointing to see how badly that trust was betrayed."

Reporters descended. CNN, NBC, the *Washington Post, People.* Hatch went silent. Spofford released an initial statement, then laid low, preferring to call employees and business associates to explain. Many had jumped to conclusions: that Granite was selling dope to the clients, then treating them. *Getting it on both ends.* That Spofford was in on it. All wondered the same two things: *Did Spofford know? And, if not, how could he have missed it?*

Spofford eventually granted a short interview to *Behavioral Healthcare Executive,* saying that he was "shocked" and "mortified" but that the treatment industry is a "business of redemption" and that Hatch had "had a relapse and made some really dumb decisions." As for Hatch, he spoke a week later, back in court. "The events around my relapse came to a head in 2017, and I have been sober since then," he said. "At that time, I was told by law enforcement I could not speak about this to anyone in my life. Not a single person in my personal or professional life knew about my relapse until several weeks ago. My employer, my family, those who are close to me knew nothing of this. I will have much more to say when I am able." After that, both men went quiet.

III. The Fallout

Three weeks after Hatch appeared in court, Spofford and I are driving north from the Salem area to the Green Mountain Treatment Center in Effingham.

Outside, the forest streams by. The farther north you get, the more rural New Hampshire becomes. The state's small, isolated communities make it a target for the drug trade. In the 2000s, it was crystal meth and heroin. Then, by the 2010s, it was fentanyl, a synthetic opioid produced in Mexico and China and brought into Massachusetts via the U.S. Mail. Since it's cheaper and more easily manufactured than heroin, street dealers began using fentanyl to cut their product or, sometimes, replace it outright. It's not an exact science, though. Mix a batch and divide it up into small baggies, and the ratio in any given dose could vary widely. Take in too much fentanyl, which is fifty times stronger than heroin, and you can die. According to the DEA, as little as two milligrams, the size of a few grains of salt, is lethal for most people.

Initially, state politicians deemed it primarily a criminal issue, but that only pushed the problem down the line. Addicts got clean through forced abstinence but then, without treatment, were dumped back onto the streets, only now with a lower tolerance. Jails filled; fatalities increased. Finally, in recent years, a movement has taken root nationally, embraced by progressive police, judges, and doctors. The approach: treatment, often medically assisted, therapy, and transitional housing, not incarceration. This is where facilities like Granite come in.

With tragedy has come opportunity. More than $35 billion is spent each year on addiction treatment domestically. Residential rehabs often charge private insurers more than $50,000 per month of treatment. Much of the industry is frighteningly unregulated. "Patient brokering"—in which rehabs give kickbacks to third parties for new clients—is rampant, as are conflicts of interest. Evidence-based care can be difficult to find.

Granite aims to stand out in the field, and Green Mountain is its flagship center. We arrive after driving up a hill past apple orchards. It's a bucolic setting; from the main building, you can see Mount Washington and Ossipee Lake.

The morning goal-setting groups are just beginning. In a bright room, three dozen men sit on chairs in a circle, sharing affirmations. Other than a few visible sores, what is striking is how unremarkable they are. They could be anyone: the dad at the soccer game, a coworker, the kids at the Twenty-One Pilots concert, the guys at your gym. At one point the session leader—a recovering addict himself—asks how many of the men are parents and having a hard time dealing with missing their kids. Almost all raise a hand.

Some have been here before. For others, it is part of the conditions of their release. Some were dropped off. Many had trigger
moments. "I don't remember the Fourth of July week," one older
man says. Humility is a running theme. Spofford talks to clients,
sharing tips. These, he says, are his people.

Spofford wishes people could see what he sees. He says this crisis
isn't about addiction but something larger: a culture of isolation
and a country where prescription meds are doled out in place of
empathy; where a company like Purdue, which will declare bank-
ruptcy within a month, has only recently been held accountable
for decades of damage. The effects ripple out. He pointed at one
of the women, walking into the cafeteria for lunch. "Right now,
while she's in here, there's a dad somewhere holding s— together.
Working his job. His kids don't know where their mom is or what
she's doing or that she's addicted to Percocet."

That afternoon, on the drive back, we talk about Hatch. Spofford says he remains stumped. He knows all the tells: raspy voice,
"pinned" pupils, incessant scratching, a personality shift, "a
jammed-out kind of junkie look." He says, "Not once did I look at
him and go, 'Is he okay? Is he on drugs? Is he f— up?'"

Spofford was there, earlier in the year, with sixty or seventy people, when Hatch got his thirteen-year medallion at AA. Spofford
thinks back, where he was at each point over the last few years.
Theoretically, he should understand addiction and relapse better
than anyone. And still, he says, "it's really, really chilling."

By now, he has pieced together a timeline. Best Spofford can
figure, Hatch used prescription meds on and off from 2014 until
a worse relapse in the summer of '17. He thinks Jeff met a woman
who introduced him to straight fentanyl and heroin, and then he
got mixed up with her dealer. Here, Hatch compounded his mistakes. "I used heroin in Lawrence, I knew the drug dealers," Spofford says. "I was involved, prior to finding recovery, in street life.
What came with that was street smarts. And Jeff does not really
have that. Jeff is a UPenn graduate that played in the NFL. He's
never been in the hood a day in his life. Never had to."

"He goes down and he picks up the dope and the dealer gives
him some for going." Spofford says, grimacing. "With all the respect in the world: *How f—— dumb can you be?*" After all, relapse is
one thing; trafficking is another. "I have to make the assumption

that he didn't really understand in that moment that the crime would carry a twenty-year sentence if he got arrested."

Spofford can only speculate, though. Spofford says he has spoken to Hatch "three or four times" since his firing. Amends have not been made. "I don't wish bad things for him," Spofford says. But he says, "Three and a half weeks ago, I thought he was my best friend and had thirteen years of sobriety, and was an upstanding citizen. So what do I know?"

IV. The Accused

It's nine the following morning, outside a two-story house on a leafy block in Manchester. A first knock goes unanswered. Same for the doorbell.

Finally, the sound of locks clunking open, followed by a face in the doorway. Jeff Hatch peers out. Behind him, the lights are off. He is wearing a black T-shirt, gym shorts, and no shoes. He is huge but fit. His black hair is shorn close to the scalp. He looks like a bouncer getting ready for yoga class. He scans the street. "Next time use the back door," he says. "We have an alarm."

He leads the way to the living room, trailed by a five-month-old Great Dane and a three-year-old pointer-lab mix. The mix belongs to his girlfriend, Lauren Grout, whom he met in recovery meetings and began dating in 2017; the Great Dane they bought together when they moved into this rental together late last year. His world is circumscribed these days, he explains, by the conditions of his plea. He says he submits to regular drug tests and meets with a rehab counselor, and without a car, he relies on Grout for rides.

At first, he is nervous. Sips water frequently. Rubs his head, displaying the William Blake cursive tattoo on his arm. He says he knows the deal with our interview, to which he had agreed the night before. "I don't expect you to tell anything but the truth and really, honestly, man, I don't want anything but the truth out there."

We start at the beginning: childhood, the first time he got stoned, as a high school sophomore, when his father invited the cops over for a "roundtable." Hatch relaxes. He leans forward and cracks jokes. Aware of how his appearance strikes others, he calls himself "an ogre" and "a mongoloid." When he agrees, he yells

"Amen!" Or "Dude, I get it." More than once, he says, "Look, let's get real." It's easy to see why he was good at his job. It's also easy to see how he could deceive people.

Take the back injury with the Giants. When pressed, he says he kept it from the team. That's why he sat out that day of rookie camp, lest he get injured. But maybe, I posit, he saw it as just doing the smart thing? "I f—— hated that, dude. You know, whether it's the smart thing or not, it wasn't the right thing. It wasn't honest."

As for what's happened the last two years, he wishes he could say more. Already, Hatch says, his lawyer and probation officer think this interview is a terrible idea.

Here's what he can say on the record. First, the relapse. It began with the knee surgery. He flushed the pills. But he says he also began using prescribed timed-release fentanyl patches, which he applied every seventy-two hours. Only he didn't stop when he was supposed to. And he didn't talk about it with anyone. Instead, he drove back monthly to Maryland to refill the prescription. But he was able to conceal his relapse. As Granite's "road guy," he rarely came to the office. And he was judicious: "I was never spending my whole day under the influence."

But by 2016 and '17, he says, he got in over his head. That's when he says he crossed certain lines—from pills to heroin, from using drugs to moving them. Each incremental step led to another, and he rationalized them as he went along. A courier was the lowest rung of the delivery system, Hatch told himself. He realizes now how this all sounds. "Dude, I f—— up, huge, man, there's no question." He can't explain his decisions. "It's not rational thought," he says. Rather, in the midst of a relapse, "I'm just thinking about staying supplied with what I need to be okay inside and . . . that always leads me to make decisions against my internal compass." It is, he says, the kind of messed-up nonlogic only addicts can understand.

In July 2017 authorities arrested a dealer above him in the food chain. "That was an opportunity for me to break away from the whole thing. And I took advantage of that." It didn't work. And so, at some point after that—he must be vague, he says—he became part of the operation, sworn to silence.

Scared straight, he got clean that fall and hasn't used since, he says. He met Lauren; they settled down together. All the while, he says, he lived in fear of the other shoe dropping. "I did not think I was pulling the wool over people's eyes, and I was not walking

around proud of what was happening. It was torture. It was f——
hell every day. And I just couldn't wait until the day I could be
honest about the relapse."

Why did he stay at Granite knowing what was coming? "They
told me not to change anything." Instead, he says, he was told to
"keep living your life as you're living it." Why didn't he call in sick
on the day of the Pence visit? "I wanted to stay as far away as possible but got pulled in. They needed me."

The rest of the story will come out eventually, he says. "It doesn't
make me look better, but it puts context on the whole thing," he
says. "I know what I did isn't right, but I'm not evil." In life, he says,
"We're all shades of gray."

A little after noon, his probation officer calls. I leave by the back
door.

V. The Reckoning

In *Dreamland: The True Tale of America's Opiate Epidemic*, Sam Quinones describes the power of opium, the root of all opioids. "Like
a lover," Quinones writes, "no other molecule in nature provided
such merciful pain relief, then hooked humans so completely, and
punished them so mercilessly for wanting their freedom from it."
Quinones then describes morphine's cruel nature—how it creates ever-higher tolerance, then fights like hell to stay in the body.
Whereas we turn most drugs into water-soluble glucose, which we
can then expel, "Alone in nature, the morphine molecule rebelled.
It resisted being turned into glucose and stayed in the body."

In the recovery world, a term exists for the addict's mindset
under the drugs' spell: insane thinking. I heard it again and again
during two days at Granite's facilities. From the mom who talked
with shame about wondering how fast she could drop off her kids
to score. From the schoolteacher who described telling herself
one thing every morning and doing the opposite every night. And
from Spofford, who told of stealing tools from his father—the
man who taught him responsibility—so he could pawn them for
heroin. When he finally tied off, Spofford said, he was crying.

Insane thinking is familiar to recovering addicts. It's also hard to
hide. Piers Kaniuka used for twenty years before he got sober, got
master's degrees in theological studies and counseling psychology,

and began helping others. As a counselor, he was the one who first got Spofford to buy in, when he was nineteen. Today, Kaniuka holds the title of spiritual director at Granite.

In Kaniuka's experience, "the celebrity athlete recovery, it never has much depth. It's always pretty shiny. Pretty Tony Robbinsish." What surprised him about Hatch's relapse was his ability to conceal it. He says, "The thing you have to understand: when I use, I lose all logic. If you could turn using on and off, we wouldn't be addicts." Then again, Kaniuka says, "He was an actor, after all."

In the weeks after my visit I reach out to dozens of people who knew Hatch. Some speak only on background. Others are unaware of what happened. Says Donald Flaherty, the director of *Brutal,* "Tell him he still has friends out here. We all screw up." Herman, his former NFL agent, says he "couldn't foretell anything that he'd get into this kind of trouble."

Many, though, decline to talk or never respond. His best friend through high school and college, presumably someone who knew him as well as anyone, declines multiple times. Al Bagnoli, his coach at Penn, sends regrets. Beckman, the high school coach, doesn't respond. Sarah Stuart, his boss in marketing at Granite, agrees and then, on the morning of the scheduled interview, begs off, texting, "I clearly know nothing about Jeff . . . his is his story to tell." A Palmetto employee whom Hatch recalls fondly says she doesn't remember him.

His family and girlfriend all say they support him. Lauren, who had her own issues with drugs and alcohol before she got clean and started working at a women's shelter, says she was drawn to Jeff when she met him because he wasn't fake, like a lot of people she meets in the recovery world.

She found out the same morning Spofford did. She says she never wavered. For one, it's not unusual in her world. ("The majority of my friends are felons," she says.) Second, the Jeff she knew was the one who'd been clean; her friends and family loved him. She's stuck by him. As for the future, she says she doesn't dwell on that. "It's about today."

Hope asks you to put yourself in her shoes. By all accounts, she and Paul raised their family with love and support. They are wonderful kids, Hope says. (Jen married a policeman and home-schools their five children on a farm in Virginia. Devout, she runs a horse ministry called Risen Ridge. In a phone interview, Jen says she can't understand what drove Jeff to do what he did but that he is, at heart, a good person.)

Paul and Hope are both sixty-nine and in poor health. She has something called orthostatic hypotension. If she stands up too quickly, she can pass out. On the morning Jeff called to break the news, he made sure his mom was lying down first.

She wants the world to know the Jeff she knows, the son who calls all the time and helps his parents around the house whenever he visits. "He's always been a good kid—well, he's not a kid, he's a man," she says. "He knows he screws up, and if he does, he owns up to it and does what he can to fix it. But he's not a wimp. He'll fight to the finish if he needs to."

Hope says, "He relapsed and now he has to pay the consequence of that. But he has always been a genuinely good human being and his unfortunate incident doesn't change that."

When Hatch and I speak again, on the phone at the end of September, he says he's "one-day-at-a-timing it," attending AA meetings, and exercising. Recently, he and Lauren went to a local monastery. It seemed "a beautiful way to live," he says. In the meantime, Hatch says he's looking for a job but having no luck. "I mean, it's tough. Nobody doesn't Google anybody these days." Online, parts of his life remain frozen. You can watch him on Netflix, in a 2015 documentary called *Prescription Thugs*. His speeches are easily tracked down. His Twitter account includes the tagline: "Living passionately and trying to put others before myself."

He turned forty recently. At points in his life, like all addicts, he has lied, hurt people, and cheated himself. He helped put a lot of fentanyl on the streets, a drug that kills people. In the arc of his life, though, it's likely—if not probable—that he has helped more than he has hurt. He can pull up messages and texts from those whose lives he bettered. No doubt his speeches resonated; he possesses the gift of genuine connection.

What sets Hatch apart are not his actions—they are not that rare in the world of addiction, which is replete with relapse—but their resonance. The 467 people who died in New Hampshire in 2017; how many of their stories are told? How many become anything other than a statistic?

For better or worse, Hatch had a platform and a voice. As

Spofford puts it, "If he doesn't play in the NFL, if Pence doesn't [plan to] visit, we're not talking right now." But Hatch did, and Pence did, and now we're here, wading through the repercussions. With his deceit, Hatch further eroded trust in an industry already short on it. He caused men like Kaniuka and Spofford to wrestle with the same feelings and negative assumptions about addicts they have long strived to banish from society. He added his name to a list of football players unable to kick the painkillers they once thought were just part of the job. And he became a cautionary tale about second chances, maybe a made-for-TV movie—one where some actor portrays the man who always dreamed of such a meaty role.

But what about Hatch, the guy with two dogs and a girlfriend and an uncertain future? On November 6, in a federal courtroom in Concord, a judge will hand down a sentence: maybe a year, maybe two, maybe none. To the outside world, the story may end there. But Jeff Hatch will still have half his life ahead of him. And, like all addicts, he will awake each morning faced with a choice. To use that day or not to use. To move forward or look back. To be the man he sees himself as, or the man he was.

MAY JEONG

Patriot Act

FROM VANITY FAIR

I. The Raid

ON JULY 6, 2018, a health inspector named Karen Herzog visited a massage parlor in South Florida for a routine inspection. She noticed that the spa worker, a young Asian woman, was "dressed provocatively," spoke "little English," and appeared "nervous." Herzog also noted suitcases, clothes, a fridge full of food, and condoms, all of which, according to the training she had received, could be signs of human trafficking. She reported her findings to the Martin County sheriff's office.

Over the next eight months, Detective Mike Fenton launched an investigation into what he believed was a large-scale prostitution ring engaged in human trafficking. Because one of the massage parlors, Orchids of Asia Day Spa, fell on the other side of the county line, in Palm Beach County, Fenton's office notified Detective Andrew Sharp of the Jupiter police, who began his own investigation in October 2018.

Orchids is located off U.S. 1, in a strip mall anchored by a Publix supermarket. Jupiter is a three-bar town that is home to what one local calls "old and quiet money." Like most spas in the area, Orchids charged $59 for a half-hour massage and $79 for a full hour. Like many spas in the United States, it's staffed by women of Asian descent.

For seven days in early November 2018, Sharp and his team staked out the spa. Almost everyone they saw enter was a man.

One day, a group of eight men who arrived in a golf cart made touchdown gestures before entering, their arms flung up to indicate that they were about to score. "At that point I understood this was not just a regular massage parlor but one that was an illicit massage business," Sharp later testified.

Sharp asked Herzog if she could survey the parlor, and on November 14, she complied.

Herzog later testified that the spa workers appeared agitated by her visit and failed to make eye contact. "As the inspection progressed, I began to feel more and more uneasy," she recalled. Herzog noted an "excessive amount of food in the refrigerator." She also noted bedding, clothing, and a flatiron. Herzog's report gave Sharp sufficient cause to search the spa's trash, and on November 14 and 19, his team found semen among the refuse. Last January, he requested what is colloquially known as a sneak-and-peek search warrant.

The warrant is a holdover from 9/11. Issued under the Patriot Act, it was initially designed to temporarily expand surveillance and investigative powers of law enforcement agencies in domestic terrorism cases. Since then, however, both the act and the warrant have been routinely used in cases that stray far from their original intent.

Sharp received the warrant on January 15, and two days later his team returned to Orchids, where they evacuated the premises, telling workers that a bomb threat had been called in. While the women waited outside, officers placed hidden cameras in the ceilings of the massage rooms.

Over the next five days, Sharp and his team watched, via a live feed, as more than twenty men received manual sex, oral sex, and anal play. When the johns left the spa, an officer would follow them and initiate a traffic stop as a pretext for identifying the men.

Among the patrons who turned up on the surveillance video at Orchids was Robert Kraft, the seventy-eight-year-old owner of the New England Patriots. Kraft, who visited the spa on the afternoon of January 19, spends part of the year in a double oceanfront apartment he owns on Breakers Row, among the most coveted addresses in Palm Beach. Earlier that day, according to a man I spoke with who asked to be identified only as Kraft's "best guy friend," Kraft had gone to the hotel spa for a massage. When he was unable to get an appointment, he conferred with his old friend Peter

Bernon, the dairy and plastics tycoon who also lives in Palm Beach. Bernon offered to drive Kraft in his 2014 white Bentley to a place he knew in Jupiter, 20 miles up the Treasure Coast.

At Orchids, according to the Jupiter police, Kraft paid cash to the spa's co-owner, Lei Wang, who goes by Lulu, and received a hand job from her and another worker, later identified as Shen Mingbi. After Kraft ejaculated, Mingbi wiped his penis with a white towel. Then she and Lulu helped him get dressed.

As Kraft left the spa in the white Bentley, Officer Scott Kimbark, nicknamed Bark, stopped the car for a minor traffic violation. Kraft asked the officer if he was a Miami Dolphins fan and showed him his Super Bowl ring, explaining that he was the owner of the Patriots. Kimbark, having accomplished his mission, let Kraft and Bernon go with a warning.

Later that day, Kraft called his friend. "You won't believe what happened to me," his friend recalls him bragging. Kraft explained how he had gone for what he thought was a regular massage, but that the masseuse had given him a hand job instead.

The friend excoriated Kraft for getting a "rub and tug." Kraft, seemingly hurt, insisted that it "wasn't like that." He said he had felt a real connection with Lulu and Mingbi.

Later that evening, Kraft received a call from Orchids, asking him to visit again. (At the time, Kraft's number in Palm Beach was publicly listed.) Kraft, according to his friend, was thrilled. He did not seem to understand that the spa was merely soliciting repeat business.

The next day, Kraft returned to Orchids, this time with a driver in a 2015 blue Bentley. He arrived before 11 a.m., qualifying for the early bird special: $15 off. He received a hand job and a blow job from Lulu, and left after fourteen minutes. That afternoon he flew to Kansas City, to watch his team play the Chiefs in the NFL playoffs. The Patriots won.

II. The Sex Ring

On February 19, after staging dramatic raids on nearly a dozen massage parlors in South Florida, Sheriff William Snyder held a press conference. Local officers, he announced, working alongside Immigration and Customs Enforcement and the Department of

Homeland Security, had busted a $20 million sex trafficking ring with tentacular reach to New York and China. Many of the women, he said, had been tricked into coming to the United States and had been working to pay off debts to traffickers before being rescued. "I don't believe they were told they were going to work in massage parlors seven days a week, having unprotected sex with up to 1,000 men a year," Snyder said.

Sex trafficking, under law, involves recruiting and transporting women by force or fraud, and coercing them to work as prostitutes. The traffickers, Snyder continued, had covered their tracks by moving the women every ten to twenty days to different spas, where they were forced to sleep on massage tables and cook on hot plates. Some were unable to leave, the sheriff said, because the traffickers confiscated their money and passports.

Snyder announced that as many as 300 men who went to the spas for sex would be charged with soliciting prostitution. "Many of the men are married," the sheriff said, adopting the moralizing tone common to faith-based groups that consider the sex industry an affront to Christian values. "Many of those men are in ongoing relationships."

Three days later, on February 22, Palm Beach County State Attorney Dave Aronberg announced that Kraft would be charged with two misdemeanor counts of soliciting prostitution. "Human trafficking is evil in our midst," Aronberg told reporters. "Modern-day slavery" can "happen anywhere, including in the peaceful community of Jupiter, Florida."

III. The Island

When I arrived in Palm Beach last spring, the weather report was threatening rain. The sky hung low and the air was loamy. If you are the 1 percent, you can opt out of most things in this world, including the weather. Many of the island's residents were packing up prior to hurricane season; covered trailers lined driveways, waiting to transport art back to Aspen or Connecticut or Long Island.

Hearings on the sex charges were ongoing; Kraft, who had pleaded not guilty, was vigorously fighting them in court. The question that the wealthy residents of Palm Beach were asking themselves was, plainly, why? Why would a man worth $6.6 billion risk getting a $59 hand job at a strip mall massage parlor?

Many year-round residents of Palm Beach attempted to distance themselves from the "nasty Krafty" scandal by dismissing the Patriots owner as nothing but a seasonal resident—one of the 20,000 or so who come to the island from Thanksgiving to Easter—and therefore not an actual member in good standing of the Palm Beach community. Others proffered the heat defense, typically reserved for explaining away acts of insanity, such as first-degree murder or third marriages. The reasoning is deterministic: the feeling that Florida itself—especially South Florida—propels men to strange deeds.

Florida has always played an outsize role in the national psyche, a shorthand for a specific aspect of the American dream. Florida is where you go when you don't want to be found, or when you have something to hide, or to escape bad debt and scandal, as did Charles Ponzi, the original defrauder. Palm Beach is the place where William Kennedy Smith was acquitted, in 1991, of raping a woman he met at a bar alongside his uncle, Senator Ted Kennedy. Where financier Jeffrey Epstein was given a "sweetheart deal," in 2008, for soliciting minors for prostitution. Where Bernie Madoff preyed on wealthy investors before pleading guilty, in 2009, to bilking his clients of nearly $65 billion.

South Florida as we know it began in 1886, when Standard Oil cofounder Henry Flagler started building railroads over recently drained swampland. It was Flagler who built the Breakers resort, to accommodate passengers on his railways, at a time when land was going for $1.25 per acre. (Now land goes by the square foot.) Flagler was also known for convincing the state legislature to allow him to divorce his second wife, whom he had committed to an insane asylum, so he could remarry.

The island of Palm Beach, sixteen miles long and less than a mile wide, remains among the most economically and socially segregated towns in America. Apart from the occasional titled European, many Palm Beach residents have been heirs to various fortunes: the Singer sewing machine, the Watson computer, Jell-O, Listerine. Ninety-seven percent of residents are white, and the median age is sixty-seven. Houses come with living rooms that can hold parties of 175, and two pools—one to catch the sun in the morning, the other to catch it in the late afternoon. Rembrandts hang in guest bathrooms.

Breakers Row—home to mostly Jewish residents, including Robert Kraft—is referred to by the island's WASPs as the Gaza Strip. The clubs are so exclusive, local legend has it, that Burt Reynolds was once turned away at the door on account of his dark skin color. Even Joseph Kennedy Sr. was reportedly spurned on account of his Catholic faith. Besides, his money was deemed too new. "It's new if it was made in the past century," explained Debi Murray, chief curator of the Historical Society of Palm Beach County.

Some residents, when I asked them about Kraft, appeared puzzled that a man of such immense wealth would feel the need to leave his valeted residence for a massage, let alone sexual services. What horrified these residents most was that Kraft had gone "over the bridge." Over the bridge is West Palm Beach, a service town on the mainland, where the support staffs live: maids, gardeners, doctors, judges—anyone who has to work for a living. It is where you go when you can't send someone else, when you have to show up in person at the hospital, or the courthouse, or the charity photo opportunity. The Publix supermarket on Palm Beach island sells Marcona almonds; the Publix in West Palm Beach only stocks the standard California variety.

Men like Kraft, after all, can have the help come to them. J'Anine, who used to work on the island as a high-end escort, told me about the many famous johns she had worked for, a list that includes best-selling authors and rock stars and titans of industry. As a professional, J'Anine charged $1,000 an hour—about thirteen times more than Orchids. But the high price did not always ensure discretion. There had been one incident, J'Anine shared, when she took too much cocaine on the job and ended up locking herself and her crack pipe in the bathroom. The client's daughter, desperate to get rid of her, had called the police for help. Two officers managed to restrain J'Anine, but not before using a Taser and a choke hold.

Jeff Greene, a Palm Beach resident who ranks 232nd on the *Forbes* list of richest Americans, told me that he could not understand why any man would want to pay for sex, but that he did understand why Kraft had chosen to go across the bridge. Everyone in Palm Beach attends the same parties, Greene explained, and wakes up the next morning to read about the selfsame parties in the town newspaper, printed on glossy paper so as not to smudge the gloved hands of its readers. "Palm Beach is a small town," Greene said. "I imagine if you want to do something you shouldn't be doing, you go out of town."

Luxury items—champagne, caviar, truffles—have no inherent value. They are made desirable through scarcity. But for the tiny stratum of society for whom nothing is unattainable, the commonplace, paradoxically, can attain a luster of its own. If calling up an escort like J'Anine is akin to ordering Wagyu beef from room service, then visiting Orchids is like swinging by the McDonald's drive-through.

Sometimes you just want a burger.

IV. The Men

Whenever I encountered men of Palm Beach in their natural habitat, in hotel lobbies, inlet tiki bars, and private clubs, they were exceedingly eager to share stories of their visits to spas like Orchids.

In midtown Manhattan, at a smoke-filled club frequented by seasonal residents like Rudy Giuliani, I fell into conversation about Kraft with a man at its mahogany bar. I explained that after many months of working on this story for *Vanity Fair*, I still could not figure out why Kraft had acted with such abandon. The man, who identified himself as the son of a famous politician, explained that men go to massage parlors for many reasons. In fact, he told me, he was heading to one himself in a few days. If I liked, I would be welcome to accompany him as his guest. (The trip did not take place.)

At a bar in Jupiter, a Patriots fan named Billy told me that he is a regular at Orchids, and had visited the spa only two weeks before the raid. His father and uncle had served in World War II, he explained, at a time when the U.S. military tacitly endorsed prostitution as good for morale. Over the years, many soldiers returned from Japan and Korea and Vietnam with a highly sexualized view of the women they met.

"Marry an Asian woman," Billy recalled being told. "You'll be happy for the rest of your life. Asian women know how to take care of a man. You come home and she cooks dinner, takes your shoes off, never complains."

Billy was forty-two when he was first taken to a "jack shack" on his way to a Patriots game in New England. After moving to South Florida, friends he made at a local bar told him about Orchids.

"A lot of my friends think Asian women are very attractive," Billy said. "That's what I think myself. The girls are beautiful. They are thin, in shape. That's why American guys like that."

Indeed, on one of my first nights on the island, I was sitting at a hotel bar, working up the courage to crash a reception for alumni of the Harvard Business School, Kraft's alma mater, that had already begun out on the deck. An older gentleman approached me and asked where the function was. I pointed to the deck. He told me he couldn't hear what I was saying. I suggested he try the deck. He became upset and walked away.

Later, the man approached me again, this time to apologize for having behaved rudely. By way of explanation, he told me that he had thought I was a member of the hotel's service staff. I introduced myself as a reporter in town on a story, and we began chatting about Kraft and Jupiter. Suddenly, he leaned toward me—this older man who only moments earlier had treated me with disdain—and began making sexually explicit comments. "I had all these fantasies about you," he confessed.

On the island, there were only two preordained roles for a young woman of Asian descent. Being a reporter was not one of them.

V. The Madam

Lulu, the co-owner of Orchids who allegedly attended to Kraft, lives a world away from her clients. From Palm Beach, you drive through West Palm Beach, past the South Dixie Highway, past laundromats advertising weekday deals and pawn shops after your gold. If you hang a right and drive north until the turnpike narrows, past billboards advertising plastic surgery and personal injury lawyers, past state prisoners performing hot, humid labor, you enter Martin and Port St. Lucie and Indian River Counties, where the rest of Florida lives.

There, upstream from the source, the story of Kraft and the

massage parlor raids has grown muddied. Flora Vera and Sean Williams, who live next door to Lulu, told me they had heard the sex workers had been kept naked so they wouldn't run away. Another neighbor chimed in, telling me it was all part of a complex global conspiracy involving President Trump, full of byzantine connections that I found impossible to follow.

Flora laughed. "Next thing you know, we are saying I saw a UFO," she said.

"Well, I did see a UFO," her husband said.

He told me that it had appeared above a Kmart parking lot at dusk, "hovering above the pines," on his way to church. He had been twelve years old. Later, Flora told me that she has precognitive dreams.

Lulu, who had been arrested at home and released after posting a cash bail of $75,000, declined my request for an interview. She has pleaded not guilty to all charges, including soliciting others to commit prostitution. But her business partner, Hua Zhang, who owns the other half of Orchids, agreed to speak to me.

Zhang was born into a "not rich but respected" family in Guangzhou, China, in 1960. After marrying and giving birth to a son, Zhang applied for a U.S. visa in 2001. Five years later, the visa came through. Zhang hesitated. She was making a good living in China as an esthetician. She knew every bend of every road in Guangzhou. The new country would be full of unfamiliar roads, and strangers who wouldn't know how to pronounce her name.

But Zhang was a mother before she was anything else, and she decided to emigrate for her son. After the family moved to Los Angeles, Zhang learned there weren't many opportunities for a middle-aged woman with no professional expertise. A friend Zhang made from her English as a second language class suggested she go to work at a massage school run by Jet Li's personal masseuse.

At the school, Zhang made another friend who later moved to Florida to work at a massage parlor there. The friend soon began calling Zhang, pleading with her to join her. Zhang was reluctant, but by that time her son was grown, and she and her husband were filing for divorce. Florida is the land of second acts, and in 2010, Zhang moved to Jupiter to begin her life anew as Mandy.

Mandy packed light; she knew everything would be provided. Businesses owned by Chinese Americans—laundromats, restaurants, massage parlors—frequently provide room, board, and transportation for newly arrived workers, who often lack the means and connections to buy or rent a place on their own.

After a few years of hard work, Mandy raised enough money to buy Orchids in 2013. She hired workers from Chinese immigrant communities across the country, placing ads in Chinese-language newspapers. Mandy also provided day care for children while their mothers were at work. By then, her son had moved to Florida, and word got out that a Chinese woman and her English-speaking son would take in your kids for a reasonable fee. Soon, Mandy was looking after as many as eleven children.

In 2017, Mandy signed over half of the spa to Lulu, one of her steadiest workers. She began devoting most of her time to her grandson, Michael—named after local resident Michael Jordan, who owns a 28,000-square-foot mansion on three acres in Jupiter.

On the morning of February 19, Mandy was making coffee at a condominium near the spa that she had rented to house her workers. Suddenly, there was banging at the door. Six police officers swarmed in, handcuffed Mandy, and booked her into the Palm Beach jail.

"At the time I thought: they must have made a mistake," she says. "It's so funny—they treat me as a treacherous criminal. I can't believe what kind of system it is. Why do you make such a big move against a family woman?"

As the co-owner of Orchids, Mandy was charged with a second-degree misdemeanor for "maintaining a house of prostitution." She was also charged with twenty-six counts of soliciting others to commit prostitution, as well as a second-degree felony for deriving support from prostitution, a crime punishable by up to fifteen years in prison. She has pleaded not guilty to the charges. A police affidavit lists the "victim" of her crime as the state of Florida. "Because it's our society as a whole that has been victimized by this prurient behavior," explains Robert Norvell, a West Palm Beach attorney who represents one of the defendants in the case. "I shit you not."

After a few weeks, Mandy was released on bail. Unable to return to the condo, where two of her employees were being detained, she was placed under house arrest in a home that a cousin of hers had put on the market. The house, on a quiet street in a gated subdivision, had not been lived in for some time, and was infested with vermin. Mandy spent six weeks scrubbing its floors. Her ankle monitor prevented her from taking out the trash or picking the ripe mangoes in the backyard, so she stared at the falling fruit from the window.

VI. The Mogul

The men who were arrested for availing themselves of Mandy's services faced no such restrictions. After his arrest, Kraft was free to live his best life. He reportedly donated $100,000 at a charity dinner at the Breakers in Palm Beach, attended the annual pre-Oscar brunch at the Beverly Hills home of Barry Diller and Diane von Furstenberg, and watched Rafael Nadal defeat Dominic Thiem in Paris to win the French Open.

Kraft was born in 1941, in the affluent Boston suburb of Brookline. In 1963, he married Myra Hiatt, an heiress to a paper box fortune whom he met at a Boston deli. They had four children. In 1994, he purchased the New England Patriots, growing the team into one of the most valuable franchises in the National Football League.

In 2010, Myra, referred to by some as the "smartest Kraft," fell ill with ovarian cancer. During the NFL lockout in 2011, Kraft spent his days negotiating with union representatives, then came home each evening to rub Myra's feet. She died later that year, and Kraft's life became a boat you forgot to tie up.

The following year, at a party in Los Angeles at the home of New York Giants co-owner Steve Tisch, Kraft met Ricki Noel Lander, an aspiring actress thirty-eight years his junior. The two began seeing each other: on, then off, then on again.

Kraft reveled in his newfound status as a single rich guy. Owning a winning football team in America gave him access to a world that money alone can't buy. He was seen at the Met Gala and the Grammys and the *Vanity Fair* Oscar party, and sometimes appeared at events alongside young women who remained uncredited in photos.

Kraft hadn't gone to Orchids on that January day because the Florida heat had driven him mad, or because he was in search of anonymity, or because he had served his country in the Far East. Born the year of Pearl Harbor, he was thirteen when the Vietnam War began. He went to Orchids, in his relatively new status as a single rich guy, to get a massage. And it was in his part as a single rich guy that he came to believe he had done nothing wrong. According to his best friend, he thought there had been something between him and Lulu. He thought she liked him. He thought that what had transpired between them had no business being discussed in a courtroom.

"If you are affluent, rules loosely apply to you," says Norvell, the lawyer representing one of the defendants. "You wear it like a loose garment."

As the owner of a six-time Super Bowl championship team, Kraft understood that sometimes the best defense is a good offense. To represent him in court, he hired William Burck, who withheld sensitive documents from Congress during Brett Kavanaugh's confirmation hearing; Alex Spiro, who defended former Patriots tight end Aaron Hernandez after he was charged with murder; and Jack Goldberger, the Palm Beach attorney who helped broker a plea deal for Jeffrey Epstein.

Epstein himself, in his twisted worldview, saw Kraft as a kindred spirit. A few months after Kraft was charged, a Fox Business reporter asked Palm Beach's most notorious sex offender if he knew that the girls he had lured to his mansion for massages and sex were underage. Epstein insisted that his own crimes weren't "that much different than what happened to Bob Kraft. Only he went somewhere, and they came to me."

Kraft's legal team bombarded the court with motions, pushing to bar the public release of the surveillance video from Orchids as an invasion of their client's privacy. "It's basically pornography," Burck told the court.

On March 28, the state attorney's office in Palm Beach offered Kraft a plea bargain. If he admitted his guilt, the charges would be dropped and his record expunged. Prosecutors extended the same offer to the other defendants in Palm Beach, a county that, despite being the home of Mar-a-Lago, votes blue. Next door, in the Trump-supporting Martin County, no plea deals were forthcoming.

Kraft rejected the plea deal.

America's criminal justice system relies on defendants taking plea deals: more than 90 percent do so. The system was not built to indict rich men, and so it was not prepared for a rich man to reject an offer of leniency. The case would have gone away quickly had Kraft not decided to devote his tremendous resources to destroying the state's case.

VII. The Rescue Industry

Florida, perhaps more than any other state, has been a leader of the Christian right's campaign to "rescue" those they consider victims of a globally syndicated criminal human trafficking ring. The first comprehensive human trafficking act passed in 2000, but it wasn't until three years later, when President George W. Bush pledged $50 million to support anti-trafficking organizations, that the campaign became a full-fledged industry.

Human trafficking is a serious problem: the Department of Health and Human Services calls it the world's "fastest-growing criminal industry." But some anti-trafficking groups, in search of funding, routinely overstate the scale of the commercial sex trade. They frequently claim that 300,000 minors are "at risk" for being sold into sexual slavery in America each year—a number that has been debunked by researchers as wildly overinflated. (The *Washington Post* dismisses it as a "nonsense statistic.") In 2018, the FBI confirmed a total of 649 trafficking cases in America, adults included.

Even more alarming, the exaggerated numbers about sex trafficking have come to inform public policy. On May 3, driven in part by spurious statistics, the Florida legislature passed a sweeping new law to combat prostitution. The measure creates a statewide "anti-prostitution registry" that is intended to list men like Robert Kraft, should he be convicted, as a john. But critics worry that the registry, which is vaguely defined, will also wind up including sex workers like Lulu and Shen Mingbi. In doing so, the anti-prostitution law could effectively end up functioning as an anti-immigration law, targeting poor women of color, many of them from Asia.

Florida's new sex registry is the latest in a long line of similar laws. One of America's first laws against prostitution, in fact, was the 1870 Act to Prevent the Kidnapping and Importing of Mongolian, Chinese, and Japanese Females for Criminal or Demoralizing Purposes, intended to protect the public from "scandal and injury." The law was a precursor to the Page Act of 1875, which aimed to "end the danger of cheap Chinese labor and immoral

Chinese women," which in turn was a precursor to the Chinese Exclusion Act of 1882—the first law to bar all members of a specific ethnicity or nationality from immigrating.

The raids on Orchids and other massage parlors in South Florida were conducted in the name of rescuing women from sex trafficking. But the only people put in jail were the women themselves. A few, like Lulu and Mandy, managed to post bail and were placed under house arrest. But others were transferred to the custody of ICE. Women who migrated to America in search of work—who chose the least bad option available to them—were being punished for what one of their lawyers calls "the crime of poverty."

The *New York Times* and other news outlets, quoting investigators, initially presented the raids as a clear-cut case of sex trafficking. Women at the spas, the media reported, were working "14 hour days" and "sleeping on massage tables." After "surrendering" their passports to spa owners, they were not allowed to leave the premises without an escort. The "wretched" women in "strip-mall brothels" were not sex workers, but rather "trafficking victims trapped among South Florida's rich and famous."

But as police subjected the women to hours-long interrogations, those claims began to unravel. The only woman alleged to have been locked up and forced to live on the premises was Yong Wang, who went by the spa name Nancy. In fact, like many other employees, Nancy had been hired from out of state, so her boss drove her back and forth from the job. When the owner fell ill, Nancy was asked if she wouldn't mind sleeping at the spa.

The one woman whose passport had allegedly been taken away was Lixia Zhu, or Yoyo. During questioning, the police repeatedly grilled Yoyo, looking for evidence of human trafficking. Did anyone else set up her bank account for her? Did anyone else have access to her account? "Did you feel like you had a choice to come down and work, or did you feel like you were forced to?"

"No one forced me," Yoyo insisted. It was the terrible winter of 2018 back in Pennsylvania, where she was living at the time, that inspired her to move to Florida.

The interrogator pressed harder. "Did you feel like you had to do this?"

Yoyo shook her head.

"Then why did you do it?"

The inquiry continued along these lines for several more hours.

It was somehow easier for law enforcement officers in South Florida to believe that the women had been sold into sex slavery by a global crime syndicate than to acknowledge that immigrant women of precarious status, hemmed in by circumstance, might choose sex work.

In the end, Yoyo told police that her boyfriend had confiscated her passport, locked it in a safe, and threatened her with a gun. He was the one, she intimated, who had forced her into sexual slavery.

Later, during a hearing conducted after she had managed to retain a lawyer, Yoyo recanted the story about her boyfriend. She told the court that she had said what she felt the police wanted to hear, in the hopes of getting a lighter sentence.

Within weeks of the raids, the state's case had evaporated. There was no $20 million trafficking ring, no women tricked into sex slavery. The things the state had mistaken as markers for human trafficking—long working hours, shared eating and living arrangements, suspicion of outside authorities, ties to New York and China—were, in fact, common organizing principles of many Chinese immigrant communities. As an assistant state attorney in Palm Beach told the court on April 12: "There is no human trafficking that arises out of this investigation."

VIII. The Mix-up

Democrats have tried, so far without success, to tie the Orchids scandal to Donald Trump. Kraft, after all, was a close friend of the president. He had attended Trump's wedding to Melania in 2005, and gave $1 million to his inaugural fund. (Trump once reportedly tried to set up Ivanka with Tom Brady, hoping to make the Patriots quarterback his son-in-law.) Li "Cindy" Yang, the former owner of the Orchids spa, also donated to Trump's campaign, and ran a consulting firm that promised Chinese business executives access to Trump and Mar-a-Lago.

On March 15, congressional Democrats on the intelligence and judiciary committees asked the FBI, the director of national intelligence, and the Secret Service to open an investigation into Yang and her alleged ties to Trump. I emailed Nancy Pelosi's office to ask why she wanted Yang to be investigated by a top intelligence agency. The speaker's press officer, Ashley Etienne, pointed me to news reports about Yang "bypassing security" at Mar-a-Lago. "This was before it broke that she's a likely spy," Etienne added.

Etienne appeared to have misidentified Yang. I asked her if she was referring to a separate probe involving a Chinese woman named Yujing *Zhang*, who had allegedly breached Mar-a-Lago security. "I am not sure what you mean," Etienne wrote back, referring me to the FBI for "more details."

I also emailed Senator Dianne Feinstein, who had signed the letter requesting an investigation. Her press person also responded by citing the case against Zhang.

"This is political prosecution with no evidence," Cliff Yi, executive director of the National Committee of Asian American Republicans, told me. "It reminds us of our experience in China. It reminds us of how we were scared, how we were oppressed."

On September 11, Zhang was convicted of trespassing and lying to federal agents. The FBI has also opened a public corruption investigation into Yang, focusing on whether she illegally funneled money from China into Trump's reelection campaign. Federal prosecutors sent subpoenas to Mar-a-Lago, demanding that it turn over all records relating to Yang.

IX. *The Double Standard*

Kraft, aided by the best defense team money can buy, seems likely to beat the charges against him. Last May, a judge threw out the video evidence that had been gathered at Orchids, ruling that the warrant had been "seriously flawed." The judge also threw out evidence from Kraft's traffic stop, calling it "the fruit of an unlawful search." The state is appealing the ruling.

Even if he is found guilty, however, Kraft has little to fear in the way of punishment. In Florida, as in most other states, the purchasing of sex is a misdemeanor. The few first-time johns who wind up being convicted typically pay a fine and perform no more than 100 hours of community service. The selling of sex, however, is policed far more severely. Sex workers are more likely than johns to face repeated arrest, increasing the odds that they will be charged with a felony and sentenced to prison, and have fewer resources to defend themselves in court. And "madams" who profit from the prostitution of others—the charge leveled against Mandy and

Lulu—can be convicted of money laundering if the proceeds are deposited in a bank, or used to pay rent, or buy milk.

While Kraft's legal team fights to have the charges against him dismissed, one of the alleged sex workers arrested in the raids, Lei Chen, remains in ICE custody. Under civil forfeiture proceedings, the state seized her J.P. Morgan Chase account, which held $2,900. Until August 21, when she was transferred to another immigration facility, Chen was held at the detention center in West Palm Beach, a half-mile from a strip club where Stormy Daniels performed, and across from the Trump International Golf Club.

Another alleged sex worker, Yaping Ren, was also held for five months, waiting to be handed over to ICE, before being released in July. Her status remains uncertain: her attorney told me that he has been unable to determine whether she is going to be deported. The county has only two court-certified Mandarin interpreters, who charge $400 an hour—a prohibitively high fee for his clients. Under Florida law, it would appear, happy endings are the exclusive property of men.

MIKE KESSLER AND MARK FAINARU-WADA

44 Years. 41 Allegations.
Now the Past Is Catching Up.

FROM ESPN.COM

IT'S A QUIET, early morning at UCLA's Drake Stadium, the sun still low. The world's greatest track athletes have run here through the years, in front of thousands of cheering fans. But on this Tuesday in June 2016, only a dozen or so anonymous men and women stretch and tick off laps.

Among them is Benjamin, a wiry, twenty-year-old UCLA sophomore. He is not on the Bruins' track team, but he is training toward his dream of making his home country's national squad. As he stretches, Benjamin (who asked that his real name not be used) sees a figure walking stiffly and deliberately toward him across the infield. The man comes into focus: early thirties, flowing blond hair, piercing blue eyes. He looks like an athlete, firm and thin, but he's wearing street clothes.

The stranger approaches Benjamin; he nods in the direction of an older man in a track jacket and white Adidas cap, perched on a folding chair about ten feet away.

"Do you train with this guy?" the stranger asks.

Benjamin hesitates, partly because his coach, a former Olympian and trainer of elite athletes, always has demanded secrecy: *Our training is our business.*

The stranger continues.

"Do you know his name?"

It occurs to Benjamin that he actually doesn't know his coach's full name.

"Coach Avondale," Benjamin says. "Look, you can go talk to him if you want."

"No, he can f— himself," comes the reply. "His name is Conrad Montgomery Avondale Mainwaring. He's a serial child molester, and he molested me when I was at UCLA.

"I trusted this guy, I thought it was okay, but what he did to me f—ed me up for the next ten years."

The stranger keeps talking, but the words are mostly a blur to Benjamin. Finally, the man turns and approaches the coach, raising his cell phone to record the encounter.

"You're going to f—ing jail!" the man says.

The man lays into the coach for what seems like forever. Benjamin tries to focus on his workout, but it's no use. He gathers his stuff and walks off the track, trying to process the stranger's words: *He molested me at UCLA.*

What the stranger didn't know was that Benjamin himself had been molested by Mainwaring—only nine hours earlier. Nor did the stranger realize that he had just pulled a thread that would begin unraveling the mystery and misdeeds of Conrad Mainwaring, a former Olympian who coached Olympic-level athletes, including a two-time gold medalist.

In June 2018, *Outside the Lines* began investigating a tip that Mainwaring allegedly had molested a twelve-year-old boy in the 1970s and might have continued such activity to the present day. The tip led to a thirteen-month reporting effort that uncovered scores of allegations spanning five decades and two continents— and sparked a police investigation that resulted in Mainwaring's recent arrest.

Those who have accused Mainwaring, now mostly middle-aged men, were interviewed multiple times each and over hundreds of hours in total. Efforts were made to corroborate their stories, including speaking with family members, friends, and spouses they had confided in over the years, as well as reviewing letters, journals, photos, official documents, and news articles.

As startling as the sheer number of accusations was the fact that for years Mainwaring—who rejected repeated interview requests—remained a cipher, a man with almost no public footprint who was able to stay one step ahead of the allegations and the law.

Until now.

A Family Secret

In May 2018, a phone rings at the Marin County, California, office of Andrew Zenoff, an entrepreneur who initially struck it big two decades ago by selling a pillow for nursing mothers. "My Brest Friend," he called his invention. Zenoff grabs his cell phone. It's a friend—a reporter—following up on an earlier conversation:

"That guy you told me about—the one you said molested your brother back in the '70s . . . what's his name again?" the reporter asks.

"Conrad Mainwaring."

Zenoff, now fifty-four, recounts the tragically short life of his older brother, Victor: They grew up on the East Coast in the 1970s. Victor was easygoing and affable. Everybody seemed to like him, and he excelled in most sports—basketball, baseball, tennis, soccer.

Each summer, starting when Victor was twelve, the Zenoff brothers went to Camp Greylock for Boys, a sleepaway sports camp in New England. There, Victor developed a close relationship with a certain counselor, a man whose distinctive qualities drew campers to him. He carried an aura of authority and spoke in a proper British accent. Most impressively, he was *an Olympian*. His name was Conrad Mainwaring.

"He was sort of like a hero figure to my brother," Zenoff says.

But Victor changed over three summers at camp. By fifteen, he was consumed by drugs and risky behavior, and the family had moved to the West Coast. One time, he rolled his car and nearly killed himself. After that, his parents bought him a used highway patrol car, thinking it would be "a safe tank," but he was pulled over driving faster than 100 miles per hour.

In the summer of 1980, Victor was approaching his eighteenth birthday—barely out of high school—when he told his mother he had been sexually abused by Mainwaring repeatedly over several summers. The next day, Victor left on a camping trip to California's Yosemite National Park with a friend he had met at a Grateful Dead show. A few days later, officers knocked on Nisha Zenoff's front door. Victor was dead, found at the bottom of a 600-foot cliff. Police deemed it a hiking accident.

Andrew says he never had Mainwaring as a counselor and was never approached by him, and he didn't learn of the alleged abuse until after Victor's death. At that point, he says, the Zenoffs were too devastated to tell anyone else what Victor had confided to his mother.

Besides, maybe Victor was Mainwaring's only victim.

"Seduced by His Interest"

In the summer of 1975, the textile hub of Leicester, England, a gloomy, downtrodden city 100 miles north of London, had little to offer fifteen-year-old Vernon Sharples. When he wasn't working as an assistant at a sporting goods store, he was smoking cigarettes and pilfering alcohol from his parents, who he says weren't very attentive.

And then one day, Conrad Mainwaring walked into the store where Sharples worked, MC Sports. "I was aware that he was going to the Olympics because he used to come into the shop and try and get a bit of stuff for free," says Sharples, now a slender, balding fifty-nine-year-old.

Though not good enough to make England's national team, the twenty-three-year-old Mainwaring was to compete as a hurdler for his native Antigua at the upcoming 1976 Summer Olympics in Montreal.

Mainwaring's athletic accomplishments interested Sharples, but he was most taken by the attention the track star heaped on him at the store. So when Mainwaring invited Sharples to train with what he called his "squad" of athletes at Saffron Lane Athletics Stadium in Leicester, the boy leaped at the chance.

"I was just seduced by his interest," he says.

The coach preached sobriety and celibacy, citing booze and girls as obstacles to athletic success. He had a word for messing around with members of the opposite sex: wenching. Mainwaring was an avid reader and classical music aficionado who seemed, at least to a kid from Leicester, to know everything. Some evenings after practice, the two would ride a bus downtown, where the coach—he went simply by "Conrad"—took Sharples to a Chinese restaurant and treated him to chicken and chips. Often, the coach would talk about a group of other select youngsters he trained —his "international squad"—at a summer camp in America.

During one of their conversations, Mainwaring explained that he was doing research in psychology and wanted Sharples to be one of his subjects. The fieldwork, Mainwaring told the teenager, involved masturbation habits. It lasted several weeks, during which time Sharples says the coach asked about frequency, timing, duration, and other aspects of self-gratification. At one point, Sharples says, Mainwaring told him to see how long he could go without indulging.

"He just kept on saying that I'm this amazing guy . . . kind of showering me with compliments," Sharples says. "And so I just went along with it."

After workouts, Mainwaring gave Sharples and other squad members massages; he called it "physiotherapy." Calling it "massage [would] really wind him up," Sharples says. One day, Sharples was the last squad member to receive treatment, lying face up on a table when Mainwaring instructed him to "think up an erection" and then "think it down." All part of the research, he was told. Sharples says this happened a few times before the sessions went to a new level: "He would rub my penis over my shorts . . . until I ejaculated."

More than forty years later, Sharples can't recall how long the alleged abuse lasted. At the time, he didn't think of it as abuse; Mainwaring used clinical language, never sexualizing the "physiotherapy." Sharples doesn't remember why Mainwaring stopped, but he says, "When it did stop, I remember feeling almost rejected."

Sharples continued to seek his coach's approval throughout the remainder of high school. Although communication diminished, the conversations were meaningful, he says. Often, talk turned to Mainwaring's international squad in America.

When Sharples turned eighteen, Mainwaring invited him to cross the Atlantic and work as a counselor at Camp Greylock for Boys in Massachusetts. Sharples didn't need much persuading; he felt honored.

By then, the summer of 1978, Mainwaring was well on his way to establishing a dramatic legacy at Greylock. And soon, he would be in America to stay.

Pitch-Black Woods

On the western edge of Massachusetts, in the heart of the Berkshire Mountains, is a summer camp where boys have gone to play for more than a century.

Camp Greylock spreads across 300 acres near the town of Becket, a bucolic setting of top-flight sports facilities—fifteen tennis courts, five baseball fields, three soccer fields, two 100-yard flag football fields, an in-line hockey rink, a nine-hole golf course, a climbing wall, a zip line, a lake, and a weight room—and cabins nestled amid abundant forest.

The camp was founded in 1916 by three brothers, who sold it to a group of former campers in the late 1940s. Those men would operate Camp Greylock for Boys for the next fifty years, until it was sold again in 1994 to a new generation of former Greylock employees. Through the years, the camp has catered to the children of wealth—the sons of entertainers and sports executives, politicians and architects. This year's tuition is $12,800 for seven weeks.

It's unclear how or exactly when Mainwaring arrived at Greylock, but he was a stalwart for at least five summers. He was a captivating figure to many of the young men and junior counselors, famous for his participation in the 1976 Montreal Olympics. Even if the campers knew he had finished last in his preliminary heats in the 400- and 110-meter hurdles, it didn't seem to matter.

That was true for David Allinson, a track star with Olympic ambitions in 1979. He was seventeen and heading into his senior year of high school in New Rochelle, New York, when Mainwaring got him a job as a junior counselor at Greylock. Allinson had been introduced to the coach the previous summer and had trained with him thereafter. Allinson admired the way Mainwaring carried himself and how he tried to be a father figure, something Allinson says he lacked at home.

But Allinson says the relationship took a dramatic turn that summer at Greylock. He remembers it this way: Soon after Allinson arrived in Becket, Mainwaring summoned him to the soccer field to work on a special athletic feat the coach liked to show off. He would leap next to a soccer goal and touch his foot to the crossbar. "If you're going to get to college and be a decathlete or get to the Olympics, you need flexibility, so we need to do this drill tonight," the coach said. Oh, and one more thing, Mainwaring added: before you come to the field, brush your teeth.

That night, after brushing his teeth, Allinson walked from his cabin to the field. It was pitch-black, surrounded by trees. He was nervous and called out for Mainwaring. "Shhh, keep your voice down," the coach said, waving a flashlight. They walked and talked a bit, did a few exercises. Gradually, Mainwaring led Allinson into the woods.

"How bad do you want the Olympics?" Mainwaring asked.

"More than anything," the boy said.

"What are you willing to do for it, how much mental energy are you prepared to give?"

The coach said the boy needed to give him a hug. He told Allinson to relax: "You need to be able to focus, and you need to learn how to slow your heartbeat down."

He then suggested Allinson think up an erection. "That is the ultimate mental test, because I'm not gay, and you're not gay, and this isn't about sex," Mainwaring said. "This is about showing me you have the mental ability to control your body."

The coach then masturbated the boy to climax.

Afterward, the coach presented another "mental challenge." He wanted the boy to kiss him, and Allinson obliged.

"Good, this has been a big test for you, and I'm happy to say you passed it and you are on your way to the Olympics," Mainwaring said.

Allinson, now a corporate executive living with his wife and children in Northern California, says after that night, "I knew my life had completely changed."

"I didn't know who I was or what I was," he says. "I couldn't even think."

Allinson says the abuse continued and eventually "started happening *in* the bunks, while the campers were out playing . . . maybe a dozen times. I remember getting emotional and saying, 'When is this going to stop?'"

He remembers Mainwaring saying, "It's going to stop when you realize what's necessary in your training, and your training isn't there. If you stop, I won't coach you."

Later, as an adult, Allinson says he contemplated suicide. He says he hid the abuse out of shame, fear, and confusion—all of which he blames for a lifelong struggle with alcohol.

In all, seven men told *Outside the Lines* they were sexually abused by Mainwaring when they were campers or junior counselors at Camp Greylock in the mid- to late 1970s.

The men who ran the camp when Mainwaring worked there are dead. After several unsuccessful attempts to reach the camp's current owners, *Outside the Lines* received an email from an attorney who said the latest iteration of the camp has never had any "affiliation whatsoever with Mainwaring." The lawyer did not respond to repeated emails seeking additional comment. Several staff members from that time period and one former camper who is now a staffer told *Outside the Lines* they couldn't recall anyone matching Mainwaring's description.

A Culture of Secrecy

By 1980, Mainwaring was twenty-eight, had landed at Syracuse University in upstate New York and was pursuing a master's degree in counseling and guidance. He worked for the school in student housing.

His latest squad was a mix of students attending the university and younger athletes he had met at local track meets while working as a counselor at a nearby high school. Mainwaring insisted the squad train in secret.

Robert Bender, a lanky freshman, met Mainwaring on his first day at Syracuse. His mom parked outside his dorm and the two were unloading boxes to take up to his room when Mainwaring approached, offering to help.

"Are you an athlete?" he asked.

Before long, Bender was part of Mainwaring's squad, lured more by his presence and attitude than by any of the physical training. The freshman was struck by how Mainwaring would "alternate between being really smiley, laughy, and exuberant," then turn on this "dead-on kind of expression [that looked] like he's kind of burrowing in to you psychologically, he's penetrating you psychologically. He had a very powerful way of pulling you in."

The coach pushed his mental training, and he was adamant there should be no girlfriends and no sex. These were things, Mainwaring said, that would dampen Bender's development as an athlete. Eventually, Bender says, the training turned physical, with the coach conducting "physiotherapy" that led to inappropriate touching. Bender says he pulled away after just a few experiences but couldn't bring himself to talk about it at the time, bowed by shame and the force of Mainwaring's message—secrecy.

"He said I couldn't talk to anyone about it. Nobody," says Bender, now fifty-seven. "I think he goes after heterosexual men, having a homosexual act with a heterosexual man, and you feel ashamed about it. You don't want anybody to know, and he relies on that horror that his victim will be equally invested in keeping it a secret as he wants it to be a secret."

Mainwaring, an avid letter writer, emphasized the need for secrecy in correspondence with Vernon Sharples in the early 1980s. "Naturally I expect you to keep my address to yourself [*Ed.'s note: Emphasis is in the original.*] as I requested in my last letter," he wrote, adding, "I do not wish anyone at all to know this." In another letter to Sharples, he wrote, "I trust that you will not tell anyone where I am or what I am doing, as for the first time I can be away from the newspaper and wagging tongues and people I cannot tolerate."

Sharples says he can't recall why Mainwaring wanted to keep a low profile. Other than a couple of 1976 clippings from the local Leicester newspaper that touted Mainwaring's spot in the Olympics, searches of old papers unearthed nothing unusual. *Outside the Lines* found no evidence of Mainwaring having trouble with the law in the United Kingdom, though criminal records there are not available to the public.

Bender and six other former Syracuse students say Mainwaring used his veil of secrecy to molest them in the dorms, using virtually identical tactics.

During his time in Syracuse, Mainwaring also kept office hours as a counselor at nearby Nottingham High School, according to two men who say they were minors when he abused them there. School district officials told *Outside the Lines* they found no records that Mainwaring was ever a staff member or a sanctioned volunteer.

Five other local high school students say they were molested by Mainwaring during the same time period. In total, fourteen men told *Outside the Lines* they were abused by Mainwaring in the Syracuse area.

Among the Nottingham students was Robert Druger, who later attended Syracuse University and ran on the track team. Now an eye surgeon and aikido instructor in Syracuse, Druger, fifty-six, says he visited Mainwaring for "sessions" in dorms where Mainwaring worked. He says the abuse went on for several years. Until recently, Druger says, he compartmentalized the darker parts of the relationship while crediting Mainwaring with helping to improve his life in some ways.

Sitting on the back deck of his home outside Syracuse last fall, Druger says the full gravity of the abuse didn't hit him until the past few years.

"It's like finding out the Wizard of Oz is only this guy behind the curtain, and instead of getting courage, a heart, or a brain, you found out he was a child predator and abused you forty years ago," he says.

A Syracuse University spokesperson told *Outside the Lines* that Mainwaring completed a master's degree in guidance and counseling and began working toward a doctorate, which he didn't complete. The spokesperson says the school wasn't made aware of any allegations against Mainwaring until this past February, at which point law enforcement authorities were notified and the school began a review of Mainwaring's time on campus.

Mainwaring left Syracuse in the summer of 1985 for Colgate University, about forty miles down the road in Hamilton, New York, where he worked in the admissions department. Several Syracuse squad members would visit him at Colgate, and new members joined. Among them was Brian, who spoke on the condition *Outside the Lines* withhold his last name. Brian was eighteen when he arrived at Colgate in the fall of 1987, a jazz guitarist and successful high school athlete who had struggled with motivation. He had partied heavily in high school and was in emotional upheaval when he got to college. A sympathetic friend said he just had to meet Conrad Mainwaring.

"He's got different degrees. He's into music. He's into sports. He's totally different," the friend said. "He knows the score, basically."

And so it was that Brian found himself in Mainwaring's office one day, challenged to attain greatness through a mental strength and therapy session. All while being touched inappropriately.

"He was very clever, very diabolically clever because he was couching it as nonsexual," Brian says now.

But within weeks of Brian arriving at Colgate, Mainwaring was leaving for his next job. A school spokesperson confirmed that Mainwaring worked for two years in the admissions department but provided no details about why he left. Mainwaring told Brian he was headed to California for a new job, gave the young man his new number, and said he could call collect anytime. In a letter to another squad member during that time, Mainwaring wrote that he was leaving for "California Institute of Technology for my new position as Counseling Psychologist and Professor of Psychology."

That was only partly true.

"Dragging It Out of Him"

California Institute of Technology is a school for geniuses, a science and engineering powerhouse in Pasadena, just a few miles down the road from the Rose Bowl. The university manages NASA's Jet Propulsion Laboratory, and it is perennially viewed as one of the nation's top tech schools—the MIT of the West.

By the end of September 1987, Mainwaring had, indeed, landed at Caltech. But he was neither a professor nor, formally, a counselor. He was hired as the associate master of student housing, essentially the No. 2 spot in the department that oversees student living at Caltech.

His arrival was covered in the student paper, which described him as "a man whom most students find easy to talk to because of his unassuming demeanor and his smooth English accent." Mainwaring, the article boasted, has "degrees in music, theology, psychology; graduate degrees in education, developmental psychology, and counseling; as well as a diploma in physiotherapy." The article said that Mainwaring's job would make him "available for more one-to-one interactions with the students."

The position came with a house near campus. Squad members visited from the East Coast, and they were impressed by his two-story digs, which had access to a swimming pool. Brian came out from Colgate, and after a workout, Mainwaring gave him a massage and masturbated him, again couched as part of mental training.

Mainwaring began incorporating a new facet into his teachings with Brian: God. By this point, religion had become a central part of the young man's life.

"I looked at him like a Christian disciple because he would intersperse his weird, whacked-out teaching with Bible aphorisms here and there," says Brian, who has a master's degree from Yale Divinity School. "Like cults use the Bible, he used it in a way that he knew had pull with me."

But things soon unraveled for Mainwaring at Caltech. His boss,

Robert Oliver, would note that Mainwaring was "very charming, but he didn't volunteer very much information, so I had to get most of what I needed to know by kind of dragging it out of him." Oliver is now dead, but in an audio oral history recorded in 1988, he clearly was describing Mainwaring when he talked about hiring an associate master of student housing who was "doing a dissertation at Syracuse."

On one hand, Oliver said, it was a smart staffing decision to hire Mainwaring, whose name he didn't use on the recording. With a new deputy, there was someone else to handle middle-of-the-night calls to the dorms. But deputizing this person was "a bad thing at the same time, because I wasn't totally aware of all the things that were going on."

"He was much too secretive about the operations," Oliver says. "Indeed, I am told that he asked the people he was counseling not to divulge information about what was going on in their counseling sessions."

One former Caltech student, who spoke only on the condition of anonymity, told *Outside the Lines* that Mainwaring quickly earned a reputation for providing informal couples counseling to students and, inevitably, urging the couples to break up. The former student says that during a session with his then-girlfriend in the spring of 1988, Mainwaring said the couple's relationship was stalled because the man's sex drive wasn't strong enough. Mainwaring said he had a fix, though, and invited the freshman to his house. Upon arrival, the man says, Mainwaring directed him to lie down on the couch. Soon, the coach's lotion-filled hands were under the man's pants and grabbing his penis. The former student says he left immediately. He didn't complain at the time, but *Outside the Lines* has learned that another student filed a complaint about Mainwaring.

Caltech fired Mainwaring on July 5, 1988, less than a year after he arrived, "following an internal investigation related to a student complaint," a school spokesperson wrote in an email. The spokesperson declined to provide details about the nature of the complaint and added, "The student was not a minor, and did not want to report the alleged incident to law enforcement." Asked if Caltech took any actions to warn other potential employers about Mainwaring, the spokesperson said the school had no further information.

In total, three men told *Outside the Lines* they were sexually abused by Mainwaring while he was at Caltech. If other students there were molested by him on or near campus, they hadn't sought justice; the Pasadena Police Department said it has no records of any complaints against Mainwaring.

In the spring of 1990, eighteen months after he was fired from Caltech, Mainwaring was hired by the University of Southern California to work in its Disability Services and Programs office. He lasted just over a year. Citing employee privacy policies, a spokesperson for USC declined to say whether the school had known about Mainwaring's dismissal from Caltech or comment on why he left.

In the decade after his departure from USC, Mainwaring kept an even lower profile than he had in the past—back when he was telling Vernon Sharples to keep his whereabouts a secret. He worked a series of random jobs and continued to coach athletes, sometimes in an official capacity. One female athlete said he coached women for a time at Santa Monica College, and a school spokesperson confirmed that Mainwaring was employed part-time as a track coach during the spring of 1996.

It is unclear how many new squad members Mainwaring began training in the 1990s. Some old members continued to visit him and stay in contact, but *Outside the Lines* spoke with only one accuser who says he met the coach during that time.

Power of the Track

Drake Stadium's nine dark azure lanes make up one of the most recognizable surfaces in track. Some of the fastest humans have run there, from Jackie Joyner-Kersee to Maurice Greene.

The power of the track was not lost on Yuri Nosenko, newly eighteen and a freshman when he was training at Drake on a fall afternoon in 2001. He was on his own—not on the UCLA track team but hoping to get there. Nosenko came from athletic cloth. His dad was once one of the Soviet Union's top 400-meter runners, and his mom was among that country's best women's tennis players.

After Nosenko had finished his workout one day, Conrad Mainwaring walked up and introduced himself as "Coach Av." Mainwaring said he noticed that Nosenko seemed serious about training, and he invited the young man to join his current squad. Some of the members were UCLA students, some were not, and some were Olympic-level athletes who had finished college. It was an open invitation. Mainwaring wouldn't charge Nosenko for his services, but there were three requirements.

"First," Mainwaring said, "no drinking or drugs. Second, no messing around with girls. And then third, you've got to come to church with me once."

The first and third didn't seem like huge deals to Nosenko, and he didn't have a girlfriend at that point, so he agreed. Above all else, he just wanted to make the UCLA team.

Initially, Nosenko loved what he found. He enjoyed the training regimen, and Mainwaring was clearly legit: to Nosenko's surprise, the squad's standout member was Felix Sanchez, the Dominican American hurdler and then-Olympic hopeful. Nosenko ultimately would be one of Sanchez's training partners in the lead-up to the 2004 Olympics in Athens.

Before long, Mainwaring taught Nosenko about mental strength and began discussing testosterone levels, the purported connection between erections and athletic performance, and the importance of abstaining from masturbation. Again, secrecy was mandatory.

"He had code words for all these things," Nosenko says. "'Coffee' was masturbation, and 'tea' was a wet dream. There was a way to call him to schedule a therapy session. Ring once, hang up. Wait, call again."

Nosenko says he never discussed this part of the training with Sanchez or other members of the squad. Sanchez says he was never touched inappropriately by Mainwaring and wasn't aware of any allegations against his former coach until three years ago. "I have heard a few comments since 2016, [but] to tell the truth, I didn't believe them," he says, adding that he was "fully surprised by the accusations." *Outside the Lines* spoke with several other men who say they trained with Mainwaring and had only positive experiences.

But Nosenko says that Mainwaring's apartment near UCLA —the same one he has lived in since 1990, according to public records—was a regular destination for many of the athletes who trained with Coach Avondale. Sometimes, squad members were at the apartment at the same time.

"There were several times when I watched him give my peers hand jobs," he says. ". . . He framed it so well as training . . . like, this is training, it's not sex."

Outside the Lines spoke with fourteen men who trained under Mainwaring at Drake Stadium or in the Los Angeles area from the mid-1990s to 2016 and say they were abused near campus, usually at Mainwaring's apartment.

One man, who spoke only on the condition of anonymity, competed for the UCLA track team from 2010 to 2013 and says he was coerced so artfully that a session occurred inside Mainwaring's apartment as the two men watched TV coverage of the Jerry Sandusky child abuse scandal.

Says the man, who also earned a law degree from UCLA: "It didn't even cross my mind that this was the same thing, that he was doing this for his own pleasure."

Beginning of the End

While Mainwaring was busy coaching at the UCLA track, his past was beginning to catch up.

Two thousand miles away, in Fort Wayne, Indiana, a man named Tym De Santo was just back from vacation in March 2010. He planned to write about the trip on his blog, where he called himself the Renaissance Guy. De Santo was a niche celebrity. He and his mop of blond hair appeared on the inaugural season of HGTV's *Design Star*, where he got his nickname because of his varied talents: designer, singer-songwriter, sculptor, photographer, mountain biker, former professional ski racer.

He wrote on the blog that he and his mother traveled to England, where the De Santo family had lived for a year when Tym was young. "My time in UK was so pleasant and inspiring!" he wrote.

De Santo described a "truly magical evening" visit to Cambridge, where he "sat in front of a long row of colleges, sipping on a cappuccino" under the "deepest indigo blue" sky he had ever seen. He concluded, "Hundreds of years of history, people, stories and events. Thank you Mom and thank you England!"

There wasn't a single mention of Conrad Mainwaring, whom De Santo met when he lived in England. Mainwaring later got him a job as a junior counselor at Camp Greylock in the late 1970s. There, De Santo says, Mainwaring molested him.

But by the time he posted about the England trip—more than three decades later—De Santo thought he had buried that past.

The blog item, probably read largely by close friends and family, sat dormant for a year. Then the strangest thing happened: a childhood friend of De Santo's named Glenn Stephens chimed in under the comments section, using an alias.

"Speaking of the UK," Stephens wrote, "I have some Conrad Mainwaring gossip for you!"

De Santo's talk of England, it turns out, had triggered Stephens to remember he had seen Mainwaring several years earlier working with a group of young men at UCLA's Drake Stadium. Stephens had briefly trained with Mainwaring decades earlier after being introduced by De Santo. He says Mainwaring once "tried a bad touch on me" during a post-workout massage, at which point Stephens cut the cord.

At the time that Stephens made his 2011 remark on De Santo's blog, Mainwaring was mostly invisible on the internet, despite having been an Olympian who coached Sanchez to a gold medal in 2004. Anyone who Googled him found little. But Stephens's blog comment would prove to be a beacon for anyone typing in Mainwaring's name. The first to speak up, in 2013, was Brian, the man who says he was molested by Mainwaring when he was an eighteen-year-old freshman at Colgate.

"I noticed a reference here to Conrad Mainwaring, who also goes by the alias Avondale Mainwaring," Brian wrote. "He has abused many boys and young men, some of whom are my friends. While eternal justice awaits him, justice now, in history, for the victims, would be a good thing . . ."

Other comments trickled in over the next few years, until the fall of 2017, when the #MeToo movement was changing the national dialogue on sexual abuse and more people found De Santo's blog and shared their experiences. The details were vague, but they began to lay bare the path of destruction—from England to Greylock to Syracuse to Colgate to Southern California.

"Crafty SOB."

"Serial predator."

"He got me and my good friend at Camp Greylock in 1977."

"He used his Olympic status to control me."

"I was abused for several years by this despicable predator."

"Grievous and utterly evil."

Some of the longest and most detailed comments came from Vernon Sharples, in the U.K. "I've had a long time to process everything," he wrote. "There is light at the end of the tunnel! We were all used and abused by Conrad. He not only stole our bodies but he stole our minds too."

The network of men accusing Mainwaring jelled. Many of them had lived in pained silence. Some had spiraled into alcohol, drug, or sexual addiction; others had considered suicide. Many had endured pervasive shame.

Now, they had found a support system. The more they connected privately through emails and phone calls, the more they discovered the similarity of their experiences—and the more emboldened they became to take action.

Andrew Zenoff sought out his reporter friend.

Others considered more direct routes to get at Mainwaring.

A Call to Repent

Brian was at his office in southern Connecticut early one morning in April 2013. It was about 8:30 on the East Coast—but he had designs on waking up Conrad Mainwaring three time zones to the west, using a number he found online. Here's how he remembers it:

After a few rings, Mainwaring, now sixty-one, picks up.

"Conrad, do you know who this is? . . . It's Brian."

Long pause.

"Do you remember me? I'm calling you to see if you repented for molesting young men and boys."

Long pause.

"Yes, I've struggled with this my whole life," Mainwaring says. "I've been in therapy since 2002."

"Have you stopped?"

"I stopped in 2002."

Brian knows this isn't true because of what he's learned through the network. He details the impact Mainwaring has had on his life.

"I ask you to forgive me," Mainwaring says.

"For what? What did you do?" Brian wants clarity.

"For ruining your life."

The call lasts about fifteen minutes. Mainwaring stumbles through, at once self-critical—"There is total hypocrisy in my life because I'm still teaching young people"—and at other times seething over the memory of a woman who supposedly betrayed him.

"You are a false teacher," Brian says. "You're deluded. You weren't following Christ."

He tells Mainwaring that if he is to truly repent, he needs to make a "wholesale confession" to all the men he wronged. Brian has a suggestion for whom to call first, and he offers a phone number.

A few days later, a man who asked to be referred to as Max is about to take a walk when his phone rings. Max says Mainwaring molested him starting when he was in high school in Syracuse in the early 1980s. He and Brian had connected through the survivor network and spent hours sharing their stories and feelings.

"This is Conrad," Mainwaring begins. "I'm calling to ask for your forgiveness."

Max asks whether the sexual part of the "training" served any legitimate purpose.

"There was no logic to any of it. It was stupid, it was wrong," Mainwaring tells Max. He says his actions were "Hitler-like. Everything I was doing was about control."

As they go back and forth, Max lays out the devastation he suffered, including thoughts of killing himself.

"There has been darkness that has been part of my life," Max says. "I went to prostitutes and massage parlors and reenacted my experience with you."

Mainwaring says that he has been in therapy for years, that he left education, that he wasn't sexually abusive anymore. He says he and a counselor he's been seeing "are pretty sure I experienced an event while I was young. That something happened with my cousins. I have flashes of it." He says his parents left him alone in Antigua until he was nine and that "some sort of molestation took place."

"That must be painful. I'm sorry for what was perpetrated on you," Max says. "I'm more sorry that you turned around and perpetrated it on others."

"Can you forgive me?"

"I don't know how to answer that question. I don't know what to do about that."

"I understand. I hope you know that I'm genuinely sorry. Good luck."

"Good luck to you," Max answers, without thinking.

The call lasts forty-five minutes, and Max immediately records everything he can remember in his journal, which he provided to *Outside the Lines*. Max writes that he felt pity for Mainwaring because he was "infected with a sickness and then infected others." Then Max feels angry and worried that he failed to convey "how much sorrow, shame and demoralization I felt over thirty years." And by finishing the call by saying, "Good luck." *What was that?*

Max writes down what he wished he had said: "Good luck as you proceed down a path for good rather than one of destruction. Good luck processing and understanding how much you've hurt young men."

In an effort both to learn about Mainwaring's family history and to address his claims of abuse as a boy in Antigua, *Outside the Lines* reached out to his brother in England and sister in New Zealand. Neither replied. But at least two things Mainwaring told Max were lies. First, Mainwaring hadn't voluntarily left education—at least not at Caltech—as he had suggested. Most notably, he allegedly hadn't stopped abusing young athletes.

Nor, apparently, would he stop.

"Something Weird Just Happened"

It's early evening, June 27, 2016, and Mainwaring is giving Benjamin a ride to his student apartment after a workout at Drake Stadium.

"I'll find parking," Mainwaring tells Benjamin. "Then I'll come up and give you the full treatment."

Over the past several months of training with Mainwaring, Benjamin has become a believer. His efforts to walk on to the UCLA track team haven't worked out, but under Mainwaring, his running times have improved, buoying his goal of making his country's national team. Sure, the talks about life and theories on training, the comments about testosterone and the connection between erections and athletic performance are weird, but they seem to fit into some grander plan.

Inside the apartment, Mainwaring has Benjamin lie on his back. Soon, he begins to work the groin area and tells Benjamin to conjure an erection. Ability to do so is an indication of high testosterone, Mainwaring says.

"The goal is to get from zero to 100," he says.

Benjamin feels uneasy, but he is oddly pleased when Mainwaring says, "Good, good, you're getting percentage quite quickly."

"The Eastern European athletes and coaches do this all the time," Mainwaring tells him. "And the Greeks used to do this."

Mainwaring works his hands under Benjamin's underwear: "To get the deep muscles, I need direct contact with the skin."

Eventually, Mainwaring masturbates Benjamin to completion. Benjamin lies there stunned, but almost hypnotized. He keeps thinking about the goal: higher testosterone levels, better performance.

After Mainwaring leaves, Benjamin replays the session over and over. He goes to his computer and searches for any information on performance and masturbation and testosterone levels. He comes up empty and texts a friend: "Something weird just happened. I need to talk with you tomorrow."

Finally, Benjamin goes to bed. He has an early workout the next day at Drake. With Mainwaring.

Around the same time, about thirty miles away, in the L.A. suburb of Agoura Hills, thirty-one-year-old UCLA alum David O'Boyle is steeling himself for the next morning. He is planning to confront Mainwaring for abusing him eleven years ago. He had kept the pain mostly to himself all these years, but then he found De Santo's blog and learned that one man who accused Mainwaring of abuse might have been just twelve years old at the time.

O'Boyle can't stay quiet any longer. He has to do something.

"It's Over for You"

Early the next morning, June 28, 2016, Mainwaring picks up Benjamin outside his apartment en route to Drake, as if nothing unusual happened the night before. And O'Boyle makes the forty-five-minute drive to UCLA.

As O'Boyle parks and walks toward the track, he hasn't decided whether he'll record the confrontation. Marching across the infield, he can see young men stretching, and he spots Mainwaring. Adrenaline floods his brain. He decides to warn the athletes before doing anything else; he wants to do for them what nobody did for him, so he approaches the group. Benjamin looks up, bewildered.

"Do you train with this man?" O'Boyle asks.

Benjamin feels paralyzed as O'Boyle turns to Mainwaring and stays on him, relentlessly, for twelve minutes, video rolling.

How are you getting away with it, you m—— f——?

How do you do it? How do you get these boys to believe in you so much? How do you get them to trust you?

You're a total master manipulator.

You're not doing this anymore. It's over for you.

Mainwaring, in a purple shirt under a black jacket, avoids eye contact. He fumbles with a stopwatch. He takes out a note pad and starts writing. He points off camera toward what appear to be some of his squad members and suggests he is going to time them.

Look in that camera. I want a good picture to show the cops.

How many boys have you molested in your life? I know at least five, maybe six.

Mainwaring tries to walk away a couple of times, with the aid of a walker he has used since having hip surgery the year before. He is carrying a large umbrella, which he uses to take occasional swipes at O'Boyle, connecting at least once.

Hittin' me with an umbrella! What are you, seven years old? Is that when it happened to you?

You're not doing this anymore. It's over for you. There's not gonna be any more boys. There's not gonna be any more molesting.

Eventually, O'Boyle is done. He goes directly to UCLA police, where he tells an officer everything, from the alleged abuse a decade ago to the confrontation that day and Mainwaring hitting him with the umbrella. He just wants something—anything—done. He writes a letter to UCLA's athletic department, demanding an investigation and insisting Mainwaring be banned from the track. Several others write letters of support.

Benjamin, in a state of fatigue and despair, goes back to his apartment. Mainwaring calls him later that day, he says, and insists O'Boyle is a disgruntled former athlete. Benjamin doesn't know what to believe, but he writes a detailed account of what happened in his apartment.

About two weeks later, Benjamin works up the nerve to tell his parents, who encourage him to file a report with authorities. So, UCLA police hear another account about Mainwaring. But according to Benjamin, officers suggest they can't bring charges because he is an adult. Any sexual contact, they say, would be seen as consensual. This contradicts California law, which states, in part, that if "the perpetrator fraudulently represented that the touching served a professional purpose, [he] is guilty of sexual battery," regardless of the age of the victim.

UCLA police took this report from Benjamin about two weeks after the runner witnessed David O'Boyle's confrontation with Mainwaring.

In a letter dated August 15, 2016, UCLA notifies Mainwaring he has been banned from campus and from working with UCLA athletes. If he doesn't comply, the letter says, he'll be subject to arrest. It reads, in part: "We recently received several complaints that you utilized as an alleged training strategy inappropriate massaging of the genital region of male athletes," which complainants consider "an assault." The letter also notes that UCLA police spoke with Mainwaring and that he "acknowledged the nature of this physical contact on more than one occasion" but "indicated it may have been inadvertent." *Outside the Lines* was unable to review the investigative files, which are protected under state law.

O'Boyle later said UCLA police informed him that the umbrella strikes didn't merit criminal charges and that the statute of limitations had expired on his claims of sexual abuse. The department declined comment to *Outside the Lines,* citing confidentiality.

Although O'Boyle's confrontation led to a small victory for those who have accused Mainwaring, none of them believed he would give up coaching. As one said, "He was like a virus, a contagion."

But they weren't through fighting him.

Detectives Catch a Break

Robert Druger, the Syracuse eye surgeon recruited to Mainwaring's squad while in high school, was at a bar mitzvah in late 2018 when he met a federal prosecutor who had handled sexual abuse cases.

Druger had buried his abuse for decades; he hadn't told anyone about it—not even his family—until he found De Santo's
blog, linked up with others who have accused Mainwaring, and
contacted *Outside the Lines* to give his account. But once Druger
opened up, there was no stopping him. His bar mitzvah conversation led to a call with a federal agent in New York, which led
to a call with the FBI in Los Angeles. Druger wanted Mainwaring
brought to justice, but it wasn't looking good.

New York's criminal statute of limitations on Druger's allegations was long expired, and there was no evidence that Mainwaring
committed a federal crime, so the FBI forwarded the case to the
Los Angeles Police Department. If Mainwaring was still involved
with boys or young men, it would be a matter for the LAPD.

Druger spoke to LAPD Detective Danetta Menifee, relaying his
experience and putting her and her partner, Detective Sharlene
Johnson, in touch with others who said Mainwaring abused them.
Still, there wasn't much the detectives could do. All of the cases
were too old.

"It was a little disheartening, listening to the victims, how they
were affected back then, how they're still affected, and knowing
that [we] couldn't do anything," Johnson told *Outside the Lines*.

But then the detectives caught a break. In December, a former
training partner of Benjamin's had encouraged him to reach out
to *Outside the Lines*. After talking with reporters, Benjamin learned
about the LAPD investigation and contacted officers, sharing his
own experience.

The report arrived just six months before expiration of California's three-year statute of limitations on sexual battery by fraud
—touching the genitals under false pretenses. With Benjamin, the
detectives had a shot at bringing a case to the district attorney. It
wouldn't be easy. Because the allegation did not include a claim of
penetration, the sexual battery was what is referred to as a "wob-
bler," meaning it might not be charged by prosecutors as a felony.

In an effort to increase their chances of getting a felony filed,
the detectives sought to show prosecutors that the alleged offense
was part of a pattern—in this case dating back to the 1970s. So
Johnson and Menifee continued chasing down men whose accounts bolstered their case.

"A lot of these men didn't even know they were victims of
crimes until more recent things started coming out in the news

about women, the #MeToo movement and what was happening to them," Johnson says. ". . . I think a lot of that has to do with . . . society being more open to what is and is not a crime when it comes to all spectrums of sexual assault."

While the LAPD was building its case against Mainwaring, *Outside the Lines* spotted him at a local track meet and learned he was still coaching young athletes at Rancho Cienega Sports Complex, a public facility in South Los Angeles.

Early on the morning of March 21 of this year, reporters found Mainwaring sitting at the track alone, waiting for his athletes to show up. It was overcast, and the rush of Exposition Boulevard traffic was audible from a hundred yards off. A reporter approached, with a TV crew in tow.

Mainwaring sprang up, grabbed his walker, and bolted, moving surprisingly fast for a sixty-seven-year-old man with hip problems. With cameras rolling and the reporter asking about the many men who accused him of sexual abuse, Mainwaring beelined across the parking lot. He refused comment, other than to accuse the reporter of harassment. Later, *Outside the Lines* attempted to contact Mainwaring by email, phone, and a letter left at his apartment. He never replied.

Early on June 19, Los Angeles police arrested Mainwaring on one felony count of sexual battery by fraud, punishable by up to four years in prison. He pleaded not guilty and was released on bail a few days later.

It is unclear who bailed him out.

Outside the Lines broke the story of the arrest—prompting several additional men to contact reporters and describe how Mainwaring had sexually abused them.

Living with the Legacy

Decades after her eldest son confided that he had been molested by Conrad Mainwaring and then died a few days later in a hiking accident, seventy-eight-year-old Nisha Zenoff sits on a couch in her Northern California home.

Her condo overlooks Richardson Bay in affluent Tiburon. It's tranquil and picturesque—a stark contrast to the dark hole in her life all these years later.

Nisha is a psychotherapist, with a specialty in grief and marriage counseling. She wrote a 2017 book titled, *The Unspeakable Loss: How Do You Live After a Child Dies?* Today, she is showing a reporter some old photos of Victor.

"Oh, this is a good one . . . I think that one was in Mexico . . ."

She sifts through the shots and smiles. "Everybody loved Victor . . . We would always say Victor had a certain sense of loving and being kind to people . . . He smiled a lot. He was happy. He had that dimple. He was easygoing."

But then: "That summer camp experience with Conrad absolutely changed him."

After Victor died, Nisha says, she vowed to her then-husband and others that she would go after "this son of a bitch, wherever he is."

But as Nisha's anger became consumed by grief, she says, her sense of urgency for justice was pushed to the background.

"I think our hearts were so broken that the most we could do was grieve his death," she says. "But for me, it was always an unfinished piece of business. Always."

Finally, she is beginning to get some answers. Her son Andrew had helped set the wheels in motion by speaking with his reporter friend, and now Nisha was hearing about what *Outside the Lines* had unearthed about Conrad Mainwaring:

There are at least forty-one men who have accused Mainwaring of abusing them. Victor was the youngest, just twelve. The men now range in age from twenty-two to fifty-nine. According to their accounts—fifteen on the record—Mainwaring carried out his abuse across two continents and four states, often while employed at prestigious institutions. A handful of the men say they tried to bring Mainwaring to justice in England and the United States, only to be met with shrugs or hindered by statutes of limitations.

The men told virtually identical stories—of being charmed, groomed, coached, and sexually molested by Mainwaring for weeks, months, or years under the auspices of sports training, mental training, spiritual guidance, or some combination of the three. They say their coach used his Olympic credentials, coaching achievements, relationships with accomplished athletes, and expertise in psychology and physiology to persuade them to train with him, often at no charge. Many said they had little or no previous sexual experience when they met him.

Collectively, they rendered a detailed and consistent picture of a con man so skilled that he often conducted the abuse without his victims even realizing they were used as tools of his perversion.

Many described a Faustian bargain driven by their desire for athletic success, combined with a sense that Mainwaring was truly their friend, their mentor, their guide on a journey toward a better life. In fact, to this day, some of the men report feeling wildly conflicted—angry and tortured by the abuse yet convinced that some of their achievements would not have been possible without him. One man still credits Mainwaring for his becoming a doctor. Another gave Mainwaring tens of thousands of dollars over the years; that man recently found himself crying alone in his car in the wake of the coach's arrest. Many invited Mainwaring into their homes to meet their parents, who were equally enamored of him. In recent years, several men banded together to raise $13,000 to help pay for Mainwaring's hip replacement.

As Nisha absorbs the breadth of the accusations and Mainwaring's lasting impact, she distills his influence to a "manipulation of the brain."

"It was a rape of the brain in that sense because it wasn't just an abuse of the body," she says. "It's abuse of the brain and the heart and the soul."

For that moment, Nisha's analysis sounds detached, more professional than parental. But then, quickly, she is inside Victor's head and overwhelmed. She's fighting back tears.

"The pain of thinking what he must have gone through internally, holding a secret like that," she says. "I really think of [Mainwaring] as a killer. I mean, that's pretty strong because I don't think he's killed anybody. But somehow, I feel like he killed Victor's spirit."

JOHN GRISWOLD

The Exiled and the Devil's Sideshow

FROM THE COMMON READER

DRIVING NORTH OUT of Baton Rouge on a beautiful Sunday afternoon in October, the sky bluer than the Gulf of Mexico, it is hard not to feel guilty for some reason, as if you have done something wrong but not been caught, or someone is waiting for you to transgress. Or maybe it is that you have the freedom to do anything you like, such as check into a nice hotel, or jump on a plane to just about anywhere, or head up to the state penitentiary to watch bulls bowl through men as if they did not exist.

Scenic Highway passes through a neighborhood with a meat market, a string of churches, and recycling centers. Many of the buildings are painted with colorful murals. "The time is always right what's right," says one. "Seek knowledge B4 vengeance."

The scene changes to chemical plants, tank farms, boxcars tagged with graffiti, then again to prairies blanketed in black-eyed Susans.

Horse country begins: multi-acre, emerald fields surrounded by white fences, coastal oaks draped in Spanish moss. A Civil War battleground and National Cemetery lie among the sea pines, and there are signs for plantations. Mississippi is ten miles away. A card table in a tangle of trees and kudzu sells JUMBO BOLLED PEANUTS [sic], but cars are going too fast to stop.

They slow rapidly on the edge of St. Francisville, a small, gentrified town in West Feliciana Parish, which also has the prison. Better not to risk it, drivers seem to be thinking. St. Francisville looks like it loves its sheriff's department. Outside of town a car is pulled over, the driver still behind the wheel but his hands pressed strangely against the windshield, forefingers and thumbs making a diamond, as a white officer stands next to his SUV.

The Sunday drive is over when the road suddenly dead-ends at the Louisiana State Penitentiary, or Angola.

Angola is the biggest maximum-security state prison in America by population, about 6,300 men, three-fourths serving life sentences. It is in what the Louisiana Department of Public Safety and Corrections calls an "extreme remote location"—18,000 acres nearly encircled by the Mississippi River—and there is no way out except this road and a ferry used only by the prison.

In the nineteenth century Angola was a slave plantation and forced-labor convict farm. As a state prison in the twentieth, it developed a reputation as "probably as close to slavery as any person could come" in a free country; "the worst prison in America"; "medieval, squalid, and horrifying"; and "bloodiest prison in the nation." In this century some things have improved, but Angola is still in the news for inhumane treatment, and an inmate was killed in a fight the day before the rodeo.

All this is why people call Angola "the Alcatraz of the South." Its reputation is nearly religious in intensity: Stygian, hellish, made for Sunday-school lessons. And its infamy is used as a threat that is all the more powerful because it lies out here, mostly unseen, at the edge of the imagination.

During Hurricane Gustav, New Orleans Mayor Ray Nagin warned, "Anybody who is caught looting in the city of New Orleans will go directly to Angola. Directly to Angola. You will not have a temporary stay in the city. You go directly to the big house, in general population. All right? So, I want to make sure that every looter, potential looter, understands that. You will go directly to Angola Prison. And God bless you when you go there." As every sweet granny in Louisiana knows, "bless your little heart" means *fuck you.*

The prison does not look all that threatening at first glance. A wooden guardhouse called "the carport" and a prison museum sit at the entrance. The Reception Center and Death Row are a hodgepodge of buildings off to the side, surrounded with concertina wire. The long allée of cypresses past the guardhouse becomes a road through green pastures where sleek, black cattle lie in repose. Someone has directed attempts to prettify the road with arrangements of gourds and geraniums and crude borders around shrubs still flowering in October.

The rodeo arena, an oval with covered bleachers, is a mile distant. It is built with steel, but the buildings and shacks around it are irregular sizes, knocked together from plywood and cinder blocks and painted different colors. An art fair and food stands sprawl under adjacent shed roofs. The impression is of firetrap, state fair, and scout camp. All of it lies within chain-link fencing and more rolls of razor wire shining like chrome, but there are a surprising number of entrances and exits and no clear security flow.

Visitors must park in an adjacent field and leave cell phones locked in their cars. Armed men patrol on ATVs. An expensive trailer marked as the sheriff's command center sits near the entrance, and a high-tech observation post a quarter-mile in the distance raises its head on a hydraulic neck to see better. Deputies, guards, and unarmed prison workers are everywhere, but there is no metal detector at the main entrance. Visitors pass through and show the contents of their pockets to two young women, who seem overwhelmed, but are not made to prove their pockets are empty. The gate attendants take my chapstick but not my collapsible metal pen, which looks like a weapon.

The Angola prison rodeo has been open to the public for fifty-one years and takes place one weekend in April and every Sunday in October. It is the last prison rodeo in the country. The prison still advertises it as "The Wildest Show in the South," but it used to be more open about how inmates, who sign releases and compete for a few bucks, would be "thrown every which way" for the crowd's entertainment. The men are untrained, and there have been many injuries and even deaths over the years.

These days the official line is about the rehabilitating effect of participation and how it provides a sense of agency. ("It really gives them a feeling of being a man and standing on their own two feet, even though they're incarcerated . . . we bring a human aspect to the way we treat them," a corrections supervisor told *Huffington Post*.) Prisoners, they say, have the chance to earn fifty, one hundred, or more dollars, if they win, which beats the four to twenty cents per hour they make at prison jobs. Net profits are meant to be used for rodeo safety, chapel construction, the Inmate Welfare Fund, and a reentry program.

But a state audit last year showed that

around $6.2 million in revenue from the rodeo just in 2014 and 2015 was being kept in a private checking account in Highlands Bank in St. Francisville, not with the Louisiana Department of Treasury where the state could account for it. Since the rodeo started in 1964, it doesn't appear the state treasury has ever held its revenue, according to the audit. This means the rodeo money hasn't been monitored by Louisiana state government since it began over 50 years ago.

The audit found that money was missing or could not be traced. In all, the public event is a tight-lipped affair, and the press is given limited access.

The stands are full this Sunday, which means a crowd of 7,500 at twenty bucks a pop. Sun and shade stripe the competition floor, which is deep in dirt. Ambulances park at both entrance-exits, and backboards are propped on walls and fences. Just inside the stands a small audience of inmates sit in a cage. A dozen guards stand with their backs to the action, facing them. Signs on the rail say standing is not permitted. As I pass to find my seat, one of the guards roars, *Siddown!!,* at an inmate, and it is hard not to react.

The bronco riding has started. Inmates do not last long and fall badly. One goes down face-first, bent at the waist, arms relaxed behind him, the way a child naps with its butt in the air. There are groans from the audience when he hits the dirt, but more laughter. The man jumps up and runs to the fence. One of the professional cowboys from the rodeo company rides to the bronc and yanks off the red flank strap that makes it buck, and the horse calms. More pro cowboys herd or lasso animals back to the pens. The real cowboys wear pink oxford shirts, cowboy boots, and hats. Competitors wait in their bullpen in striped prison shirts, jeans, tennis shoes or boots, ballistic vests, and sometimes helmets with wire faceguards.

For the next event, cowboys walk several prisoners into the ring and stand each in a hula hoop on the dirt. "Be very, very still," the announcer says, but when the bull is set loose, professional rodeo clowns run among them, waving their arms. The bull head-butts the prisoners, runs over the top of them, tramples them under his hooves. Bodies fly the way people do when hit by cars—ten feet in the air, twenty feet distant—and land awkwardly as mannequins. The men get up and run, looking over their shoulders. One falls flat before the bull reaches him and though disqualified refuses to move. The announcer mocks him and the crowd jeers.

After that, a semi-tractor with WILD THING painted on it pulls out into the dirt. Music blares and the announcer shouts incoherently on the PA. The crowd waits to see what will happen next—or maybe I am the only one in the arena not to know—and what happens is that Bighorn rams run into the ring, chased by monkeys riding dogs. I know I am at a rodeo, in a penitentiary, in the deep South, where men have their spines bent back double and their organs tenderized for our entertainment by animals the size of Hyundais, but now, for some reason, is when my weird-shit-o-meter pegs; the plane of reason is departed; things get mystical.

The bobbling, worried Capuchins wear cowboy shirts, chaps that indicate an endorsement deal, and little hats. They "ride" border collies—sit atop them, more accurately, holding on for dear life—that do not give a flip about them and focus on herding the mountain sheep into a pen and then, for some reason, onto the roof of the semi. For comic relief, a yapping Aussie pup named Cujo helps out at the end. Confused applause.

Tim "Wild Thang" Lepard, their owner, is dressed as gaudily as any American showman. His blue shirt has a giant white star on its back, like a magnification of the U.S. flag. He takes a knee, another symbolic move, hugs a dog-monkey and speaks into his mic. He introduces the dogs. One was in *Sports Illustrated*, another raised money for breast-cancer awareness. He formally introduces the monkeys. One is named Little Elvis.

Lepard wants us to slow down and consider this: as a boy in Tupelo, Mississippi, he dreamed this very dream, and *it came true.* "This," he says, indicating the dog-monkeys and semi-sheep, "is what dreams are all about." He wants badly for us to chase our own dreams.

In 2000, Lepard's bad muffler killed every one of his animals —monkeys, dogs, and sheep. "I started again," he said, "and in four weeks' time trained brand-new animals. Went to Oklahoma City and won Act of the Year." A reporter, "distressed" that one of Lepard's Capuchins had been professionally bobbling for *twenty-*

six years, was told, "We love our animals. And the real people can tell you that."

Now Wild Thing stands, hobbles painfully across the ring—he used to be a bull-rider himself—and speaks directly to the real people in the arena.

"I am not a Republican," he says. "I'm not a Democrat. But I can tell you that it is time to put God back in the USA!"

Thunderous applause. I have the fleeting but distinct feeling I have slipped backwards, maybe to Shakespeare's time. *Exeunt* monkeys.

In the next event two inmates hold a horse with a rope while a third tries to mount it. (No one manages it.) Then "Lady barrel racers," the announcer says, will race in "the only event with someone not in prison." There is bull-riding; not a single inmate stays on to the buzzer.

There are two rounds of "Convict Poker," a variation of the hula-hoop game and much loved by the crowd and YouTube. Four prisoners sit at a table in the ring, pretending to play cards, while a bull is set loose and taunted until it bowls through them, the chairs, and the table. Last man sitting wins. Bodies fly, the crowd roars. The plywood table with two-by-four legs is smashed to pieces both times and replaced.

There is "Bull-Dogging," in which teams of inmates try to catch and pin young cattle as they come racing out of chutes. "Get the nose, get the nose, you gotta get the nose!" the announcer cries. Five of sixteen teams manage it, usually when their steers are flipped all the way over and land on their backs. Most of the men get trampled and a few are dragged until they give up.

There is a corny and risqué magic show by Rudy The Clown, with the mounted MC as his straight man. ("That was a cheap trick, Rudy," the cowboy MC says disapprovingly after one dumb bit. Rudy points to a woman in the audience and says he thought *she* was the cheapest trick there. "*RUDY!*" the MC shouts.) At the merciful end, Rudy releases two white doves from their confinement in a serving dish. They fly in confused lines no farther than the tin roof of the arena and sit there.

In the "Chariot Races," professional horsemen drag prisoners around the ring on scraps of sheet metal. The prisoners lie flat on their backs and hold clear-plastic pitchers of colored water.

Whoever makes it back with the most water wins. Riders gallop like hell for a distant barrel, make the turn, and gallop back to the pens. One rider always speeds up just as the sled comes around the turn—a sadistic joke that makes a cash prize impossible—and slings his prisoners sideways, rolling violently, still clutching their empty pitchers. Two of ten finish.

There is "Wild Cow Milking," but spectator fatigue is setting in. Do the cattle even have teats? Pizzles? It is hard to see in the dust and sinking sun. Is this another joke, meant to parody what ignorance yields in the hardness of life? In any case, no one wins anything.

Finally, all competitor inmates walk into the ring for "Guts and Glory": "A chit (poker chip) is tied to the meanest, toughest Brahma bull available," the rodeo website says. "The object here is to get close enough to the bull in order to snatch the chit. This is the last event of the day, and perhaps the most exciting." Their boldfaced emphasis is on danger. The mounted announcer says the inmate who grabs the chit will win $1,500 this day, due to a bump by a local business sponsor, and the crowd gasps.

The bull is a brindle with horns painted satanic-red. He is a massive, bulging animal, biggest of the day and in an evil mood. The inmates look at each other, and many watch from the far fence. Others rush the bull and get knocked aside or trampled for their ambition. When the bull has them down he does the dance that grinds them in with his hooves and hooks them again and again. His horns have been tipped slightly, so there may not be penetration. With less than thirty seconds left, a man grabs the chit and trots away, limping.

Outside the arena, families wait their turn for a Ferris wheel barely taller than a man. They line up for funnel cakes and nachos. I want to see the art fair, which provides a *roundedness* to the day. A warden must have thought hard: What is the opposite of a violent stomping? Art, I guess. Maybe he was thinking of those girls from good families in a Faulkner story with their "boxes of color and tedious brushes and pictures cut from the ladies' magazines."

Hundreds of stands display all manner of inmate work. Paintings range in quality from First Night Class, to Holiday Inn–style work, to wooden signs painted with photo-realistic branding, such as the LSU TIGERS and TONY CHACHERE'S ORIGINAL CREOLE

SEASONING. A few pieces have the spark of outsider art. Other stands sell decorative turned bowls, sailing ships, leather goods, fabricated barbecue grills, rustic tables and chairs, and a much-duplicated double-rocker with a table between the seats, which is impractical but poignant, given the setting.

Trustees (ten years in prison and good conduct) in non-striped uniforms mix with visitors at their stands. "Medium-custody" prisoners sit behind chain-link fences with their wares on the public side. Maximum-security prisoners cannot take part in the art fair or the rodeo.

Inmates keep sales tickets on hand with their names, Department of Corrections numbers, and space to fill in descriptions of items. When you buy, the prisoner gives you the ticket to take to a shack where non-prisoners run your card or take your cash and stamp the ticket with a red star. You return it to the seller; he takes one of the carbonless copies, and you get your item. Trustees wheel large items to the front gate.

One trustee is selling colorful sculptures made of tack-welded nuts, bolts, pistons, wrenches, and other found metal. A praying mantis figure is beautifully executed but weighs forty pounds. A smaller Uncle Sam with a skull head sits on the edge of a table, saluting. His body is a lawnmower carburetor and limbs are made from rebar. The artist has real talent. He says they call him Pork Chop. He has calm eyes and is easy to talk to. He says he works a prison job, goes to school for HVAC, and makes sculptures with his buddy when he has time. He asks fifty bucks for Uncle Sam, and I buy it and say I would like to put him in touch with an art-dealer friend, if he is open to commissions. He writes out his real name and prison address on a spare ticket. We shake hands.

Across the pavilion a rough guy and his rough buddy are behind a chain-link fence in their striped uniforms. They are selling airboat models, which are on my side of the fence. The boats are to scale but are not models really; they are two- and three-feet-long sculptures made of cypress, cedar, and walnut inlay. The rudders move on ingenious linkages. The first guy tells me to "mash down that thing where the driver sits," and I find that both accelerator and electric propeller work. He is a big, angry-looking dude who looks like a white nationalist. He may have called me Pal. He says the smaller, prettier boat, which he made, had started at $300 but is reduced to two. I shake my head at the beauty of it. It reminds

me, in its delicate ornateness and whiff of cedar, of Vietnamese
woodwork. He mistakes my headshake for a no.

"I'm in a selling mood," he barks. "You in a buying mood? One-
fifty."

His buddy spins on him and whispers, "You sure?"

"Yeah, *fuck it*," my man says, and I buy it for my dealer friend.

Why do I feel surprise, later, when I learn by internet this man
is in prison for life, with no hope for parole, because he made
drugs more than once, while Pork Chop broke into his former
girlfriend's place, strangled her to death in her bed, tried to have
sex with her corpse, then dumped her naked body in the ivy off a
road? I cannot seem to retain the chief lesson of leaving the plane
of reason: things do not have to make sense.

With difficulty I carry the airboat and Uncle Sam to the front
gate, where a big guy in a guard uniform—all the guys are big guys
—checks my sales tickets to see if I stole anything.

The prison art fair is good but alone would not draw thousands
up from the cities, down from Mississippi, over from Alabama and
Georgia and Texas. No, it is the rodeo that sells: powerful animals
stripped of will and forced to participate; men without defenses
hurt by them; the surreal spectacle of dog-monkeys chasing Big-
horns onto a semi.

Having won dominion over most of what walks, creeps, flies,
and swims, we cannot simply leave other animals alone, even when
there is no good reason to mess with them. What is the line that
runs back through rodeo, bullfight, circus, organ grinder, cock-
fight, bear-baiting, horse-and-dog blood sports, and the forum?
Nothing makes Twain's town loafers as happy as a dogfight, "unless it might be putting turpentine on a stray dog and setting fire
to him, or tying a tin pan to his tail and see him run himself to
death."

These prisoners, who did not leave others alone, mess with animals not left alone, for a prize many of us would not call in to a radio station for. It is a spectacle of servitude, cruelty enacted, a passion play about the hard and irrational. It is predicated on pain.

The Angola Rodeo survives when other prison rodeos have
closed because, of all places in America, Angola is the perfect
stage. Can you imagine it taking place in the state capital? Or on
the National Mall? No, this sort of bald-faced admission of who we

are is best left to the sticks, the former slave plantation, the prison, the place with the worst possible reputation. And for half a century the state government has sanctioned, organized, and made money from the spectacle.

The Angola Rodeo seems like the sort of thing you would find in a distant province of some empire now gone. After weeks of hard travel by steamer and coach and by foot in the mud, across versts of inhospitable country, you arrive at a penal colony with cruel justice and an odd ritual performed for visitors. Its pageantry invokes God and praises the king, though neither church nor palace discuss it in polite conversation.

But this is the United States of America, *anno Domini* 2018, when the source of a particular neutrino has just been discovered to be an elliptical galaxy many light-years distant, with a supermassive black hole at its center.

It is disorienting. I leave Angola under the gaze of guards and deputies and drive north. In minutes I am in Mississippi. The narrow road twists through the forest, as in some dream. The sun gets weird. Trees have fallen in the road, and road signs are riddled with bullets. Later, on the main highway a lighted billboard advertises an odd URL, *IsHeInYou.com,* and Jesus, in the spotlight, looks away, looks away, looks away, somewhere else.

KENT BABB

Olympic Cyclist Catlin Was Driven to the End

FROM THE WASHINGTON POST

ON THE DAY he'd bury his daughter, Mark Catlin stepped out of a chapel and into the fresh air.

"Nice day for a walk," he said, looking up, and on this morning in late March, the weather was flawless: cloudless, crisp, a bright blue sky.

He took a breath and set off, heading down the cemetery's path and falling behind the procession of cars ahead, talking as gravel crunched beneath his shoes. He asked if the memorial service, laboriously planned near the lakefront cycling trails Kelly Catlin had explored before becoming a silver medalist in the 2016 Olympics, had been good enough. He apologized if it had been too sad. The afternoon reception, he assured friends and visitors, should be more lively.

A few paces up the winding path, a longtime friend shook his head. Mark, the friend whispered, would do anything to distract himself—he always had—in this case to avoid facing "the darkness": Kelly's suicide two weeks earlier, her thoughts during those final days and weeks, the way she'd planned her death in the same meticulous, results-oriented way she'd lived her life.

Back on the walkway, Mark wore a blank expression as he accepted condolences and told people about his plans for the coming weeks. Eventually he reached a gravesite surrounded by mourners, and he stopped at the rear of the group as if happening upon a stranger's funeral.

Gradually the faces turned, and after a moment Mark noticed his wife and two other children waiting near a charcoal-colored casket.

"I guess we'll go lay her to rest now," he said, stepping forward.

Next to the computer in the basement of his home, Mark has a notebook labeled "To Do: Kelly" with seven projects listed: photos to organize by year, sixty hours of video to edit, a bio to write, calls to make, and emails he'll send after jolting awake most nights around two. But now he's working on No. 1: the enormous memorial he's designing alongside a touch-screen information kiosk, like something at a museum, he imagines at Kelly's graveside.

"So people can remember," he says.

He wants people to know Kelly wasn't just the daughter of Carolyn and Mark, the triplet sister of Christine and Colin. She was more than an intelligent but socially awkward twenty-three-year-old from the Twin Cities. Kelly built herself into an Olympian and a three-time world champion in the four-rider group race known as the team pursuit. She was fluent in Chinese and had been first-chair violinist in her high school orchestra, a competitive pit bull who folded origami and played badminton with the same joyless ferocity that she brought into a velodrome or classroom.

Kelly's father wants you to know all of it: she took classes at the University of Minnesota in eleventh grade, notched a perfect score on the SAT, had enrolled last fall in the computational mathematics program at Stanford's graduate school. This was a young woman who had become convinced, like so many of her high-achieving peers, that pedaling to the peak of one mountain only meant a better view of the other, taller ones in the distance.

"The very characteristics that made you successful will be self-destructive," Mark says he has realized, though he prefers to keep himself busy than think too deeply about it, and indeed as much as his daughter was an outlier in life, she was part of a trend in death.

Mark is a retired medical pathologist, and he has learned these past few months that young people in the United States —and, in particular, young women and girls—are killing themselves at a rate the Centers for Disease Control and Prevention considers a national health crisis. Between 2007 and 2015, according to a CDC study, the suicide rate doubled among females aged fifteen to nineteen and reached a forty-year high.

Major depressive episodes and suicide attempts have skyrocketed among women under thirty-five, according to a twelve-year analysis by the National Survey on Drug Use and Health, as a society fixated on collecting and comparing achievements seemingly has conditioned a promising generation of young people to ignore emotional alarms—insomnia, anxiety, and depression—and work toward the next goal.

Sometimes that pressure comes from family or peer groups, and it can manifest itself in ways good and bad: pushing certain individuals to astonishing heights and others to alarming depths. Kelly, though, found herself at both extremes—climbing the Olympic medal stand three years before taking her own life in the bedroom of her Stanford apartment—and seemed determined from an early age to prove herself in increasingly intense arenas, only exacerbating her best and worst tendencies.

And even that, mental health experts say, is more and more common as suicide has been on a consistent rise among individuals born between 1982 and 1999. Kat Giordano, Kelly's former roommate at Stanford who discovered her body, has experienced the highs and lows of existing in a culture that seems to have convinced its young people that being average is unacceptable—leading some to grow up believing they must be exceptional or die trying.

"I am someone who thrives under pressure, but . . . you're surrounded by it," said Giordano, a Stanford Law School student who in 2018 graduated magna cum laude from Princeton. "It feels like the best motivation and something dangerous simultaneously."

On the day of Kelly's funeral, Colin Catlin sat on a nearby tombstone and watched the gravediggers bury his sister. He had taken photographs of her casket, crouching and experimenting with angles to find the perfect light. He'd picked up handfuls of dirt and let it slide through his fingers.

"With her to the very end," he'd say later, going on to point out it was just his way of coping.

His sister Christine's, though, was to bolt toward a car once the eulogies concluded. If her father and brother had somehow found ways to channel the emotions of the previous weeks, Christine felt engulfed by them: despair, anger, regret. None, though, was as prevalent as guilt, and considering the family she was born into, she knew lingering at the grave would lead to a breakdown—exposing her yet again as the black sheep of the Catlin flock.

"I was," she'd say later, "the weak one."

Triplet siblings are often measured against one another from birth—Kelly won her first race by being the first to enter the world, a minute ahead of Christine—and the competitions and labeling never stop. Kelly was the cyborg, ruthless and analytical by third grade, and Colin was the bohemian: a beekeeper, Eagle Scout, and gardener. Christine, though, was the crier. She'd fly upstairs after a cross word or remark about her being underweight, sobbing and reading alone. She'd disappear from conversations and ruminate on what had been said, channeling her feelings into short stories and plays.

During those early years, Kelly would act out the roles in Christine's imagination—she took home theater as seriously as everything else—but as time passed, the competitions became more intense. Mark, for reasons the triplets wouldn't understand until much later, seemed fixated on his children growing into highly successful adults. His own father had been a heavy drinker, and Mark and his seven siblings had grown up in poverty and fear. His dad died young, and Mark beat his family's odds by putting himself through medical school and entering the most emotionless of specialties: looking through a microscope. And for decades his charge was finding answers that, to others, were invisible—but, if he zoomed in enough, were there somewhere.

Along the way he decided that when the time came, he'd raise his own kids by surrounding them with activities, reminding them of traps, exposing them to sports and the arts and travel and culture—everything, it would seem, but the possibility of failure.

Mark enjoyed his job, and it allowed him a vacation home and time to indulge his many hobbies—"I used to call them obsessions," Carolyn would say, though she remained supportive of her husband's interests and largely deferential to his parenting decisions—and introduce his children to the methodical pursuit of results. That pursuit, the parents reminded the kids, could even be a matter of life and death: exercise and determination enrich and extend lives, but certain distractions—alcohol and a lack of focus—could derail or perhaps shorten them. The kids would say later they grew up learning anger and intensity were acceptable but crying was a show of weakness.

"We didn't do touchy-feely," Colin says now, adding in a separate interview that "the three of us stopped looking to the parents for affection."

Carolyn and Mark insist the kids began resisting their parents' embraces around middle school, but although Mark admits granting his children space, Carolyn would approach Kelly with a bear-hug sneak attack.

"It's too hard to resist," Carolyn would say.

Still, the triplets learned the art of strategy and the way to properly build things: Mark's seventy-foot retaining wall, a modest field of hop plants, a sprawling tomato garden. Mark coached their soccer teams and introduced them to culture during trips to Italy, South Africa, and England. Watching television was forbidden, and the siblings were allowed to watch movies only while using an exercise machine. When they were eight, Christine says, their $20 monthly allowance depended on whether they exercised thirty minutes a day, five days a week. They had to log their totals on a chart that required a parent to initial it.

Time passed, and at least on the surface the plan was working: Colin carefully tracked his workouts at age fourteen, and his grape jelly recipe won third place in the Minnesota State Fair. Christine was thirteen when she published her first book, a kids' guide to raising monarch butterflies, and was a distance runner with a resting heart rate of forty-five beats per minute. Kelly, to her siblings' constant discouragement, excelled at most everything she took on —skiing, fencing, competitive shooting—and the kids learned that their parents were supportive, though earning their approval was sometimes a different matter.

"A pet peeve of mine: so many parents just automatically say, 'Good job,'" Carolyn says even now. "Their kids are successful getting a fork to their mouth: 'Good job!'"

Kelly, pursuing whatever it was she was pursuing, simply amplified her intensity and determination, seeming to never break. But Colin looked forward to his classical guitar lessons because the instructor allowed him to cry. Christine increasingly felt like an outsider, once writing a story about a family of opera-singing mice from the perspective of the one mouse who couldn't sing.

Christine moved out when she was a teenager, searching for belonging in Maine and California and New York. The siblings had all been pushed, but Kelly—the one pushed hardest—had won the household Olympics, Christine decided. Leaving everything behind, Christine assumed her sister was embarrassed by her, so she stopped calling. She stopped texting and emailing. Kelly did the same.

Until one day this past February, Christine was watering plants at home when her phone rang. She saw "Kelly Sista" on the display and answered immediately.

The years passed, Kelly's intensity grew, and Mark felt equally fascinated with and alarmed by his daughter.

"She has created this lofty image of herself that she is forced to maintain and live up to," he wrote to a friend in 2010, when Kelly was fourteen. "We have talked to her about starting over in high school—not sure if she can."

She was spending an increasing amount of time alone, staying home on weekends to study or put in extra hours on an indoor training bike. She recoiled if anyone touched her and locked herself in her room for violin practice, vowing to become first chair, and after her death relatives would struggle to reconcile a certain dichotomy: these were the extremes that made Kelly *Kelly*, but they were also the things that would cost them Kelly. Should they have stopped her? *Could* they have? She'd refuse to admit defeat or even to feeling stress, preferring to write in one of her three diaries and add to "The Code," a list of personal guidelines she'd begun honing in third grade.

"A fact about who I am: I do *not* cry," she'd write.

Sticking to what would eventually become her thirteen commandments—"Fear not physical discomfort" and "Never use coarse or vulgar language" among them—would propel her to the mountaintop; any deviation or show of weakness, she'd come to believe, could topple her. Four of her rules pertained to her belief that socializing was, like crying, a display of submission.

"Never allow yourself to become close enough to another," she'd write, "that their actions or inactions might cause you (any amount of) distress or pain."

Kelly read science fiction novels as she brushed her teeth and crafted meticulous to-do lists. She simplified her meals—lunch most every day was a sandwich with deli meat and hummus, two clementine oranges, and yogurt with chocolate, her favorite food —and usually wore black.

"She always wanted to basically be this monolithic, terrifying force of power," Colin would say, and after a while family members and acquaintances didn't just avoid touching her. Many of them stopped talking to her. One longtime cycling coach, Charlie Townsend, sometimes wondered if she even enjoyed the activities she seemed to obsess over; the only time he saw her smile, he'd say, was on the medal stand.

Mark watched his daughter as she'd disappear for a twelve-hour study session or a sixty-mile bike ride, preferring to be alone with only her thoughts and Beethoven's Fifth Symphony as company. Olympians, she believed, were made and not born. She would make the sacrifices and maintain focus and get into Harvard or Cambridge or Stanford. She would.

"Never give or receive touch of a romantic or sexual nature," The Code instructed.

"Never engage in a relationship that could be defined as having a significant other. (In my case, a so-called 'boyfriend.')"

"Never love."

Kelly stepped off the medal stand in Rio de Janeiro, and soon after her smile was gone. It wasn't just the end of a long and grueling journey; she hadn't felt this connected to something since the triplets began drifting apart in middle school.

Kelly returned to Minnesota and her solitary discipline, back to the things that made her, and looked toward an uncertain future. Following her graduation from the University of Minnesota, where she completed degrees in biomedical engineering and Chinese, she applied to Harvard and Stanford for graduate school. Kelly wrote essays, recommitted herself to the violin and writing, made her lists—"loaf of bread (28 pieces for breakfast and lunch)"— and sometimes planned her outfits weeks in advance.

She joined a professional road cycling team, Rally UCH, and planned for the international cycling schedule: races in Canada, Chile, Belarus, the United Kingdom. She traveled with teammates but often remained disconnected, and if the talk turned to gossip or relationships, Kelly would leave the table. If she said anything, it was to point out that these discussions were pointless and that dating was, a teammate would recall, a "waste of resources." When a new cyclist introduced herself with hugs, the veterans said nothing as the rookie approached Kelly, who recoiled with such disgust that the teammates wondered if she might throw a punch. If there were team-building exercises or games, Kelly could usually be found in her room.

They were in Belgium when the group learned Kelly had never seen *Mean Girls* or *High School Musical,* and a few of them arranged a two-night viewing and hounded Kelly until she joined them on the sofa. They were in London when some teammates wouldn't stop talking about seeing *School of Rock* on the West End, and Kelly complained all the way to the theater before singing "Stick It to the Man" all the way back.

The weeks and months passed, and Kelly eased out of her room, slowly removed her earbuds, occasionally spoke. If Kelly had once been a curiosity, now she was entertainment, and she was best in debate mode: speech quickening, legs pacing, hands directing the traffic of her restless mind. Kelly and Christina Birch, a cyclist with a PhD from MIT, bonded over academics and the feeling that no matter what either of them accomplished, they never felt complete. There was just more to do—more, more, more—and the antidotes to fear were harder work and force of will.

"She got to the top and found that it wasn't what she was expecting," says Birch, who wasn't the only person who wondered if Team USA's silver medal—Britain won gold by 1.02 seconds—had somehow been a disappointment to Kelly. "It still sucked. It still wasn't enough."

The teammates talked sometimes about the things that define a meaningful life and whether it was possible to actually reach the height of human potential. Kelly hated talking about the future—in her mind marriage and career representing such clichés—and a teammate would recall that she once admitted a preference for "disappearing into the mist." She blushed when teammates joked about her secret crush on Lionel Messi, the Argentine soccer star, and laughed when they'd slip Kelly, as averse to coffee as alcohol, a caffeine gel. Kelly brought dinner once to Sara Bergen, a Canadian cyclist who'd suffered a concussion after a crash, and kept her company on a training bike. She joined in the occasional trivia contest against the male cyclists and, on Valentine's Day, thanked Birch for sending her an anatomically correct chocolate heart.

The countries and trails changed, and somehow so did Kelly. She recoiled and disappeared less often—even standing there, arms dangling, when Bergen insisted on celebrating the end of a stage by wrapping each of her teammates in a big, sweaty, fifteen-second hug.

"She wouldn't hug back," Bergen says. "But she wouldn't run from them anymore."

In the fall of 2018, Kelly had come to Stanford, posted a welcome note from Giordano next to an Olympic flag on her dresser, and leaned into a future she was unsure she wanted. But she was here, another box checked, and she tried to overpower her doubts as she always had. She made her lists, chopped away at her violin, repeatedly cleaned her bicycles.

And that was part of the problem: cycling was a chore now, not an escape. In October, she crashed and broke her arm. Another crash led to a concussion. She had opened herself to new friend-ships, sure, but what about the politics of being an Olympian? She had begun to dread the grind, forty days at a track camp between November and December 2018, and when she returned to school, a mountain of work waited. It felt overwhelming, and one day last year she at last allowed herself to cry. She nonetheless filled recovery days with studying and makeup tests, and though she'd been admitted to one of her dream schools, she was never there for the classes, the guest lectures, the networking events. The 2020 Olympics in Tokyo, which she saw as a correction of Rio and a chance to win gold, were on the horizon. She couldn't just stop, and indeed Kelly wept not because there were no worlds left to conquer but because there were so many.

Late last January, with a chocolate chip cookie at her side, Kelly stood at her desk and began typing, "Well hello, one and all!"

In what eventually became an eight-page letter to six people —Mark and Carolyn, Christine and Colin, a cycling coach, and a former high school classmate—Kelly included a confession: Yes, she cried. More and more often she'd wake in the night, feeling no guilt, and just let it rip.

On this evening, she typed that she felt "somehow unequal" to Stanford and that she had sent a collectible dagger out for sharp-ening, intending to stab herself in the heart. She was curious about the sensation of bleeding out, she wrote, going on to explain a fan-tasy of becoming a serial killer with an elaborate and meticulous ritual. "Oh, the drama I could create," she wrote.

Instead, she had rented two cylinders of compressed helium

and waited for the halls to clear before dragging them to her room. She ordered supplies to construct an "exit hood," and on the evening of January 25, she began writing her email. She was planning to end her life in six days because, on January 31, she was scheduled to meet the queen of Spain. Instead, she'd be dead, and even Kelly Catlin's suicide note had to be perfect. "I really did want a nice hook opener," she wrote.

She kept typing, 470 words in the email's body: instructions for Colin, final wishes, the phone number for the Santa Clara County medical examiner's office. In addition to the eight-page document was a separate nine-page personal addendum. She listed twenty-seven songs and their corresponding links on YouTube, a playlist meant to accompany the reading.

"In truth my mind has conquered me," the document read. "Its never ending spinning spinning spinning would not rest. Always, always was it sprinting a marathon, thoughts never at rest, never at peace. It just wouldn't stop."

She suspected that she had major depressive disorder, though to her seeking therapy was another show of weakness. "I would rather suffer than ask for help," she wrote, going on to describe her delight in the problems her death would cause Team USA and some thoughts about her upbringing.

"I suspect a large part of why I am the way I am—both 'good' and 'bad'—is our childhood environment," she wrote. "We are triplets. And we are, none of us, truly functional . . . Those parched for affection from a young age do not quickly heal. I shall say no more."

Kelly finished her documents and waited her six days. On January 31, she gave herself the morning off from training, and before sliding in her earbuds and twisting the helium valve, she had one last thing to say.

"I was dancing before the end. Just so you know," she typed before hitting Send. "I woke up, danced a dance, played my fiddle, and died."

But then, hours later, she woke up.

In the moments and hours after Kelly's suicide attempt, those who'd received her email tried to make sense of it. Was this, as Colin initially suspected, a dark and elaborate prank? Her parents, panicked after having been alerted by the high school classmate, called Stanford police. Kelly had never been evaluated for anxiety

KENT BABB

or depression, her father would say, and none of her family members would recall Kelly ever mentioning suicide.

Kelly, according to relatives, was perhaps as confused by her survival as anyone. She had done as her research suggested, and indeed the helium had caused her to drift off. But after a while, she'd write in her journal later, she simply regained consciousness; the first thing she remembered was standing fully clothed in the shower. Colin would say authorities had arrived, discovering Kelly's materials and rushing her to Stanford Hospital, where she'd spend seven days on an involuntary hold. Kelly either couldn't remember or wouldn't reveal much else.

"What I can say with certainty," she'd write later, "is that I have indeed been given a second chance and I do not intend to waste it."

She vowed to graduate from Stanford, to read autobiographies of suicide survivors, to study and adopt their lessons. Kelly promised her family she had no intention of a second attempt—"Her word was her bond," Carolyn would write later—and after her parents returned from California, Kelly and her mother spoke by phone every few days. She never said anything about lingering feelings of hopelessness or depression, Carolyn would say. Christine texted Kelly and mailed books to her hospital room, which —despite what was meant as a mandatory rest period from cycling and classwork—she often escaped each day to spend a few hours on the facility's stationary bike. The hospital recommended Kelly remain under supervision another week, Mark Catlin would say, but Kelly felt frustrated and trapped before threatening legal action and being released to her apartment.

Attempting to resettle into a new routine, Kelly wrote a letter demanding equal pay for female cyclists and had an essay published in *VeloNews*. She met with faculty advisers and agreed to reduce her academic load to one class for the remainder of the spring term. She told Colin of her renewed optimism and a willingness to cast aside social inhibitions.

But as the weeks passed, Colin suspected that something was gnawing at her: for perhaps the first time in her life, Kelly had put her mind to something—truly committed to it—and fallen short.

"I suck," she told her brother, going on to describe the fellow students in her mandatory group therapy sessions who, she believed, only wanted attention when they had threatened or attempted suicide. Those students, Kelly told Colin, hadn't been as dedicated—as serious as she'd been—and it became clear that, even here, it wasn't empathy she felt but a desire to compete.

"She wanted to prove that she was not one of them," Colin says now, and when Kelly brought up her frustration, he tried to change the subject.

During Carolyn's phone calls with Kelly, they'd discuss politics or she'd talk about something lighthearted to make Kelly smile. Mark occasionally heard anger in his daughter's voice when she described her suicide attempt, and he assured her it wouldn't be long before she'd be back on her bike.

But he didn't get it. Nobody seemed to. By then it was mid-February, and it seemed clear Kelly just wanted someone to listen, so she called a number she hadn't in a long time.

"I could relate," Christine would say later. "It makes perfect sense."

Kelly had become increasingly alarmed that either her concussion or her suicide attempt had caused permanent brain damage, and she remained anxious about life after cycling and school. She had, after her hospital discharge, exchanged emails with a staffer at Stanford's student health center, and the staffer expressed increasing concern that Kelly hadn't scheduled an appointment with a mental health specialist.

Kelly had, she emailed back to the staffer, called a telephone counseling service contracted by the U.S. Olympic Committee but hung up after being put on hold for twenty minutes; a subsequent email to the service, Kelly wrote, yielded only plans to look into potential treatment. A USOC spokesman said extensive efforts were made to provide support following Kelly's initial suicide attempt. Olympic athletes are required to complete intake surveys, whose questions include asking individuals to self-identify symptoms of depression and anxiety, though potential treatment is up to each athlete's service providers.

During the sisters' phone call, Christine kept listening. Eventually she reminded Kelly that she was twenty-three; she didn't have to plan the rest of her life as she did her meals and outfits. Painful as it had been, Christine told Kelly, detaching her identity from writing —from the expectations of others—had been liberating. Kelly could do the same: quit cycling, leave school, live for her own happiness.

Kelly said she'd think about it, though when it was time to end the call, she casually mentioned that if things didn't change in a month, she might again attempt suicide. Christine begged her sister to reconsider, and after they hung up, she called their parents and sounded the alarm. She says they told her she was overreacting.

"They didn't take me seriously at all," she'd say, and though it's common for parents of suicide survivors to remain in denial, Mark and Carolyn would say later they had no idea which words or behavior might signal a second attempt—or whom to call if they suspected Kelly might break her promise.

In the days after calling Christine, Kelly wrote out the pros and cons of living and dying. One day she was reminding herself of her strength—"I *can* fight through this," she wrote. "I *can* live for tomorrow"—and the next she was chastising herself for delaying the inevitable.

At one point, she filled four pages with her thoughts.

"Principle: If I am not an athlete, I am nothing," she wrote at the end. "Principle: If I am in therapy, I have failed."

In her journal she typed out her to-do list for a week in early March and identified the day Giordano, her roommate, would be studying and absent from their apartment.

Monday: ". . . packages sometime, assemble hood."

Tuesday: "train, practice run with ear-buds."

Wednesday: "train, practice run with earbuds."

Thursday: ". . . tuck sheets under, switch Verizon to DO NOT DISTURB, meditate . . . set out DNR note and Helium note and printed/signed letters, start exit by 11."

In the weeks after their call, Christine kept texting, kept reminding Kelly she was still there. She sent an article about the Italian town where Stradivarius violins are made, shipped her a Chinese string instrument called an erhu, began planning a road trip to Northern California. Though Kelly had mentioned a second possible suicide attempt as an aside, Christine believed her sister had given her a deadline. Christine would, before the month was out, drive west with Scottie, her chihuahua mix, and surprise Kelly at Stanford. Christine would listen as long as it took.

Then, on March 8, Christine's phone rang again. This time, Kelly had done what she'd set out to. She always did.

Almost immediately after Kelly's death, Mark Catlin kept himself busy. There was a funeral to plan and photographs to sort. He had

a shooting competition in Arizona, chores on the farm, a memorial bike ride to think about.

The family donated Kelly's brain to Boston University's CTE
Center, which in the past two years has seen an uptick in the brains
of women. Mark studied his daughter's medical records and requested the Olympic Training Center's post-concussion protocol.
A lawyer had to talk him out of suing Stanford, which he said
wouldn't offer treatment for Kelly because she wasn't a varsity athlete. (The Stanford spokesman said the school's follow-up is the
same for athletes and non-athletes.)

"You create a barrier in your mind," Mark says, "and the barrier
is between normal activities and thoughts about Kelly."

The triplets were teenagers when Mark told them about his own
father. He hadn't been much older than them when his own dad
died from a gunshot; though the official cause of death was a hunting accident, Mark says, he always suspected his father had taken
his own life.

"How could anyone get there?" he'd wonder, and he dealt with
his trauma by ignoring it: Mark skipped the funeral, devoted himself to self-improvement, became convinced alcohol and misplaced
priorities were to blame. Mark, using force of will, would defy the
odds; he'd become the only one of his siblings to graduate college,
the only one who'd never have a drink. With the advantages Mark
could offer his children, they would succeed at an even higher
level than he had. They would.

But his plan had ended in tragedy, and now Mark reached into
a bedside table one night around 2 a.m. and removed the four-
page letter Kelly had written shortly before her death. Mark, again
attempting to overpower emotion, had avoided reading it until
that moment.

"So what do I want?" she had written. "Love."

Mark, feeling a need to understand what Kelly had felt—his answers, as they'd been while he was a pathologist, were down there
somewhere—kept reading.

"I do desire to be valued, to be special, to have great power and
responsibility. But, beyond all else, I desire 'love and connection.'"

By now the darkness was all-consuming, and he kept sinking,
kept absorbing his daughter's final words.

"I cry," Kelly wrote, "because I only ever truly desired Love.

Kindness. Understanding. Warmth. Touch. And these things shall be denied, for eternity."

Overcome, Mark will say later, he considered his own suicide.

"Just dwelling on our failures and what I feel is *my* failure," he'll say. "That made me so sad: there were things I could've done."

But then, he says, he thought of Christine and Colin and Carolyn. He couldn't go quite as far as Kelly had gone. But in his mind, he'd felt what she had. He had his answer.

"I could pull myself back, and she couldn't," Mark says, and that night he lay in bed and cried for a long time.

Maybe no emotion is more complicated, or personal, than grief: not just the inevitable questions about how and why, but the thoughts and actions that begin the march forward.

In those first days after Kelly died, Christine and Mark knew they needed to talk but were uncertain they even knew how. They were either too different or too similar, depending on whom you asked, and years ago daughter and father struggled to be honest with each other unless they were on their bicycles, quarantined on some faraway trail.

And so, at the beginning, their actions were to delay: Mark sending his emails, designing his models, imagining having Kelly cloned. Christine, her instincts telling her as always to flee, would disappear to Cuba and California, attempting to drown guilt with silence or noise.

"I just ran out of time," she kept saying, and that was among the sentiments she shared with Mark.

Eventually they'd conclude there was something about Kelly they both admired and feared, and it's what pushed her to the top and her bottom: once she made up her mind on something —anything—there could be no changing it.

"To be so obsessed with something," Mark says, "that you can't give it up."

When Christine came home to Minnesota for her sister's funeral, most of the snow had melted. The ground had begun to thaw. Family and friends had gathered to hold Kelly's silver medal and eat chocolate and tell stories. Colin made jokes, believing Kelly would've hated a somber memorial, and Carolyn tried to hide her overwhelming despair.

"The devastating consequences of our trust," she'd write in an email months later, overcome with regret because she'd believed Kelly's promise.

At one point in the day, Mark and Christine slipped out of the reception without telling anyone, heading out to do something necessary—a thing they hadn't done in years. The trails would be muddy and treacherous, but out there the air wouldn't feel so heavy. So a little after noon, they pulled on their tights and helmets, taking their first steps away from a fractured past and toward an uncertain future, setting off, just the two of them, to go for a ride.

AMY RAGSDALE AND PETER STARK

What It's Like to Die from Heatstroke

FROM OUTSIDE

END OF THE dirt road. You brake to a stop, swing your leg over the scooter, and kick the stand into place. The effort makes your head throb. The scooter wobbles. Your sunglasses slide down the mixture of sweat and sunscreen on your nose. You adjust them, look up tentatively at the fiery orb in the deep blue sky, and flinch. You chide yourself for staying out so late the night before, for not getting an earlier start this morning. The sun already feels too hot. But this is your only chance to surf Emerald Cove. It's gonna be okay, you tell yourself. You're in good shape. You've got the stamina to hike the five miles over the ridge and down to the beach before the tide comes in.

That glaring sun, of course, is essential for life on this planet. But its thermal energy, which we feel as heat, is a force both benevolent and cruel. The human body employs a spectrum of physiological tricks to maintain the steady internal temperature—98.6 Fahrenheit—at which it thrives. There is about eight degrees of difference between an optimal level of internal heat and the limit the body can endure. This threshold is referred to as the critical thermal maximum. Exactly when one reaches it depends on individual physiology, exertion, hydration, acclimation, and other factors. Estimates place it at an internal temperature between 105 and 107 degrees. Heat is a giver of life, but when the human body gets this hot—or hotter—terrible things occur.

Emerald Cove is on an island off the coast of South America.

You'd flown over a couple of days ago, after a trek in the mainland's cool interior highlands. You wanted to take in those thousand-year-old stone statues you'd heard so much about, plus you figured you could cap off your vacation with a couple days of surfing. You're just a beginner, and already you're hooked, but it's hard being a newbie. The locals are reluctant to let you into the lineup. What you need is that perfect undiscovered break, no people, no pressure.

Last night you walked into a popular surf bar and pulled up a stool next to two guys you'd seen in the water that day. If you wanted to find a secret spot along this spectacular wave-battered coast, you figured these guys would be the ones to know. They gave you a cursory nod and continued their conversation.

"*Huevón*," one was saying to his pal (or at least that's what you think he said). Your Spanish is okay, but you're not catching all the slang. He was talking about a point break.

"*Qué bacán!*" Rad! "And there's nobody there. Nobody. You have to try it."

"Nobody where?" you asked quietly, leaning in.

"*La Cala Esmeralda.*" He barely turned his head to look at you.

"Emerald Cove?" you repeated.

It had taken a long time, a lot of patience, and too many piscolas—pisco and Cokes—to pry out where it was, but the effort was worth it. It'd be the perfect end to a perfect trip, something to talk about to your well-traveled friends back home. "Seriously, you've never been there?" you'll say to them, acting surprised. "You should definitely check it out. But it's kinda hard to get to, and the trail's a secret."

You had to ask the surfers to repeat themselves, just to be sure you understood. They'd finally turned and looked at you full on.

"Dude," one said, "I'm not sure I'd try it if I were you."

Heat-related illnesses in the U.S. claim more lives annually than hurricanes, lightning, earthquakes, tornadoes, and floods; there were over 9,000 heat-related deaths between 1979 and 2014. The fatalities tend to peak during heat waves and hotter-than-average years, and they're expected to rise as climate change affects global temperatures. One of the deadliest heat waves in modern times swept Europe in 2003, killing over 30,000 people as temperatures soared to 100 degrees for days on end.

The human body is much less tolerant of rises in internal temperature than drops. The lowest body temperature a human has been known to survive is 56.7 degrees, nearly 42 degrees below normal. Anna Bagenholm, a twenty-nine-year-old Swedish woman, was backcountry skiing when she broke through eight inches of ice into a frozen stream. Her upper body was sucked down, leaving only her feet and skis visible, but she managed to find an air pocket and was able to breathe. After eighty minutes, she was finally rescued. Bagenholm remained in a coma for about ten days and was in intensive care for two months but ultimately suffered only minor nerve damage. On the other end of the spectrum, the highest body temperature measured was only 17 degrees above normal. Willie Jones, a fifty-two-year-old Atlanta man, was rescued from his apartment during a heat wave in 1980. His internal temperature was 115.7. He spent twenty-four days in the hospital before being released.

While there is some debate, studies on women in the military have shown that they may be more susceptible to heat illness than men due to their higher body-fat content and lower sweat output. Whether the heatstroke victim is male or female, the odds of surviving depend on the duration of overheating and, once their condition is discovered, how quickly they can be cooled down—most effectively by immersion in ice water within thirty minutes. Survival, moreover, doesn't guarantee full recovery. A powerful heat wave in Chicago in 1995 caused 739 deaths and 3,300 emergency-room visits. A study reviewing 58 of the severe heatstroke victims found that 21 percent died in the hospital soon after admission, 28 percent died within a year, and all the remaining subjects experienced organ dysfunction and neurological impairments.

An average-size male at rest generates about as much heat as a 100-watt light bulb simply through metabolism. During moderate exercise, temperature increases nearly ten degrees every hour unless you cool yourself by sweating or some other means. You risk a variety of illnesses, starting with heat edema, which entails swelling of the hands and feet and can begin at body temperatures close to normal. No precise temperature marks the onset of the various other heat illnesses, and the order of symptoms varies between individuals, but they may include heat syncope (dizziness and fainting from the dilation of blood vessels), heat cramps (muscular clenching due to low salt), and heat exhaustion (identified by muscular weakness, rapid heartbeat, nausea, headache, and possible vomiting and diarrhea). Finally, an internal temperature of 105 marks the lower boundary of heatstroke territory, with outward symptoms of extreme irritability, delirium, and convulsion. Because of individual variation in how these symptoms appear, and because some may not appear at all, athletes in particular can be overcome quickly and with little warning.

There are two kinds of heatstroke: classic and exertional. Classic heatstroke hits the very young, the elderly, the overweight, and people suffering from chronic conditions like uncontrolled diabetes, hypertension, and cardiovascular disease. Alcohol and certain medications (diuretics, tricyclic antidepressants, antipsychotics, and some cold and allergy remedies) can increase susceptibility as well. Classic heatstroke can strike in the quiet of upper-floor apartments with no air-conditioning.

Exertional heatstroke, on the other hand, pounces on the young and fit. Exercise drastically accelerates temperature rise. Marathon runners, cyclists, and other athletes sometimes push into what used to be known as the fever of exercise and is now called exercise-induced hyperthermia, where internal temperatures typically hit 100 to 104 degrees. Usually, there's no lasting damage. But as body temperature climbs higher, the physiological response becomes more dramatic and the complications more profound. The higher temperature can ultimately trigger a cascading disaster of events as the metabolism, like a runaway nuclear reactor, races so fast and so hot that the body can't cool itself down. A person careens toward organ failure, brain damage, and death.

It's February, the height of summer in the Southern Hemisphere. You'd planned to get up early but didn't hear your alarm after the late night at the bar. Now the sun is well into its arc. The temperature is supposed to hit 93 degrees by midday.

Pulling the keys from your scooter, you sling your rented surfboard onto your back, thread your arms through your chest pack, and hear the reassuring slosh of the water bottle inside. You have a seat on the twice-weekly plane that leaves tomorrow, returning you to the mainland. If you're going to do this, the moment is now. You launch up the trail, a faint unmarked path on the gentle, grassy slope. You're not surprised you're the only one around. The surfers said to follow the volcano's right flank until you gain the ridge, then drop down a cleft in the rocks to the sea. Good luck finding the cleft, they seemed to say. Maybe they were just trying to deter you. You see the slope steepen as it rises toward the sharp crest, where chunks of volcanic rock protrude like broken dinosaur scales through velvety green nap. No trees, not a wisp of wind. Ancient cultures deforested this island centuries ago and mysteriously disappeared, leaving not a sliver of shade under the tropical sun.

You feel the quick flex of your quads, the push of your glutes, the spring of your calves propelling you up the winding path, and hear the steady mantra of your breathing. You have to make time. The guys at the bar said the shore bristles with stone *dientes*, teeth — get there at low tide. That gives you just under two hours.

Within only a few steps, your body begins to respond to the sun's radiation, the moist air pressing against your skin, and the heat generated by your own rising metabolism. Blood coursing through your arteries begins to grow warmer. At less than one degree Fahrenheit above your normal internal temperature, receptors in your brain's hypothalamus start to fire, signaling the circulatory system to shunt more blood toward your skin's surface for cooling. Other messages tell peripheral blood vessels to dilate, opening up to allow greater blood flow. Still other signals activate millions of tiny coils and tubes embedded in your skin — your sweat glands. Concentrated within your head, palms, soles, and trunk, the glands pump water from a tiny reservoir at the base, pushing the salty liquid up a long tube through layers of skin to erupt in a miniature gusher at the surface.

Several hundred yards up the grassy slope, sweat is popping onto your face. You feel the slick, dark blue fabric of your shirt sticking to your back, despite its breathability. You wish it was looser, and a lighter color that didn't so readily absorb the sun's rays. A trickle of sweat runs down your forehead and into one eye, stinging with dissolved salts, blurring your vision.

The air is smothering, thick with moisture, like a greenhouse. The dripping sweat should bring some relief. Usually, the body's cooling system operates remarkably efficiently; blood rushes to carry the excess heat from your core out to your sweat glands, which squeeze warm fluids to the surface, where air moving past your skin evaporates the moisture. Your excess heat literally blows away in the wind. But for this to work properly, the sweat must evaporate. When the air lies close and unmoving, heavy with humidity, sweat evaporates more slowly. If the air is saturated enough, or if impermeable fabric—or, in your case, a surfboard and a chest pack—trap the sweat against your skin, the moisture won't evaporate at all.

High school athletes are often afflicted by heatstroke, which ranks as one of the top three leading causes of death among that demographic. And according to an investigation done by the HBO show *Real Sports with Bryant Gumbel,* since the year 2000, at least thirty college football players have died of heatstroke during practice, when remedies as simple as immersing the overheated player in ice water were available. Minnesota Vikings offensive lineman Korey Stringer died of heatstroke during a preseason practice in 2001, and now the University of Connecticut's Korey Stringer Institute, established in 2010, specializes in sudden-death prevention in athletes, soldiers, and laborers.

Runners, cyclists, and hikers routinely succumb to heatstroke. If properly acclimated, trained, and managed carefully, the human body can endure grueling events in high temperatures, like the Badwater—a 135-mile running race in California that begins in Death Valley, traverses three mountain ranges, and ends at Mount Whitney—and the six-day Marathon des Sables in the Sahara. However, experts say that due to the high intensity of the pace on shorter courses, heatstroke is more common in races of thirty to ninety minutes than in longer events. Three years ago at the annual Falmouth Road Race, a 12K running event in Massachusetts in August, forty-eight out of more than 10,000 finishers suffered from heatstroke and another fifty-five from heat exhaustion. (All of them survived without incident due to the extensive cooling procedures available at the race's finish.)

The National Weather Service now issues warnings when excessive temperatures are expected and gives predictions of the heat index, which takes into account both temperature and humidity as experienced by a five-foot-seven, 147-pound person walking at a speed of about three miles per hour in a six-mile-per-hour breeze. Like the windchill index, the heat index conveys what it feels like outside. For instance, at the Hot Trot Half Marathon, which is held in Dallas in August, the day is often 97 degrees but can have a heat index of 116 degrees because of the 60 percent humidity.

*

You pull your water bottle from your pack—a full liter shimmering inside a translucent blue Nalgene—take a warm swig, and strike upward again toward the broken scales of the ridge. For the next hour you push at a fast walk, pausing only occasionally to drink. You know the importance of hydration. What you don't know is how remarkably fast the human body can expel water to cool itself —one and a half liters or more per hour. (Highly efficient, heat-acclimated marathoners can lose close to four liters per hour while they run.) The human gut, however, can absorb only a little over one liter of water per hour. That means that during maximum rates of water loss, it's possible to drink steadily and still become dehydrated.

Your core temperature has now climbed to 101.5—three degrees above normal—but you're still in the exercise-induced hyperthermia zone. Your head throbs. You wish you hadn't drunk quite so many piscolas last night. In doing so, you unwittingly tricked your body's water controls. Alcohol is a small molecule that slides easily through the walls of the gut, into the bloodstream, and up into the brain, where it suppresses the release of antidiuretic hormone, or ADH. This is the hormone that inhibits urination, in effect closing your dam's spillway in order to keep your reservoir full. Typically, when you become dehydrated, the percentage of salt in your blood rises, triggering your pituitary gland to release ADH. But under the sabotaging influence of alcohol, your body may sense that your water stores are being depleted but blithely ignore the warning. Thanks to those piscolas, rather than prehydrating for today's climb, you started the day in the red.

The incline grows steeper. The grass gives way to a light, loose volcanic rock called tuff. The scrappy path has now completely disappeared, but still you labor toward the ridgetop—two steps up, slide, one step down. You're panting now. The rocks crunch under your feet. Each footstep produces a gritty dust that crusts your bare legs, which are coated in a paste of sweat and sunscreen. The arteries protruding on your forearms look like grapevines wrapped around a post. Your blood vessels are dilating, trying to move as much overheated blood to the surface as possible. Your heart pumps madly, trying to keep the vessels full, but it can't keep up. Not enough blood—and the oxygen it carries—reaches your brain. You pause to rest. You feel lightheaded and faint. Your vision dims and narrows. You feel wobbly and strange—the onset of heat syncope (or orthostatic hypotension), a temporary loss of consciousness from falling blood pressure.

Fainting from orthostatic hypotension poses a distinct problem for those whose sworn duty requires standing still for hours in the sun, as it does for Britain's royal guards. In their bearskin hats and thickly layered uniforms, which are designed to hide sweat, they topple with surprising regularity flat onto their faces, breaking teeth and smashing noses, fainting at full attention with their arms and rifles still rigidly glued to their sides.

But you decide to sit on the rocks, and so you do not topple. You finish your water. You feel limp, like a wrung-out rag. You have a single thought: make it to the ridge and descend to the cool of Emerald Cove. Thirty minutes to go.

At 103 degrees internally, you're pushing into the upper limits of exercise-induced hyperthermia and into heat exhaustion. Your brain is no longer able to deal with large numbers.

One hundred four. Get over the ridge, you tell yourself. Get over the ridge.

Above you the jagged lava rocks begin to distort, reshaping into those ancient giant stone statues erected along the island's shore. They face you, their enormous heads silhouetted against the blue sky, as if to say, Go back!

But you don't.

Over millennia, people exerting themselves in hot environments, like the nomadic Maasai of Kenya, have genetically adapted, selecting for tall, slender, long-limbed body types that offer the maximum ratio of cooling surface area to heat-generating body mass. You are not Maasai.

When you finally crest the ridge, your core temperature is pushing 105. You are weak, hot, and thirsty, and you are confused but don't know it. Gazing back down the way you came, you see the dropping sweep of green. It seems surreal, removed and stylized, like an old hand-painted postcard. Just ahead, the cliff's edge drops away to crashing ocean far below.

The guy at the bar had said that the top of the trail was marked by a divot where the rock is worn like a V. You walk carefully along the broken ridgetop, afraid to peek over the airy drop. Where's the guardrail? Your body feels unwieldy.

Maybe it was a mistake to come here straight from the interior highlands, with their evening breezes and cool air. You'd heard that the human body needs time to fully adjust to heat. What you didn't know is that it generally needs about seven to fourteen days. By gradually building your exercise time outdoors in heat and humidity, your body learns to activate its cooling response at lower temperatures. It learns to increase the rate of sweat production and to trigger a mechanism to conserve sodium, which, along with potassium, is essential for fluid regulation and transmission of nerve signals. (The evolution of this mechanism was honed by our hunter-gatherer ancestors, who struggled to consume enough sodium in their diets.) Acclimation would have slowed your heartbeat but boosted the volume of blood circulated with each contraction to help maintain your blood pressure as your vessels dilated.

But you didn't acclimate. You relied on the fact that you exercise five days a week at home—also a hot, humid place in the summer. Your heat-addled mind drifts back to those summer days. Instead of this blazing light, you see the tinted windows of your SUV. Instead of this heat smothering your skin, you remember the hair-tingling chill of your car's air-conditioning, the dim, dank spaces of a parking garage, the cold blasts washing over the treadmill in the climate-controlled gym. It begins to dawn on you that all your life you have relied on artificial sources to keep you cool. You've never had to change your behavior or alter your ambitious schedule to accommodate the natural diurnal cycle. You've always carried your bubble with you. You've never had to truly confront the punishing heat of the midday sun.

And then: you've found it! You see a scuffed notch on the ridgetop and, far below, the glint of water. This is why you came! Delirious, you begin to scramble down. You slip, skid on your side, dragging and scraping your hands. You regain your feet and steady yourself against smooth boulders, leaving a bloody handprint. The bloodstain looks like a bird, you think, in acrylic paint, textured and thick—another effect of dehydration. Suddenly you notice that a bird (does it have four wings or six?) is swooping toward you, its talons reaching for your face. You try to swat the heat-induced hallucination away, first with your hands, then with your board, but it keeps coming back. You toss aside your board and stumble downward to get out of range.

You come to a ledge. Beyond it is pure drop and yes, there's the beach, several hundred feet below. You just need to fly, you think foggily, but sense that you have no choice but to climb back up. Your chest pack feels impossibly heavy, as if you're hauling the thirteen-ton head of one of those ancient statues. Irritated, you shimmy clumsily out of the straps and watch, mesmerized, as your pack tumbles over the edge and drops into the ocean.

Free at last, you begin to crawl back up. But you feel yourself sliding down the loose tuff. It's so much easier than climbing. You give in to the sensation of increasing speed, like a plane accelerating down a runway. You always loved that. You spread your wings and topple backward down the slope. As your head hits the tuff, you feel the coarse lava grit stick to the drying saliva of your lips and mouth. The ledge stops your descent. And then you feel no more.

It could be a small measure of good fortune that confusion, semiconsciousness, or coma overcome victims as they succumb to severe heatstroke. The damage about to ensue wreaks so much havoc that almost no major organ escapes untouched. At 105, your metabolism accelerates, so your cells generate heat at a rate that is 50 percent faster than normal. In other words, as your internal temperature rises, rather than cranking your air conditioner, you fire up your furnace. The only effective remedy is to douse the fires with immediate and extensive cooling.

Each heatstroke victim responds differently to these extreme internal temperatures, but a sequence of events might go like this: at 105 to 106 degrees, your limbs and core are convulsed by seizures. From 107 to 109, you begin vomiting and your sphincter releases. At 110 to 111, your cells begin to break down. Proteins distort. Liver cells die; the tiny tubes in your kidneys are grilled. The large Purkinje neurons in your cerebellum vanish. Your muscle tissues disintegrate. The sheaths of your blood vessels begin to leak, causing hemorrhaging throughout your body, including your lungs and heart. There is now blood in your vomit. You develop holes in your intestines, and toxins from your digestive tract enter your bloodstream. In a last-ditch effort, your circulatory system responds to all the damage by clotting your blood, thinking your vessels have been severed. This triggers what physicians call a clotting cascade.

As your insides melt and disintegrate, purple hemorrhagic spots appear on your skin. Those, the bloody vomit, and your convulsions are the only external hints of total internal annihilation.

*

"Is that a person down there?" the surfer from the bar asks his friend, skidding to a halt in their quick descent through the rocks.

Following the line of a pointing finger, the friend peers at a dark splotch on a ledge far below and a bit to the left, off the winding path and down through the steep rocks.

"Looks like that dude from the bar last night," he continues.

They continue scrambling down toward the cove, their wide-brimmed hats flapping, surfboards strapped to their backs. As they get closer, they see it *is* you. They drop their boards and clamber across the rocky slope. When they reach you, you look dead —limbs askew, eyes staring. One of them touches your bare arm. The skin is clammy. He feels for a pulse. It's faint and quick, like the heartbeat of a bird.

"He's still alive," he says. "But he's way too hot," he adds, shaking his head. "Let's get him to the *agua dulce.*"

Lifting you carefully, they drape you over the stouter surfer's back and shoulders. You're several pounds lighter than your normal weight due to dehydration. They scramble down the precipitous path, kicking free tuff that bounces ahead. Ignoring the shimmering water and the sculpted waves curling off the point, they haul you across the beach to a grove of palms against the foot of a cliff. A spring spills from a crevice in the rocks into a clear, quiet pool. *Agua dulce.* Sweet water.

It's much cooler than the tepid ocean—almost cold. They slide your body in and hold you there, immersed, cradling your head above the surface. Two minutes pass, five minutes, ten.

"*Está muerto,*" says the stouter one.

"No," says the other, carefully scooping handfuls of cooling water over your head.

Your eyes show a flicker of movement.

You hear splashing, faint at first, from somewhere far away. It comes closer, growing louder, until you realize that it's right around your ears. You feel the sensation of cold all over your body. When you open your eyes, you can't make sense of what you see—two faces framed by drooping palm fronds and deep blue sky.

"*Descansa,*" one says. Rest.

You close your eyes again. A hand brings water to your lips. You drink. You are lucky. With an internal temperature of 106, you peaked within your critical thermal maximum. It's not yet clear what lasting damage you may have sustained, but you are alive.

Right now, however, all you know is that you're so very tired. You'll have to be carried out of here, by stretcher or helicopter or boat. Your thirst feels like a cavernous hollow at your core. You don't know where you are or where you have been. You remember leaving the scooter and starting up a long grassy slope toward a volcanic ridge. After that there was only the relentless weight of the sun overhead, the heat-blasted lava rock underfoot, and the sense that you were being crushed between them with nowhere to run or hide, a fragile creature of flesh and bone, blood and water, trying to escape the enormity of this force that gives life but, you now understand, can so easily destroy it.

* * *

Act Fast

Exertional heatstroke can cause devastating damage, but it can also be treated quickly—P.S.

"The key thing for people's outcome is the number of minutes their temperature is over 105 degrees," says Douglas Casa, CEO of the University of Connecticut's Korey Stringer Institute, named after the Minnesota Vikings offensive lineman who died of heatstroke during an August 2001 training camp. Survival is highly likely if the core temperature is brought below 104 degrees within thirty minutes. Here are Casa's tips on prevention and treatment.

1. Avoid exercising in high temperatures, or choose cooler parts of the day and stay in the shade. If you do exercise in the heat, wear pale-colored, loose-fitting, lightweight clothing, and acclimate to the conditions by gradually increasing your output over seven to fourteen days.
2. How much water to drink is the subject of some debate. For recreational athletes, Casa suggests hydrating based on thirst. High-level endurance athletes should account for other factors, such as sweat rate. Avoid drinking alcohol before and during strenuous outings.

3. Heatstroke symptoms vary. Many victims are still conscious, and some have seizures or vomit while others do not. Suspect heatstroke if the person can no longer support their body weight, speaks irrationally, or is hyperirritable or confused. (Casa knows of heatstroke victims who punched a police officer at the finish line of a race.) To get a true reading of core temperature, use a rectal thermometer.

4. "Cool first, transport second" is the operable concept when it comes to heatstroke. With mere minutes to act, a victim should be cooled down before being taken to an emergency room. Immersing the body in a cold bath lowers temperature the fastest, dropping it one degree every three minutes if the water is circulating.

5. Exertional heatstroke in the backcountry presents additional challenges. Anything that cools the victim is helpful, but the best options are to immerse them in a lake, river, or stream, or wrap them in fabric drenched with ice water from a cooler. It's important to cool as much of the body's surface area as possible. In the absence of cold water, seek shade, wet the person's clothing with your water bottle, and fan them.

ANDREW KEH

The Champion Who Picked a Date to Die

FROM THE NEW YORK TIMES

I: *An Appointment to Die*

DIEST, BELGIUM — Champagne flutes were hastily unpacked from boxes, filled to their brims and passed around the room. Dozens of people stood around inside Marieke Vervoort's cramped apartment, unsure of what to say or do. This was a celebration, Vervoort had assured her guests. But it did not feel like one.

Eleven years earlier, Vervoort had obtained the paperwork required to undergo doctor-assisted euthanasia. Since her teenage years she had been battling a degenerative muscle disease that stole away the use her legs, stripped her of her independence, and caused her agonizing, unrelenting pain. The paperwork had returned some sense of control. Under Belgian law, she was free to end her life anytime she chose.

But instead, she just went on with it—seized it with new vigor, even. Within a few years she reached uncharted heights in her career as a wheelchair sprinter, winning a gold medal at the Paralympics. She became a celebrity at home and abroad, appearing in the pages of international magazines and newspapers, sitting for interviews on television shows. She traveled the world telling her life story, unspooling it as an inspirational narrative.

But she still had that paperwork. And now, after more than a decade of uncertainty and pain and joy, of opening her private life to friends and strangers and reporters, of inspiring others, of vexing them, of wishing for the end of her life and at the same time fearing it, Vervoort had invited her loved ones to her home for the most heart-wrenching of reasons:

In three days, she had an appointment to die.

"It's a strange, strange, strange feeling," her mother, Odette Pauwels, said as she scanned the party.

Vervoort's guests sipped their drinks and made small talk, struggling to oblige her request for everyone to be happy. There were toasts. There were wails of anguish.

There was, also, a faint feeling of uncertainty in the air—an unspoken question of whether this really was the end, a nanoscopic hope that it might not be. Almost three years had passed since two journalists from the *New York Times*—the photographer Lynsey Addario and I—began spending time with Vervoort to chronicle the end of her life, to observe a top athlete taking control of her destiny in an extraordinary fashion.

Being around her during that time sometimes felt like one extended, indefinite goodbye.

She had come close to scheduling her euthanasia on multiple occasions, but had always switched course, found a reason to put it off. Something would come up. Conflicts would emerge. There would be another date to look forward to, another reason to live.

Her friends and family had observed this tug of war longer than anyone else, the endless seesawing between her mounting pain and whatever small fulfillments she could experience in however much time she had left.

"You're still hoping something else would happen, that she would change her mind," said Jan Desaer, one of Vervoort's best friends. "You know the date, but you're denying it. You don't think it's real."

This time, Vervoort, forty, seemed resolved. Over the previous week, she had been discussing the procedure with a degree of clarity and seriousness that those who knew her best admitted they did not often see.

"I'm looking forward to it," she said of her death. "Looking forward finally to rest my mind, finally have no pain." She paused. "Everything I hate will be over."

II: The Pain

The guests who came to the farewell party in Vervoort's apartment in Diest, a tranquil town forty-five minutes east of Brussels by car, were surrounded by reminders of her achievements: four medals from the Paralympic Games strewn over a beanbag chair; Champagne bottles from earlier celebrations lined up triumphantly atop the refrigerator; shiny trophies standing sentry along a windowsill.

On a wall beside her kitchen table were three framed pictures of her strapped into a sleek racing wheelchair. In the first, her face is snarled in effort. In the second, her biceps bulge as she punches the air with joy. In the third, she smiles broadly with a gold medal in her hand.

The triptych captures the moment when Vervoort catapulted to national fame: the finish of the women's 100-meter final at the 2012 Paralympics in London, where she dramatically held off a late surge from the defending champion, Michelle Stilwell, to claim the gold medal.

Paralympic athletes rarely enjoy anything close to mainstream renown, but Vervoort captivated Belgian sports fans with her displays of power on the track and charmed them with her unadulterated screams of elation beyond the finish line. Her colorful personality helped too—as did the presence of her loyal sidekick, a service dog named Zenn.

Soon, those fans learned of the melancholic story behind her competitive success, and of the debilitating hardships that lay ahead.

What had begun for Vervoort as a happy childhood—loving parents, a younger sister, long days playing sports on a dead-end street—had grown complicated by her teenage years, when the pain that plagued her for the rest of her life first appeared. It emerged initially as a tingling in her feet. The tingling over the years turned to pain, smoldering up her legs, sapping their strength. She spent her teens on crutches. At twenty, she was in a wheelchair.

Doctors were bewildered. They attached labels to her worsening condition—reflex sympathetic dystrophy, progressive tetraplegia—and noticed a deformity between her fifth and sixth cervical vertebrae. But they could never fully understand why the pain had started, or why her eyesight was failing, or why she was having intermittent seizures. All the while her pain grew, often feeling like a muscle cramp coursing through her entire body.

With her childhood dreams of becoming a teacher derailed by her precarious health and the uncertainty that accompanied it, Vervoort, by her twenties, had come to find some meaning in sports: wheelchair basketball, scuba diving, triathlons. But the constant pain and fear eventually plunged her into deep depression. At age twenty-nine, she determined her disease was too heavy a burden to bear. She began hoarding pills at home. That was how she would end things, she thought.

As a last resort, a psychiatrist suggested she speak to Dr. Wim Distelmans, the leading advocate for euthanasia in Belgium.

The right to end one's life with the assistance of a doctor has been legal in the country since 2002, available to patients who exhibit a "hopeless" medical condition with "unbearable" suffering, including mental illnesses or cognitive disorders. No country has more liberal laws for doctor-assisted death than Belgium, a nation of 11 million people, where 2,357 patients underwent euthanasia in 2018.

Until then, Vervoort said, the prospect of euthanasia had never crossed her mind. On her best days, she still had an almost childlike embrace of life, an impish sense of humor and visions beyond a fledgling athletic career. People were drawn to her, to her jokes, to her easy, squealing laughter. She was the mischievous ringleader of a large, loose association of friends she christened the Dafalgan Club, named after a brand of dissolvable painkiller. But their preferred fizzy medicine, they said, was Champagne.

And even as the choice to undergo euthanasia had become more common in Belgium, there were still many, including Vervoort's parents, who were philosophically uncomfortable with it.

But she kept the appointment with Dr. Distelmans, and he, after a close examination, granted her the preliminary approval to end her life. He added, though, that she did not quite seem ready to follow through with it.

She agreed.

"I just wanted to have the paper in my hands for when the time comes that it's too much for me, when, day and night, someone has to take care of me, when I have too much pain," she said in one of a series of conversations we had over three years of reporting. "I don't want to live that way."

III: Taking Control

In Vervoort's telling, the euthanasia papers allowed her to wrest back some control of her life. She no longer feared death because she could hold it in her hands at any time.

Newly empowered, she said she found herself approaching sports with a different level of focus. She reoriented her nascent wheelchair racing career from triathlons and marathons toward sprinting. She thrived.

The pain was still there, deepening. But she also imagined herself using it as fuel for competition. Her days were no longer consumed with dark thoughts of how her life would end. Mentally, she felt free.

"Because of those papers," she said, "I started to live again."

Unencumbered by old anxieties, she produced an extended run of excellence in her small corner of wheelchair sports. She became known as the Beast From Diest.

Along with the gold medal she won at the 2012 Paralympics in London, she took home a silver in the 200-meter event. After that came three gold medals at the 2015 world championships in Doha, Qatar, and then two more medals—a silver in the 400 and a bronze in the 100—at the 2016 Paralympics in Rio de Janeiro.

The victories changed her life. Suddenly in the spotlight, she blossomed.

A year after the London Games, King Philippe of Belgium named her a Grand Officer of the Order of the Crown, one of her nation's highest honors. She gave motivational speeches to corporate audiences and picked up sponsors. One of them delivered meals to her home. Another gave her a car with her picture on the side. She went on shopping sprees at the Belgian headquarters of Nike.

It was under more inelegant circumstances, however, that she reached her highest point of fame. During the Rio Paralympics in 2016, her life story became distorted and sensationalized through a sort of morbid game of telephone.

A newspaper in Belgium had reported that she was considering euthanasia. The report was picked up by other news outlets, first at home, then abroad, and incrementally simplified and sensationalized. Her decision to undergo euthanasia was not only possible, but imminent, the story went, until those watching her in Brazil were convinced that they were observing the final days of her life. "'I'll Go for Gold, Then Kill Myself,' Says Paralympian Hopeful," one British tabloid headline blared during the Games, manufacturing something Vervoort had never said.

Embarrassed, she decided to correct the assumptions at a news conference. No, she said, she was not planning to kill herself immediately after the competition. But, she added, it was true that she would do it one day, and that knowledge was helping push her through her pain and depression. More countries should allow doctor-assisted suicide, she said.

It was a stunning sight: a world-class athlete sitting before a room of journalists, charismatically serving as an advocate for euthanasia. Her vivid accounting of her life and worldview—not to mention her quick humor while surrounded by microphones and bathed in the television cameras' bright lights—immediately inspired a new round of international news media coverage. "I don't want to suffer when I'm dying," she told the reporters that day between smiles. "I want to go in a peaceful mood, in a peaceful way, with the people around me that I want, the people that I really love."

I first contacted Vervoort in the fall of 2016, a few months after she returned to Belgium from Rio, and only a few weeks after I moved to Berlin as the *Times*'s European sports correspondent. An email turned into a phone call, which quickly turned into a trip to see her in Diest. She was eager to share her story. Over the ensuing three years, she allowed Lynsey, our photographer, and me to document the final chapter of her life.

We visited Vervoort at her home and in the hospital, followed her on errands around town and on trips overseas. She opened hidden corners of her life to us, revealed vulnerabilities that even those closest to her never saw. We had countless calls on the phone and over FaceTime, shared meals and traded jokes. We helped push her wheelchair when needed. Many, many times, we watched her cry.

It was an undulating process, intellectually and emotionally. Her parents and close friends told us that seeing her in pain forced them to confront their feelings about her decision, and I was forced to probe my own. At times I wondered—as others did—about her real intentions. She declined to let us view her medical records or speak with her doctors to learn more about her condition. Other times, even as we were committing time and effort to documenting her final days, I found myself hoping she would pull back from the brink.

She asked me more than once when she might see our finished article. I needed more than one attempt to explain, awkwardly, that we hoped to follow her through the end of her life—that, ultimately, she would never read what I would write about her life, never see all the photographs Lynsey was taking of her.

Eventually, as she told us on many occasions, she came to trust us. She made clear over time that she wanted people to see the full picture of her life, the pain and sadness and toil hidden behind the inspirational images and motivational talks, the profound loneliness beneath the jokes and laughter.

While accompanying Vervoort on a bucket-list trip to Japan in the spring of 2017, I watched her simmer with anger and embarrassment one afternoon after being forced to crawl along the floor of a crowded tour bus that was not equipped for wheelchairs, so many sets of eyes watching her. That night, she left a group dinner fifteen minutes early so she could board the bus before anyone else.

A year later, on another night that lingers in my memory, I sat in her apartment as she lit two dozen candles and brought out packs of premade sandwiches, which we washed down with cans of soda. Vervoort had hosted a parade of visitors throughout the afternoon—a local journalist, nurses, her parents—and now, nearly alone, she was trying to soothe herself. We sat on her couch and talked about her past relationships: how she began dating women when she was thirty, how those relationships had fallen apart, and her belief that, perhaps, she was happier without a companion.

"I'm alone," she said, matter-of-factly, "but I like it."

IV: Descent

The Rio games brought her a new rush of attention, and it was obvious she enjoyed it. She welcomed every interview, every television and radio appearance. She became an object of fascination in the Belgian tabloid press and was trailed by a documentary filmmaker. She posted minute details about her life on a Facebook page followed by tens of thousands of people and talked openly about her desire to have a museum built to memorialize her life.

The mesmerizing specter of mortality hung over everything, creating a tension that could not be ignored.

Her celebrity came with a dark twist: the prospect of her dying by euthanasia brought her more renown than she ever imagined, and yet it would, in time, bring everything to an end. Many athletes endorse shoes or soft drinks; here was a gold medalist effectively endorsing doctor-assisted suicide.

If the Rio Paralympics were a launching pad for her fame, their aftermath, her official retirement, would symbolize a turn toward the dark and inevitable.

The pain intensified. She had long traveled with a rattling green toolbox of pills, but by mid-2017 she was openly addicted to morphine, taking several doses daily. Her days, once filled with training and appearances, became a blur of hospital stays, pain treatments, and drug-induced naps.

"This is a difficult period for her," her father, Jos, said in late 2017. "Last year, she had sports. Now, most of the time, when we see her at her house, she's laying down on the couch, sleeping."

By the time she returned from her trip to Japan—which had been paid for by a radio station that had been tracking her story —Vervoort was relying heavily on a circle of friends who were beginning to function more like caretakers. "It was always bad; now, it's very, very bad," said Patricia Doms, one of several friends who drove Vervoort around town after she grew too weak to do it herself. "It's hard to see as her friend."

Those closest to Vervoort could see her eyes sag under the weight of the drugs she took to ease her pain. They heard her speech slur, filled in the gaps when she would forget entire conversations, sat patiently when she nodded off midsentence.

Her parents cried at seeing her suffer. But they also lived in fear of receiving a telephone call that something had happened to her, or that she had made concrete plans, at last, to undergo the procedure. Their stance on euthanasia became more complicated as their daughter inched toward it.

"We don't support it," Jos Vervoort said, "but we understand it."

They were among those who held out hope that she would change her mind. Some days, their daughter was her bright former self. She tried picking up new hobbies. She spent time with friends, peppering them with sophomoric jokes, filling the spaces around her with laughter.

But increasingly the fundamental demands of daily life were provoking in her an obscure weariness. She fell unconscious at a child's birthday party in late 2017 and left feeling helpless and embarrassed. She sneered at people who accused her—often in the online comment sections of news reports about her—of exaggerating her pain or faking it for publicity. She found herself lacking the strength to respond to friends' messages.

The Paralympic champion was withering in plain sight.

"I really try to enjoy the little things," she said. "But the little things are getting so little."

Picking a day to die, though, proved difficult. Beyond the grand, existential questions, there were more banal conflicts like birthdays or unexpected family illnesses that regularly popped up to complicate the scheduling. Her paperwork lapsed—it legally expires every five years—and she was forced to renew it.

"I want to die," she told me once in the summer of 2018. "I pray to die. But it's so hard to say, 'This is the day I want to go.' Choosing a day is already dying a little bit."

She wrote dozens of goodbye letters to friends and family members. She planned her funeral. She said she did not believe there was an afterlife, but confessed she wished she could view the ceremony from above.

By this fall, it became clear she was growing impatient. Her doctors were struggling to coordinate a date, and she was convinced that they were finding reasons to stall.

"When they tell me the day," she said, "I will be the happiest person on earth."

V: The End

Vervoort convened her so-called goodbye party at her apartment on short notice for a Saturday in October. Barring a last-minute postponement, she was scheduled to die the following Tuesday.

The night of the party, with dozens of people in her home, Vervoort barely moved. She wore a loose, orange sweatshirt, and her hair—short, spiky, and bleached blond at the height of her athletic career—was matted to her head in her natural muted brown.

She stationed her wheelchair outside her bedroom, and one by one her guests crouched down to meet her eyes and squeeze her head, whisper into her ear. After the party, she asked to be returned to the hospital; the unending stream of visitors and roiling waves of emotion had become too much.

Three days later, on the Tuesday, her parents drove her home, this time to die. She asked that they swing by the pet store so she could buy treats and stuffed animals for Zenn and a second service dog, Mazzel. They were set to be adopted by friends of hers. They stopped at the pharmacy to pick up the euthanasia drugs, which by law the family must purchase itself.

Back at her apartment, another small group of people gathered to say their goodbyes, but Vervoort seemed only partly aware of their presence. She sought out and held her nephew, Zappa, her sister's first child, who was less than a month old. She had scheduled her death for after his birth, so that she could meet him. Then she climbed out of her wheelchair, lay on her couch, and fell asleep.

When Dr. Distelmans arrived two hours later, most of the guests were gone. Vervoort was sipping cava and munching on Maltesers chocolates, a guilty pleasure. She offered him one.

Dr. Distelmans and another doctor wheeled Vervoort into her bedroom, where pictures of her in her racing days had been taped to the door, and helped her into bed. She spent a final moment with her parents, her godmother, and two of her best friends.

"Are you sure you want to continue?" one of the doctors said.

"Yes, I want to continue," she said.

The time of death was recorded as 8:15 p.m. The doctor touched a stethoscope to her skin. The family called the undertaker.

The next morning, Jos Vervoort awoke to find he was still talking to his daughter. "Where are you now, Marieke?" he said.

Slowly he forced himself out of bed. He eventually ventured into town. It was cool and sunny. He stopped himself at a newsstand. His daughter's face beamed from the front pages of half a dozen Belgian newspapers, her name in the headlines one final time.

Jos Vervoort bought a copy of each one, went home, and laid them out carefully on the family's kitchen table.

EMILY GIAMBALVO

A Second Chance

FROM THE WASHINGTON POST

KANAB, UTAH — Not long before lunchtime, Mya's wagging tail splashes as she waits for the tank to drain. The bowlegged black pit bull just finished a three-minute hydrotherapy session, guided by treats offered from a staffer reaching down into the apparatus. But while Mya walks slowly on the submerged treadmill, she notices Laura Rethoret's car through the window. Once the tank empties, Mya scurries down the ramp as fast as she can with her weakened legs, which have splayed more as she has aged.

"Good morning, beautiful!" says Rethoret, who embraces Mya with a towel. "I'm right here!"

Rethoret loads Mya and her runmate, Curly, into her car and drives to the quiet office where the dogs hang out a few times a week. These dogs are reminders that even now, twelve years later, survivors of former NFL quarterback Michael Vick's dogfighting operation live on in pockets throughout the country, including here at Best Friends Animal Society's 3,700-acre sanctuary.

Vick pleaded guilty in 2007 to running an illegal dogfighting ring in southeastern Virginia, a scandal that cast a spotlight on the problem of dogfighting rings around the nation. But for forty-seven dogs pulled from Bad Newz Kennels, there was another, less publicized development that helped change how dogs taken in large-scale dogfighting busts are treated. Rather than being euthanized, the Vick dogs were given a chance to live.

The dogs became ambassadors, tail-wagging proof of what's possible through rescue and rehabilitation. In doing so, they changed how the public — and some prominent rescue organizations — view dogs freed from fighting rings. Dogfighting remains prevalent, but now, in large part thanks to these dogs, others seized in fight busts are evaluated to see whether they can become pets.

The *Washington Post* tracked down all forty-seven dogs and compiled a comprehensive look into their post-adoption lives and the families they joined. They landed in homes from California to Rhode Island, embraced by people with jobs ranging from preschool teacher to attorney. Some adopters love sports. Others had never heard of Vick, once the highest-paid player in the NFL who at the time of the bust starred for the Atlanta Falcons. Some of the dogs struggled to heal emotionally and remained fearful through their lives. But they all found homes far more loving than the horror-film kennel that made headlines around the globe.

"While Michael Vick [was] a deplorable person in a lot of ways, the fact that he was the one that got caught was really a big boom for this whole topic and for these animals," Best Friends cofounder Francis Battista said. "It just catapulted it into the public eye."

In late August, just a few weeks after her therapy session, Mya spent her final moments lying on blankets and surrounded by Best Friends staffers, including Rethoret, whose face turned red as Mya slipped away. She's one of five of the Vick dogs who have died in recent months, leaving just eleven survivors. They are poignant reminders of their tragic beginnings but also of the grace, patience, and unexpected opportunities that followed.

When Vick's dogfighting operation was broken up, animal rescues from around the country understood the gravity of the case but also the opportunities it presented because of the NFL star's fame. Eight organizations received custody of the animals. Some groups placed a single dog into a foster home. Best Friends agreed to give the twenty-two most challenging cases a place to recover and, for some, a permanent home.

The organizations worked to redefine what made a dog adoptable. The dogs were seen as victims, not irreparably damaged. They weren't just pit bulls or fight dogs. They became Mya and Curly, Frodo and Zippy.

"Michael Vick brought dogfighting into the living room of every American," said Heather Gutshall, who adopted Handsome Dan and later founded a rescue organization that aims to help survivors of dogfighting. "Am I glad it happened? No. Am I glad, that if it was going to happen, that it happened the way it did? Absolutely. They changed the landscape."

Moment in Animal Welfare

In southern Utah, the city of Kanab makes the NFL feel like a distant enterprise. The feature of the town, which has two stoplights and fewer than 5,000 residents, is that it once served as the backdrop for Western films.

As the highway curves from the tiny town center and through a scenic southwestern landscape of vast skies and towering orange cliffs, one right turn leads into Best Friends, a haven for second chances that is home to 1,600 animals, including dogs, cats, horses, and birds. Dogs cruise by with caregivers on golf carts. The chorus of barking chaos quiets as you venture deeper through the sandy trails. It's busy and boisterous yet vast and peaceful.

John Garcia, who at the time of the Vick case co-managed the Dogtown at Best Friends, grew up in a neighboring town without a TV. He doesn't watch sports. Garcia only learned of Vick through his case, but he remembers the message from the rescue's senior leadership: "Hey, if we get involved in this, it's a big deal," he said. "We may be able to change the world."

The pressure to help the dogs—and to prove they could indeed be helped—was palpable. Because Vick's fame turned the dog-fighting bust into a national story, not just a conversation in the animal welfare community, many watched with curiosity or skepticism, wondering whether a dog from a traumatic past could ever live normally in society.

BADRAP, an Oakland-based organization, emerged as an early voice advocating for the dogs. People for the Ethical Treatment of Animals (PETA) and the Humane Society of the United States thought they should be killed, in keeping with their long-standing belief that the emotional trauma such dogs had suffered would be too much to overcome. Of the fifty-one dogs listed in court documents, just one needed to be euthanized for behavioral reasons. One, named Rose, was euthanized for medical reasons, and two died in care.

BADRAP had worked with individual dogs seized from fighting

situations many times, which gave the organization confidence. Donna Reynolds, the director of BADRAP, said once staff members met the dogs for evaluations in Virginia, there was a sense of relief—"wiping brow with back of hand," she called it. They knew they would be able to work with them.

Pit bulls continue to face breed discrimination, with blanket bans in parts of the country. As of this year, however, twenty-two states have provisions against this type of legislation, and Best Friends has spearheaded initiatives to increase that number. Rehabilitating the Vick dogs has helped further the argument that the owner, not the breed, dictates a dog's behavior. And this marquee moment in animal welfare preached values that extend beyond just pit bulls and into the overarching no-kill movement.

"This is what really excites me because it goes to that pushing the boundaries and the demonstration of what is adoptable," Best Friends CEO Julie Castle said. "That flag has always been something that we've held."

Most involved with the Vick case, from the adopters to rescue staffers, express indifference toward the former quarterback himself. Visitors often ask Michelle Weaver, who once co-managed Dogtown and now oversees all animal care at Best Friends, what she thinks about the quarterback who abused dogs such as the ones that have lounged in her office for years. Her answer: she doesn't think about Vick. Her energy usually goes toward the dogs. Is Curly feeling okay? He has been slowing down lately. How's Cherry, whose photo hangs near Weaver's desk, doing in his Connecticut home?

"There's not the anger. I think in the early days there was," said Stacy Dubuc, a Green Bay Packers fan who adopted Ginger from the SPCA for Monterey County in Northern California. "Honestly at this point, I hate to say it, but somehow [Vick] is involved in my life. And I have the best dog possible because of it. He was the face of dogfighting. It took a celebrity to become that. And I don't talk about him."

Vick, who paid nearly $1 million restitution for care of the dogs, says he regrets it all and didn't have the strength to stop what he realized was wrong about a year before he was caught. Vick, thirtynine, retired in 2017 and is an NFL analyst with Fox Sports. He has advocated for stronger animal cruelty laws and works to educate children.

"I think people have moved on," Vick said in a telephone interview. "I think they've moved past it. It's been twelve-plus years since it all happened, so I don't get any questions about it anymore. People don't talk about it. They don't ask me about it. Life is kind of normal. But I still have a responsibility, and that will never change."

Treated as Individuals

Mel's life was not normal.

Mel trembled whenever strangers entered Richard Hunter's suburban Las Vegas home, the emotional scars from his time at Bad Newz Kennels still evident twelve years on. But Hunter always emphasized the progress Mel had made, though he let the dog's continued struggles serve as a reminder of what Vick did.

Every night, Hunter walked Mel and his two other dogs. It would take Mel a minute to get going. He would pause in the short driveway, look in each direction, take slow steps, assess the situation, and only then decide he was ready to walk. The stories of all these dogs, Hunter said, shouldn't be reduced to a Disney-style tale.

"Everybody is great in a lot of ways now," Hunter said in July, shortly before Mel's death following a brief and unexpected illness. "But you better believe the ghosts of what Vick did to him and did to those other dogs stays with them to this day and always will."

When Mel and the other twenty-one Best Friends dogs arrived at the Utah sanctuary, they surprised the staff with their shyness. While some of Dogtown's newest residents, dubbed the Vicktory dogs, were overconfident and aggressive, many seemed undersocialized and afraid. For at least six months, the dogs had twenty-four-hour care. Garcia slept on the concrete floor of the building that housed the dogs for a month straight.

Progress was gradual. The issues varied. Georgia, a former dogfighting champion, reacted to other dogs a football field away. Others loved canine companions, and socializing with dogs helped them get closer to people. Many had never walked on a leash. They hadn't lived in a home environment. They needed to learn how to play.

"It was clear," Weaver said, "that their world was pretty small before."

Once in homes, the dogs still had their own quirks, which in many ways exemplify the legacy these dogs will leave—that all animals, even from a fighting background, should be treated as individuals. Layla, who died in June, needed her collar removed when she ate. The clanging of her tag hitting the stainless steel food bowl frightened her. Shadow, one of the eleven still alive, remains terrified of ladders, making his family wonder whether he saw dogs being hanged. His adopters don't think Shadow fought, but the fights took place on the second level of a shed, accessible by a ladder.

Public Facebook pages have chronicled the dogs' post-adoption adventures for thousands of followers. (Handsome Dan's page has 546,000 likes.) Adopters shared successes and the dogs' lives in a world that slowly became more comfortable.

"I almost forget where he came from because he's such a typical dog now," said Melissa Fiaccone, who adopted Cherry. The dog's confidence has surged through the years. Cherry spent a week this summer in a cabin with more than a dozen people, including many children. The family posted a photo of Cherry on a dock with his eyes squinting and his massive tongue flopping happily. He frequently attends public events and loves greeting everyone. Fiaccone's husband, Paul, says Cherry "took on the rock star persona."

They Were Game-Changers

About a year after the Vick dogs were dispersed around the country, a North Carolina man pleaded guilty to dogfighting. All 127 dogs seized—and the puppies born during the legal proceedings—were euthanized. Leaders from across animal welfare met to confront the issue, and it prompted the Humane Society to adjust its stance on dogs seized from fight busts. The experience with the Vick dogs, Battista said, was pivotal in that policy change.

PETA's stance "remains firmly the same as it was in 2007," Senior Vice President Daphna Nachminovitch said in a statement, adding that dogs from these situations can be "unpredictable" and a danger to other animals and humans.

Dogfighting continues to be a problem in the United States,

but Janette Reever, a senior specialist for Humane Society International's global anti-dogfighting program, said she believes it's declining. Dogfighting is an underground enterprise, however, so there's not comprehensive data to prove that.

Since 2008, dogfighting has been a felony in all fifty states, and Reever said law enforcement has realized animal cruelty is often joined by other illegal activities, providing an additional incentive for police to look into reports of fighting rings.

Uba, a Vick dog who lives with Letti de Little in Northern Virginia, has a housemate named Jamie, a dog from a 2013 multi-state fight bust in which 367 dogs were seized. The Missouri 500, a 2009 seizure of more than 400 dogs, is still the largest fight bust in U.S. history, and "thank God it happened after the Vick case," said Ledy VanKavage, a senior legislative attorney for Best Friends whose dog, Karma, was among those rescued.

"She would be dead but for the Vick dogs," VanKavage said. "I have no doubt. They were game-changers."

Across from a small church in rural Virginia, Vick's property has been purchased by Dogs Deserve Better, an organization that focuses on rescuing chained and penned dogs. On a summer day, dogs run in the fenced yard and the mood feels cheerful.

Then there are the four sheds, where Vick kept and fought his dogs. All are painted black, even the windows, to make them less visible at night. The group decided to preserve these relics of the dogfighting operation for educational purposes. The kennels inside one of the buildings still show claw marks on the walls. But there's hope and remembrance, too, through memorial candles and trees dedicated to each dog planted in a grassy field out back.

"They've gone through so much, and they've changed so much," Garcia said. "They'll never be forgotten."

Garcia now works as the safety and security manager at Best Friends. Sometimes during night shifts, he wanders up to the sanctuary's cemeteries, where hundreds of wind chimes ring at different pitches in the breeze and intensify into a song when a strong wind arrives. It's peaceful and quiet.

A number of the Vicktory dogs rest there, with small memorial stones towering into mountains on top of their graves. One has a toy golf cart, representing how the dog loved riding around with caregivers, along with an old tennis ball. A couple of the adopters brought their dogs' ashes back to Best Friends, the place that gave them a chance. That's what felt right, and it helps preserve their legacy as the dogs fade further from the public eye.

But far from this canyon and across the country, other dogs live because of these forty-seven. So as time eventually defeats them all, the message on a slab of stone in the cemetery carries hope and truth.

"Do not stand by my grave and cry," the poem reminds those who enter through the ornate gates. "I am not there. I did not die."

ELIZABETH MERRILL

Whatever Happened to Villanova Basketball Star Shelly Pennefather? "So I Made This Deal with God."

FROM ESPN.COM

SHE LEFT WITH the clothes on her back, a long blue dress and a pair of shoes she'd never wear again. It was June 8, 1991, a Saturday morning, and Shelly Pennefather was starting a new life. She posed for a group photo in front of her parents' tidy brick home in Northern Virginia, and her family scrunched in around her and smiled.

All six of her brothers and sisters were there—Little Therese, in braided pigtails; older brother Dick, tall and athletic with Kennedyesque looks. When Shelly came to her decision, she insisted on telling each of them separately.

Dick had the loosest lips in the family, so she'd told him last. Therese, twelve years old and the baby of the family, took the news particularly hard. She put on a brave face in front of Shelly, then cried all night.

They crammed a lot of memories into those last days of spring, dancing and laughing, knowing they would never do it together again. Shelly went horseback riding with Therese and took the family to fancy restaurants with cloth napkins, picking up all the tabs.

Twenty-five years old and not far removed from her All-America days at Villanova, Pennefather was in her prime. She had legions of friends and a contract offer for $200,000 to play basketball in Japan that would have made her one of the richest players in women's basketball.

And children—she was so good with children. She had talked about having lots of them with John Heisler, a friend she'd known most of her life. Heisler nearly proposed to her twice, but something inside stopped him, and he never bought a ring.

"When she walked into the room," Heisler said, "the whole room came alive.

"She had a cheerfulness and a confidence that everything was going to be okay. That there was nothing to fear."

That Saturday morning in 1991, Pennefather drove her Mazda 323 to the Monastery of the Poor Clares in Alexandria, Virginia. She loved to drive. Fifteen cloistered nuns waited for her in two lines, their smiles radiant.

She turned to her family.

"I love you all," she said.

The door closed, and Shelly Pennefather was gone.

It's been twenty-eight years since Pennefather left home to become Sister Rose Marie of the Queen of Angels, and I'm standing outside the family's house in Manassas, Virginia, on a warm June day, searching for answers.

I spent eight years in Catholic schools, with lessons in history from Sister Agnes Marie and kindness from Sister Rosetta. We knew that on Sundays, if you're breathing, you'd better be at Mass.

But I cannot grasp what Pennefather—now Sister Rose Marie—has chosen to do. The Poor Clares are one of the strictest religious orders in the world. They sleep on straw mattresses, in full habit, and wake up every night at 12:30 a.m. to pray, never resting more than four hours at a time. They are barefoot twenty-three hours of the day, except for the one hour in which they walk around the courtyard in sandals.

They are cut off from society. Sister Rose Marie will never leave the monastery, unless there's a medical emergency. She'll never call or email or text anyone either. The rules seem so arbitrarily harsh. She gets two family visits per year, but converses through a see-through screen. She can write letters to her friends, but only if they write to her first. And once every twenty-five years, she can hug her family.

That's why we are here in early June 2019, to witness the twenty-five-year anniversary of her solemn profession and the renewal of her vows.

The Poor Clare nuns enter this radical way of life because they believe that their prayers for humanity will help the suffering, and that their sacrifice will lead to the salvation of the world.

But why would someone with so much to offer the world lock herself away and hide her talents? Who, staring at a professional contract that would be worth the equivalent of about $400,000 today, would subject herself to such strict isolation and sacrifice? Imagine Kansas legend Danny Manning quitting basketball to become a monk.

Perhaps the best person to answer this is the woman who stood next to Shelly in that goodbye photo in front of the house, who wrapped her arm around her daughter and smiled while her heart must have wanted to stop.

Mary Jane Pennefather is the matriarch of the family, a seventy-eight-year-old who mows her own lawn and rises every morning to walk to church. When Shelly entered the monastery all those years ago, she left behind a note. Mary Jane is the strongest person Therese knows, but when she read the letter, she broke down and cried.

Mary Jane was a cheerleader once, but is steeped in a generation of Catholics who did not believe in drawing attention to themselves. She opens the door to her home and leads me to a room full of religious statues and images, which the family calls the Blessed Mother room. Her husband, Mike, died in this room. He had skin cancer, which had spread too far when doctors found it, but he went quickly, which Mary Jane considers a blessing. Sister Rose Marie couldn't go to her father's funeral back in 1998. She was in the monastery. But she wrote a letter that they read out loud, and her brother Dick says it was probably the most touching part of the service.

Surely, Mike Pennefather had hoped to hold his daughter again on her silver jubilee. But Mary Jane would be there. The week leading up to the Mass was stressful. How do you prepare to hug your daughter for the last time?

Nuns are by no means an anomaly in today's society. The 2018 Official Catholic Directory lists 45,100 sisters in the United States. But cloistered nuns, with all of their combined orders, account for only a fraction of that number. The Poor Clare Colettines, according to the directory, have about 160 sisters in this country.

There were hints, all along, that Pennefather was different.

In sixth grade, a teacher asked the class an ordinary question: What do you want to be when you grow up?

The teacher wasn't prepared for Shelly's answer.

"I'm going to be a saint," she said.

The whole class laughed, assuming she was joking. Pennefather liked to regale her friends with jokes and magic tricks.

Her childhood might have inadvertently prepared her for life as a cloistered nun. Mike Pennefather was an Air Force colonel, taking the family to Germany and Hawaii and New York, so she'd already seen a lot of the world by her twenties.

Her mom was—and is—about as anti-technology as a person can be in 2019. Mary Jane doesn't own a cell phone, she could go on for hours about how cell phones are destroying the human experience, and a few decades ago, she was saying pretty much the same thing about television.

Children of the '70s often have stories of their forays into alcohol or drugs; the Pennefathers' illicit pursuits centered mostly on the forbidden television. They'd wait until Mary Jane was gone, pull it out of the closet, rig up a coat hanger for an antenna, and stand in just the right spot to get reception.

"I think my sister watched *Fantasy Island* and got caught and got in trouble," Therese said. "You had to invent your own entertainment, and we did all kinds of stupid stuff.

"I absolutely wouldn't trade any of it."

The Air Force gave the Pennefathers new playgrounds every few years, and assured that they would almost always be safe. Want to play kick the can at eleven o'clock at night? No problem. Leave the base lights on and go ahead and invite twenty other Air Force brats.

Mary Jane might have seemed strict, but Mike was actually more intimidating. He was a bear of a man with a loud voice and a physics degree. Mike Pennefather did not tolerate foolishness. He taught all seven of his children how to shoot a basketball, and when he had finished with that, he taught other people's children how to do it too.

The Pennefathers had six children in eight years, and Shelly was born between two brothers, two basketball playmates. The elbows and charges she took made her unstoppable when she finally played against girls.

At nighttime, Mary Jane would gather the whole family together to pray the rosary. It didn't matter if it was midnight; she waited until everyone was home.

The rosary is considered one of the most powerful symbols in Catholicism. Each of the fifty-nine beads represents a prayer. The Hail Mary is said fifty-three times during the rosary. The repetition is intended to bring spiritual contemplation and peace.

At the Pennefather house, after the last prayer was said, each child gave Mary Jane and Mike a kiss goodnight.

Coach Harry Perretta also prayed the rosary every day, a practice that came in handy in his pursuit to lure Pennefather to Villanova. If Pennefather played today, her recruitment might have been as big as that of Breanna Stewart or Elena Delle Donne.

Pennefather went 70-0 in her first three years of high school at Bishop Machebeuf in Denver and won three state championships. When her dad was transferred to upstate New York her senior season, nothing changed. Utica's Notre Dame High went undefeated too.

Pennefather had no interest in the recruiting process. She hated the attention that it brought, and didn't like talking on the phone. So it was hard for any coach to get a read on her. Perretta talked to her about his devotion to the Blessed Mother Mary, and they connected. She committed to Villanova, the oldest Catholic university in Pennsylvania.

Their bond was tested early. Her freshman year, they clashed constantly. "She was a very lazy basketball player at first," Perretta said. "She didn't work hard on the court when she came here."

He said it wasn't necessarily her fault; she was so good in high school that she probably didn't know what playing hard meant. But he had to get through to her. He yelled at her and kicked her out of the gym, and nothing seemed to work. In her sophomore season, Pennefather considered transferring.

She'd leave campus on weekends, seeking solace at teammate Lisa Gedaka's house in New Jersey. Gedaka, a freshman, would go back a lot because she was homesick.

"I always remember hearing about how she was searching," Gedaka said. "Was this the right place to go? What is the meaning? Why is she here? And I remember saying to her once, 'Shelly, did you ever think that maybe this is God's will that you should be with us here at Villanova? This is where you're meant to be.'"

Somehow, some way, Pennefather and Perretta finally clicked. "God gave you this gift," Perretta told her. "You're not really using it to the fullest extent."

From there, she didn't hold anything back. There was one game, junior year, when she was so overcome with menstrual cramps that they were almost debilitating. As the team left for the gym, Perretta told her to just stay at the hotel.

A couple of minutes before tip-off, Pennefather emerged from the locker room, in agony, with her sneakers still untied. "I'm going to try to play," she told him. She mustered enough strength to tie her shoes when the horn sounded. There was no time for any warm-up. She made all nine of her shots in the first half.

The Wildcats' teams in the mid- to late 1980s were lucky. They were a collection of people who knew, when they were freshmen, that they'd stay friends forever. They demanded the best of each other.

It was a different time, before NCAA-regulated practice schedules and transfer portals. "We could say stuff to each other," said former Wildcats point guard Lynn Tighe. "If somebody was being a pain in the butt, I had no trouble telling them, and if I was a pain in the butt, I was told about it. We were open to each other, and nonsense didn't fester."

Pennefather was roommates with Tighe, and you can imagine her glee when she found out her point guard had a small television. Pennefather had one movie she would watch constantly on the VCR. *The Sound of Music.* She subjected everyone to it, belting out Julie Andrews songs on the team bus.

"I wouldn't say she had a good voice," Tighe said. "But it wasn't bad. She knew every word to every one of them."

But Pennefather did have the most beautiful shooting touch in all of women's basketball. She scored 2,408 points, breaking Villanova's all-time record for women and men. She did it without the benefit of the three-point shot, and the record still stands today.

In 1987, she won the Wade Trophy, given to the best women's college basketball player. She eventually threw away all of her trophies—"I don't think she cared about them at all," said her sister, Therese—but spared one, the Wade Trophy. She gave it to Perretta.

The WNBA did not exist when Pennefather graduated from Villanova, but women's professional basketball overseas offered good money. She signed with the Nippon Express in Japan, the place where her whole life would change.

The pace in Japan was much slower—the Express played just fourteen games in the span of four months—and it jolted Pennefather. Away from her college teammates and the daily chaos of her large family, she felt homesick and alone in a faraway city. Her team started 0-5. If they finished at the bottom of the division, she would need to stay in Japan for another two months to play a series of round-robin games.

She desperately wanted to go home, and vowed that if her team could finish in the top six, allowing her to go home rather than stay those two months, she would spend that time doing volunteer work.

The Express turned their season around and finished third. Pennefather returned to the U.S. and fulfilled her promise by working in a soup kitchen at the Missionary Sisters of Charity in Norristown, Pennsylvania. In a convent full of tiny nuns, the six-foot-one basketball player stood out.

She felt even more out of place that next season in Japan. She did everything she could to keep busy, reading books, learning Japanese, teaching English. But Pennefather still felt a deep emptiness.

"She was forced to go into solitude," said John Heisler, her childhood friend. "There was nobody else, just her and God."

Heisler was sort of a mystery man for many years. Pennefather's teammates used to say that they thought she'd do one of two things in her life—marry this guy she spent summers with or become a nun. But not a cloistered nun, of course.

Sports Illustrated did a story on Pennefather's rare sacrifice in the late 1990s, but Heisler's name wasn't mentioned. He was nowhere near being ready to talk about her back then.

But now Heisler is really helpful. He wants people to understand, even if he still doesn't completely get it himself.

"It's a mystery to me too about why they'd take somebody so talented, so giving, so energetic," he said. "She could help so many other young ladies to be women . . . to be strong too, in their identity. Why should she be so hidden now? I've been really thinking . . . about the mystery of the stars. They're so distant, yet they're so beautiful."

They met in grade school on a base in Wiesbaden, Germany. He'd never met a girl like her—confident yet self-effacing; strong but kind enough to defend anyone who was being picked on.

Heisler came from a large Catholic family too. At one point, the families prayed the rosary together. They eventually were shipped to different places, but they always seemed to find each other. Heisler had three passions growing up: sports, comic books, and stories about saints. He was fascinated by St. Francis of Assisi, who eventually helped St. Clare start an order called the Poor Clares.

When he got older, Heisler developed another interest: Shelly Pennefather. Heisler went on to the Air Force Academy, and one morning he woke up content with his life and the fact that he flew F15s but also plagued by one question: What if God has another plan for me?

In a move that was both bold and not very well thought out, he withdrew from his classes at the academy, went back to his family's home in Maine, then drove to Villanova to see Pennefather.

They'd spend their summers together white-water rafting and talking about anything.

Despite their affection for each other, they were never intimate. John Heisler, you see, was battling his own inner voice, the one that told him he should become a priest.

If a calling came from a booming voice above the clouds, like in the movies, it would be easy. Heisler's was a gnawing pain. He went back to school to become an electrical engineer, and pursued Pennefather through different stops in their lives, but that pain just wouldn't go away. It was like a kill switch that told them they'd never be together.

In early 1991, during her third season in Japan, she called

Heisler and asked him to meet her in Virginia so they could talk. "What's going on?" he asked.

"Well, I'm entering the Poor Clares," she told him, "and this is our last time . . . to spend time together."

Heisler's heart dropped. But in a way, it was freeing. Father John Heisler had nothing holding him back. Eight years later, he was ordained.

When Pennefather got back from Japan in 1991, she wanted to tell her closest friends about her decision in person. She traveled to New Jersey to tell Lisa Gedaka and to Pennsylvania to tell Lynn Tighe.

Tighe owned a deli back then, and she and Pennefather were peeling potatoes when her former teammate dropped the news. Pennefather never stopped peeling.

"Lynn, I would never choose this for myself," Pennefather told her. "I would never leave my family and my friends. But this is what I'm called to do. I know it. God is calling me. And I'm going to do it."

But Tighe, Karen Daly, and Kathy Miller, all part of the same Villanova class that met each other as freshmen in 1983, wanted more answers. They insisted on going to the monastery and talking to the mother superior. They wanted to know everything they could about the life of a cloistered nun.

They wanted to make sure their teammate would be okay.

Pennefather gave her friends a couple of questions to ask too, a true sign she had little idea what she was getting herself into.

Miller said that they struck a deal with the mother superior that day: that in 2019, the three of them would be able to hug Pennefather during her silver jubilee. Just like family.

Seasons passed for everyone but Sister Rose Marie. Tighe became an associate athletic director at Villanova; Lisa Gedaka got married, had children, and became a high school basketball coach. Her oldest daughter plays basketball too, and now Mary Gedaka is a forward at Villanova, playing under an older and somewhat mellower Harry Perretta.

Perretta also brokered a backdoor deal with the Poor Clares. He'd bring the sisters some much-needed supplies every summer in return for his own yearly visit with Sister Rose Marie.

So every June, he drives three hours down I-95 to the monastery, delivering necessities such as ginger ale and Reese's peanut butter cups. Sometimes, he'll bring along one or two of her old teammates to (wink, wink) help. They can see her through the screen and hold their hands up to hers.

One time, Perretta was visiting Sister Rose Marie when his phone rang.

"What's that?" she asked.

She'd never seen a cell phone.

If Perretta or any of Sister Rose Marie's teammates are struggling, they can call the monastery and ask the mother superior to pass along prayer requests. They pray for humanity and the things they can't see.

They prayed for the victims of 9/11 even though they never saw any pictures of the towers falling or knew the names of the people who died.

"I didn't understand it at first," Perretta said. "But if you believe in the power of prayers, then they're doing more for humanity than anybody."

It rained on June 9, the day of Sister Rose Marie's jubilee Mass. The bishop of Arlington, Virginia, came, and people in Sunday suits and dresses scurried to find seats in the monastery's tiny chapel. Perretta's two sons, strapping young men, stood in the back and craned their necks to see the altar. They weren't even born when Pennefather left.

Shortly after the homily, two wooden doors opened and the whole chapel let out a silent gasp. There she was, fifty-three years old, standing before them, with no screen. Without even scanning the crowd, she immediately fixed her eyes on the pew where her mother sat. Her face lit up.

Sister Rose Marie renewed her vows. Then a procession line formed in front of her. Mary Jane was first. Sister Rose Marie held her hands out as her mother drew closer. The Pennefathers have never been a touchy-feely family, but when mother and daughter embraced, it seemed to last an eternity. Neither one wanted to let go.

"I'll be here at 103 if you can hang in there," Mary Jane told her daughter.

"I'll try," Sister Rose Marie said.

She hugged nieces and nephews she had never touched before. She embraced siblings whose hair had turned from dark to gray.

Perretta got his hug. Tighe, Daly, and Martin weren't sure whether anyone would remember that deal they made with the mother superior so many years ago. But they slipped into the back and hugged her too.

And in that receiving line stood Father John Heisler. He saw the woman he had known and loved for most of his life, and they gave each other a knowing smile and an embrace.

"We made the right decision," she told him.

"No regrets," he said.

Most of her teammates knew, going in, that they weren't going to get a hug because it was supposed to be for family only. But they didn't want to miss this moment. They traveled from Washington State and points up and down the Eastern Seaboard.

One ex-Syracuse player who met Shelly at a camp more than three decades ago drove three hours to see her too. She means that much to people, Marita Finley said.

A few hours after the Mass, Sister Rose Marie's teammates were allowed a visit. It was the first time they'd been together in decades. They didn't know what to expect.

When she appeared behind a screen, the whole room erupted in cheers.

"I just want to say one thing," Pennefather told them. "I've heard every comment you said about me at alumni gatherings in the past. These will have eternal repercussions."

Everyone laughed.

A woman who spends twenty-three hours a day in silence seamlessly launched right into conversation. There were no awkward gaps. It was as if they picked back up after seeing each other at the last team reunion.

"I mean, it doesn't really surprise me that some of us should have ended up incarcerated," she deadpanned. "The surprise was that it was me."

The years had been kind to Sister Rose Marie. She lifts weights three times a week and stretches on the other days, except, of course, on Sundays. No, she does not play basketball, but every so often, the sisters will engage in a game of stickball.

With her old teammates around her, clinging to each other's

words, they caught up on families and careers, then, without being asked, Sister Rose Marie shared a story. Her story.

She was in Japan that first year and wanted to go home. "So I made this deal with God," she said. She told them that the missionary work moved her so much that she went back every summer after that. One year, she was invited to a retreat, where she was asked to read a Bible verse, John 6:56: "Whoever eats my flesh and drinks my blood remains in me, and I in him."

And that, she said, is when it hit her. She felt that God was right there, twenty feet in front of her. She kept reading, and when she closed the Bible, she said a silent prayer. She was stunned. She walked into church the next day, genuflected at the tabernacle like she always did, and realized that she was no longer alone.

"You can look back now and you see how providentially our Lord just kind of took me and put me there in that place where I could just develop, you know?" she told them. "And then I just kind of felt that he was asking me to serve this sort of radical kind of call, which is the hardest thing I ever did. But I'm grateful I did, and here I am. Incarcerated."

But she never really left them. Her letters got them through marriage problems and deaths and child-raising crises. Some of the women brought their children to the monastery, just to see her.

"I love this life," she told them. "I wish you all could just live it for a little while just to see. It's so peaceful. I just feel like I'm not underliving life. I'm living it to the full."

The Pennefathers threw a jubilee reception at a Knights of Columbus hall. They could have catered it, but Mary Jane wouldn't have it. She spent weeks making everything, the lasagna and chocolate cake and orange slush. Maybe if she kept moving, she wouldn't have to think about the finality of the hug.

If anyone is going to make it to 103, her children say, it's Mary Jane. She's lost a husband and two grandchildren, but she is constant, like the spring cherry blossoms up the highway.

Sister Rose Marie's sacrifice was Mary Jane's sacrifice. She no doubt was filled with pride and sorrow when Shelly made her decision. She keeps a box at the house that contains her daughter's hair. It was cut after she went into the monastery.

Mary Jane isn't sentimental about it; she doesn't open the box to feel closer to her daughter. But she's kept it, and Shelly's letter, after all these years.

Mary Jane does not want to share the letter. It's too personal. But she will recite one line, from memory.

"I realize that I won't hear the laughter of my brothers and sisters anymore."

Shelly's younger sister, Jean, also became a nun. She's not cloistered and can hug her family, use a cell phone, and drive.

Mary Jane does not want people to think that someone who chooses either of these lives is an oddball. But she knows that no matter what she says, people will not understand.

She got out of her seat in what they call the Blessed Mother room and searched through some drawers and pulled out a photo album. She stopped at an old picture of a young girl wearing a veil.

"That's me," Mary Jane whispered. "I entered too."

She was fourteen years old in the picture. The convent was vast, and two and a half hours away from her home in Louisiana. Nine months in, it dawned on her. *I shouldn't be here.* She went home, finished high school, went to college, met Mike, and never looked back.

She, too, has no regrets.

"Well," she said, "look at the fruits of my life."

Contributors' Notes

Notable Sports Writing of 2019

Contributors' Notes

KEVIN ARNOVITZ has covered the NBA for *ESPN* since 2008. His work has spanned stories on the mental health of top athletes, the dysfunctional front offices of NBA franchises, and a profile of Billy Kennedy, the NBA's only openly gay referee. His piece on Nancy Lieberman was anthologized in 2012 in *Jewish Jocks,* edited by Franklin Foer and Marc Tracy. Prior to joining *ESPN,* he was an editor and producer at National Public Radio. He cohosts *Pack Your Knives,* a *Top Chef* podcast. He is completing a half-marathon in all fifty states, and as of publication, he has run fourteen. He is a native of Atlanta, a graduate of Columbia University, and a resident of Los Angeles.

KENT BABB is a sports features writer for the *Washington Post* and the author of the 2015 Allen Iverson biography *Not a Game* and the forthcoming *Across the River,* a book about gun violence and high school football in New Orleans. This is his third appearance in *The Best American Sports Writing.*

CHRIS BALLARD was a senior writer at *Sports Illustrated,* a lecturer at the UC Berkeley Graduate School of Journalism, and the author of four books, most recently *One Shot at Forever.* He lives in Berkeley, California, where he does a passable job of coaching his daughter's basketball team. This is his seventh story to be included in *The Best American Sports Writing,* an anthology series that inspired him and countless others to enter this field and to see sports as about so much more than just people playing games.

BRYAN BURROUGH has been a special correspondent at *Vanity Fair* for twenty-eight years. Based in Austin, Texas, Burrough is the author of *New York Times* best-sellers *Barbarians at the Gate, Public Enemies,* and *The Big Rich.* He made his first trip to India to write "Shooting a Tiger," fell in love with the country and its people, and hopes to get back to see more of it soon.

EVAN DRELLICH worked at the *Houston Chronicle* and *Boston Herald* before joining *The Athletic*. A New York City native, Evan is a graduate of Friends Seminary and Binghamton University. He has a forthcoming book on the Astros.

MARK FAINARU-WADA is a graduate of Northwestern's Medill School of Journalism and is an investigative reporter for ESPN. He is the co-author of *Game of Shadows* and *League of Denial*.

ROBERTO JOSÉ ANDRADE FRANCO is a freelance writer. Among other places, his work has been published in *Texas Monthly, ESPN,* the *Los Angeles Times, Bleacher Report, Yahoo Sports, D Magazine,* and *Deadspin*. He lives in Arlington, Texas, and spends as much time as he can in the El Paso–Juárez borderland. Arriba Juárez!

EMILY GIAMBALVO is a staff writer for the *Washington Post*. She grew up in Easley, South Carolina, and graduated from the University of Georgia in 2018.

MARK GOZONSKY'S writing has appeared recently in *The Sun, Lit Hub, Craft,* and the *Austin Chronicle*. He lives with his wife in Los Angeles, where he teaches English at Grand Arts High School. Gozonsky.com archives his stuff: shmarkozonky.school, his students' academic writing + doodles.

JOHN GRISWOLD is a staff writer at *The Common Reader,* a publication of Washington University in St. Louis. His most recent book is *Pirates You Don't Know, and Other Adventures in the Examined Life*.

JOSHUA HAMMER spent fifteen years as a *Newsweek* bureau chief and correspondent at large on five continents. Since 2006, he has been an independent foreign correspondent based in Berlin and a regular contributor to *Smithsonian, Outside,* the *New York Review of Books, GQ,* and the *New York Times Magazine*. He won the National Magazine Award in 2016 for his reporting about the Ebola crisis in West Africa and is the author of five nonfiction books, including the *New York Times* 2016 best-seller *The Bad-Ass Librarians of Timbuktu*. His latest book, *The Falcon Thief,* was published in 2020.

MAY JEONG has been awarded the South Asian Journalists Association's Daniel Pearl Award and the Prix Bayeux Calvados Award for War Correspondents for her reporting from Afghanistan. Her work has also been recognized by the Kurt Schork Awards, the Livingston Awards, and the One World Media Award. She is best known for her investigations into the 2015 attack on the Médecins Sans Frontières hospital in Kunduz, Afghanistan, for which she snuck into a besieged city as a stowaway on a helicopter, had a gun held to her head, and traveled disguised through Taliban country.

CHLOÉ COOPER JONES is a philosophy professor, writer, and journalist. Her first book, *Easy Beauty,* will be published in the spring of 2021. She lives in Brooklyn, New York.

ANDREW KEH is a reporter for the *New York Times.* He has covered Major League Baseball and the NBA, reported from the World Cup and the Olympics, and was an international correspondent based in Berlin. He lives in New York City.

MIKE KESSLER has twice been a finalist for the National Magazine Award and in 2017 was a Knight-Wallace Fellow. He is senior editor of investigations and projects at *KPCC/LAist.*

A native of Chennai, India, AISHWARYA KUMAR is an international writer at ESPN.com, where she has worked since graduating from Northwestern University's Medill School of Journalism in 2016. She writes about race, identity, and global culture using sport as the vehicle. Previously, she worked for the *New Indian Express,* a national daily newspaper in India, covering culture, food, and sport. She now lives in Hartford, Connecticut, with her boyfriend, Jack Sullivan, who is a teacher of foreign languages.

TIM LAYDEN is a writer-at-large at *NBC Sports.* For twenty-five years, from 1994 to 2019, he was a senior writer at *Sports Illustrated,* where he worked as a feature writer and also covered college football and basketball, the NFL, and every Olympics since 1992. Previously, Layden worked at *Newsday,* the *Albany Times Union,* and the *Schenectady Gazette.* He lives in Connecticut and is married with two grown children. This is his fourth appearance in *The Best American Sports Writing.*

STEVEN LECKART is a writer, director, and National Magazine Award finalist. His writing has appeared in *Wired, Esquire,* the *New York Times, Popular Science, Playboy, Maxim,* and *Men's Health,* among others. His film credits include writing *What's My Name | Muhammad Ali,* a two-part HBO documentary. Leckart also wrote and was a co-executive producer for *Inside Bill's Brain: Decoding Bill Gates,* a three-part Netflix documentary.

ELIZABETH MERRILL is a senior writer for *ESPN.* A graduate of the University of Nebraska at Omaha, she has covered football for the *Omaha World-Herald* and the *Kansas City Star.* She started at *ESPN* in 2007 and works in the Digital Storytelling Group.

NICK PAUMGARTEN has been a staff writer at *The New Yorker* since 2005. Prior to that, he was an editor of "The Talk of the Town." He has reported on a wide range of subjects, including politics, finance, art, music, food, technology, mountaineering, sports talk radio, elevators, boxer-bartenders, commuters, and canoes.

BILL PLASCHKE has been an *LA Times* columnist since 1996. He has been named National Sports Columnist of the Year seven times by the Associated Press, and twice by the Society of Professional Journalists and National Headliner Awards. He is the author of five books, including a collection of his columns entitled *Plaschke: Good Sports, Spoil Sports, Foul Ball and Oddballs.* Plaschke is also a panelist on the popular ESPN daily talk show *Around the Horn.* For his community service, he has been named Man of the Year by the Los Angeles Big Brothers/Big Sisters and has received a Pursuit of Justice Award from the California Women's Law Center. Plaschke has appeared in a movie (*Ali*) and in a dramatic HBO series (*Luck*), and in a crowning cultural moment he still does not quite understand, his name can be found in a rap song, "Females Welcome," by Asher Roth. In case you were wondering—and he was—"Plaschke" is rhymed with "Great Gatsby."

STEVE POLITI is the sports columnist for *NJ Advance Media.* The former paperboy for the *Star-Ledger* achieved a lifelong dream when he joined the newspaper's staff as a sports enterprise reporter in 1998. His work has appeared on its pages and on NJ.com ever since. He and his wife, Nancy, live in Montclair, New Jersey, with their two children, Julian and Sara.

AMY RAGSDALE began her career as a modern dancer, choreographer, and professor of dance. After thirty years in dance—performing in Boston and New York, directing the University of Montana's program, and founding and directing two dance companies, she transitioned into writing. Her articles have appeared in *Mamalode, High Desert Journal,* and *Outside Online,* where she was an originator of the "Raising Rippers" columns. Raised in Wisconsin and abroad, she is an avid traveler and has lived with her husband Peter Stark and their two children in Spain, Mozambique, and Brazil as well as gone on numerous adventures to Africa, Southeast Asia, and Greenland. Her travel memoir *Crossing the River* was published in 2015. She lives in Missoula, Montana, with her husband and black lab, Maggie.

KEN ROSENTHAL has been the senior baseball writer for *The Athletic* since August 2017. He began his career at the *York* (Pennsylvania) *Daily Record* in 1984 and later moved to the *Courier-Post* (New Jersey), before joining the *Baltimore Sun* in 1987, *The Sporting News* in 2000, and Foxsports.com in 2005. He also appears on television with Fox Sports and MLB Network.

DAVY ROTHBART is a best-selling author, Emmy Award–winning filmmaker, the creator of *Found Magazine,* a frequent contributor to public radio's *This American Life,* and the author of a book of personal essays, *My Heart Is an Idiot,* and a collection of stories, *The Lone Surfer of Montana, Kansas.* His latest film, *17 Blocks,* which spans twenty years in the life of a family in Southeast Washington, D.C., premiered at the 2019 Tribeca Film Festival and will soon be released by MTV Documentary Films. His previous film, *Medora,* about a resilient high school basketball team in a dwindling Indiana town, was executive-produced by Steve Buscemi and Stanley Tucci, aired on the acclaimed PBS series *Independent Lens,* and won a 2015 Emmy Award. Rothbart is also the founder of Washington To Washington, an annual hiking adventure for city kids. He lives in Los Angeles, California.

PETER STARK is an adventure writer and exploration historian. Born in Wisconsin and based in Montana, Stark's travels on magazine assignments and book research have taken him from the Inuit hunters of the world's farthest-north villages to the yak-herding nomads of the Tibetan Plateau to the first kayak descent of an African wilderness river. His travels in Greenland for *Outside* magazine, where he is a longtime correspondent, inspired him to write the "as-if-you-were-the-victim" account of the physiology of hypothermia, "Frozen Alive," an article that still attracts many readers each winter twenty years after its publication. This article further inspired his book, *Last Breath,* as well as this essay on the physiology of heatstroke, cowritten with his wife, Amy Ragsdale. His most recent books are the *New York Times* best-seller *Astoria* and *Young Washington,* a finalist for the 2018 George Washington Book Prize.

KURT STREETER covers sports at the *New York Times.* He primarily writes features and essays and has a particular interest in stories related to race, gender, and justice. Prior to coming to the *Times* in 2017, he was a senior writer for *ESPN.* He also covered the inner city for the *Baltimore Sun* and spent fifteen years at the *Los Angeles Times,* where he wrote about everything from crime to transportation to religion and also was a columnist. He was a captain on the tennis team at UC California–Berkeley, which won the national indoor title in 1989.

ELIZABETH WEIL lives in San Francisco. Her profile of the skier Mikaela Shiffrin appeared in *The Best American Sports Writing 2018.*

Notable Sports Writing of 2019

SELECTED BY GLENN STOUT

THE BEST AMERICAN SERIES®

FIRST, BEST, AND BEST-SELLING

The Best American Essays

The Best American Food Writing

The Best American Mystery Stories

The Best American Science and Nature Writing

The Best American Science Fiction and Fantasy

The Best American Short Stories

The Best American Sports Writing

The Best American Travel Writing

Available in print and e-book wherever books are sold.

Visit our website: hmhbooks.com/series/best-american